FROM
CAMP DAVID
TO
THE GULF

To Dost Tarik Ismail with best wishes and kind regards

[signature] 2001 1863

To my brothers and sisters

FROM CAMP DAVID TO THE GULF

NEGOTIATIONS, LANGUAGE & PROPAGANDA, AND WAR

Adel Safty

BLACK ROSE BOOKS

Montréal/New York

Copyright © 1992. BLACK ROSE BOOKS LTD.

No part of this book may be reproduced or transmitted in any form, by any means, electronic or mechanical, including photocopying and recording, or by any information storage or retrieval system, without written permission from the publisher, except for brief passages quoted by a reviewer in a newspaper or magazine.

BLACK ROSE BOOKS No. V180
Hardcover ISBN: 1-895431-11-5
Paperback ISBN: 1-895431-10-7
Library of Congress Catalog No. 92-72624

Canadian Cataloguing in Publication Data

Safty, Adel, 1953-
  From Camp David to the Gulf

Includes index.
ISBN 1-895431-11-5 (bound) —
ISBN 1-895431-10-7 (pbk.)

1. Israel—Arab conflicts. 2. United States—Foreign relations—Middle East. 3. Middle East—Foreign relations—United States. 4. Persian Gulf War, 1991. I. Title.

DS63.1.S24   1992   327.73056   C92-090363-0

Cover Illustration: *Isfahan, Madrasah-vi-Madar Shah, tile decoration*

Mailing Address

BLACK ROSE BOOKS
C.P. 1258
Succ. Place du Parc
Montréal, Québec
H2W 2R3 Canada

BLACK ROSE BOOKS
340 Nagel Drive
Cheektowaga, New York
14225 USA

A publication of the Institute of Policy Alternatives of Montréal (IPAM)

Printed in Canada

Contents

PREFACE

The history of contemporary relations between the industrialized West and the Arab World can be characterized not only as one of domination, but more importantly as one of ignorance and deliberate disinformation. At the heart of this situation, the Palestinian-Israeli confrontation provides one important justification, an excellent excuse, and the occasion for such a relationship. The desire to control such a strategically important geographic area, with its oil reserves, is the other fundamental aspect of this relationship. Although the author of this book does not put it that bluntly, this impression is conveyed by the wealth of facts he has patiently gathered and articulated, to form an eloquent picture of the kind of bond that ties the Arab world to the West.

Indeed, beyond the details of the diplomatic manoeuvring that has been taking place around the various Middle Eastern political issues and which are patiently recorded and decoded in this book, the question of the *relationship* between the West and the Arab World stands out as a fundamental issue. The material presented draws its meaning and relevance from the fact that it is of utmost importance to understand the nature of that relationship.

Discussing this relationship requires that the parties involved be clearly identified. What "West" are we talking about? Certainly not that represented by the many solidarity groups, and by the many individuals who have taken a clear position supporting the rights of the Palestinians, or those who have voiced dissent regarding the aims of, and justifications for, the war against Iraq. Unfortunately, these groups and individuals are not a majority, and in some cases they are quite marginal, which is not to say of course that their work is not important. But the *dominant* political tendencies in the industrialised West have consistently upheld and defended positions that were, by and large, in line with the official Israeli policies.

The intellectual elites have tended to follow suit, and the dominant ideology has incorporated a deeply-rooted bias for Israel, to the extent that any departure from the official Israeli line, however slight, is usually labelled "pro-Arab," and costs its author a reprobation of one sort or another. To the many instances of such biases in the media, analysed in chapter three, one could add many more in the various fields of intellectual activities, academic and scientific as well as artistic, or in the field of entertainment.

So, this is the "West" that has a determining role — for the time being and likely for quite a while — in defining the kind of relationship it desires with the Arabs.

It is constituted by the *dominant* political and ideological tendencies in the Western industrialized countries, primarily the U.S.

This, of course, does not prevent those Westerners who hold a more balanced or pro-Arab position or even the Arabs and Palestinians themselves who have migrated to the industrialized Western countries, from benefitting materially from the unequal relationship established with the Arabs living in the Arab world. And as far as those on the Arab side are concerned, those who maintain such a relationship with the West, and who — supreme subservience on their part, supreme humiliation for the people they represent — thank the West for it, are precisely those Governments that are maintained in power because of the military, political and economic support of the West. For example, the war launched against Iraq by the U.S.-led coalition was, first of all, a war to maintain the existing Arab order by direct military intervention, which included keeping the Kuwaiti ruling family in place and preventing the rise of a regional power no longer useful to Washington. It had nothing to do with punishing a dictator (after all, the U.S. had supported a number of dictators, including Saddam Hussein, when this served their interests) or protecting international legitimacy (which the U.S. also violated when it suited its interests).

Today, the archaic systems of power in the Gulf States have the protection of the U.S. Government and many of these monarchies have even adopted American methods of social control such as the recent discovery of Macarthism demonstrates: A memorandum circulated by the Gulf Cooperation Council to the Gulf newspapers and magazines lists a number of prominent Egyptian writers and journalists who should be prevented from publishing in any of these papers because of their opinions about the Gulf war. Some newspapers have already started to refuse articles by those appearing on the list.

But if those who maintain this subservient relationship are the Arab governments, those who suffer from it are the whole Arab people, and in particular the Palestinians...So this is the other pole of the relationship. It should be noted that this relationship stands in total contradiction to the values supposedly held by the Western governments, and loudly proclaimed by them on every occasion.

As a result of this unequal relationship, a dominant power has managed not only to gain the control of a whole cultural area, with the active support of local elites maintained in power by it, but also to portray the Palestinian victims as the aggressors, to actively support the crushing of their society and prevent its reconstruction, to destroy one Arab capital, Baghdad, on prime time television, and to assist in the destruction of another one (Beirut, 1982), while claiming to act in the name of international legality and in defense of human values.

How did that become possible? The studies in this work shed light on the aspects, or manifestations, of that complex relationship that bonds the Arab world to the industrialized West. They provide us with tools to analyse the processes by which such a relationship is maintained and reinforced.

Starting with an analysis of the Palestinian-Israeli conflict, the author reminds us of the fundamental issue at stake. He argues convincingly that a major injustice has been committed against the Palestinians, and reminds us that enough Israeli documents exist, by now, to establish that the displacement of the Palestinians by the Zionist forces was a deliberate action, followed by the total destruction of close to 400 Palestinian villages. He also discusses the conditions that are necessary to realize a just and durable peace. He then proceeds to show that the Camp David negotiations did not provide the necessary conditions for a just and enduring peace; they were dominated by an inadequate decision-making process on the part of Sadat, who kept thinking that the U.S. administration would come forward and support a just solution. Not only did the U.S. administration fail to endorse a just solution, but President Carter even failed to stand up to his own ideas about the appropriate solution, in spite of the fact that his views already carried a pro-Israeli bias, yielding further to Israeli pressures, and admitted to doing so.

This state of affairs was facilitated by a dominant public discourse on the Palestine question that was — and still is — fundamentally biased. In spite of the many instances where the dominant interpretations on the question of Palestine were challenged, a number of myths — known to be false among Arab, American and Israeli specialists and decision makers alike — have survived. The book documents many of these instances where the dominant media interpretation of the Palestine question was challenged by verifiable facts, but where dominant discourse continued to propagate the same myths.

The author then continues with a careful analysis of the factors that put Iraq and the U.S. on a collision course. With the weakening of the Soviet Union, the threat to U.S. interests no longer came from the ex-superpower, but from rising regional powers. Safty shows how, long before the Iraqi invasion of Kuwait, this was indeed the reading the U.S. Government made of the international situation. It had identified the rise of regional powers in the third world as the source of future threats to its interests, it had determined that the adequate response to this threat would be "medium-intensity warfare," and it had identified Iraq as such a likely threat. Accordingly, measures to weaken the Iraqi economy have been adopted by the U.S. and executed in part by Kuwait, provoking the ill-conceived response of Iraq. The author does not, however, fall into the trap of treating Saddam Hussein as a victimized hero of the Arab cause, and shows instead the rather cynical set of miscalculations that led him to precipitate a confrontation that turned out to be devastating for his country. He analyses the factors that led the major players to come to the decisions they took, even when this represented a reversal of previous alliances, such as was the case for King Hussein on the one hand, and for Syria and the Soviet Union on the other hand. Safty also offers an excellent analysis of the events that resulted in this disastrous war, identifying the different actors, their margins of manoeuvre, and the logic behind their decisions.

Concerning the particular relationship between Israelis and Palestinians, the author notes the asymmetry between the existential conditions of these two national identities which, he says, "nourishes and maintains the conflict," as it has allowed the Israelis not only to destroy Palestinian society, but also to prevent "its reconstitution in a reduced Palestinian Arab state." This notion of asymmetry is also clearly, but implicitly, present in the rest of the book. However, a few additional comments about this asymmetry deserve to be expanded upon.

One brand of the Zionist discourse on the Middle East, often defining itself as liberal and being perceived as such, has made a very systematic use of the notions of symmetry and asymmetry in the Israeli-Palestinian conflict to then propose a *symmetry of rights* between two social groups whose very existence on the land of Palestine was at stake in an asymmetric conflict: one group used its position of military and political strength to expel the other and then to propose to share the land with those left. This discourse presents, therefore, the just solution as something that falls half-way between the demands of the Israeli extreme right-wing, and the Palestinian moderates.

To illustrate this pernicious use of the "moral" notion of symmetry of rights, let me recall an incident that took place in the Jerusalem suburb of Silwan in the fall of 1991, an incident involving the same dynamics as those during the creation of the State of Israel: In the middle of the night, a group of Gush Emunim militants dug a hole in the roof of a Palestinian house and burst into it, armed with machine guns, and ordered its inhabitants out. The Palestinians refused of course and alerted the neighbours; the Israeli police intervened and kicked *everybody* out, including the original inhabitants, until a court settled the issue. The Israeli court divided the house in two, one half for the original owners, and the other half for the Gush Emunim settlers. Since the settlers wanted the whole house, this allowed Israeli official and unofficial spokespersons to claim that there is a legal system in Israel that opposes the claims of the Israeli right-wing and that imposes the rule of law on everybody alike. And of course, this new instance of Israeli racist behaviour did not make headlines.

This misconception of symmetry has been the official guiding principle behind most radio and TV programmes, with only a few exceptions (particularly during the Gulf war). Being "fair" and objective meant precisely forgetting the fundamental asymmetry between Israelis and Palestinians.

The way the film "Deadly Currents," by Toronto film maker Simcha Jacobovici has been reviewed is an excellent illustration of this situation: the film, which equates the violence of the Palestinian children of the *intifada* with that of the heavily armed settlers who kill them, has been judged extremely "fair" and "courageous" by most reviewers. It is also on the basis of a similar definition of fairness that diplomatic offers are judged, and that, for instance, Sadat and Begin have both been given the Nobel Peace prize in 1979. And it is also on the basis of this same definition of fairness that stories and documentaries are selected for distribution, and that experts are retained as commentators. Fortunately this logic has not been adopted universally, and viewers did have the opportunity to listen to alternative analyses such as the ones offered by Dr. Safty.

Given the resilience of the myths referred to above about the contemporary Arab World and the Israeli-Palestinian confrontation, this book is a welcome addition to the literature on the Middle East, original in its approach and in many of the facts reported.

The author must be credited for his extremely rational and well-documented analysis. He must also be credited for the restraint in his tone, even when the reported facts — documented and comprehensive — suggest justifiable outrage by any reader with a minimum care for humanity and decency.

Rachad Antonius
Cairo
August 1992

INTRODUCTION

I started my research for this book in 1986 when I was teaching Political Science at Simon Fraser University. I was interested primarily in the Camp David negotiation process and its consequences — which were having a dramatic impact on the Arab-Israeli-Palestinian conflict — and, secondarily, in the question of consistency and contradictions in United States foreign policy. But as is often the case with the Arab-Israeli-Palestinian conflict, I found that its events and developments have a dynamic of their own which defies compartmentalization and categorization so often found in academic writings.

When the Palestinian uprising erupted in December 1987 I became interested in its developments and in the way public opinion makers easily established norms and historical frames of reference reflecting discredited myths about the conflict. After the end of the Iran-Iraq war in 1988, a confrontation developed between Baghdad and Washington; it took on crisis proportions and was exacerbated by miscalculations and by conflicting conceptions of balance of power in the post Cold-War era. It culminated in the war against Iraq. Just as it would be difficult to write about the Arab-Israeli-Palestinian uprising — and how public opinion and policy makers in the West reacted to it — it would be impossible to critically examine the question of consistency and contradictions in American foreign policy without reference to the war against Iraq. These two themes imposed themselves and the scope of the book was expanded to deal with the period from Camp David to the Gulf.

It was a typical period of the on-going saga of the West's relationship with the Arabs and the Zionists' encounter with the Palestinians. From the Napoleonic campaign in Egypt at the end of the eighteenth century, French occupation of North Africa, British occupation of Egypt, the Balfour Declaration in 1917 and the arrival of the Zionist commission in Palestine in 1918, the bloody repression of Arab nationalism by French and British colonialism after World War I, the forcible establishment of Israel in 1948, to the Anglo-French-Israeli invasion of Egypt in 1956, the West's and the Zionist-Israeli's relationship with the Arabs were predicated on and moved by the fundamental assumption of inequality of relations. Language and propaganda, power politics, the balance of power game, and the use of force were all necessary instruments for the realization of goals, the imposition of will, the fulfilment of aspirations, and the accomplishment of grand designs — none more successful than the Zionist design to seize Palestine — whose *raison d'être* emanated from Western and Zionist-Israeli perceptions. The period from Camp David to the

Gulf may be inscribed in the same register. It contained and was dominated by elements of propaganda, diplomacy, and violence, and by the successful use Israeli and American leaders and public opinion makers made of them. Thus, the language was skilful and purposeful; the politics and diplomacy manipulative and effective, the balance of power game experienced and efficaciously divisive, and the instruments of violence — from the Israeli invasion of Lebanon in 1982 to the war against Iraq in 1991 — massive and overwhelming. The result was remarkably predictable: the unequal and coercive relationship with the Arabs became more sharply defined and continued to be governed, more unambiguously than ever, by the interests of the West, more particularly as conceived by the various American administrations and their partnership with Israeli governments.

This further exacerbated the Arab predicament and its contradictions which have never been more painfully glaring: growing material and human resources and diminishing effective collective power. Powerlessness and frustrations inhered in such a condition. Its dramatic manifestations culminated in the helplessness of the Arab nation as two Arab capitals were systematically destroyed, first Beirut in 1982, then Baghdad in 1991.

And thus the themes that intersect and intermingle in this book became those of unequal relationships, of questionable diplomatic strategies, of conflicting definitions of peace, and of a crisis almost doomed to be resolved by the most modern of instruments of violence, given the parameters that traditionally defined the Arabs' relationship with the West.

In doing research for this book I was helped and inspired by a number of people and would like to particularly recognize the contributions of two individuals who were both sources of information and intellectual motivation: the first is the late Allan Cunningham whom I knew from my days at Simon Fraser University where he taught history. Allan was well-known for his public speaking and media interviews and I greatly admired his lucidity and courage in speaking out in support of the justice of the Palestinian cause. So when my friend and University of British Columbia colleague Professor Jean Cunningham, Allan's wife, approached me and asked if I would be interested in consulting the research notes her late husband had been preparing for a future book on the Arab-Israeli conflict which would have been entitled *The Closing of the Doors,* I readily accepted. Allan's thesis was that the process of dispossessing the Palestinians was so far advanced that the time was fast approaching when there would be nothing left to talk or negotiate about; when the doors would be completely closed. He deeply deplored American and Israeli policies which made possible the occupation, continuous dispossession, and denial of Palestinian humanity, but he urged the Palestinian leadership to seize all opportunities to make their just claims heard and to reach a negotiated settlement. Had he lived, he would have been pleased to see Israelis and Palestinians sitting at a negotiation table, although, I think, he might have regretted the neutral role to which the United Nations has been reduced. I share both sentiments.

I found professor Cunningham's notes valuable and would like to acknowledge not only a research debt but also an inspirational debt for the example he set as an untiring believer in and defender of justice. He was one of the few university professors from non-Middle-Eastern backgrounds who recognized the justice of the Palestinian cause and had the courage to speak out in its support long before it acquired the recognition it now seems to enjoy.

To the question *Can There Be a Just and Enduring Peace in the Arab-Israeli-Palestinian Conflict?* I truly believe that the answer depends on the future direction the recently-elected Labour leadership will give to Israel and to its relations with its Arab and Palestinian neighbours and peace interlocutors. In the post Cold-War era Israel can no longer automatically count on its traditional role as a strategic asset in an American geostrategic system solely preoccupied with communist threats to the Middle East and its oil resources; nor can it maintain the claim that Arabs and Palestinians are bent on its destruction and will never reconcile themselves to its existence. Israel's choice has never been more crystallized, more sharply in focus; its alternatives never more publicly exposed: either it lives in peace with its neighbours and concludes peace treaties based on some justice for the Palestinians, the destruction of whose society Zionist leaders bear primary responsibility, and on the accepted norms of international legality requiring the end of the occupation of Arab territories; or it continues to rely on force to defend a status quo of occupation and continued subjugation in one form or another. This latter alternative is rejected by the international community and, increasingly, by American public opinion.

The Palestinians suffered through the destruction of their society and the dispersal of their community. This injustice is neither denied nor mitigated by arguments claiming that the Palestinians are to blame because they refused to share their country with European Jewish immigrants, or that Israel is a democracy while Arab regimes have traditionally been corrupt and dictatorial, or that many Palestinians engaged in misguided and counterproductive acts of terrorism and therefore the Palestinian leadership is not a worthy interlocutor. No amount of obfuscation, linguistic manipulation, legal hair-splitting, creative historical reconstructions or invocation of divine right can obscure or diminish the reality of Palestinian victimization. The Zionists themselves did not deny this reality; they simply rationalized it on the basis of the principle of the "lesser evil:" the destruction of the Palestinian society is a lesser evil than the non-fulfillment of the Zionist goal of a Jewish State offering a haven to the persecuted Jews of Europe.

In the first chapter I examine some of the basic elements of the Arab-Israeli and Israeli-Palestinian conflicts and set out principles for a just and enduring peace that recognizes the Palestinians' right to independence and freedom and guarantees the security of all peoples in the region including the Israelis and the Palestinians. I believe that in the long run only peace that is just and appears to be just, can provide an enduring basis for peaceful Arab-Israeli and Arab-Palestinian relationships. The injustice suffered by the Palestinians must be at least partly redressed and the conditions allowing illegal occupation removed before such a peace can be established. This first chapter benefitted from the historical research of the late Professor Allan Cunningham, and is dedicated to his memory.

My second intellectual and motivational debt goes to Mohammed Ibrahim Kamel, the former Egyptian Foreign Minister who accompanied Sadat to the Camp David Conference in 1978 and resigned at Camp David to protest Sadat's negotiating style and unusual concessions to the Americans and Israelis. I met Minister Kamel in Cairo in 1990 and spent many hours talking with him, listening to him recall in detail some of the significant events in which he participated and the discussions he had with Sadat during his term as Minister of Foreign Affairs which began in late 1977 and ended with his resignation at Camp David in September 1978. Kamel embodied for me the image that Sadat wanted but, I think, failed to give to Egypt: modern, forward-looking, rational-thinking, independent, and possessing a great sense of integrity. I greatly admired and respected Minister Kamel's love for Egypt and the strength of his convictions. He represented for me a modern reincarnation of Saad Zaghlul, nationalist but democratic and non-ethnocentrist, assertive but not belligerent, dedicated to Egyptian independence but ready to cooperate with the West on a basis of mutual respect and tolerance, realist but still animated by the self-less ideals of his revolutionary days. In short, Kamel was a modern Statesman animated by practical idealism and enlightened realism. When I told him this he modestly played down the comparison.

As Egyptian Minister of Foreign Affairs in 1977, Kamel accepted the publicly-stated premise of the Sadat strategy, i.e.; that Egypt could not fight the United States which was committed to ensuring Israeli military superiority; Egypt had therefore to opt for a negotiated settlement of the conflict; such a settlement must be just and comprehensive, based on the withdrawal of Israel from all the occupied Arab territories in return for full peace agreements, and providing for the recognition of the Palestinian people's right to self-determination. But when Kamel discovered wide discrepancies between what Sadat was saying in public and what he was actually willing to settle for in private, he developed strong reservations which he courageously articulated to Sadat. But Sadat was a one-man show whose love for the limelight was only equalled by his aversion to dissension from his political views and decisions. The relationship between the two men deteriorated until in the end Kamel found it impossible to endorse what Sadat had agreed to at the Camp David conference in September 1978. He preferred to tender his resignation on the spot as the American, Egyptian and Israeli delegations were getting ready to leave Camp David for Washington. Last-minute appeals from Secretary of State Vance for Kamel to reconsider failed, and Kamel refused to attend the White House signing ceremonies.

The chapter on Sadat's road to Camp David, his negotiations and decision-making from Sinai to Camp David and Blair House, analyzes Sadat's position on the conflict, his assessment of the operational environment and the forces at play, and critically examines his negotiating and decision-making style. By his own repeated statements, Sadat set out to achieve a comprehensive peace based on UN resolutions providing for withdrawal from the occupied Arab territories and recognition of Palestinians' rights to self-determination in return for full peace agreements with Israel. He achieved a separate peace which isolated Egypt and helped Israel consolidate its occupation of the Arab territories, as is evidenced from the accelerated pace of Jewish settlement activities that followed Camp David; the separate agreement also freed Israel to pursue a bloody military "final solution" to the Palestinian question, as became clear from the Israeli invasion of Lebanon. For this chapter, I am greatly indebted to Minister Mohammed Ibrahim Kamel. Two articles based on that chapter have already appeared in the *American Journal of Economics and Sociology* and in *International Studies*.

The chapter on the Camp David order and its consequences examines the reactions to Camp David mainly in Egypt, whose defection from the Arab camp greatly modified the balance of power in the region. The term balance of power never really means, and I doubt it ever meant when practised with consummate art by imperial Britain, what a straightforward meaning would suggest, i.e., balance or equilibrium. It often means a distribution of relative power between competing entities which is favourable to a certain military and political order. This is the operative definition used throughout this book, although often balance of power simply means an imbalance of relative military and political power favouring Israel and the United States. Thus, with Egypt realigned along American foreign policy orientations in the same camp as Israel and the conservative Arab regimes of the Gulf, the Arab front which Egypt traditionally led, and which included Syria, Jordan and the Palestinians — to various degrees opposed to Camp David — found itself deprived of any option other than the one dictated by American ascendency in the region. If the new power relations resulting from Camp David had been used to bring about a comprehensive resolution of the Arab-Israeli and the Israeli-Palestinian conflicts on the basis of UN resolutions, peace agreements based on Israeli withdrawal from occupied Arab territories in return for peace treaties could have been concluded with Syria, Jordan and the Palestinians. But no sooner were the Camp David accords signed that the Israeli leaders set out to violate the accords' provisions with regard to the West Bank and Gaza which the Israeli cabinet claimed to be part of Eretz Israel (greater Israel). The pace of Jewish settlements in the occupied territories was increased and even the Syrian Golan Heights were annexed. It became clear, as Israeli Minister of Defense Ezer Weizman noted, that whereas Sadat and Carter hoped that the withdrawal agreement with Egypt would be the model for other withdrawal agreements on the Syrian and Palestinian fronts, Israeli leaders saw them as the end of any withdrawal from the occupied Arab territories. In effect, Camp David was used to separate Egypt from the Arab camp and strengthen, rather than terminate, Israeli occupation of the Arab territories. Dispossession of the Palestinians was accelerated and an invasion of Lebanon was launched to liquidate the Palestinian question once and for all. These actions shook any remaining Egyptian faith in the possibility of a comprehensive Arab-Israeli peace and Egyptian opposition to Camp David and its process of "normalization" increased. Shortly after Sadat's assassination, Egyptian President Hosni Mubarak began the process of bringing Egypt back to the Arab camp.

I greatly benefited from my discussions with many Egyptian intellectuals, most of whom basically accepted the premise of peaceful co-existence with Israel on the basis of the principles of justice and international legitimacy embodied in UN resolutions; but all rejected the notion of normalized relations with Israel as long as it continues to subjugate the Palestinian people and occupy Palestinian, Syrian and Lebanese territories.

One of the often-neglected dimensions in the Zionist-Palestinian encounter and the conflict that resulted therefrom is situated at the linguistic level. Socially, culturally, politically and linguistically, the Zionists and the Palestinians spoke different languages and in one sense it was inevitable that their encounter would be defined by the coercive language of imperial, financial, and propagandistic power. Language and its creative use have played a crucial role in advertising the benefits of political Zionism to British imperialism, in obfuscating its intentions vis-à-vis the Palestinian Arabs, and, after the establishment of Israel, in presenting a carefully-constructed set of myths essentially absolving Israel of any moral responsibility for the destruction of the Palestinian society. After the conquest and the occupation of the rest of mandated Palestine and additional Arab territories in 1967, the creative and manipulative use of language was put to the service of the ideological

enterprise of further historical reconstruction to justify and perpetuate Israeli occupation of Arab territories. Thus, Israeli leaders claimed that Arab territories were
not occupied territories but rather "liberated" territories; Jerusalem was not annexed but rather "Israeli laws were extended to Jerusalem," Palestinian lands were
not confiscated but rather "seized." The powerful support Israel enjoyed in the
West ensured that its perspective on the conflict and the linguistic representations
of its views, beliefs and aspirations remained the contextual reference for Western
media "coverage" of the Palestine question. But the Israeli invasion of Lebanon
and the horrific images of the siege of Beirut in 1982 upset the Israeli-derived
Western interpretative framework of the conflict. And this, because it showed a
side of Israel many Westerners did not suspect existed at all.

The chapter on language and propaganda and the linguistic management of
challenges to media interpretation of the Palestine question has been inspired by
the propaganda model constructed by Noam Chomsky and Edward Herman in
their book *Manufacturing Consent*. They applied their propaganda model to different conflicts in Central America and South East Asia. I used this particular model
to examine how, despite growing public support for the Palestinian cause, media's
views and perspectives on the Palestine question remained informed by the traditional pro-Israeli assumptions which served as the only permissible context for
analyzing and reporting on the Palestinian uprising that erupted in 1987. The
realities of subjugation and revolt against dispossession and oppression, made
graphic by daily images of unequal confrontations between young Palestinian
stone-throwers and the Israeli army of occupation, were discursively and
psychologically subordinated to the imperatives of an "official" interpretative
framework in which it was often possible to blame the victim. I am particularly
grateful to Noam Chomsky for having read a first draft of this chapter and for
giving me encouraging comments both for my analysis and for my book project. I
am also grateful to him for sharing with me information about the *New York Times'*
refusal to print statements about the real position of the PLO rather than the convenient propaganda-derived "official" position. An article based on this chapter on
language and propaganda has already appeared in *Arab Studies Quarterly* in 1991.

Part Two of this book, which deals with the war against Iraq, critically examines the similar but inherently conflictual balance of power visions of Iraq and
the United States, and analyzes how these led to a confrontation that Iraq was
bound to loose. It is clear to me that a negotiated settlement to the crisis precipitated
by the Iraqi invasion of Kuwait could have been achieved. But the Bush administration was bent on a course of confrontation: either force a politically costly
and humiliating unconditional retreat upon the Iraqis, or launch a destructive war
to cut down to seize Baghdad's regional ambitions. In challenging the new balance
of power which resulted from Camp David — which enormously enhanced Israeli
military domination of and American ascendency in the Middle East — Saddam
Hussein was challenging the two traditional American foreign policy priorities in
the region: the security of pro-American conservative petromonarchies which ensures ready and cheap American access to their oil resources, and the military superiority of Israel over all its Arab neighbours combined. If allowed to succeed,
Saddam Hussein's challenge could have upset a balance of power favourable to
the United States and its regional allies with significant repercussions for the political, economic and military order in the Middle East; therefore, American policy

makers argued, it had to be confronted and eliminated; in the process, the vast military deployment and the massive war against Iraq displayed awesome technological power, thus enhancing American claim to undisputed superpower status, and serving as an example for all regional powers tempted to challenge American interests. In short, it was a unique opportunity to, in the words of Secretary of State James Baker, "lay down and solidify the ground rules of the new world order." A negotiated withdrawal from Kuwait could have resolved the Iraq-Kuwait crisis peacefully but it would have left Iraq free to mount future challenges. The Bush administration decided to foreclose the possibility of a negotiated settlement, successfully managed public consent, and persuaded reluctant allies to fall in line and form an American-led coalition to wage a massive war against Iraq and put to rest its regional ambitions. This chapter benefited from extensive interviews I conducted with some of the actors directly or indirectly involved in the drama. These included American, British, French, Soviet, and Arab diplomats. As well, I greatly benefited from my meetings with Dr. Boutros Ghali while he was still Egyptian Deputy Prime Minister for Foreign Affairs. I am also indebted to Egyptian Foreign Minister Amr Moussa who was gracious and generous with his time with me while he was still Egypt's Ambassador to the United Nations, and after he became Foreign Minister. I would also like to acknowledge a debt to the Yemeni Ambassador to the United Nations Abdallaah al-Ashtall, the only Arab ambassador at the Security Council during the crucial weeks of the war against Iraq. He was both lucid in his analysis and unfailing in his generosity with his time. Prince Seilman al-Sabah of the ruling Kuwaiti family provided me with valuable information particularly about the aborted attempts to reach an Arab-negotiated solution to the crisis in the days that immediately followed the Iraqi invasion of Kuwait. I am also indebted to dozens of UN officials, especially Under-Secretary-General Martti Ahtisaari, for their help in providing me with documents and responding to my endless queries.

This chapter has also been influenced by my own experience. During the Gulf crisis I had given a number of interviews to radio and television stations, but from the first day of the war I was retained as a political analyst by two television networks on which I appeared practically every night. It was an interesting, instructive and demanding experience. It gave me a first-hand and painful knowledge of the extent to which Zionist supporters of the hard-line Israeli rejectionist policy would go to try to silence critics, an unpleasant reality which Noam Chomsky, Edward Said, and a number of American and British journalists and politicians (Michael Adams and Christopher Mayhew, *Publish it not...The Middle East Cover-Up,* and former Congressman Paul Findley, *They Dare to Speak: People and Institutions Confront Israel's Lobby*) have documented and condemned. I can only add my voice to theirs; irrational and anti-democratic behaviours will not make the reprehensible reality of Israel's subjugation of Palestinians and the illegality of its occupation of Arab territories disappear. To their credit, the office of the President of the University of British Columbia, the office of the Dean of Education, and CBC and UTV television networks have resisted pressures to silence me or interfere with my freedom of expression. But it is instructive to note that CBC television took care to ensure that whenever I appeared they also invited someone who supported the war; very often it was military analyst Gwyn Dyer via satellite from Montreal. He remained a supporter of the war from the very beginning of our television debates, and often surprised me by insisting until practically the end of the war that the United States was fulfilling a UN mandate and had no other political objectives in this war beyond the eviction of Iraqi troops from Kuwait. A claim that even the White House and the Pentagon had stopped making as early as January 20 when the White House and military officials spelled out the destruction of Iraqi industrial-military complex as a basic American war aim.

My media experience also focused my attention on the extent of public ignorance about the Middle East in general and the Arab and Palestinian issues in particular. It is truly depressing when one thinks of the amount of work required simply to rehabilitate the Arabs as human beings in the popular North-American perceptions, shaped by traditional representations of the Arab-Israeli conflict from the Israeli point of view, and heavily affected by a mixture of ignorance and crass propaganda successfully depicting the Arabs as oil-vendors, blackmailers and terrorists. Only by reducing the Other to this base level of inhumanity would it be possible to objectify the massive destruction, the suffering and the killings the war brought to the Iraqi people.

As a footnote, my media experience also allowed me to have a brief claim to fame for having the luck of predicting from the first days of the war that the Iraqis would probably attempt to hide their air force in Iran, long before the major American television networks discovered that the Iraqis were doing precisely that. Although this may have briefly enhanced my media profile, it also put additional pressure on me to keep up with every little detail and be "on top" of events, all while trying not to allow the impressive and dazzling display of advanced weaponry, and the media's tendency to reduce complex issues to simplistic dimensions, make one lose sight of the tragic human drama the peoples of Iraq and Kuwait were living.

I would like to express my thanks to the anonymous reviewers who evaluated the manuscript and recommended its publication. I would also like to gratefully acknowledge the financial assistance provided by the Office of the President of Simon Fraser University. Finally, while I am grateful to all those who helped me in the process of gathering information, any error or omission contained in this book are entirely my responsibility.

Adel Safty
Vancouver, British Columbia
1992

PART I

PEACE, NEGOTIATIONS, LANGUAGE AND PROPAGANDA

CHAPTER ONE

Can There Be A Just and Enduring Peace in the Arab-Israeli-Palestinian Conflict?

Thomas Hobbes suggested in his classic work *Leviathan* that peace was a state obtaining between times of war and conditions of war. This negatively defined conception of peace essentially remains dominant and largely unchallenged in international politics. But it is an inadequate conception predicated on the erroneous assumption that war and conflicts are the normal state of affairs between nations. And that is why it is of limited usefulness as an intellectual concept and as an analytical tool. On the eve of the twenty-first century, we can no longer define peace reductively and negatively as the absence of war; we must define it positively and relate it to such fundamental and universal concepts as human equality and justice.

Defined positively, peace may be said to be a state of existence governed by a community of interests and shared values between nations. For instance, according to this definition, one can say that there is peace between Canada and the United States. There is no war between Israel and Syria but one cannot say that there is peace between them. There is a peace treaty between Egypt and Israel but the failure of "normalization" shows that the "peace" between them is an absence of belligerency which has not been translated into shared values. A community of interests and shared values are thus the most enduring and reliable basis of peaceful co-existence among nations. In addition, an enduring peace is, to appropriate Paul Valéry's notion, a peace of satisfaction which is and appears to be based on commonly accepted principles of justice. An imposed peace that is unjust and perceived to be unjust is often an interlude between violent confrontations resulting from conflicts over fundamental values.

The first article of the Charter of the United Nations prescribes that the purposes of the UN are, *inter alia,* to bring about, by peaceful means and "in conformity with the principles of justice and international law," the resolution of conflicts. Kesler pointed out that: "If we may judge by the wording of Article I, paragraph I of the Charter, the 'principles of justice' are something distinct from international law."[1] It is not by accident that the principles of justice are given precedence over the principles of international law. This is because law without generally accepted norms of justice is a tyrannical concept serving the interests and advancing the views of those who made it and have the means of enforcing it. Thus, the law often discriminates against women, minority groups and Blacks in the United States; it discriminates against the Palestinians under occupation and inside Israel, and against the Blacks in South Africa. The concept of justice, on the other hand, is universal and unlike international law, is much less subject to interpretation.

Given the injustices inherent in the destruction of the Palestinian society, and the opposition of Israel and the United States to its free and unhampered reconstitution even on a portion of its former land, and given the illegality of the continued Israeli occupations of Arab territories, there can be no just and enduring peace between Israelis and Arabs without the removal of these conditions of injustice and illegality. The current absence of armed conflict between the parties in the Middle East can only be described as a condition enforced by Israel's militaristic hegemony over the region. Because this condition is not based on shared values, it will likely continue to be challenged by the aggrieved parties, who have at their disposal enormous human and material resources which can ensure effective continued moral protest. A lasting resolution of the Palestinian-Israeli and Arab-Israeli conflicts can only be guaranteed by peace agreements based on universally recognized principles of justice, and in conformity with generally accepted principles of international law. Arab governments and the Palestinian leadership in exile have accepted that the conflict be resolved on the basis of normative criteria compatible with the principles of justice and international legitimacy. The Israeli leaders have reluctantly and after considerable American pressure agreed to come to the negotiation table but have done so only after ensuring that the representative of international law, the United Nations, were excluded from the negotiations. The basis of the Middle East peace negotiations became therefore more related to the balance of relative power of the parties than to a set of agreed principles and shared values.

Violation of Justice

The State of Israel bases its juridical existence on the Balfour Declaration of 1917 and on the UN partition resolution of 1947. Both instruments represented a violation of the principles of justice for the Palestinian Arabs. The Balfour Declaration was issued by England, a foreign power that did not posses any sovereignty or right of disposition and was not even in physical occupation of Palestine at the time of the declaration. The British government's promise to use its best endeavors to facilitate the Zionist project in Palestine amounted to a promise to give to the Zionists what England did not have, in violation of the established legal maxim *Nemo dat quod non habet* (nobody can give what he does not possess). By viewing "with favour" the establishment in Palestine of a Jewish national home, as the Balfour Declaration stated, Britain was denying the Palestinian Arabs, who represented 92 percent of the population of Palestine, their natural and political rights to self-determined and self-governed national existence. And this at a time when Britain was already committed to respecting these rights in the Anglo-Arab compact of 1915 which preceded the Balfour Declaration, in the British Declaration to the Seven of 1918, and in the Anglo-French Declaration of the same year in which the British and French governments undertook that no regime would be set up in the Arab territories unless it was based on the "principle of the consent of the governed."[2] Moreover, the Balfour declaration conditioned the promise of a national home for the Jews by the obligation to safeguard the rights of the Moslem and Christian Arab majority in Palestine.

In its fourth clause, Article 22 of the Covenant of the League of Nations made clear that with regard "to certain communities formerly belonging to the Turkish Empire [which] have reached a stage of development...their existence as separate nations can be provisionally recognized subject to the rendering of administrative advice and assistance by a Mandatory until such time as they are able to stand alone. The wishes of these communities must be a principal consideration in the selection of the Mandatory." The same clause created what was called type A Mandates to which Palestine belonged, and through which the League of Nations was in effect provisionally recognizing the independence of Palestine subject only to "the rendering of administrative assistance."

The wishes of the people of Palestine were perfectly well-known to the drafters of the Palestine mandate. At the Paris Peace Conference in 1919, American President Woodrow Wilson had opposed Anglo-French calculations to divide the Middle East among themselves according to their secret agreements and in violation of their various pledges to the people of the area to support independent Arab governments established on the basis of the consent of the governed. Wilson shocked the two colonial powers by insisting that the only acceptable settlement in the Middle East was one based on what the people themselves wanted. Accordingly, he formed a Commission of Inquiry which the Zionists and the French strongly opposed and the British failed to support. The Commission was finally composed of two Americans, Dr. Howard King and Mr. Charles Crane. The King-Crane Commission went to the Middle East, visited 40 towns, interviewed hundreds of delegations and received 1800 petitions. In their final report the Commissioners recommended "serious modification of the extreme Zionist programme for Palestine of unlimited immigration of Jews, looking finally to making Palestine distinctly a Jewish State. The Commissioners began their study of Zionism with minds predisposed in its favour, but the actual facts in Palestine, coupled with the force of the general principles proclaimed by the Allies and accepted by the Syrians have driven them to the recommendation here made...The fact repeatedly came out in the Commission's conferences with Jewish representatives, that the Zionists looked forward to a practically complete dispossession of the present non-Jewish inhabitants of Palestine." Repeating President Wilson's July 4, 1919 commitment to the principle of self-determination, the Commissioners wrote: "If that principle is to rule, and so the wishes of the Palestine's population are to be decisive as to what is to be done with Palestine, then it is to be remembered that the non-Jewish population of Palestine — nearly nine-tenths of the whole — are emphatically against the Zionist programme...No British officer consulted by the Commissioners, believed that the Zionist programme could be carried out except by force...That of itself is evidence of the strong sense of the injustice of the Zionist programme."[3]

Yet, in formulating the terms of the Palestine mandate, Britain ignored the Palestinian Arab majority's rights to, and expressed demand for, self-determination. Instead, the British government took into account Zionist designs on Palestine by formulating the terms of the mandate in close consultation with European Zionist leaders. This resulted in the inclusion in the mandate of the Balfour declaration's clauses about the establishment of a Jewish home in Palestine (not the transformation of Palestine into a Jewish home as the Zionists initially wanted during the negotiations that led to the Balfour declaration), and the safeguarding of the rights of the Arab majority inhabitants of Palestine; this latter important safeguard clause was reinstated after the Zionists had succeeded in having it removed from the first draft of the mandate. Although specifically entrusted with the development of the well-being of the inhabitants of Palestine, British mandatory rule of Palestine permitted, against the will and despite the opposition of the majority of Palestinians, massive Jewish immigration, mostly from Eastern Europe. This, as Ibrahim Abu-Lughod has shown in his extremely useful work *The Transformation of Palestine,* resulted in radical demographic changes in Palestine and violated the expressed reservation in the Balfour Declaration committing Britain to ensure that nothing would be done which might prejudice the rights of the Moslem and Christian majority. But deception and duplicity, as Walid Khalidi has shown in his classic anthology *From Haven to Conquest,* were part and parcel of the policy which enabled the British to keep the Palestinian Arab majority captive while the Zionists developed such demographic, political and military conditions in the country as to allow the ultimate seizure of Palestine from its inhabitants. Then British Foreign Secretary Lord Balfour himself candidly admitted that duplicity was inherent in Britain's policy toward Palestine from the beginning: "The Four Great Powers are committed to Zionism...What I have never been able to understand is how it can be harmonized with the declaration [Anglo-French of November 1918], the Covenant, or the instructions to the Commission of Inquiry...In short, so far as Palestine is concerned, the Powers have made no statement of fact which is not admittedly wrong, and no declaration of policy which, at least in the letter, they have not always intended to violate."[4]

Still, a basis in international law was provided for the existence of an independent State of Palestine which remained deprived of the institutions of self-government and of the power to establish them. Having violently suppressed the Palestinian rebellion of 1936-39, Britain was unable to apply the same repressive methods to bring to an end the Jewish terrorist campaign orchestrated by members of the Irgun and the Stern gang in the 1940s, and directed against the Palestinian Arabs and the British occupation. Nor was the British government more successful in brokering a negotiated settlement to the Palestinian-Zionist conflict over Palestine. The Palestinian Arabs wanted an end to Jewish immigration which was transforming the demographic composition of their country and slowly turning it into a Jewish State while the Zionists by now, after the 1941 Baltimore programme, would settle for nothing less than a Jewish State. With a devilishly successful media and public relations campaign, the Zionists dramatically advertised the plight of the European Jewish refugees whom they successfully used to pressure the United States to throw its weight against the British policy of controlled and more limited Jewish immigration to Palestine. Unable to withstand the pressure from the United States, unwilling to shoulder the growing financial burden of continued occupation in Palestine, and no longer enjoying the power of its former imperial days, Britain decided to pass the Palestine problem to someone else. In 1947, the British government turned over its Palestine mandate to the United Nations.

A strong Zionist campaign pressured the American government and the Truman White House to "persuade" members of the United Nations into changing their known opposition to a UN General Assembly resolution recommending the partition of Palestine into a Jewish State and an Arab Palestinian State. Truman, although strongly supportive of the Zionist cause, complained of overwhelming Zionist pressure: "I do not think I ever had as much pressure and propaganda aimed at the White House as I had in this instance. The persistence of a few of the extreme Zionist leaders — actuated by political motives and engaging in political threats — disturbed and annoyed me. Some were even suggesting that we pressure sovereign nations into favorable votes at the General Assembly. I have never approved of the practice of the strong imposing its will on the weak whether among men or among nations."[5] But Truman's daughter Margaret reported in her book *Harry S. Truman* that her father did not tell the whole truth about the pressure he had been subjected to by the Zionists because he was afraid if he did he and the entire American government would look pathetically ridiculous. In reality, the Truman administration did browbeat independent nations into changing their votes. Six vulnerable nations which had indicated their intentions of voting against the partition resolution became the target of intense pressure: Haiti, Liberia, the Philippines, China, Ethiopia, and Greece. All except Greece were "persuaded" to change their vote.[6] The last-minute change of votes of Liberia, Haiti and the Philippine assured the necessary two-thirds majority for the adoption of the partition resolution.

The Palestinian Arabs rejected the partition of their country and questioned the competence of the United Nations to partition their homeland and destroy its territorial integrity. The partition resolution suffered from several moral and legal problems which may be briefly summarized: a) the resolution was adopted by a body that had no sovereignty over Palestine nor the right to deprive its people of their right to independence; b) the refusal by the General Assembly to refer the question of the UN jurisdiction over Palestine to the International Court of Justice represented "avoidance of international law," and this constituted a denial of justice which deprived the resolution of juridical value; c) it violated the internationally recognized status of Palestine as a "provisionally independent" State; d) it violated the principle of self-determination of the people of Palestine; and e) it represented a gross injustice to the majority of the people in Palestine. The partition resolution attributed to the Jews, who constituted less than one third of the population most of whom were recent immigrants, and who possessed less than 6 percent of the land, 57 percent of Palestine. This left the Palestinian Arabs, who owned 94 percent of the land with only 43 percent of their own homeland.[7]

J. Bowyer Bell wrote: "Surely, the Arab argument had much justice...Whittled down to basics, the Zionist position was that, given the Palestine dilemma, they would settle for half whereas the Arabs unfairly continued to demand all. It was ingenious, it was evil, and it threw the entire Arab argument into the wrong frame of reference. More devastating still, it proved effective."[8]

Israeli Leaders' Responsibility

Israel's responsibility for the destruction of the Palestinian society, and the prevention of its reconstitution in a reduced Palestinian Arab State has now been documented by a number of Israeli writers. It is now clear that the dominant thinking among Zionist leaders on the eve of the establishment of Israel was informed by Ben-Gurion's conviction, impressed upon the Zionist leadership in 1937 that "military faits accomplis 'are' the basis for political achievements." Pragmatically,

Ben-Gurion urged that the partition of Palestine be accepted for now as a first step toward the achievement of Zionist goals. He pledged: "After the formation of a large army in the wake of the establishment of the State, we will abolish partition and expand to the whole of Palestine."[9]

Thus, after the partition resolution was adopted in November 1947, the Zionist forces quickly moved to implement their plan to seize Palestine and forcibly establish a Jewish State. Prepared in advance, the so-called Plan D (Plan Dalet) was put into action on March 10, 1948, after several Zionist operations of "aggressive defense" shattered the morale of the Palestinian society. Plan D, as Simha Flapan wrote, provided for "seizure of areas in Galilee and on the way from Tel-Aviv to Jerusalem that had been assigned to the Arab State or included in the international zone." Founded on these aims, the plan dealt in detail with "the expulsion over the borders of the local Arab population in the event of opposition to our attacks." Flapan concluded: "In retrospect it can be seen that the aim of the plan was annexation — the destruction of the Arab villages was to be followed by the establishment of Jewish villages in their places."[10] Outnumbered, ill-prepared and poorly equipped, the Arab armies belatedly attempted on May 15, 1948 to save the rest of Palestine from falling under Zionist control. They were roundly defeated and by the end of 1949 the Jewish armies controlled the area defined as a Jewish State by the partition resolution as well as 50 percent of the area which the same resolution defined as the Palestinian Arab State. Over 800,000 Palestinians had fled in terror or been expelled by the advancing Jewish armies. Drawing from previously unpublished Israeli cabinet and army papers, Israeli writers have also recently documented what Arab and European writers reported about the Zionists leaders' responsibility for the expulsion and dispossession of the Palestinian people. In his book *The Birth of the Palestinian Refugee Problem: 1947-49* Israeli historian Benny Morris "shatter[ed] Palestinian exodus myth"[11] by showing Zionist leaders' and Jewish armies' responsibility for the expulsion of Palestinians, with the help of the occasional massacre between 1947 and 1949. In a television interview in Israel, Morris dismissed the long dominant, and uncritically accepted in the West, Israeli propagandistic version of the events and said: "people's minds have been warped by 40 years of nonsense."[12]

Admission of Jewish responsibility for the expulsion of Palestinians was deleted by Israeli censorship from Defence Minister Yitzhak Rabin's Hebrew version of his published memoir.[13] Similarly, Ben-Gurion's biographer Michael Bar-Zohar quotes one Israeli officer's description of the prime minister's first visit to Nazareth during the 1948 war: "He looked around in astonishment, saying, 'Why are there so many Arabs? Why didn't you drive them out?'" These accounts appeared only in the Hebrew version but were deleted from the English version of the biography.[14] In an article describing some of the Jewish military operations which resulted in "carnage" and "slaughter" of Palestinians in Lydda and Ramle, in 1948, Benny Morris wrote that when Ben-Gurion was asked: "What shall we do with the Arabs?" Ben-Gurion made a dismissive, energetic gesture with his hands and said: "expel them (garesh otam)."[15] Israeli writer Simha Flapan wrote that "the myth of a voluntary Palestinian exodus in response to Arab 'orders from above' has survived with an astounding perseverance. In retrospect, the myth can be seen as the inevitable result of the denial of the Palestinians' right to national independence and Statehood, a principle that guided Zionist policies from the very beginning."[16]

Zionist policies were also able to rely on another carefully-constructed myth propagated with devastatingly effective impact: the myth about Arab refusal to negotiate with Israel. The myth was effectively propagated and kept alive by Israeli propagandists and their media, and political supporters in the West, partly as a result of the pathetic ineptitude of Arab regimes to adequately put forth the facts and explain their case to Western public opinion. Typical of what Israeli leaders and their media supporters have been saying to the Western and particularly North-American public with hardly any refutation, is the statement made by Israeli Labour leader Yitzhak Rabin, in the September/October 1982 issue of the *Harvard International Review*. The "facts speak for themselves," wrote Rabin, "the main reason — the heart of the Arab-Israeli conflict — was and still is, the fact that except for Egypt, there has been no readiness on the part of the Arab leaders to reconcile themselves with the existence of Israel as a viable, Jewish, independent State — regardless of its boundaries." Even peace with Egypt came as a totally unexpected surprise, according to the carefully-reconstructed version of reality put by Rabin to educated American audiences and dutifully supported by countless editorials and news "analyses" in the elite media as my chapter on language and propaganda will show.

The reality is, as always, more complex than the mythology and at times may be its exact opposite. Thus, while the public positions of the Arab regimes were traditionally one of commitment to a struggle to liberate Palestine, the private and real positions differed substantially. Israeli writer Tom Segev documented in his book *1949: The First Israelis* how Arab countries sought peace with Israel in 1948-49 but their attempts were rebuffed by Israeli leaders who preferred the status quo and the state of siege. "The Arabs 'recognized' Israel and were ready to discuss peace," Segev wrote, "but Israel did not accept the conditions"[17] of allowing the Palestinian refugees to return and permitting the establishment of a Palestinian Arab State as provided for by the United Nations resolution. That is still what Arab and Palestinian negotiators are demanding today and Israeli leaders are continuing to refuse. Simha Flapan stated at the beginning of his book that he wrote it "in the hope of sweeping away the distortions and lies that have hardened into sacrosanct myth…and had become accepted as historical truth."[18] About the myth of Israel's commitment to peace and Arab dedication to rejectionism, he discovered from declassified Israeli documents that: "On the contrary, from the end of World War II to 1952, Israel turned down successive proposals made by the Arab states."[19] Moreover, even the revolutionary Egyptian officers who overthrew King Faruk in 1952 were prepared to make peace with Israel. As early as 1955, a year before the Israeli-Anglo-French attack on Egypt which convinced Egyptians of Israeli expansionist designs and led to preparations for the next war, Egyptian President Gamal Abdel Nasser was making it clear that he was ready for peace with Israel on the basis of United Nations resolutions.[20]

Israeli leaders also bear responsibility for the injustice and illegality inherent in the process of dispossessing the Palestinians under occupation since 1967. Shortly after conquering the rest of Palestine in the June 1967 war, the Israeli government used a combination of measures to accomplish the Judaization of Palestinian territories through systematic confiscation and expropriation of land. The occupation authorities used the repressive British Defence Emergency Regulations of 1945 which the British mandate authorities had enacted to deal with Arab and Jewish clashes. Relying on Article 125 of these regulations, the Israeli military authorities typically declare a given area "restricted" for security reasons which they never fully have to justify. Palestinian farmers are then barred "for security reasons" from the area and are not allowed to cultivate their own land. After three years of forced exclusion, the Israeli authorities, invoking a Jordanian law, claim that this area had not been cultivated for three years and therefore must be declared "abandoned property" and expropriated as State land. In addition, shortly after the 1967 conquest of Arab territories, the Israeli government enacted a law similar to the Absentee Property Law of 1950 by which the Israelis were able with the fictitious appearance of legality to seize Palestinian property and land abandoned after the 1948-49 exodus. Through the "Abandoned Property of Private Individuals Order" of July 23, 1967, the Israeli authorities instituted in the West Bank and Gaza a "legal" framework for a replay of the process of expropriation and confiscation. Thus, all land areas and buildings whose owners left the country before, during or after the 1967 war — and the Israeli authorities did their best to prevent their return — were declared "abandoned property" and taken over by the military authorities. The land thus confiscated, expropriated or "seized," to use the term preferred by a Menahem Begin anxious to avoid the negative connotation of expropriation, was used for an energetic settlement policy aimed at completing the Judaization of the West Bank.[21] An international Commission of Jurists found that "the settlements have, to a substantial extent, been established through the expropriation or confiscation of private property."[22]

The process of Judaization was embodied in a number of Master Plans for the future of the occupied Palestinian territories. The Labour Party's vision was expressed in a 1970 government publication entitled "Judea and Samaria: Guidelines for Regional and Physical Planning." The document stated: "in the course of the Six Day War, new territories to the north, center, and south of the *former* boundaries of the State of Israel were *liberated*. For the first time in twenty years, the West Bank of the Jordan has become a *natural entity*." The central objective of the plan was spelled out as: "the development of the periphery of Samaria and Judea so that it may become integrated with the rest of the country."[23] With the Likud in power in 1977 there was no longer any pretence of returning any Arab territory and the World Zionist Organization (WZO) was called upon to draft a new master settlement plan. The Drobless plan (named after its author, the head of the WZO's settlement division) was finalized in 1981. It stated that: "there is to be not a shadow of doubt regarding our intention to remain in Judea and Samaria. A dense chain of settlements on the mountain ridge running southwards from Nabuls to Hebron will serve as a reliable barrier on the eastern front. This buffer zone of settlements will also create security for settlers in the Jordan valley. Both areas between concentrations of the minority [Arab] population and the area around them must be settled to minimize the danger of the rise of another Arab State in the region." The plan was updated in 1983 and the declared objective of the revised plan known as "Master Plan for 2010" was to "disperse maximally large Jewish population in areas of high settlement priority, using small national inputs and in a relatively short period by using the settlement potential of the West Bank and to achieve the incorporation [of the West Bank] into the national [Israeli] system."[24]

During his Middle East tour following the American-led war against Iraq, U.S. Secretary of State James Baker met twice with a Palestinian delegation in Jerusalem. At their second meeting with Baker on April 9, 1991, the delegation presented him with a memorandum which, inter alia, warned against the continued Israeli policy of creating facts on the ground in the occupied territories to render the peace negotiations useless:

> In the last year, an estimated 15,000 new settlers have moved into the occupied territories and every day brings an average of 50 new settlers. Already, the Jewish population in East Jerusalem equals the Arab population of 150,000, while the Jewish population in the rest of the occupied territories exceeds 100,000.
>
> The stated position of the Israeli Ministry of Housing that 'only' 10 percent of new housing starts are taking place in the occupied territories is disingenuous and disguises its true intent — to erase the 'green line' and to establish facts on the grounds in order to sabotage a negotiated settlement.
>
> Since the beginning of the Gulf war, and the imposition of a blanket curfew on the occupied territories for six weeks, Palestinian villages have received notices declaring thousands of dunums 'state land' and ordering them to cease farming or face 'trespassing' charges.
>
> By the mid-1980s, Israel had already seized over 50 percent of the land base of the West Bank and Gaza for exclusive Jewish use, and every year since, confiscation orders are issued to another 1-2 percent of this land. The clearing of these lands for Jewish housing and road construction has also resulted in the uprooting of 100,000 olive and other fruit-bearing trees. All this is happening in a period when thousands of workers dismissed from their jobs in Israel have returned to farming as their only source of subsistence.
>
> "...our land is being pulled out from under our feet. The destruction of our farming land and the transfer of large numbers of Israeli civilians onto this land are creating almost insurmountable obstacles in the path of peace."[25]

According to Israeli Knesset members Dedi Zucker and Chaim Oron, the current construction activities in the occupied Arab territories are designed to provide an additional 12,000 new housing units within the next three years with the aim of enlarging the Jewish populations in the occupied territories by another 50,000 settlers.[26] Israeli leaders reason that with about 200,000 Jewish settlers in the West Bank and Gaza there would be no force or power on earth which could remove them in any peace agreement by which Israeli occupation of Palestine is terminated. The Camp David peace process had played a role in facilitating the realization of that goal by allowing the Israelis to consolidate their occupation, intensify their settlement activities, and multiply by tenfold the number of Jewish settlers in the occupied Arab territories. Prime Minister Shamir planned to use the latest U.S.-sponsored peace-talks for similar purposes. After his defeat in the June 1992 election, he admitted that he had planned to drag the peace talks with the Palestinians for ten years until he brought 500,000 Jewish settlers to the occupied Arab territories. By then there would be little or nothing to negotiate about. Significantly, at their 1992 peace-talks, Israeli negotiators were telling their Palestinian counterparts that Camp David was irrelevant now because "things have changed since 1978."[27] Camp David may be dead as a framework for a comprehensive peace in the region but the Zionist strategy of "military faits accomplis as the basis for political achievements," is alive and well.

This policy of expropriation, dispossession, and plantation of alien groups in the occupied Arab territories is a violation of both justice and international law. Palestinians who lived on the land for centuries are being uprooted to make room for an alien people invoking a right based on divine promise and historical connection. The international community and international law do not recognize the validity of divine promises in inter-State relations. Nor do they recognize the principle of "historical right" which, if accepted, would theoretically call into question the legal existence of most modern nation-States. Articles 42-56 of the Hague Regulations, and Articles 47-78 of the Geneva Convention deal with the rights and duties of a military occupation in occupied territories. Article 49 of the Fourth Geneva Convention specifically prohibits the occupying power from "deporting or transferring any of its own civilian population to the occupied territories."

Israeli leaders have claimed that international law does not apply to the occupied territories and advanced, in support, a number of specious arguments based on semantic obfuscations such as the notion that these territories were not occupied, they were "liberated," or that they fell into Israel's hands as a result of a war of "defensive conquest." These arguments are rejected by the entire international community including the United States. The international community has repeatedly called on Israel to apply and respect the Hague Regulations and the Geneva Convention and refused to recognize the legality of its Jewish settlement actions. The international community has also repeatedly condemned Israeli violations of human rights, acts of collective punishment, house-demolition, arbitrary arrest and detention and the continued process of dispossession and deportation of Palestinians.[28] UN General Assembly Resolution 3092 specifically stated:

> "The General Assembly...expresses its grave concern at the violation by Israel of the Geneva Convention relative to the Protection of Civilian Persons in Time of War as well as the other applicable international conventions and regulations, in particular the following violations:
>
> (a) The annexation of certain parts of the occupied territories;
> (b) The establishment of Israeli settlements in the occupied territories and the transfer of an alien population thereto;
> (c)The destruction and demolition of Arab houses, quarters, villages and towns;
> (c) The confiscation and expropriation of Arab property in the occupied territories and all other transactions for the acquisition of land between the Government of Israel, Israeli institutions and Israeli nationals on the one hand, and the inhabitants or institutions of the occupied territories on the other;

(e) The evacuation, deportation, expulsion, displacement and transfer of the Arab inhabitants of the Arab territories occupied by Israel since 1967, and the denial of their right to return to their homes and property;

(f) Administrative detention and ill-treatment inflicted on the Arab inhabitants;

(g) The pillaging of archaeological and cultural property in the occupied territories;

(h) The interference with religious freedom, religious practices and family rights and customs;

(i) The illegal exploitation of the natural wealth, resources of the occupied territories...[29]

The situation has worsened since the resolution was adopted in 1978; Israel continued to consolidate its repressive occupation, expropriate Palestinian land, inflict collective punishments on entire communities, intern and deport Palestinian nationalist leaders, and expand the Jewish settlements in the occupied territories in defiance of the international community.[30]

Arab and Palestinian Positions

There is no attempt here to argue that the Arabs welcomed the establishment of the State of Israel or that they were gladly willing to embrace its ideological convictions and connections with former colonial powers. On the other hand it is plainly misleading to abstract Arab enmity to Israel from all causality and historical context in order to better compare it to European anti-Semitic persecution of Jews. Like all nationalisms, Arab nationalism was not free from ethnocentricity and parochial tendencies of rigid thought and irrational actions. But its negativism did not spring from some sort of decontextualized aberrations of the "Arab mind" or "Muslim violence" as pro-Israeli academic cold-warriors such as Walter Laqueur or Bernard Lewis like to suggest. It was the product of a specific historical experience which pitted the indigenous Arab people against European colonialism and imperialism and against Zionism as an extension of these movements in its conquering drive and subjugating intentions. Even critical accounts of Arab nationalism such as that by Sylvia Haim in her *Arab Nationalism* recognizes its role as a political weapon against European domination. Violence inhered in such unequal and coercive relations. The violence of oppression generated violence from the anger against inequality and the revolt against subjugation.

Jewish nationalism itself was the product of a dialectics of conflict between liberal assimilationist ideals and political Zionism's assertions of ethnocentricity. Theodor Herzl, the founder of political Zionism, idealized struggle and conflict as supreme channels of human redemption. And in the end, Zionism was able to achieve its goal of a Jewish State in Palestine not through the ideals of humanist Zionists like Ahad Ha-am and Judah Magnes who preached equality in a binational State but through the activism of a Ben-Gurion and the violence of a Vladimir Jabotinsky and his followers. The seizure of Palestine from its original inhabitants necessarily implied violence on a massive scale. The destruction of an entire society is not mitigated by the refusal of this society to acquiesce in a project condemning the majority to a status of minority. Arab nationalism, often appropriated for selfish reasons by corrupt and dictatorial Arab regimes, confronted political Zionism as an extension of European imperialism and clashed with Jewish nationalism, itself a revolt against European liberalism, and its exclusionist State-supported manifestations after the establishment of the State of Israel. The result was a state of permanent belligerency interrupted by periods of preparation for the next conflict. The logic of the Zionist sword imposed a reluctant *de facto* acceptance of the reality of a nationalist Jewish State which negated the nationalist aspirations of the Palestinian people and by extension, but mainly by military force, that of the Arab nation.

To say that the Arabs were prepared to recognize Israel, as many Israeli historians are now saying, does not mean that, had they had a choice in the matter of establishing a Jewish State at the expense of the Arab Palestinian society, that they would have welcomed the extinction of Arab Palestine. It simply means that behind the rhetoric and propagandistically-useful mythology, there is a documented historical record showing that a negotiated settlement could have been reached in the Israeli-Palestinian conflict, and if it were not it was not because the Arabs were not willing to entertain the notion of peaceful co-existence with Israel. What has been often misunderstood, and frequently deliberately distorted by Israeli leaders for propaganda purposes in the West, has been the extent of Arab realism in terms of accepting, grudgingly to be sure, the reality of the imposed injustice on the Palestinian people. As early as 1949 Arab leaders were prepared to come to terms with this reality on the basis of a reasonable reparation of the injustice inherent in the destruction of the Palestinian society and the dispersal of its people. However, Israeli leaders predicated then, as they do now, the national existence of Israel on the denial of a national existence of Palestine.

Humiliated politically and decimated militarily after the 1967 Israeli attack and the occupation by the Israeli army of major portions of Arab territories, Arab regimes publicly rejected any possibility of peace with Israel. But they readily admitted to themselves the failure of the military option which up till 1967 was believed to be inevitable given Israel's refusal to repatriate the Palestinian refugees or to withdraw from the territories occupied in the 1948-49 war. After 1967, Arab leaders agreed to pursue a diplomatic solution to the conflict which now focused on Israeli withdrawal from its latest conquests in 1967. Egyptian President Nasser and King Hussein of Jordan were to lead the Arab effort in this direction.

Both Nasser and Hussein stated their readiness to end the state of war with Israel and *de facto* recognize its existence within the pre-1967 lines. This came in a historic meeting between Nasser and Hussein in Cairo on September 30, 1967. The two leaders agreed on a five-point political programme defining the Arab position:

1. We would be willing to recognize everyone's right to live in peace and security in the area, including Israel's.
2. We agreed to bring an end to the state of belligerency and the war.
3. We agreed to open the international waterways, including the Suez Canal, to all nations.

In return for these concessions, the two leaders agreed to insist:

4. That the Israelis withdraw from the territories occupied
    during the June 1967 conflict;
5. That a real solution is found for the living symbol of our con-
    tinual state of war — the refugees: that they would be given
    the right to return to their land, or adequate compensation
    in accordance with the earliest resolutions of the United Na-
    tions.[31]

Thus, in October, Nasser told British Labour MP Sir Dingle Foot that he was ready to negotiate a political settlement with Israel through the United Nations.[32] In November, King Hussein toured European capitals and went to Washington to make the case, on behalf of Nasser and himself, for a political settlement of the crisis. He stated that they were prepared to recognize Israel's right to exist in peace and security and to allow freedom of navigation to Israeli shipping even through the Suez Canal, provided Israel withdrew from all the Arab territories it conquered in the recent war and accepted to negotiate on the basis of UN resolutions a just solution to the Palestinian refugees. As had been their wont in the past, the Israeli leaders shifted the blame on the Arabs for "starting" the war and claimed that Arab leaders must accept the responsibility of the loss of their territories which ensued from a war Israel claimed it fought in "self-defense." In addition, Israeli leaders claimed that the war — which they in fact had started — had relieved them of any obligations to respect the General Armistice Agreements with Egypt, Jordan and Syria. They would therefore no longer recognize the validity of these agreements and would not cooperate with any related UN machinery such as the Mixed Armi-stice Commissions or the United Nations Truce Supervisory Organization. Israel also defiantly told the UN that it no longer recognized the old demarcation lines or the demilitarized zones separating Israel from Egypt, Jordan and Syria. In short, Is-rael seemed to be serving notice that thanks to its new military conquests it was unilaterally abrogating the legal obligations it contracted in the various armistice agreements of 1949. In addition, it also seemed determined to turn the latest faits accomplis into a new and permanent reality that the Arabs and the world must learn to accept. Naturally, the United Nations rejected the preposterous proposi-tion that a war started by one party can relieve that party of its international obliga-tions. But Israeli leaders believed that time was on their side. Thus, Prime Minister Levi Eshkol summed up the Israeli position in the following manner: "We need not be in a hurry about anything. We are staying put until the Arabs make the first con-crete move (and the later that is, the better it is for us). The intransigent Syrians and Algerians are doing the work of 'Zionist agents', if only they realised it."[33]

In 1970, Nasser publicly stated his readiness for full peace negotiations leading to "durable peace" with Israel in return for Israeli withdrawal from the occupied Arab territories and a just settlement of the problem of Palestinian refugees.[34] It should be noted here that the Egyptian peace offer did not mention the political rights of the Palestinians whose problem was still viewed in the humanitarian terms of repatriation to their homes and land or compensation for property lost, and not yet in terms of independent national existence. Israel did not respond to Nasser's offer. Similar peace offers were made by Egypt in 1971 and by Jordan in 1972, and turned down by Israel.[35] Subsequent Arab peace plans such as the Fahd plan of 1981 and the Fez peace plan of 1982 based on security guarantees for all States in the region including Israel and self-determination for the Palestinians were opposed by the United States and Israel. At the Casablanca Summit in 1989, the Arab heads of State for the first time since 1947 collectively and publicly endorsed the concept of two States in Palestine (Israel and Palestine) and also collectively endorsed UN Security Council Resolution 242.

From 1974 on, the Palestinian position gradually evolved away from the idea of a secular democratic State in all of Palestine until in 1981 the PLO formally notified the United Nations of its acceptance of a solution based on United Nations resolutions. The UN General Assembly formally recorded, in December 1982, the PLO position and stated that it took "note of the declaration of the Palestine Liberation Organization of 19 April 1981 to pursue its role in the solution of the Question of Palestine on the basis of the attainment in Palestine of the inalienable rights of the Palestinian people in accordance with relevant resolutions of the United Nations."

Until recently the PLO had refused to accept UN Security Council Resolution 242 because of the failure of that resolution to recognize the political rights of the Palestinians to whom the resolution referred as simple refugees. In addition, Resolution 242 presented other legal problems. It emphasized the inadmissibility of the acquisition of territories by war and called for the establishment of a "just and lasting peace in the Middle East" based on the application of the following two principles: a) withdrawal of Israeli armed forces from territories occupied in the recent conflict; and b) termination of all claims or states of belligerency and respect for and acknowledgement of the sovereignty, territorial integrity and political independence of every state in the area. In requiring Israel to withdraw only from territories occupied since 1967 and requiring the Arab States to recognize Israel's sovereignty and territorial integrity, Resolution 242 was in fact legalizing the Israeli occupation of the territories of Palestine seized by Israel in 1948-49 in excess of the area of the Jewish State as defined by United Nations 1947 partition resolution. This violates resolution 242's own preamble which reaffirmed the principle of "the inadmissibility of the acquisition of territory by war." Israel does not possess title over the Palestinian territories acquired during the 1948-49 war, and its armistice agreements with Egypt, Lebanon, Jordan, and Syria in 1949 did not lay down political boundaries. These agreements specifically provided that the armistice lines were delineated "without prejudice to the ultimate settlement of the Palestine Question."[36]

The Palestine National Council, meeting in Algiers on November 15, 1988 officially and explicitly accepted the principle of two States in Palestine: Israel and Palestine. It adopted a historic declaration of Palestinian independence which it grounded in the Palestinian people's natural and historic rights in the land of Palestine as well as in two specific instruments of international legality. The first was Article 22 of the Covenant of the League of Nations which provided a basis in international law for Palestinian independence subject to rendering administrative assistance to the Palestinian people. The second instrument of international law serving as a specific basis for Palestinian independence was the United Nations General Assembly Partition Resolution 181 of November 29, 1947. Significantly, the Palestinian Declaration of Independence stated: "Despite the historical injustice done to the Palestinian people by their dispersion and their being deprived of the right of self-determination after UN

General Assembly Resolution 181 of 1947, which partitioned Palestine in two States, one Arab and one Jewish, that resolution still provides the legal basis for the right of the Palestinian Arab people to national sovereignty and independence."[37] In accepting the injustice inherent in the partition resolution and using it as a basis for Palestinian independence, the Palestinian leadership was also unambiguously recognizing the existence and the legality of the State of Israel. PLO leader Yasser Arafat was anxious to leave no ambiguity as to the import of Palestinian acceptance of the partition resolution; he clarified his previous declarations and statements by emphatically saying that the Palestinian leadership had recognized "the right of all parties concerned in the Middle East conflict to exist in peace and security, and, as I have mentioned, including the state of Palestine, *Israel* and other neighbors…"[38]

The Declaration also set forth guidelines for the nature and constitution of Palestine:

> The State of Palestine is the state of Palestinians wherever they may be. The State is for them to enjoy within it their collective national and cultural identity, theirs to pursue within it a complete equality of rights. In it will be safeguarded their political and religious convictions and their human dignity by means of a parliamentary democratic system of governance, itself based on freedom of expression and the freedom to form parties. The right to minorities will be duly respected by the majority, as minorities must abide by decisions of the majority. Governance will be based on principles of social justice, equality and non-discrimination in public rights, men or women, or grounds of race, religion, colour or sex under the aegis of a constitution which ensures the rule of law and an independent judiciary. Thus shall these principles allow no departure from Palestine's age-old spiritual and civilizational heritage of tolerance and religious coexistence.[39]

The Palestine National Council also issued a political statement which, significantly, made no mention of the PLO National Charter which had called for the dismantlement of the Zionist State in Palestine. The omission was by design. The declaration of Palestinian independence was explicitly based on UN General Assembly Partition Resolution 181 which provided a juridical basis for the establishment of Israel and Palestine. Accepting the resolution necessarily meant accepting its legal basis in its entirety as applicable to both Israel and Palestine and this essentially rendered inoperative the principle of a secular democratic State in all of Palestine. Yasser Arafat later described the PLO charter as null and void. Further, the PNC political statement remained silent about the content of "armed struggle" and reaffirmed "the determination of the PLO to arrive at a comprehensive settlement of the Arab-Israeli conflict and its core, which is the question of Palestine…in such a manner that safeguards the Palestinian Arab people's rights to return, to self-determination, and the establishment of their independent national State on their national soil, and that institutes arrangements for security and peace for all states in the region," through a negotiated settlement at an international peace conference on the basis of UN resolutions 242 and 338 and Palestinian national rights.[40]

The PLO also made additional concessions which were reported by the Israeli newspaper *Jerusalem Post*. In December 1989, a close associate of Arafat told a London audience that the PLO had "no objections to mutually agreed border modifications in so far as they may be necessary for genuine Israeli security concerns and needs."[41] The Palestinians were prepared to settle for less than the whole of West Bank and Gaza, that is less than 23 percent of mandated Palestine.

The positions of the parties are thus clearly defined. Arab governments and the PLO are ready for a negotiated settlement of the Arab-Israeli-Palestinian conflict on the basis of universally accepted principles of justice and of international legality embodied in the various UN resolutions. It should be axiomatic that no process or accords that ignore these two fundamental values can hope to achieve a lasting peace in the region. This was underlined by the UN General Assembly's rejection, in 1981, of the Camp David accords and any accords "that ignore, infringe, violate or deny the inalienable rights of the Palestinian people, including the rights of return, self-determination, national independence and sovereignty in Palestine."

Conditions for a Just and Enduring Peace

Given Israel's responsibility for the injustices inflicted upon the Palestinians, and given the international community's recognition of these responsibilities and UN resolutions adopted to deal with the conflict, and in view of the Arab and Palestinian positions on the conflict, it is now commonly accepted by the international community that peace based on justice and international legitimacy must satisfy the following conditions:

1. Repatriation of or compensation to the Palestine refugees: the United Nations has been reminding Israel since December 1948 of its obligation to allow the Palestine refugees to return to their homes as required by international law and the Universal Declaration of Human Rights (1948, article 13) which provided that "everyone has the right to return to his country." Resolution 194 of December 11, 1948 provided that " refugees wishing to return to their homes and live at peace with their neighbors should be permitted to do so at the earliest practicable date, and that compensation should be paid for the property of those choosing not to return and for loss or damage to property which, under principles of international law or in equity, should be made good by the Government or authorities responsible." Since 1981, the General Assembly has declared in several resolutions that "the Palestine Arab refugees are entitled to their property and to the income derived therefrom, in conformity with the principles of justice and equity."

2. Recognition of the Palestinian people's rights to self-determination, to independence and to sovereignty. These rights have already been recognized by the international community; only Israel and the United States continue to oppose them. But Israel cannot claim the validity of its juridical existence on the basis of UN Partition Resolution 181, of 1947 and continue to violate its provision for the establishment of a Palestinian State.

3. The end of Israeli occupation of Arab territories is a *sine qua non* condition for a peaceful settlement. Under the Hague Regulations of 1907 and the Fourth Geneva Convention of 1949 the occupant is regarded as an "administrator" of the occupied territory. The UN has emphasized by several resolutions the principle of

the inadmissibility of the acquisition of territory by war. Now, the absence of prescription in international law means that the passage of time cannot legitimize Israel's annexation of occupied Arab territories. Only when there is a complete absence of protests and claims can the passage of time make the new state of affairs part of the accepted international order. It is self-evident that Israel's occupation of Palestine and of other Arab territories in Lebanon and in Syria is not accepted, and that no lasting peace can be established in the region unless Israel accepts to end its occupation of Arab territories. In pursuing his separate negotiations, Egyptian President Sadat believed, as he rightly emphasized in his speech to the Israeli Knesset in November 1977, that total Israeli withdrawal "was a logical and undisputed fact" without which peace and security would be meaningless.[42]

4. The transformation of the legal, demographic and institutional structures of Jerusalem is accepted neither by the Arabs nor by the international community. In this respect, the General Assembly and the Security Council have declared that all legislative and administrative measures and actions taken by Israel which tend to change the legal status of Jerusalem are null and void and must be rescinded. The official American position on Jerusalem, spelled out by Ambassador Arthur Goldberg on July 14, 1967, rejected Israel's claims: "With regard to the specific measures taken by the Government of Israel on June 28, I wish to make it clear that the United States does not accept or recognize these measures altering the status of Jerusalem."[43] Ambassador Charles Yost was even more specific and stated before the UN Security Council on July 1, 1969: "The expropriation or confiscation of land, the construction of housing on such land, the demolition or confiscation of buildings, including those having historic or religious significance, and the application of Israeli law to occupied portions of the city are detrimental to our common interests in the city. The United States considers that the part of Jerusalem that came under control of Israel in the June war, like other areas occupied by Israel, is occupied territory and hence subject to the provisions of international law governing the rights and obligations of an occupying power."[44]

Far from paying any attention to protests and injunctions from the international community, various Israeli governments have been accelerating the pace of Jewish settlements in Jerusalem in a determined effort to eradicate the Arab character of the city. Israeli leaders have also been sponsoring and supporting Jewish infiltration and seizure of Muslim and Christian properties in Jerusalem, on the assumption that, as Israeli mayor of Jerusalem Teddy Kollek put it: "with enough pressure, the Arabs will gradually pack up and leave." After regretting the Israeli government role in the Jewish settlers' takeover of a Christian compound, and its involvement in helping Jewish settlers infiltrate Arab districts, Kollek described the familiar ritual of dispossession in the latest example of Israeli expropriation of Arab property in the Jerusalem Arab district of Silwan: "evicting Arab families in the middle of the night, the sad and helpless faces of the Arab residents mocked by the settlers' gleeful singing and dancing."[45]

All of this underlines the importance of ensuring that an equitable solution to Jerusalem, sacred city to all three monotheistic religions, must reflect the interests of the three communities. Such an equitable solution is embodied in the principle of equal communal representation envisaged by the 1947 partition resolution; it provided for the formation of a tripartite communal administration composed of an equal number of Christians, Moslems, and Jews.[46]

5. A just peace must provide for the security of all States in the region including Israel and Palestine. The latter will be in greater need of security guarantees than the former. No respected strategist or military thinker can accept the claim that a Palestinian State would pose a threat to Israel's survival. The Israeli Center for Strategic Studies at Tel-Aviv University, headed by mainstream military establishment figures, reports that Israel has a mobilizable manpower of 540,000, some 3,800 tanks, 682 aircraft, and thousands of artillery pieces and missiles supported by one of the most sophisticated electronic systems in the world. In addition, Seymour Hersh documented in his recent book *The Samson Option* the extent of sophisticated Israeli nuclear arsenal which has essentially made Israeli territories inviolable sanctuaries. The PLO has 8,000 men in scattered places, no tanks, no aircrafts, and no missiles. A detailed American study of the security question concluded that "a settlement based on an independent Palestinian State which meets certain minimal conditions actually constitutes a recommended strategic choice for Israel."[47] Strategic territorial depth may have made sense in nineteenth century's warfare doctrines; in the missile age it has become an anachronistic concept, its irrelevancy dramatically demonstrated by recent Middle East wars. The argument advanced by Israeli leaders that continued occupation of Arab territories is necessary for security reasons is clearly a spurious argument designed to cloak and justify expansionist policies driven by ideological and religious beliefs, not security considerations.[48] Abba Eban, former Israeli Foreign Minister, commented in the *New York Times,* that: "If there were to be an Arab-ruled entity in a large part of the West Bank and Gaza...it would be the weakest military entity on earth...To call such an entity a threat to Israel's survival is preposterous. It is the survival of the Palestinian nation that could be threatened by irredentism."[49]

Conflict over Fundamental Values

The Israeli-Palestinian conflict is essentially a conflict over fundamental values and so long as these values remain incompatible no genuine peace is likely to come to the region. The most fundamental value of a people living in a nation-State is that of its national existence and so it is logical that both the Israeli people and the Palestinian people consider their respective national existence as their most fundamental value. But it is the asymmetry between the existential conditions of these two fundamental values, and the Israeli view of the necessity of such asymmetry, that nourish and maintain the conflict. Israel's national existence is militarily secured, politically and legally dynamic and organically linked to Jews outside of Israel. The Palestinians' national existence has been destroyed by the partition resolution, the forcible establishment of Israel, and Israeli leaders' policy of expulsion, dispossession and destruction of Palestinian Arab villages. (In 1975 Israeli human rights activist Israel Shahak counted 350 Palestinian Arab villages destroyed by Israel since 1948.)[50] In addition, the reconstitution of Palestinian national existence is being opposed by Israel with the active support of the United States. Despite the moral and legal arguments against the partition resolution of 1947, it has now been accepted by the Palestinians as a basis for a peaceful settlement. This, however, is opposed by the Israeli leaders who view Palestinian national existence as incompatible with Israeli national existence and Zionist goals. This view is reinforced by Israel's legislated commitment to the primacy of Zionist ideology through its organic and legal link with the World Zionist Organization.[51]

Unlike any other State, Israel's partnership with the World Zionist Organization creates a sort of dual sovereignty whereby the two entities, the State apparatus and the organization, work together for the well-being of a national constituency described as "the entire Jewish people." Israel's link to the world Zionist organization and its commitment to a national constituency which extends beyond its borders is reflected in a number of "Fundamental Laws" such as the "Status Law," the "Law of Return" and the "Law of Nationality." These laws establish the Zionist character of the State of Israel and guarantee its bond to the "entire Jewish people." The Status Law states that: "The mission of gathering in the exiles…is *the central task* of the State of Israel and the Zionist movement in our days."[52] This means that the State of Israel's primary responsibility is not to *all its citizens* (certainly not to its Moslem and Christian citizens) but rather to *all* the Jewish people, i.e., the Jews within and without Israel. Such a responsibility is to be reflected in Israel's achievement, in cooperation with the World Zionist organization, of its central task of bringing to Israel the Jews of the world.

The Law of Return states that "every Jew has the right to come to this country" and automatically be granted Israeli citizenship. In essence, people who are Jews and citizens of other countries will automatically be granted priorities and rights in Israel which are denied to Moslem and Christian Palestinians born in Palestine. With the Eichmann trial judgement in 1961, Israel alleged that the "Jewish people" enjoyed a nationality status wherever they were, and consequently were legally linked to the State of Israel. In 1964, Israel and the Zionist Organization — which enjoys a governmental status within Israel — issued a joint communique which warned all Jews living abroad against "the danger of assimilation," and promised to work to implement, in public law, Zionist nationalism wherever Jews lived. When the anti-Zionist American Council for Judaism pressed the State Department for its position on the status of Jews living in America, the official letter of reply clearly stated that the United States government "does not regard the 'Jewish people' concept as a concept in international law."[53]

The Israeli Law of Return meant of necessity that Israel's Moslem and Christian citizens had to be subjected to various forms of discrimination the nature of which has been authoritatively documented and explained by Sabri Jiryis in his book *The Arabs in Israel*. It also meant that the commitment to Jewish immigration to Israel was automatically accompanied by strategies to encourage Arab emigration from Israel, and from occupied Palestine. The notorious Koening Plan recommended several strategies to encourage Arab emigration. In the field of education, for instance, it recommended "to make it easy for the Arabs to go abroad for studying and to make it difficult for them to return and find a job — that policy might help their emigration."[54]

As a matter of policy and by law Israel is therefore committed to the Zionist ideological tenet which provides that Israel is the State of all the Jews in the world. The Zionist ideology is believed to be both a national interest and also a fundamental value of the Israeli State. Thus, in addition to national existence which all modern nation-States share as the most fundamental value, Israel holds the Zionist ideology as another fundamental value. This explains the dominant thinking among Israeli leaders who seem to sincerely regard additional territories as a Zionist objective necessary for the absorption of future Jewish immigrants. This dynamic view of Israel's political boundaries has been a basic component of dominant Israeli strategic thinking and finds its source in conceptions articulated by, among others, David Ben-Gurion who viewed the proposed partition of Palestine within such a context: "We shall accept a state in the boundaries fixed today — but the boundaries of Zionist aspirations are the concern of the Jewish people and no external factor will be able to limit them."[55] Thus, Israel's commitment to the basic tenet of the ideological Zionist view of nationality and its concomitant commitment to territorial expansionist concepts explain the refusal to grant Palestinian refugees their universally recognized right of repatriation and also explain the negation of the Palestinian people's right to self-determination in their own country.

These ideological views are embodied and reflected in the dominant thinking of all mainstream Israeli leaders. What distinguishes the Likud leaders from others is mainly the fact that Likud leaders are particularly outspoken and frank in stating time and again that there is nothing to negotiate about with the Palestinians, except perhaps various forms of continued Israeli occupation. The new Labour government is willing to make concessions on the form of autonomy to be granted to the Palestinians under occupation, but insist, in the name of strategic considerations, on denying the Palestinians their right to self-determined national existence.

Israeli Leaders' Positions

After a visit to the Middle East in 1989 former President Jimmy Carter concluded: "All of the participants in the Middle East dispute are ready to go to an international conference except the leaders of Israel."[56] Israeli leaders show no sign of interest in a negotiated settlement which recognizes Palestinian national rights and involves Israeli withdrawal from the occupied Arab territories. Such a negotiated settlement continues to be considered by most current Israeli leaders as contrary to Israel's national interest and to its commitment to the political objectives of the Zionist ideology.

The dominant thinking in Israeli Labour and Likud camps today is no different from the ideological convictions which dominated Zionist thinking on the eve of the establishment of Israel in 1948. The recognition of Palestinian political rights continues to be viewed as incompatible with the national existence of Israel given its partnership with the world Zionist organization and its *central task* of gathering in the exiles. The late Israeli historian Simha Flapan wrote that an essential part of Israeli strategy has been "the elimination of the Palestinian people as contenders for, and even inhabitants of the same territory...These objectives took precedence over peace."[57] Neither Likud nor Labour leaderships show any signs that the vastly different international and regional environments, and the unilateral concessions made by the PLO, have significantly affected their thinking, their commitment to rejectionism or their view of Palestinian national rights.

Labour's public acceptance of the formula "land for peace" dates back to 1970 when Israeli Foreign Minister Yigal Allon outlined a plan for partial Israeli withdrawal from the occupied Arab territories and for the establishment of a chain of Jewish colonies along the Jordan River, the Rift Valley and the "Judean" desert.

A 1970 Labour government publication entitled *Judea and Samaria: Guidelines for Regional and Physical Planning* revealed Labour's thinking on the question of occupation of Arab territories. It stated: "in the course of the Six Day War, new territories to the north, center, and south of the *former* boundaries of the State of Israel were *liberated*. For the first time in twenty years, the West Bank of the Jordan has become a *natural entity.*" The Guidelines go on to state that the central planning objective must be "the development of the periphery of Samaria and Judea so that it may become integrated with the rest of the country." The northern part of the Gaza strip and the densely-populated parts of the West Bank not colonized by Jewish settlers under the Allon Plan were to form part of a Jordanian-Palestinian federation under Jordanian rule from Amman. The Allon plan was never officially approved but continued to provide guidelines for Jewish colonization of the West Bank and Gaza until Labour was voted out of power by the Likud in 1977.[58]

The mainstream Israeli Labour leadership has remained frozen since the Yigal Allon Plan and has shown neither the courage nor the willingness necessary to honestly confront the question of long-denied Palestinian rights. The bankruptcy of its thought was exposed at the 1988 meeting in Madrid of Socialist International. In his long-awaited speech, Israeli Labour leader Shimon Peres presented a peace position which confirmed fundamental agreement with Likud's ideological and rejectionist thinking. He made no reference to Palestinian rights, no mention of PLO, and stated that "a Palestinian state already exists in Jordan." European socialist leaders were outraged by the hypocrisy and anachronism of these views. One by one they took the floor to lambast Peres who angrily stormed out of the meeting. The late Bruno Kreisky, vice-President of the International and respected former Premier of Austria, later issued a communique which read: "Israel is a semi-fascist state…The leaders of the (Israeli) labour party, and particularly Shimon Peres, have betrayed the Socialist International."[59]

There is an identity of views and beliefs between Labour and Likud when it comes to fundamental questions of Palestinian rights to their land. Both ground their convictions in divine authority above all man-made laws even if Labour leaders are more circumspect in advertising the Bible as the convenient basis of their political convictions. But occasionally Labour leaders make explicit statements of their position in a manner identical to that routinely used by the right-wing and extreme-right wing leaders; such was the case when Peres stated that "since the Bible made no distinction between Judea and Samaria, we have the right to settle in both" and "there is no argument in Israel about our historic rights in the Land of Israel. The past is immutable and the Bible is the decisive document in determining the fate of our Land."[60]

Israeli leaders responded to the challenge of the Palestinian uprising with unrestrained repression, organized and coordinated by Labour Leader Yitzhak Rabin, responsible for the so-called iron-fist policy of bone-breaking, shooting at unarmed demonstrators, and routinely subjecting entire communities to collective punishments.[61] In response to international public opinion's outrage, Israeli leaders proposed a "peace plan" conditioned upon the termination of the Palestinian uprising. It proposed election without freedom and "peace" with occupation. It completely ignored the concessions made by the Palestinian leadership at the 19th PNC Congress, made no mention of withdrawal, no mention of Palestinian right to self-determination and no mention of negotiations with the Palestinian leadership. The Shamir Plan was endorsed by the Labour group and thus represents a common denominator between the two currents of official Israeli thinking. In an interview with Leslie Stahl from CBS *Face the Nation* on November 19, 1989, Israeli Prime Minister Shamir, who had opposed even the Camp David accords, explained the latest Israeli proposals:

> Shamir: "We have some differences of view with the United States...The Americans believe that the end solution has to be something in the spirit of land for peace."
>
> Stahl: "Camp David."
>
> Shamir: "It's not Camp David."
>
> Stahl: "Land for peace."
>
> Shamir: "Excuse me, it's not Camp David."
>
> Stahl: "Land for peace?"
>
> Shamir: "In our opinion, we have to resolve the conflict, *but the territories are part of our national heritage.*" (emphasis added.)[62]

Although the official and dominant myth in the West held that successive Israeli leaders had always been ready to negotiate with their Arab neighbours without prior conditions, Secretary Baker found out otherwise. In his long-drawn negotiations with Israel following the American-led war against Iraq he was presented with a set of conditions before Israeli leaders could agree to show up at the International Peace Conference: Israel must have the right to veto choice of Palestinian delegates, to exclude from the agenda any Palestinian claims; to neutralize the European presence at the peace conference and reduce to silence the United Nations, and by extension its resolutions on the question of Palestine. The United States gave in to Israel on all of these demands. The peace conference which was finally convened in Madrid in October 1991 was, as Secretary of State James Baker would later recognize, "basically constructed on Israel's terms."[63] It thus became a replay of the Camp David process which Shamir had publicly opposed and which denied the Palestinians self-determination. Shamir brought with him to Madrid his peculiar vision of history and historical rights and a "peace plan" which he himself had once derided as being designed for public relations purposes.[64]

The day following Labour Leader Yitzhak Rabin's victory in the June 23, 1992 Israeli election, Shimon Shamir, of Tel-Aviv University and former Israeli Ambassador to Egypt, appeared on PBS television. He told the interviewer that there were substantive differences between the defeated Prime Minister Shamir and the victorious Labour leader Rabin. The latter was ready to show flexibility on the autonomy issue in the peace negotiations. He was willing to hold elections in the occupied territories (something that Shamir promised several times and reneged on several times), and then negotiate with the elected Palestinians the ultimate status of the territories. But this "substantive" difference still rejects the notion of negotiating with the PLO, denies that the Palestinians in exile have a stake in the conflict, rejects the internationally-supported concept of right of return, and reduces the negotiations to modalities of autonomy for the Palestinians under occupation only. There was another "substantive" difference, professor Shamir informed the American viewers, between Yitzhak Shamir and Yitzhak Rabin: the former insisted on building settlements for political reasons, the latter values the settlements for strategic reason. But regardless of their *raison d'être* the Jewish settlements have been built in violation of international law and on land confiscated from its rightful owners. Likud leaders are on the record (December 1989) as being committed, if the American-Israeli "peace process" failed, to push for other solutions. Likud Knesset members favour the "Jordan is Palestine" option. Prime Minister Shamir said Palestinians' national aspirations can be satisfied in Jordan. Many agreed, but Binyamin Begin, son of former Prime Minister Menahem Begin, drew attention to the danger that the mere mention of Palestinian national rights "implies accepting the argument that (the Palestinians) *have* national rights."[65] A dangerous heresy which, if repeated often enough, could contaminate Zionist ideological thinking.

With the influx of Soviet Jews, who were reportedly arriving in Israel at a rate of 5,000 a month in 1990,[66] although their numbers have been falling recently, Israel's attention to *its central task* necessarily took precedence over other issues. Thus, Yitzhak Shamir candidly told Israeli television that "Jewish immigration to Israel in the next few years will make Israel stronger and bigger. Israel's greatest mission in the foreseeable future consists in giving priority to the absorption and the settlement of Jewish immigrants."[67] In light of Israel's organic and legislated commitment to Zionism, it is not surprising that Yitzhak Shamir should feel justified in saying: "the next wave of immigration will resolve everything…In five years everything would have changed," and in affirming that great immigration required a great Israel because: "We need the space to shelter all these people."[68] The similarity with the *Lebensraum* reasoning used by German Fascists to justify expansionist policies is too palpably patent in policy statements, implemented decisions and advertised designs to represent an isolated aberration.[69] In fact, Prime Minister Shamir's political affinity and past association with fascist ideological beliefs is common knowledge in Israel. Israel Eldad, one of the leaders of Shamir's terrorist organization Stern Gang, admitted to the Tel Aviv newspaper *Yediot Aharonot* (February 4, 1983) that the Stern Gang had contacted representatives of Nazi Germany during the war and pleaded with them for an alliance between the Fascist New Order in Europe after the triumph of Nazism, and a Jewish Palestine led by the Stern Gang. The *pourparlers* came to a halt when one of the Stern Gang negotiators was arrested in the offices of the Nazi secret services in Damascus and when Shamir himself was arrested by the British, in December 1941, for "terrorism and collaboration with the Nazi enemy."

The geopolitical ideas which were at the basis of German fascism are strikingly evident in the Zionist Plan, an ambitious grand design for redrawing the political map of the Middle East to better ensure Israel's domination over its neighbours. The Zionist Plan as formulated by an official of the Israeli Foreign Ministry calls for "breaking Egypt down territorially into distinct geographical regions…[with] a Christian Coptic State in Upper Egypt alongside a number of weak states," and for "Lebanon's total dissolution into five provinces serv[ing] as a precedent for the entire Arab world including Egypt, Syria, Iraq and the Arabian peninsula...The dissolution of Syria and Iraq later on into ethnically or religiously unique areas such as in Lebanon, is Israel's primary target on the Eastern front in the long run."[70] The peace treaty with Egypt may have tempered somewhat the enthusiastic and boundless ambitions of these Zionist planners, at least with regard to Egypt, but the overall ambition of ruling over the region through the old imperial device of divide and conquer is clearly a basic principle of the Zionist Plan for the Middle East. Zionist ideologues have traditionally been practical and pragmatic men. Weizmann's gradual approach and Ben-Gurion's strategy of creating facts on the grounds find expression and continuity in the policies of today's Zionist leaders. The treaty with Egypt brought undeniable practical advantages to Israel and in no way can it be presented as proving the end of Zionist territorial ambitions. As former Israeli Foreign Minister Ezer Weizman suggested, the withdrawal from the Sinai may have been judged an acceptable price to pay for what must have seemed as an opportunity to perpetuate Israel's rule and facilitate the realization of Zionist aspirations in all of Palestine.[71]

These strategic objectives elaborated in the Zionist Plan for the Middle East are also the logical and natural extension of earlier plans elaborated by Ben-Gurion and others for the dismemberment of Lebanon and Jordan in 1955 and 1956. They all reflect an adventurist and dangerously expansionist tendency which acquires its own momentum, defies political solutions, and thus ensures the perpetuation of the conflict. Former Israeli Prime Minister Moshe Sharett, who resigned over differences with Ben-Gurion over the latter's plan for the dismemberment of Jordan, candidly admitted that the realization of Israel's real objectives in the region required systematic use of Orwellian language to present to the West an acceptable explanation of Israel's expansionist policies. He wrote in his memoirs: "I have learned that the state of Israel cannot be ruled in our generation without deceit and adventurism. These are historical facts that cannot be altered."[72]

It is, therefore, crucially important that Israeli peace plans and negotiating proposals not obscure the fundamental contradiction between Israel's proclaimed desire for peace and its practised policies. In his monumental work *Paix et guerre* Raymond Aron observed that in swearing *Delenda est Carthago* Rome was committed to absolute enmity with Carthage whose very existence had to be eliminated in the name of *Pax Romana*. As currently defined by its leaders, Israel's desire for peace is doubtless genuine but inherently unproductive because of its exclusionist definition of a peace denying the legitimacy of the very existence of the Other. In defining Palestinian nationalism as an *absolute* enemy, current Israeli peace conceptions exclude any genuine reconciliation because the very existence of Palestine becomes an act of aggression in itself justifying the violence inherent in various forms of domination in the name of *Pax Herbaica*.

Conclusion

A lasting resolution of the Arab-Israeli and the Palestinian-Israeli conflicts may be achieved on the basis of commonly accepted principles of justice and international legitimacy. This will require that the injustices suffered by the Palestinians who lost their homeland and the injustices inherent in the destruction of a society and the subjugation of an entire people be redressed, or at least partly redressed. It will also require that the illegal conditions of Israeli occupation and annexation of Arab territories be removed.

This is not likely to happen as long as Israeli leaders continue to espouse an ex-clusively-defined conception of peace based on dynamic views of Jewish national existence and of the unfinished Zionist project, the realization of whose poten-tialities are presumed to require new territories. The paramount importance that this conception enjoys in dominant Israeli political thinking is not likely to diminish as long as the United States continues to effectively, if not officially, finance the building and consolidation of Jewish settlements in occupied Palestine, and acquiesce in the continuation of Israeli occupation of Arab territories. Recently released secret memoranda of understandings between Israel and the United States suggest an American acceptance of Israeli annexation of certain occupied Arab territories.[73] This is tantamount to endorsing the principle of acquisition of territories by war, in clear violation of international law, pertinent United Nations resolutions, the international consensus on the solution to the Israel-Palestinian conflict, and even the official American position.

Although the Bush administration turned down the Shamir government's re-quest for $10 billion in loan guarantees, the election of a Labour government is like-ly to improve Israeli-American relations, including American financial support for Israeli occupation of Arab territories to which it is officially opposed. Raanan Weitz, the retired chairman of the Jewish Agency Settlement Department pointed out with refreshing candour the inconsistency in the traditional American position of official opposition to, but effective support of Israeli occupation of Arab territories: "U.S. law prohibits the use of American Jewish money in the territories but American Jews tolerated the establishment of a separate WZO (World Zionist Or-ganization) Settlement Department that could devote Israeli funds to the West Bank — funds that would not be available were it not for American UJA [United Jewish Appeal] money making up the shortfall. A legal fiction, in other words. It encouraged Begin and Sharon to direct money we could not afford. And the American government was just as inconsistent. They oppose the occupation but instead of enforcing their view by applying pressure as they have a right to do, they keep granting massive aid. This relieves pressure so Israel can pour millions into the territories."[74] With equal candour, retired Israeli Major General Mattityahu Peled told an American magazine that it was the duty of all those Israelis opposed to the expansionist and annexationist policies of the Israeli government to "call upon the United States to stop giving money to Israel." [75]

The Palestinians have now accepted resolution 181 which partitioned their homeland and are prepared to settle the conflict on the basis of the two-State solu-tion. They have accepted to come to the international conference and agreed to negotiate in good faith on the basis of a gradual move toward real and effective self-determination in the West Bank and Gaza, less than half of the territories allocated as a reduced Palestinian State by the 1947 Partition Resolution, and a mere 23 per-cent of the territories of mandated Palestine. This is a fundamental and courageous concession on the part of the victim, the original majority inhabitants of Palestine. But thus far it has produced no significant changes in the position of the Israeli leadership. Hani al-Hassan, a top Arafat aid, shared with a London audience, before the Iraqi invasion of Kuwait, his reading of the Arab and Palestinian mood in view of Israel's intransigence: "There is taking place on the Palestinian side and in the hearts and minds of the Arab masses, a slow but sure erosion of support for the idea of compromise with Israel. It is no exaggeration to say that in the absence of peace, the Arab world is an explosion of frustration and despair waiting to happen."[76] Israeli negotiators at the international peace conferences convened after the war against Iraq, have been presenting to their Palestinian counterparts positions that represent a retreat even from Camp David which they argue has been overtaken by events. Indeed, the continuous Israeli dispossession of the Palestinians has increased the number of Jewish settlements in the occupied Palestinian territories tenfold since Camp David. The elimination of Egypt through Camp David and the elimination of Iraq as a potential deterrent to Israeli military hegemony over the region have dramatically changed the situation since Camp David. Israeli leaders felt confident enough to refuse even to discuss at the peace negotiations basic principles such as the formula "land for peace" or the Palestinians' right to repatriation or compensation.

The two-State solution offers the possibility of resolving the contradiction between Israel's Zionist goals and the Palestinians' national existence. This is because it can partially redress the violent asymmetry between the Israeli and the Palestinian existential conditions, providing the Palestinians with a territorial basis, albeit significantly reduced, for the reconstruction of their shattered society, while leaving Israel free to pursue its Zionist goals within defined political borders that are not dynamic and expansionist. Repeated statements by former Prime Minister Shamir to the effect that God gave these territories to the Jewish people forever suggested that Israel's commitment to the realization of exclusionist Zionist aspirations in occupied Palestine takes precedence over the settlement of the conflict on the basis of justice and international legitimacy. The election of a Labour government is likely to modify the ideological and religious nature of the political discourse. Labour leaders are said to be prepared for more flexibility on the question of autonomy for the Palestinians under occupation. But even this position precludes a peaceful resolution of the conflict on the basis of shared values. And this is because although the Palestinians have accepted the political reality of the existence of Israel they cannot accept the Zionist ideology of permitting any Jew from anywhere in the world to settle in occupied Palestine while Moslem and Christian Palestinians are denied the right to live freely in their own country. Rational calculations of self-interest and political realism may have prompted the Palestinians to give up their claim to the half of Palestine on which Israel was established. The instinct of self-preservation suggests that the Palestinians cannot possibly accept Israel's exclusionist Zionist ideology for all of Palestine without negating what is left of their very own national existence.

Given the garrison State mentality of Israeli leaders and the widespread assumption in Israeli political establishment that a state of siege and permanent tension actually serves the national interest by mobilizing material support from abroad and consolidating national cohesiveness and the fighting spirit at home; and given traditional Israeli doctrines of preponderance of power and overwhelming superiority over all Arab States combined, it may not be realistic to expect Israel to agree anytime soon "to become a non-aligned state, denuclearized, and renounce even certain prerogatives of sovereignty in order to achieve collective security agreements…"[77] It may also be equally problematic to plan for the future on the expectation that Zionist leaders, whose very ideology rejected assimilation into the Liberal Western societies in favour of active affirmation of nationalist and ethnocentrist views of the world, may substantially modify their views of themselves as subject of history while relegating "all others to the status of objects of history."[78] It may be more realistic, however, to expect new and younger generations of Israeli leaders to evolve a view of Zionism which departs from the anachronistic historical dichotomy of a form of haven for Jewish refugees and many forms of oppression for the Palestinians. There is little doubt that many Israeli leaders now realize that the Palestinian people cannot possibly accept the Zionist ideology for the rest of Palestine without essentially signing a certificate for their national extinction. And yet that is precisely what Israeli leaders seem to be asking the Palestinians to do under the guise of autonomy arrangements where autonomy may be eventually granted to the inhabitants of the West Bank and Gaza but denied to the land which Israeli leaders would like to keep under Israeli control "for ever." Strongly-held ideological views, as Karl Mannheim reminded us in his classic work *Ideology and Utopia* tend to harden the dominant group's intensively interest-bound thinking to the point of being blind to facts and realities which could undermine their sense of domination. Surely, though, there will be other Israelis who, having realized that the Palestinian people cannot be expected to acquiesce in their national self-extinction, will sooner or later conclude that a new form of evolving Zionism is possible without the total denial of the national rights of the Palestinian people in whatever is left of Palestine.

The resolution of the fundamental contradiction between Israel's Zionist convictions and views of itself on the one hand, and, on the other hand, the rights of the people on whom it imposes its views is prerequisite for the peaceful resolution of the conflicts. Unless the dominant party, Israel, is capable of generous concessions, a settlement based on the realities of power relations between the various parties will be perceived as an unjust settlement and may in the end amount to no more than an interlude until the imposed status quo is challenged again. The Palestinian offer of peaceful co-existence, on the other hand, makes possible a peace of satisfaction which is politically and existentially accommodating, and presents a more reliable basis for a just and enduring peace.

Notes

1. See Hans Kesler, *The Law of the United Nations* (New York, Praeger, 1950), p. 18.
2. See the authoritative account by George Antonius, *The Arab Awakening: The Story of the Arab National Movement* (New York, Capricorn Books, 1965).
3. See the full text of the King-Crane Commission Report in ibid., pp. 443-458; see also Harry N. Howard, *The King-Crane Commission: An American Inquiry in the Middle East* (Beirut, Khayat's, 1963).
4. See Doreen Ingram, *Palestine Papers 1917-1922: Seeds of Conflict* (New York, Gorge Braziller, 1972), p. 73.

5. Harry S. Truman, *Memoirs: Years of Trial and Hope*, vol. II (New York: Doubleday, 1958), p. 225.
6. Kermit Roosevelt, "The Partition of Palestine: A Lesson in Pressure Politics," *The Middle East Journal*, vol. 2, no. 1 (January 1948), pp. 1-16, p. 14.
7. See Henry Cattan, *The Palestine Question* (London, Croom Helm, 1988), pp. 38-39.
8. J. Bowyer Bell, *The Long War: Israel and the Arabs since 1946* (Englewood Cliffs, N.J., Prentice-Hall, 1969), p. 67.
9. See Simha Flapan, *The Birth of Israel: Myths and Realities* (New York, Pantheon Books, 1987), p. 53.
10. Michael Bar-Zohar, *Ben-Gurion*, p. 704, quoted in ibid., p. 42.
11. See Ian Black in *The Manchester Guardian Weekly*, March 23, 1986.
12. Quoted in ibid. See also the debate between Norman Finkelstein, Nur Masalha, and Benny Morris in the autumn 1991 issue of the *Journal for Palestine Studies*. Finkelstein and Masalha argue that Morris is now trying to play down the conclusions that derive from his own research. Finkelstein wrote: "Morris's central thesis that the Arab refugee problem was 'born out of war, not by design' is belied by his own evidence which shows that Palestine Arabs were expelled systematically and with premeditation." (Normal Finkelstein, "Myths, Old and New," *Journal of Palestine Studies*, vol. XXI, no. 1, Autumn 1991, pp. 66-89; the quote comes from p. 67.) In his rebuttal Morris reported that "in the Hebrew version of *Birth* [of the Palestinian Refugee Problem, 1947-1949] (published in March 1991), I changed the first para-graph of the 'conclusion', which Finkelstein, Masalha, and most other reviewers and critics found quoteworthy:

    > The Palestinian refugee problem was born of war, not by design, Jewish or Arab. It was largely a by-product of Arab and Jewish fears and the protracted, bitter fighting that characterized the first Israeli-Arab war; in part, it was the result of deliberate, not to say malevolent, actions of Jewish commanders and politicians; in smaller part, Arab commanders and politicians were responsible for its creation through acts of commission and omission.

    Morris then added: "I was impelled to make this change...by my discovery, after com-pleting *Birth* in mid-1986, of fresh Israeli and UN documentation that tended to amplify and magnify the role of the Yishuv in the Palestinian exodus in certain parts of the country (Jezreel Valley, Majdal, etc.)" Ibid., pp. 98-114; the quote comes from p. 114. See also Norman Finkelstein, "Rejoinder to Benny Morris," *Journal of Palestine Studies*, vol. XXI, no. 2, winter 1992, pp. 61-71.
13. See Ellen Cantarow and Peretz Kidron, "Israel Talks of a New Exodus," *Inquiry Magazine*, Washington, D.C., December 8, 1980, reproduced in *The Zionist Plan for the Middle East*, translated and edited by Israel Shahak (Belmont, MA, AAUG, 1982).
14. Ibid, p. 22.
15. Benny Morris, "Operation Dani and the Palestinian Exodus from Lydda and Ramale in 1948," *The Middle East Journal*, vol. 40, no. 1 (Winter 1986), pp. 81-109. The quote comes from p. 91.
16. Flapan, op. cit., p. 117.
17. Tom Segev, *1949: The First Israelis* (The Free Press, New York, 1986), p. 23.
18. Simha Flapan, *The Birth of Israel: Myths and Realities* (Pantheon Books, New York, 1987), pp. 4-8.
19. Ibid., p. 10.
20. See Jean and Simone Lacouture, *Egypt in Transition*. Translated by Frances Scarf, (Criterion Books, New York, 1958), p. 462.

21. See Ian Lustick, "Israel and the West Bank after Elon Morch: The Mechanics of de facto Annexation," *Middle East Studies*, vol. 35, No. 4 (Autumn 1981), pp. 557-577; see also Ian Black, "Land Grabbing on the West Bank," *New Statesman, vol. 95, June 9, 1978, p. 769; see also Ann Mosely Lesch, "Israeli Settlements in the Occupied Territories, 1967-1977,"* Journal of Palestine Studies, vol. 7 (Autumn 1977), pp. 26-47.
22. Quoted in Jan Metzger, Martin Orth and Christian Sterzling, *This Land is Our Land* (London, Zed Press, 1983), p. 26; see also Ligue internationale pour le droit et la libération des peuples, *Dossier Palestine. La question palestinienne et le droit international* (Paris, La Découverte, 1991).
23. Rami S. Abdulhadi, "Land Use Planning in the Occupied Palestinian Territories," *Journal of Palestine Studies*, vol. XIX, no. 4 (Summer 1990), pp. 46-63, p. 47; on Israel's efforts to complete the Judaization of the area of Palestine which became Israel, see Gazi Falah, "Israeli 'Judaization' Policy in Galilee," *Journal of Palestine Studies* vol. XX, no. 4 (Summer 1991), pp. 69-85.
24. Rami Abdulhadi, op. cit., p. 48.
25. Palestinian Nationalists from the Occupied Territories, Memorandum to Secretary Baker, Jerusalem, April 9, 1991, reproduced in *Journal of Palestine Studies* vol. XX, no. 4 (Summer 1991), pp. 164-166; see also Nadav Shragay's article on the Israeli government policy of "fleshing out" existing settlements, "A Report on Jewish Settlements in the Occupied Territories," *Haaretz*, June 22, 1990, translated from the Hebrew by FBIS on June 29, 1990 and reproduced in *Journal of Palestine Studies*, vol. XX, no. 1 (Autumn 1990); pp. 178-179; see also U.S. Department of State, "Israeli Settlement in the Occupied Territories," Washington, D. C., March 21, 1991, in which it is stated that: "Over 200,000 settlers now reside in some 200 settlement locales, rural and urban, in the occupied territories including expanded East Jerusalem...About one-half of the land in the West Bank has been dedicated by the Israeli authorities for Israeli use...About one-third of the land in Gaza has been reserved for Israeli use. In the West Bank, roughly 90,000 settlers reside in approximately 150 residential communities...In the Gaza Strip, 15 settlements house about 3,000 settlers. On the Golan Heights, about 12,000 settlers reside in some 30 settlements. In East Jerusalem and the expanded boundaries of the municipality, about 120,000 Jews reside in 12 Jewish neighborhoods." The document is reproduced in *Journal of Palestine Studies* vol. XX, no. 4 (Summer 1991), pp. 185-189.
26. See the report by Israeli Knesset members Dedi Zucker and Chaim Oron, "Report on the construction of Jewish settlements in the Occupied Territories 1991-1993," Jerusalem, February 13, 1991, reproduced in *Journal of Palestine Studies* vol. XX, no. 3 (Spring 1991), pp. 151-153.
27. *Globe and Mail*, (Toronto), February 29, 1992.
28. See Ann M. Lesch, "Israeli Deportation of Palestinians from the West Bank and the Gaza Strip: 1967-1978," *Journal of Palestine Studies*, vol. 8 (Winter 1978), pp. 101-132, and (Spring 1978), pp. 81-111; see also Ian Black, "Punishment for the West Bank," *New Statesman, 97, June 29, 1979, p. 949; see also Michael Adams, "Israel's Treatment of the Arabs in the occupied Territories," *Journal of Palestine Studies*, vol. 6 (Winter 1977), pp. 19-40; see also Amnon Kapeliouk, "Israel Picks on the Landless Peasants," *New Statesman*, vol. 103, no. 2662, April 2, 1982, p. 11.
29. UN General Assembly, Resolution 3092 (XXVIII), Wilhelm Wengler and Josef Tittel, (eds.) *Documents on the Arab-Israeli Conflict: The Resolutions of the United Nations Organization* (Berlin, Berling Verlag), 1978.
30. For more recent examples of Israeli repression and oppression of the Palestinians, see "The Resolution of the European Parliament on Repression in the Israeli-Occupied Territories," Strasbourg, France, January 18, 1990 reproduced in *Journal of Palestine Studies*, vol. 19, no. 4 (Summer 1990), pp. 134-136; see also the statement issued by the

heads of state of the twelve members of the European Community at the Dublin Summit, June 26, 1990, and reproduced in the Mideast Mirror on June 27, 1990; see also Norman Finkelstein, "Israel and Iraq: A Double Standard," *Journal of Palestine Studies*, vol. XX, no. 2 (Winter 1991), pp. 43-56; see also "Country Reports on Human Rights Practices For 1990, Israel And the Occupied Territories," US Department of State, U.S. Government Printing Office: Washington, D. C., February 1990: pp. 1477-1496, reproduced in *Journal of Palestine Studies* vol. XX, no. 3 (Spring 1991), pp. 98-111.

31. Hussein of Jordan: My "War" With Israel, As told and with additional material by Vick Vance and Pierre Lauer, (New York, William Morrow, 1969), p. 118.

32. *New York Times*, October, 15, 1967.

33. Quoted in Jon Kimch, *There Could Have Been Peace* (New York, The Dial Press, 1973), p. 262.

34. Eric Rouleau, *Le Monde* (Paris), February 19, 1970.

35. Amos Elon, *Haaretz* (Israel), November 13, 1981, quoted in Noam Chomsky, *The Fateful Triangle: Israel, the United States and the Palestinians* (Black Rose Books, Montreal, 1984), p. 64.

36. See Henry Cattan, *Palestine and International Law* (London, Longman, 1976).

37. Quoted in Rashid Khalidi, "The Resolutions of the 19th Palestine National Council," *Journal of Palestine Studies*, vol. XIX, no. 2 (Winter 1990), pp. 29-42, p. 34.

38. See Muhammad Muslih, "Towards Coexistence: An Analysis of the Resolutions of the Palestine National Council," *Journal of Palestine Studies*, vol. 19, no. 4 (Summer 1990), pp. 3-29, p. 25.

39. Declaration of Palestinian Independence, *Palestine Post*, no. 43, November, 1989.

40. Rashid Khalidi, op. cit., p. 37.

41. *The Jerusalem Post*, December 23, 1989.

42. *The New York Times*, November 21, 1977.

43. Arthur Goldberg, "Statement by Ambassador Goldberg," *Department of State Bulletin*, July 31, 1967, p. 149.

44. Charles W. Yost, "United States Reaffirms Position on Jerusalem," *Department of State Bulletin*, July 28, 1969, pp. 76-77.

45. See Teddy Kollek, "Unsettling a unique city," *Guardian Weekly*, January 19, 1992.

46. See Henry Cattan, *Jerusalem* (Croom Helm, London, 1981); see also Rouba Housary, "Jérusalem, la ville sainte qui devient ville-forteresse," *Le Monde Diplomatique*, (January 1992), pp. 22-23; see also Ligue internationale pour le droit et la libération des peuples, *Dossier Palestine. La question palestinienne et le droit international* (Paris, La Découverte, 1991); see also Gérard De La Pradelle, "Vers le partage en deux capitales?," *Le Monde Diplomatique* (January 1992), p. 23.

47. See Mark A. Heller, *A Palestinian State: The Implications for Israel* (Cambridge, MA, Harvard University Press, 1983), p. 5.

48. See Norman Moss, "Israel Security: Myth and Reality," *New Outlook*, August, 1990, reproduced in *Shalom Hayom*, vol. 4, (Fall 1990), pp. 7-8.

49. *The New York Times*, January 2, 1989.

50. Israel Shahak, *Le Racisme de l'Etat d'Israël* (Guy Authier, Paris, 1975), p. 156. Palestinian scholar Walid Khalidi wrote in 1990 of the destruction of 400 Palestinian villages. See Walid Khalidi, "The Half-Empty Glass of Middle East Peace," *Journal of Palestine Studies*, vol. 19, no. 3, (Spring, 1990), pp. 14-38.

51. See Joseph Badi, (ed.) *Fundamental Laws of the State of Israel* (New York, Twayne Publishers, 1961), p. 285.

52. See W.T. Mallison, Jr. "The Legal Problems Concerning the Juridical Status and the Political Activities of the Zionist Organization/Jewish Agency: A Study in Interna-

tional and United States law," *William and Mary Law Review* vol. 9, no. 2 ; Spring 1968, pp. 556-629.

53. Wilburn Crane Eveland, *Ropes of Sand: America's Failure in the Middle East* (London, Norton and Company, 1980), p. 65.

54. See *Palaces of Injustice* available from Americans for Middle East Understanding, Room 771, 475 Riverside Drive, N. Y. 10027.

55. Ben-Gurion, *Memoirs*, vol. 4, p. 151., cited in Flapan, op. cit., p. 53.

56. *The Washington Report on Middle Eastern Affairs*, August 1989, p. 6.

57. Flapan, *The Birth of Israel*, op. cit., p. 49.

58. See Rami S. Abdulhadi, "Land Use Planning in the Occupied Palestinian Territories," *Journal of Palestine Studies*, vol. XIX, no. 4 (Summer 1990), pp. 46-63, p. 47.

59. See Jean Ziegler, "Les Socialistes français isolés au sein de l'Internationale," in *Le Monde Diplomatique*, August, 1988.

60. Quoted in Norman Finkelstein, "Israel and Iraq: A Double Standard," *Journal of Palestine Studies*, vol. XX, no. 2 (Winter 1991), pp. 43-56, p. 45.

61. See the 1,000-page, 3-part report put out on May 15, 1990, by the Swedish Save the Children, "The Status of Palestinian Children during the Uprising in the Occupied Territories," *Journal of Palestine Studies*, vol. XX, no. 2 (Winter 1991), pp. 136-149.

62. Walid Khalidi, "The Half-Empty Glass of Middle East Peace," *Journal of Palestine Studies*, vol. XIX, no. 3 (Spring 1990), pp. 14-38, p. 19.

63. The MacNeil-Leher News Hour, *PBS Television*, April 1, 1992.

64. Statement broadcast by the Israeli radio on June 26, 1989, quoted in *Le Monde Diplomatique*, April 1990, pp. 22-23.

65. *The Jerusalem Post*, December 23, 1989.

66. *The Christian Science Monitor*, February 23 March 1, 1990. Shamir imposed a military censorship on the issue of Soviet Jewish immigration to Israel; see Joseph Al-Ghazi, "Qui a peur des immigrants soviètiques?," *Le Monde Diplomatique*, April, 1990.

67. *Al-Ahram* (in Arabic) (Cairo), May 1, 1990.

68. *The Middle East*, February, 1990. p. 10.

69. On the relationship between fascism and Zionist thought see Lenni Brenner, *Zionism in the Age of the Dictators* (London, Croom Helm, 1983).

70. Oded Yinon, "A Strategy for Israel in the Nineteen Eighties." It originally appeared in Hebrew in *Kivunim, A Journal for Judaism and Zionism*, issue no. 4, February 1982. It was translated and edited by Israel Shahak and appeared as *The Zionist Plan for the Middle East* (Belmont, MA, AAUG, 1982) the quotations come from pp. 8-9.

71. See Ezer Weizman, *The Battle For Peace* (New York, Bantam Books, 1981), p.190-191.

72. Moshe Sharett, *Personal Diaries* (Hebrew, Tel Aviv, 1978), November 16, 1956, vol 7; p. 1958, quoted in Flapan,*The Birth of Israel* op. cit., p. 52.

73. See "Can Israel Exist and Live Next to a Palestinian State?" released by the Institute of Advanced Strategic Studies in Jerusalem and by the Weizenthal Institute in Los Angeles, and translated and reported by *Al-Ahram*, (in Arabic) (Cairo), May 1, 1990.

74. *Moment* magazine (January-February 1987) quoted in Walid Khalidi, "The Half-Empty Glass of Middle East Peace," *Journal of Palestine Studies*, vol. XIX. no. 3 (Spring 1990), pp. 14-38, p. 32.

75. "United States: Stop Giving Us Money," An Interview with Matti Peled, *The Progressive*, reproduced in *Shalom Hayom*, February 1992, pp. 4-6, p. 5.

76. See David Hirst, "the Politics of Armageddon," *The Manchester Guardian Weekly*, April 29, 1990.

77. Mohamed Sid-Ahmed, "Pour qu'un règlement au Proche-Orient débouche sur une paix durable," *Le Monde diplomatique*, November, 1989, pp. 22-23.

78. Mohamed Sid Ahmed, in *The Middle East Monitor*, vol. 6, no.1, 1989.

CHAPTER TWO

Sadat's Road to Camp David — Negotiations and Decision-Making: From Sinai to Camp David and Blair House

On September 17, 1978 the Camp David agreement was signed by Egypt, Israel and the United States. It consisted of two documents, one establishing the guiding principles for "a just, comprehensive, and durable settlement of the Middle East conflict," and for the resolution of the Palestinian problem "in all its aspects." The other provided a framework for a peace treaty between Egypt and Israel. U.S. President Jimmy Carter told the invited guests assembled to witness the signing of the Camp David agreement in the East Room in the White House: "When we first arrived at Camp David, the first thing upon which we agreed was to ask the people of the world to pray that our negotiations would be successful. Those prayers have been answered far beyond our expectations. We are privileged to witness tonight a significant achievement in the cause of peace, an achievement none thought possible a year ago, or even a month ago, an achievement that reflects the courage and wisdom of these two leaders (Sadat and Begin)."[1] Describing his own decision-making approach, Egyptian President Anwar Sadat wrote: "I always know what I am doing and calculate all the possible consequences of every step I take."[2]

This chapter will closely examine the Egyptian-American-Israeli negotiation process, which started in 1973 and culminated in the Egyptian-Israeli treaty of 1979, and answer the following questions: How did the Camp David decisions reflect Sadat's perceptions, beliefs, and decision-making approach; and how do Egyptian decisions at Camp David reflect Egyptian, or more accurately President Sadat's bargaining strategy?

Conceptual discussions of what has been loosely termed decision-making "theories" (claiming to be scientific but lacking verifiability) identified a large number of factors, assumptions, and relevant variables, and highlighted the behaviour of political leaders as decision-makers. The fundamental postulate underlying decision-making theory is that "decision-makers act in accordance with their perception of reality not in response to reality itself."[3] Leaders' decisions are influenced by their perceptions of the national, regional and international environments, as well as by the temperament, psychological make-up and the personal proclivities of the leaders themselves. Harold and Margaret Sprout conveniently grouped these factors in two categories: the "psychological environment" and the "operational environment,"[4] the latter being a reference to the decision-maker's reality as it exists "objectively" (such a determination being in itself an epistemological problem). The key to understanding decision-making lies in understanding the factors which influenced the decision-makers' definition of their situation.[5]

In his analysis of Third-World decision-making, Bahgat Korany deplored the scarcity of appropriate models of analysis. He argued that the inapplicability of the bureaucratic model (in which foreign policy decisions are influenced by bureaucratic interests; the pluralist-bureaucratic model includes, in addition to bureaucratic interests, group interests and institutional interests) essentially meant that the psychological-perceptual school, with its "one-sidedness and reductionism," continued to dominate Third-World foreign policy analysis. Korany believes that the psychological-perceptual school (in which foreign policy decisions are reflections of the psychology and perceptions of leaders as decision-makers) has tended to exclude the operational environment. He argued that its reliance on simple answers to complex psychological questions has complicated rather than eased the problem of data accessibility in Third-World foreign policy analysis. He urged that more attention be paid to the operational environment.[6] In his analysis of the alliance decisions of the October 1973 war, Korany concluded that Sadat's October war decision was basically out of character and that "it was the operational environment's potency that pushed toward the war."[7] This conclusion is supported by the fact that Sadat was basically interested in reaching a negotiated agreement but that Israeli refusal to withdraw from the occupied Arab territories and American failure to act as intermediaries as long as Egypt remained the defeated party, pushed Sadat to the military option.

In a more recent work, Bahgat Korany and Ali Dessouki go further and identify the constraints inherent in the operational environment of Third World countries. They group them around three major issues: a) aid/independence dilemma (the trade off between the need for foreign aid and the necessity of maintaining national independence); b) the resource/objective dilemma (the ability of foreign policy makers to pursue objectives within the realm of their country's capabilities); and c) the security/development dilemma (the difficulty of having to choose between guns and butter). They propose a framework for Third-World foreign policy analysis based on domestic environment, foreign policy orientation, decision-making process, and foreign-policy behaviour.[8] Dessouki used such a framework to analyze Sadat's rapprochement with the United States and peace with Israel and concluded that they were motivated by economic troubles at home and the desire to attract foreign investments.[9]

The Korany-Dessouki framework has merits particularly in its emphasis upon the relatedness of opportunities and constraints inherent in the foreign policy alternatives available to Third World countries. Similarly, Dessouki's application of the framework to Egypt is appropriate particularly with regard to the interaction of historical, geographical and domestic factors with the cluster of constraints inherent in Egypt's operational environment. His conclusion that "Sadat's decision to visit Israel was largely motivated by economic considerations"[10] is, however, inadequate. And this for a number of reasons. First, it assumes that Sadat's decision to visit Israel was a major foreign policy orientation whereas in fact it would be more appropriate to view it as a strategy, as Sadat himself has repeatedly argued. The general foreign policy orientation involved was to pursue the path of a negotiated settlement and sue for peace. The decision to pursue such a policy having been made by Sadat in February 1971 when he offered to sign a peace treaty with Israel on the basis of withdrawal from the Arab territories occupied in 1967, we must view all his subsequent actions as strategies designed to accomplish the foreign policy goal of bringing about a negotiated settlement. Even the October 1973 war was part of that strategy since it did not seek to liberate occupied Egyptian territories but was rather a limited war with the stated objective of reactivating Middle-East diplomacy and bargaining from a less helpless position. This general foreign policy goal of bringing about a negotiated settlement of the Arab-Israeli conflict may indeed have been partly motivated by economic considerations but these can not convincingly be said to be behind Sadat's specific strategies such as his visit to Israel in 1977, or his decision to pursue a separate agreement with Israel, or his specific negotiating strategies with the Americans and the Israelis.

Second, Dessouki's conclusion seems to be based on the postulate of a static relationship between the operational environment and the psychological environment in which the former has an unalterable and unvaried impact on the latter when the relationship is really dynamic and as evolving as the two environments themselves. For instance, President Nasser himself had accepted the foreign policy orientation of a negotiated settlement as early as 1955 and again clearly and emphatically in 1970, but it is reasonable to assume that his psycho-perceptual analysis, and therefore his strategies, would have been different from Sadat's. Further, the operational environment which prevailed in 1971 when Sadat offered to accept a partial settlement with the Israelis and reopen the Canal was vastly different from the operational environment of the Egyptian-Israeli disengagement agreements in 1974-75, and still more different from that prevailing at the time of Sadat's visit to Jerusalem, and still even more different at the time of the signing of the Camp David and Blair House agreements. The significant differences between these environments presented opportunities which a realistic assessment of opportunities and constraints as well as of the forces, alliances and strategic factors at play, could have exploited in a manner which transcended the static means-capabilities postulate of the economic determinism framework. Third, the economic factors explanation presents some of the drawbacks Korany himself invoked in his criticism of the psychological-perceptual model, such as an exclusionist and reductionist emphasis on one factor to the detriment of other relevant factors. While the resource/objective dilemma is certainly germane to and may be a fundamental factor in the operational environment of Egyptian decision-making, it does not adequately explain Sadat's decision-making approach, certainly not his bargaining and negotiation strategies. For instance, his decision to accept a cease-fire mediated by the United States in October 1973 to the consternation of Arab allies, particularly the Syrian comrades in arms who were preparing for a major offensive, fits more convincingly within the psychological-perceptual framework within which he operated. His highly personalized approach to negotiations with the Americans is more a function of Sadat's own perceptions and beliefs in the perspicacity of his strategies and vision than a reflection of a sober analysis of Egypt's economic situation. In fact, an economic framework may not be of much help when core values are at stake in inter-State conflicts. For instance, despite the obvious preponderance of American power and the gross inequality in resources, the Vietnamese nationalist forces drove a hard bargain and pressed for and obtained complete American withdrawal in 1973.[11] This may be because "an asymmetry in the evaluation of stakes may offset an asymmetry in the national power of the participants in a struggle."[12]

The major objective of bargaining is to behave in such a way as to accomplish at a minimal cost the goals established by the decision-makers. In all bargaining situations credibility is of paramount importance. Thomas Schelling emphasized the importance of credibility without which threats, promises and commitments will carry little weight with the other party. He recognized the value of making and clearly communicating overt commitments from which no retreat is possible. Sadat seemed unable to do this as the contradictions between his public statements and what he actually accepted clearly revealed.[13] Further, by isolating himself from potential allies, supporters, and even his own ministers, and negotiating and making decisions alone, first with the Americans and later with the Israelis, he drastically reduced his margin of maneuverability. Given the balance of power prevailing between the negotiating parties he took on, Sadat ensured that the negotiations would necessarily be between grossly unequal parties. In their exhaustive review of almost a thousand social-psychologist studies, Jeffrey Rubin and Bert Brown reached the following conclusion about negotiations between unequal powers: "Under conditions of unequal relative power among bargainers, the party with high power tends to behave exploitatively, while the less powerful party tends to behave submissively, unless certain special conditions prevail (specifically, coalition formation by the weak)."[14] Sadat did not want to behave submissively, but, given their powerful positions, the Americans and the Israelis should have been expected to behave exploitatively. And this meant that Sadat placed himself in the uncomfortable position of either behaving submissively to accommodate the exploitative behaviour of the stronger parties or withdrawing from the negotiations and recognizing the failure of his initial analysis. Sadat had a penchant for dramatic gestures of largess and grandeur which characterized his negotiation style, but in sacrificing the coalition power Egypt derived from its Arab and Soviet alliances, Sadat's grand gestures became face-saving devices that poorly masked helpless and submissive positions with negotiating partners determined to make the most out of a good opportunity. Accepting the validity of the conclusion reached by Rubin and Brown, I found Snyder's framework emphasizing the primacy of a proper definition of one's situation very useful. Similarly, the framework provided by Lerche and Abdul Said has considerable merits, particularly in its emphasis on the importance of a proper assessment of the pattern of forces in a given situation, of the relevant policies of other States active in the situation, and of the capability of the State of carrying out various policies given the situational context defined by the first two cluster of factors.[15]

It may be tautological to say that the outcome of the Egyptian-American-Israeli negotiations reflected the relative balance of power between the three parties. But the balance of power is not a static construct. It is a dynamic reality at any given moment, now reflecting a certain distribution of power between competing entities, now connoting an *imbalance* of power in favour of one of the competitors. The art of diplomacy and negotiations is partly how to achieve the best possible results given the reality of the balance of power at a given moment. The helplessness of the Egyptian position during the negotiations at Camp David was largely the result of the strategy of the Egyptian President who started from a relatively decent position following the Arab show of solidarity in 1973 and systematically worked to place himself in isolated and vulnerable positions until he was forced at Camp David, in 1978, to confront the helplessness of his predicament and settle for what he could get. The story of these negotiations and of the results obtained by the Israelis and the Americans support the realist view of international relations propounded chiefly by Hans Morgenthau in his classic study *Politics Among Nations*. Within this realist context of international relations, the general criteria for rationality in defining one's situation derive from a hard-nosed and well-reasoned calculation of options most likely to maximize utility and make effective use of one's power to achieve stated goals.

The Egyptians may have believed that they were doing just that, but in allowing Egyptian decisions and negotiating strategies to be largely the reflections of one man's psycho-political perceptions and beliefs and not necessarily the result of a realistic assessment of the operational environment and the real and potential balance of power, they were placing enormous faith in one individual as the sole guardian of the national interests. The result tends to confirm the validity of the traditional model of Third-World foreign policy analysis in which foreign policy decisions are largely influenced by the perceptions and beliefs of the leader as a decision-maker. The new operational environment largely created by the decisions which flowed from President Sadat's psycho-political perceptions created its own momentum and chains of action-reactions dynamics, negatively affecting the balance of relative power between the parties, making it more difficult to achieve stated policy objectives, and in the end making it almost unavoidable that Sadat negotiate from a position of increasing vulnerability. Thus, his decisions and negotiation strategies almost ensured that the stronger parties, Israel and the United States, would interact exploitatively with the weaker party, Egypt.

Sadat's Strategic Assessment of the Forces at Play

Upon becoming president of Egypt following the sudden death of the immensely popular Gamal Abdel Nasser, Sadat's first assessment of his local environment in Egypt presented him with a number of dilemmas: how to eliminate his rivals from the left and establish a reliable power base; how to terminate Israeli occupation of Egyptian territory; and how to cope with Egypt's perennial economic problems. Sadat mounted a counter-revolution which essentially de-Nasserized Egypt; internally by replacing socialism with ill-regulated capitalism, and externally by replacing Nasser's Pan-Arab alliances with a coalition with conservative and "moderate" Arab regimes. The concomitant reorientation of Egyptian foreign policy resulted in the termination of the privileged relations with the Soviet Union and the offering of Egypt as a candidate in the American camp. More specifically, Sadat heard Washington's stated objective in the Middle East as formulated by Henry Kissinger: "We are trying to get a Middle East settlement in such a way that the moderate regimes are strengthened and not the radical regimes. *We are trying to expel the Soviet military presence.*"[16] In 1972, Sadat expelled the Soviet advisors from Egypt, wooed American corporate power by granting exploration contracts to Exxon and Mobil Oil, and a multimillion dollar pipeline deal to the Bechtel Corporation. In February, 1973, Sadat sent Hafez Ismail, his Deputy Prime Minister, to convey to Washington Cairo's sense of desperation for a negotiated settlement. Washington seemed unmoved, and shortly after Ismail's visit, more American phantoms were promised to Israel. In coalition with the newly forged Conservative Arab order, Egypt and Syria fought the 1973 war and scored some military successes and an important psychological victory.

Following the Arab armies' decent showing in the October war and the Arab States' unprecedented show of political and economic solidarity, Sadat seems to have correctly assessed the growing political, financial and strategic importance of the Arab world. And it is all the more surprising that he decided to sacrifice the potentialities of the military and political unity achieved in 1973-74 and opt for an exclusive reliance on the United States. By the end of 1974, Kuwait had opened credits worth $ 818 million, Saudi Arabia $616 million. Some estimates put Saudi Arabia's financial help to Egypt between 1973 and 1978 at $7 billion. Sadat was aware and proud of the financial and political power inherent in the Arab show of unity. He correctly understood that one of the most important achievements of the October war was the unprecedented Arab military, political, and economic coordination of human and material resources for the realization of a set of common objectives. He told Hedly Donovan of *Time* magazine in March 1974: "I regard Arab unity as the greatest achievement of the glorious days of October. When I speak of unity, I do not mean well-defined legalistic forms. What we have accomplished was a genuine Arab unity, which showed that during difficult moments our ranks closed, and I think that we shall pursue this course."[17] In a speech delivered on April 16, 1974 before representatives of Egyptian students abroad, Sadat gave an assessment of the new forces at play which confirmed his acute awareness of the importance of Arab political and military power. In fact, his sense of pride in Arab power was so strong he could not resist the temptation of exaggeration: "October 6," he said, "has changed the world militarily, economically and politically. The balance of power was altered and so was the map of the Middle East. We are now driving to equilibrium in our relations with the Great Powers…We are now endeavouring to build our self-reliant forces in all of the military, political, economic and scientific domains. October 6 has brought about a new Arab condition, which constitutes the greatest achievement in centuries."[18] He delighted in the notion that the Arab world may have become the world sixth power. In an interview with the Egyptian magazine *Rooz-al-Yussuf* in September 1974, Sadat said: "I regard Arab solidarity in the October War, as one of the most glorious elements of this war, and the most important of its results. Suffice it to look at the admission by strategists throughout the world, that the Arabs have become after October, the sixth world power. They said so, not I."[19] Sadat readily accepted and proudly used the assessment of the Arab world as the sixth world power in many of his subsequent speeches.

And yet, Sadat followed a strategy which clearly set out to reorient Egypt's alliances, extricate it from Pan-Arabism, and emphasize an "Egypt first" philosophy. Egyptian nationalism was played up at the expense of Arab nationalism; Arab leaders who disagreed with Sadat were persistently denigrated, belittled and insulted. With Sadat setting the tone and calling Arab leaders "pygmies," "dwarfs," and "psychopaths," the government-controlled media emphasized Egypt's sacrifices for the Arab cause and attacked the Arab millionaires and the Palestinians and Syrians who "profited from the conflict." The political and intellectual climate was propitious for the growth of an "Egypt first" attitude as a prelude to the separation of Egypt from its Arab environment. The attack on Egypt's Arab nationalist orientation, which Nasser had carefully built and cultivated since coming to power in 1952, was led by, among others, Egyptian writer and Nobel-Prize winner in literature, Naguib Mahfouz. He reminded Egyptians that Egypt's history did not start with Nasser. In his novel *El Karnak* (a café in Cairo), Mahfouz wrote, through the reflections of one of his characters: "I thought that Egypt's history began on the 23rd of July (the date of the 1952 revolution), it was only after the debacle (the 1967 defeat) that I began to look for what preceded it."[20] The campaign against Egypt's traditional Arab orientation culminated in an outright call for the rejection of Egypt's Arabism launched by Egypt's "dean of letters" Tawfiq al-Hakim. In a series of six articles published between March and May 1978 in the Egyptian newspapers *Al-Ahram* and *Al-Akhbar*, al-Hakim argued that "Egypt will not have peace of mind, will not have stability, and will not be able to feed its hungry except through one path:...neutrality"[21] in the Arab-Israeli conflict.[22] The depth and strength of Egypt's Arabism and of the Arab nationalist sentiments of most Egyptian intellectuals were made evident by the "storm of opposition" which greeted al-Hakim's call for Egypt's neutrality. Out of the dozen or so Egyptian intellectuals who participated in the debate only one supported it, two agreed but expressed reservations, and the rest clearly rejected it or opposed it.[23]

One may wonder why, despite his correct assessment of Arab real and potential power and despite the strength of Egyptians' Arab nationalist sentiments, Sadat embarked on the path of separating Egypt from its Arab character. It may be that denial of Egypt's Arabism was viewed as a necessary component of a political strategy which implied the detachment of Egypt from the Arab Camp opposed to separate peace with Israel. Such a strategy was supposed to prove to Washington Egypt's new "moderate" orientation and what Sadat called ideological openness, in order to better facilitate Egypt's integration in the American-led geopolitical and strategic system in the region. Further, there is little doubt that Washington desired to see Egypt's Arabism weakened. And that is because of the assumption of American foreign policy makers that "Arabism" automatically meant "radicalism" and "nationalism" which were perceived as threats to American interests in the region. The Egyptian political establishment under Sadat and the Egyptian intelligentsia understood that Sadat's policy of distancing Egypt from the Arab world was designed to please Washington. "There is a great power," observed the prominent Egyptian writer Ahmad Baha Elddin, "which no doubt wants Egypt out of the Arab world."[24]

On the other hand, Sadat may have genuinely believed that his strategy of separating Egyptian nationalism from Arab nationalism would ultimately prove to be not only best for Egypt but also for the Arab cause. He believed that only the United States could solve the Arab-Israeli conflict and it was important therefore to prove to Washington that Egypt was no longer committed to the armed struggle many Arabs thought might still be inevitable given Israeli refusal to withdraw from the occupied Arab territories. And one way of proving his sincerity to Washington was to show that Egypt had broken with its Arab link and was looking forward to a new relationship with the United States. Indeed, Sadat gave many indications of how Egypt under his guidance was no longer committed to the old ways of thinking which used to be chief characteristics of the Arab States' approach to the Arab-Israeli conflict. In an interview in 1975 he repeated a familiar theme: "Unfortunately, we in the Arab World, still think in emotional terms. I have said that in Kuwait. Even without Resolution 242, Israel has become a fait accompli within her 1967 boundaries, for the simple reason that both superpowers, who share the mastery of the world, defend this fact."[25]

Sadat's public position on the Palestinian question was, throughout the period under discussion, i.e.; from 1974 to 1979, compatible with the Arab consensus reached at the Rabbat Summit in 1974. Throughout his negotiations with the United States and subsequent negotiations with the Israelis he publicly supported the position he summarized during an interview with French Radio and Television: "I must say that since the Rabat Conference the Palestinians should henceforth speak for themselves. This is a fact. But if you want to know my personal opinion, I can tell you that the core problem in the Middle East is the Palestinian issue. If the Palestinian problem is not settled there will be no peace in this area. To my mind a Palestinian State should be set up in the West Bank and Gaza. I think this is the correct way to settle this problem and to bring peace to the region."[26] When his critics charged that his agreements with the United States and Israel seemed to be violating his public commitments to the Arab cause, Sadat simply reiterated his assurances that he would respect the principles agreed upon at the Rabat Arab Summit Conference, i.e.; that the PLO would be the sole and legitimate representative of the Palestinians, and that the Arabs should remain united in their determination not to yield territories to Israel. But he argued that he wanted the freedom to pursue what he called his "triangular strategy," a strategy whose basis is commitment to agreed Arab principles but whose apex would be flexible enough to give him the tactical maneuverability he needed to accomplish Arab goals.

But this was precisely the problem, namely: the contradiction between stated goals and policies apparently incompatible with these goals and ostensibly designed to achieve separate agreements which would fall short of the agreed upon goals. Deprived of the use and the threat to use the military option, increasingly bereft of Arab political support, contemptuous of the Soviet Union and unwilling to mend fences with it, Sadat seemed to believe that his faith in Washington would enable him to achieve his stated goals and would ultimately vindicate the wisdom of his strategies. But a more realistic assessment of the nature of the American-Israeli relations and of the respective positions and relative power of Israel and the United States should have tempered Sadat's overly optimistic assessment.

But realism does not seem to have influenced the strategy Sadat devised to deal with Israel, nor did it seem to significantly influence his assessment of his ability to substantially modify traditional American foreign policy orientation in the region. Thus, Sadat saw Israeli leaders as divided and unable to make up their minds about peace with the Arabs. He claimed that his strategy was flexible and gave him the option of refusing anything he did not like, but he failed to explain what he would do in case his strategy failed. He seemed to have no contingency plans other than the belief that if his peace initiative failed it would be because of Israeli opposition to peace. And this would expose Israeli intransigence to the world. But how exposing Israeli intransigence to the world was supposed to lead to concrete results given the little importance Israel assigned to world public opinion Sadat did not explain, probably he had no idea as the following exposition of his strategy reveals. In an interview with a Kuwaiti newspaper on April 11, 1975 he claimed that: "Disunity is now plaguing the Israeli society, which is in a state of confusion. The mood that reigned in our midst after the 1967 War is now prevailing in Israel, and it poses a question mark on their future. These uncertainties had never come up during the past 26 years. Israel used to live according to her philosophy of security, which asserted that she was an invincible country, able to strike at anything. These talks are now over...The Israeli government, like the Israeli people, are now in a state of confusion...Should Kissinger succeed, all is right. If he fails, we shall go to Geneva. The same applies to Geneva. If it is successful, all is right. If not, we will have exposed Israel before the world. We are in a position to say 'Yes' and 'No', from the vantage point of our interests."[27]

Sadat believed that only the United States could bring about a resolution of the Arab-Israeli conflict. He repeatedly emphasized his belief that Washington held 99 percent of the cards in the Arab-Israeli and the Palestinian-Israeli conflicts. He made no secret that his entire strategy hinged on what he believed and hoped America would do by way of placing pressure on Israel for a negotiated settlement of the two conflicts. In an interview with the BBC on June 9, 1975, Sadat repeated his by-now familiar assessment of American power: "All the cards of this game are in the hands of the U.S., because...they provide Israel with everything, and they are the only ones who can exert pressure on Israel."[28] In an interview with a Lebanese magazine on June 22, 1975, Sadat repeated the same assessment, but also betrayed signs of frustrations that the U.S. was not behaving according to his strategic analysis: "The Headquarters is America, and Israel is just a branch. If we can solve our problems with the Headquarters, the Israeli problem will be thereby resolved too. Whether we like it or not, all the cards of this game are in U.S. hands, because the U.S. grants Israel everything from bread to weapons. Thus, the only party who could pressure Israel is the U.S....However, if the U.S. is the major factor, why does she not take a clear position and settle the conflict?"[29] A question that may have already started to unsettle Sadat but he was too proud and too optimistic to draw any conclusions that might expose flaws in his strategic thinking.

Despite clear signs that the United States was not responding as he had hoped, Sadat continued to keep faith in Washington and to enthusiastically follow its step-by-step approach, ignoring the persistent criticisms that his policies were separating Egypt from the Arab camp. He continued to respond to his critics by claiming, without convincing evidence, that he had seen a fundamental shift in American foreign policy in the region. In his *October Paper*, Sadat reported an interview with the American television network ABC on April 29, 1974 in which he repeated the claim that "The U.S. not only guarantees the cease-fire but also the implementation of (Security Council Resolution) 242. This is a new position on the part of the U.S. and a total shift in her attitude towards us and towards peace in our region."[30] Both conclusions were clearly mistaken.

Kissinger, the architect of the policy which elevated Israel to the status of American strategic asset during the Jordanian crisis of September 1970, seems to have easily manipulated Sadat into believing that the United States was embarking on a wholly different Middle-East policy and that he (Kissinger) should be trusted to carry it out in the best interest of the parties concerned. In an interview with Arnaud de Borchgrave of *Newsweek* in March 1974 Sadat, not realizing that Kissinger himself was the first supporter of Israel as a gendarme for American interests in the region, gave the following instructive and flawed assessment of Kissinger's views:

"My talks with Dr. Kissinger convinced me that he rejects the simplistic notion of some of your strategists who see — or saw — Israel as the American gendarme in this part of the world." "Kissinger," continued Sadat, "is a man of his word. I trust him completely. He is the first U.S. official who has dealt with our problems, who has proved himself to be a man of integrity—direct, frank, and farsighted. We have suffered a lot with American officials in the last two decades...Kissinger, under the guidance of President Nixon, — and you cannot separate the two — has revolutionized the thrust of U.S. policy in our area, and before that in the rest of the world. What Nixon and Kissinger did in China and the USSR was unthinkable a few years back. They are now doing the unthinkable in the Middle East. Kissinger is a man of vision, imagination and, perhaps most important of all, trust."[31] On both counts, the thrust of American foreign policy in the region and Kissinger's view of Israel, Sadat's assessment was supported neither by the historical record nor by a realistic assessment of the prevalent realities. In fact, Sadat himself occasionally betrayed his disappointment and frustrations with American actions which were blatantly at odds with what he had been telling his people. Thus, in the same BBC television interview mentioned above, Sadat impatiently demanded: "It is time the U.S. state its policy quite clearly...for a final solution...It is a pity [that the U.S. does not seem to have a policy at all]; moreover, there are two governments now in America, one in the White House and the other on Capitol Hill...On the contrary, quote me, I am not asking America to abandon Israel. I am not asking America to drop Israel...nor sever her special relationship with Israel. But I am asking America: Is she going to protect and defend Israel in its own borders or in its conquests?"[32] The question was both pertinent and poignantly put, but Sadat raised it only rhetorically because he seems to have sincerely believed that America could not possibly protect Israel in its conquests because this would be contrary to American assurances and to the United States' official position on the Israeli occupation of Arab territories. Sadat's understanding of and admiration for the American political culture made it impossible for him to conceive that an American government could pursue a policy which was effectively contrary to its officially stated position. Sadat's frustrations with American inaction were therefore derived from his impatience with what he believed to be the slow pace of American diplomacy rather than from any realization that his faith in what Washington could do for him might be misplaced.

Thus, in an interview with the editor of a Lebanese newspaper Sadat expressed more frustrations with the position of the United States, but stopped short of drawing any conclusions about his strategy: "It is time that the U.S. define her position, because of her responsibility for everything in Israel: arms deliveries, checks and covering Israel's budget deficits...What is important to us at this point is that the U.S. tell us her views...the U.S. should adopt a policy that makes sense to us in the Arab World and in the international arena."[33]

Still, Sadat kept faith in Washington. More significantly, perhaps, he continued to have an unshaken belief that his own vision, cunning, political dexterity, bargaining skills, and "strategic thinking" were so superior that his Arab and Egyptian opponents could not even hope to begin to understand its intricate components. And this belief must have figured prominently in his assessment of his psychological environment and naturally in the decisions which flowed from it. For instance, during his meeting with American President Gerald Ford on June 1,

1975 in Salzburg, Austria, Sadat agreed that the Suez Canal would be reopened for navigation even though the Israelis refused to meet his eminently reasonable demand that they withdraw to a safe distance from the water-way. The Suez canal was reopened on June 5, 1975, thus effectively constituting a first concession to Israel's demand for a non-belligerency agreement since the reopening of the Canal with Israeli troops stationed on the other side deprived Egypt of the option of resumption of military hostilities to recover occupied Egyptian territories. To his critics who claimed that he had submitted to American and Israeli extortions, Sadat responded with unconvincing arguments about his superior grasp of the science of diplomacy: "Many things and distortions are said. This is not the first allegation of this sort that we hear. Similar things were said when I began the restoration of the Canal cities. They said that Sadat shall no longer wage war, because he pulled his troops back from the Canal, and that is the end of it. However, on June 25, 1974, I reviewed the Second and Third Armies in front of the entire world. I am sure that Israel has photos of that event, because the U.S. takes pictures from her satellites; they must have seen the Second and Third Armies in a state of alert on the West Bank of the Canal, fully equipped and manned. Thus, let us not waste time on talks of this sort. I wish to teach them (the critics) one lesson, that is in diplomacy, the use of a bargaining card can be reversed...I say that in the science of diplomacy you can reverse the use of your cards, by causing world interests to hinge upon you. The reopening of the Canal will bring us better results than its closure. Reopening might bring about the most glorious outcome, while closure breeds negative results."[34] In effect Sadat answered the charge that he deprived Egypt of the option of military action even as a bargaining chip by saying that he reviewed the Second and Third Armies in front of the entire world. The logic was dubious, but the action was vintage Sadat: resorting to grand gestures to hide increasingly helpless positions. But neither dubious logic nor grandiose assertions about superior grasp of the science of diplomacy could hide the reality of a president restricting his options and weakening his negotiating power.

Sadat's exaggeratedly inflated assessment of the perspicacity of his "strategic thinking" and of his unique mastery of the science of diplomacy led to unwarranted conclusions and unrealistic evaluations, a shaky basis for any strategy let alone a grand strategy. His initial claim that his policies had given Egypt a new stature in the world and gave him a well-deserved reputation as an important world leader were partly justified. But the more the Western media courted him the more he felt that he had transcended to a position of world leadership and the more he credited himself with extraordinary and unbelievable achievements, making statements bordering on the ridiculous. Thus, Sadat told the Egyptian people that he and his policies were to be credited for: "overcoming the dangers of the Cold War, the easing of international tension...the elimination of colonialism, furtherance of the war against racial discrimination, and the promotion of a democratic conception of international relations."[35] With these achievements to one's credit one might justifiably develop a view of one's diplomatic prowess which escapes self-criticism and transcends the realities of one's predicament.

The political culture in Egypt and the nature of the regime significantly affected decision-making and influenced the type of negotiating strategies that were permissible. Thus, the authoritarian nature of the Sadat regime and the strongly personalized approach to decision-making resulted in significant differences with the bureaucratic-professional elites in Egypt, particularly the foreign policy elites. Yet, these differences could not be aired publicly and if and when they were made public, they did not result in making Sadat more accountable, not even to the foreign policy professional elites. Thus, whereas Ismail Fahmy, Egypt's Foreign Minister, wanted to avoid excessive foreign policy reliance on any one country, Sadat adopted a strategy founded exclusively on the hope that Washington would pressure Israel to withdraw from the occupied Arab territories; whereas Fahmy wanted to work for Arab unity under Egypt's leadership, Sadat took Egypt's leadership for granted; whereas Fahmy urged the development of a counter-balancing relationship with Moscow, Sadat decided in March 1976, despite difficulties in getting modest arms supplies from Washington, that it was time to abrogate the Friendship Treaty with the Soviet Union. Cabinet decisions were often reversed "as a favour" to the American friends; Egyptian negotiators were sent to important negotiating sessions, such as the Political Committee meeting in Jerusalem in January 1978, without proper preparation, and, perhaps most significantly, important decisions were made by Sadat, alone and without the prior knowledge of his ministers, in private meetings with American and Israeli leaders. Sadat's personalized approach and his unorthodox analysis of his situation was succinctly summed up by the prominent Egyptian writer Mohamed Heikal who was for a brief period close to the Egyptian President. "Sadat failed to recognize the magnitude of the victory that was now (1974) within his grasp," observed Heikal, "He held all the trumps. The oil weapon was his to command; public opinion among the Arabs and in much of the rest of the world was solidly behind him; the Soviet Union was still prepared to support him. But he turned his back on all this. Instead, he opted for the victory parades and the cameras, and, ignoring his Arab allies and friends, resolved that he would rebuild the area alone with his new friend, Henry Kissinger."[36]

The two Egyptian-Israeli disengagement agreements of 1974 and 1975 started Sadat on the road to the American-sponsored peace, the price of which Sadat must have known to be the establishment of an Egypto-American-Israeli strategic alliance at the expense of Egypt's traditional role in the Arab world. Having accepted this premise, Sadat allowed his alternatives to narrow and bargaining power to diminish until they almost exclusively and entirely rested on what the United States and Israel were prepared to offer. To the extent that Henry Kissinger's overall strategic goal was to separate Egypt from Arab and Palestinian aspirations and further isolate the "radical" forces in the region, thus weakening Soviet influence and paving the way for a settlement acceptable to Israel, the American negotiator achieved his goal, with hardly any opposition from Sadat. In fact, in his eagerness to accelerate his admission into the American camp, Sadat adopted negotiating strategies and made concessions that dismayed his Cabinet ministers, astonished his American friends and delighted his Israeli enemies.

Replying to his critics who charged that his exclusive reliance on Nixon and Kissinger diminished his options, Sadat denied that he was "putting all my bets on one spot" and insisted that "under Nixon and Kissinger, there is a real shift in U.S. policies toward peace." Yet, a little further in the same *October Paper* he admits: "I have always put my trust in personal relationships, especially as I found a Secretary of State who knew the issues inside out, who had a clear insight into our problems, and whom we could trust...I am a strategist and so is he."[37] This highly subjective assessment of American foreign policy, its thrust in the Middle East, the intentions of its architects, and the intensely personalized approach to diplomacy, help explain why Kissinger had no difficulties selling to Sadat policies that even Kissinger himself, in his most optimistic scenarios, did not believe would be acceptable to Egypt.

Sadat's Negotiation Strategies with the United States

The prominent Pakistani intellectual Eqbal Ahmad observed that all governments "do on occasion manipulate allies, mislead enemies, and misinform the public. But only rarely have they considered systematic deception, cynical manipulation, and calculated betrayal as the primary instruments of policy. The Nixon-Kissinger government belonged in that category."[38] Kissinger perceived successful diplomacy as a function of astute manipulation and elaborate deceptions. He admired the Austrian Foreign Minister Prince Metternich who reached the height of his power during the Congress of Vienna in 1815, gathered to re-establish the ascendency of the conservative order shattered by the French revolution and the Napoleonic wars. Metternich was the embodiment of the conservative values of the *ancien regime* which he was dedicated to defending and preserving from being contaminated by the French revolutionary ideals of liberty and self-determination. To this end he built a system of alliances and balance of power which managed to preserve the crumbling status quo until the wind of European revolutions finally swept it aside. Kissinger admiringly wrote that the agility of Metternich's performance sometimes overshadowed the fact that "its basis was diplomatic skill and that it left the fundamental problem unresolved, that it was manipulation not creation...For diplomacy can achieve a great deal through the proper evaluation of the forces of international realities and their skillful utilization."[39] Like his hero, Kissinger played the balance of power game; moreover he excelled at manipulative strategies unencumbered by moral, ethical, or legal considerations. Ted Szulc has shown the extent of Kissinger's manipulation and deception strategies in negotiating American withdrawal from Vietnam.[40] Ismail Fahmy, the Egyptian Foreign Minister who participated in the American-Egyptian negotiations and observed Kissinger's dealings with Sadat, was frequently irritated by Kissinger's "tendency to manipulate people, his constant attempts to take advantage of Sadat's trust and impulsiveness to extract major concessions from him, and his tendency to present Israeli papers as American proposals, only to disavow them quickly when we refused to accept them."[41]

Kissinger came to Cairo on November 7, 1973 to discuss with Sadat how to bring the Israelis to withdraw from the new positions they had occupied in violation of the cease-fire ordered by UN Security Council Resolution 338 on the October 22 lines. Sadat rejected the advice of a joint meeting between the two Egyptian and American negotiating teams and preferred instead to have tête—à-tête meetings with Kissinger. In his first meeting with Kissinger, Sadat went straight to the point and exposed his cards from the outset. He told Kissinger: "Do you think I am going to argue about the cease-fire lines of 22 October or about disengagement? No, Dr. Kissinger. You are a man of strategy, I am a man of strategy. I want to talk to you at the strategic level."[42] Sadat said that he got along very well with Kissinger: "For the first time I felt as if I was looking at the real face of the United States (!)...Anyone seeing us after that first hour in al-Tahriah Palace would have thought we had been friends for years."[43] Kissinger presented to Sadat Israeli demands with regard to exchange of prisoners and the ending of the Egyptian naval blockade of Bab El-Mandeb in return for agreeing to return to the October 22 lines "within the context of an agreement on the disengagement of forces." In effect, Kissinger was asking Sadat to pay a substantial price and make significant concessions including a military agreement with potentially significant political implications to get the Israelis to abide by the cease-fire they had officially accepted on October 22, and allow the resupply of the Egyptian Third Army which the Israelis had entrapped after violating the cease-fire agreement. Kissinger apparently had no difficulty getting Sadat to agree to Israeli demands. To help Sadat accept the concessions he was being asked to make, Kissinger resorted to his favourite approach: secrecy. He suggested to Sadat that limitations on Egyptian forces in the Sinai and Sadat's private assurances on Israeli cargoes transiting the Canal could be handled in secret memos of understanding.[44] Kissinger took out from his briefcase the paper on which Israeli Prime Minister Golda Meir's six points were written — points which Kissinger had told her when she was in Washington he was sure Sadat would reject. Sadat glanced at the paper and said: "All right; I accept." Sadat's negotiating approach taxed the incredulity of Kissinger who could not believe his luck and the ease with which he got Sadat to agree to these important concessions. Kissinger wrote that he could not understand why Sadat "did not haggle or argue. He did not dispute my analysis, he did not offer an alternative, violating the normal method of diplomacy — which is to see what one can extract in return for concessions."[45] Sadat made the concessions demanded by the Israelis and later that day he told the waiting journalists that he and Kissinger had agreed "on *my* six points, and without bating an eyelid handed out copies of Golda Meir's proposals as his own."[46] (emphasis added).

At another tête-à-tête meeting, on December 11, in Aswan, Upper Egypt, Sadat astonished and delighted Kissinger by agreeing to more important concessions. He agreed to much lower levels of Egyptian military presence in the Sinai than Kissinger had thought would be acceptable to Egypt. Kissinger had argued with the Israelis that Egypt could not accept anything less than 250 tanks in Sinai.[47] At the Aswan meeting, Sadat told Kissinger that he was prepared to maintain only 30 tanks. When the full Egyptian and American delegations met, Kissinger announced the agreement he had reached with Sadat at their private meeting. General Gamsy, the Egyptian Chief of Staff who had not been consulted, felt that he and the Egyptian army had been betrayed. Sadat decided to go even further, and, as "a goodwill gesture" he grandly offered to withdraw the token Egyptian force from Sinai. An Israeli observer wrote that Sadat "must have felt that it would be more degrading for him to fight for the positioning, with Israeli consent, of a mere 30 tanks in Sinai than to put on a show of largesse by offering to put no tanks there at all. That was Sadat."[48] An Egyptian participant at these talks reported that "General Gamsy...could not believe his ears. 'What a heavy price we paid to get our tanks into Sinai,' he said. Thirty tanks was a ridiculously low figure, but to reduce that to none...! He went over to the window, and I saw that he was in tears."[49] Another Egyptian participant at the talks commented: "Sadat had single-handedly given away all that the Egyptian army had won with great sacrifice.

Without consulting anybody, he had caved in to the Israeli request that the Egyptian military presence east of the Canal be reduced to nothing."[50]

At a press conference at Asswan on January 18, Sadat shared with reporters his assessment of the role played by the Nixon-Kissinger team whom he credited with crucial contributions to the success of the Sinai disengagement agreement: "I had the opportunity to talk with Nixon on the phone, when he phoned to greet me [for the disengagement agreement]. I told him that his wise policy, coupled with the efforts of his friend Kissinger, were instrumental in bringing about the agreement, and therefore more greetings were due to him than to me...Previously, the U.S. had been advocating direct negotiations, and refrained from making any suggestions, but Kissinger has more guts than any American Secretary before him, and he came up with an American proposal."[51] Furthermore, Sadat seems to have convinced himself that the fact that Kissinger presented to him some American proposals — regardless of how close to the Israeli ideas these proposals were — proved his point about the new shift in American foreign policy. In a speech to the staff of a frontline air-base in the Port Said area in June 1974 Sadat claimed: "The U.S. position has changed to such an extent that when we concluded the disengagement agreement in Asswan, and I rejected all Israeli proposals, while Israel rejected all my suggestions, the U.S. stepped in and said: 'We are submitting a specific American proposal and we are seeking your — that is both parties — views on it'. This means that the U.S. no longer entirely aligned (sic) with Israel. No! She has moved to occupy a position of equidistance between the parties."[52]

The ease with which Kissinger sold Sadat on many of the ideas he presented to him may also be partly explained by the temperament of the Egyptian President. Sadat liked to think of himself as a strategist, not a tactician, a man in pursuit of a vision with no time for short-term objectives, a leader of actions and grand designs with no patience for small and cumbersome details. He tended to reach a general decision and cared little for details, some of which had significant political implications. For instance, at a meeting in Egypt between the American and Egyptian delegations, on September 4, 1975, Kissinger requested that Sadat sign the documents of the second disengagement agreement. A member of the Egyptian delegation reported that "Sadat as usual welcomed the idea and gave his approval immediately." The Egyptian Foreign Minister intervened and said: "No, President Sadat will not sign the agreement." Sadat was astonished: "Why, Ismail, I have already signed the first disengagement." Foreign Minister Ismail Fahmy told Sadat that he had not signed an agreement with Israel, but American proposals. Sadat then changed his mind: "Yes, Henry, Fahmy is correct. I did not sign any papers with Israel, only American papers."[53] Kissinger asked Fahmy to sign but the Egyptian Foreign Minister refused and urged Sadat to postpone the conclusion of the accord until Egypt reconsidered its options. Sadat rejected the suggestion, and seeing that his Foreign Minister was refusing to sign, he called Mahmoud Salem, the Egyptian Prime Minister, and ordered him to sign. Salem readily complied and signed the disengagement documents.

Sinai II, as the second disengagement agreement came to be known, was more than a military agreement between Egypt and Israel. It had significant political implications, notwithstanding Sadat's and Fahmy's assertions to the contrary. Egypt pledged itself to abstain from the use of military force to solve the Arab-Israeli conflict, and this essentially represented the end of belligerency which Israel had demanded. Thus, the agreement marked Egypt's military abandonment of its commitment to the right to liberate occupied Arab territories. Sadat also agreed to honour the pledge he had made to Ford in Salzburg to allow the United States to establish and operate an early warning system in the strategic Milta and Giddi passes. The Israelis had wanted to operate the system themselves but their presence in the Sinai would have been unacceptable; the presence of the Americans, however, would serve the purpose of the Israelis but without arousing the same hostility. At any rate, the concession represented another significant reduction in Egypt's sovereignty over its own territory. In an address to a joint session of the People's Council and the Central Committee of the Arab Socialist Union on September 4, Sadat admitted that Sinai II fell short of achieving what he set out to accomplish but justified the signing of the agreement on the grounds that it was better than the stalemate situation: "I must tell you with similar frankness and straightforwardness that this disengagement agreement did not achieve what I wanted. But its value, in addition to what I have already said, lies in the fact that it is another step forward and that it ends the likelihood of stagnation. As you can see it is not linked with political conditions, except when it is linked to an overall settlement in this region."[54] On the important charges made by his Arab critics that Sinai II ended the state of belligerency and represented an abandonment of Egypt's right to liberate occupied Arab territories, Sadat offered, once more, vague reassurances that he did not accept any formal end to belligerency: "[Israel] asked for the termination of the state of belligerency, and that was a new element that had not been raised in the Nixon Era. When Kissinger was here in the Summer of 1974, it was agreed with Israel that the question of ending the State of war was a taboo that could not be brought up for discussion. My view regarding the termination of the State of war was, and still is, that if I were to concur, I would thereby be inviting Israel to continue to occupy my land in tranquillity. I had repeated that view many times over, throughout the Arab Nation. Why, then, all the turmoil, the shouts and the demonstrations?...We rejected the first attempt at disengagement because Israel saw it as an opportunity to sow disunity in the Arab world; therefore, she insisted. But when Kissinger came to see me, I said: 'Sorry, it is all over...'"[55]

Kissinger was more candid about, and rightly proud of his accomplishments. He told the U.S. Senate Foreign Relations Committee that the disengagement agreements he engineered had effectively detached Egypt from the Arab-Israeli conflict. The Israelis of-course made a similar assessment. When, on January 24, 1976, a Lebanese Magazine editor confronted Sadat with Kissinger's remarks, Sadat reacted angrily: "Do not quote me Kissinger's words to the Foreign Relations Committee of the American Congress, or Rabin's speech in the knesset. Everyone speaks his own mind. Ask me about my strategy; I know the others' strategy and way of reasoning...Egypt has not abandoned the battle, and no force in the world could detach her from it."[56]

Still, Sinai II helped bring about some significant modifications in the political and military balance of power in the region, and not only because it effectively removed Egypt from the Arab-Israeli conflict. Israeli leaders extracted meaningful "compensations" from the U.S. for agreeing to disengagement which effectively enhanced their strategic and military domination of the region. Washington pledged "an uninterrupted flow of modern weapon systems to Israel," and undertook to refrain from pressuring Israel for "withdrawals from the Golan or from the

West Bank," and to "withhold recognition of the PLO" until it accepted Resolution 242. Kissinger also committed the United States government to "consult closely" with Israel in the event of a threat to the stability of the region either by Egypt or "an outside power."[57] The American economic, political and military commitments to Israel took the form of an "executive agreement" which was not published, and therefore escaped serious Congressional scrutiny, but committed the United States government to unprecedented involvement on the side of Israel.

Sadat was acquainted with and approved Kissinger's secret pledges to Israel.[58] He thus knew as early as 1975 that the United States had become more committed than ever to maintaining a strategic and military balance of power more overwhelmingly favourable to Israel than ever, and knew the role that the disengagement agreements he signed played in making this possible. He defended his decisions by emphasizing that his strategy was too grand for most people to understand and that it was based on a vision whose long term benefits could not be doubted; but he was reluctant to talk about his strategy and its long term implications. Thus, he told a Saudi newspaper on February 20, 1976: "I am not afraid about what I say or do, and my people know that…As for the rest of our strategy, I wish to match the Basel Conference convened by Herzl. They planned and concluded a scheme for an entire century. They waited 50-75 years until they began applying their plans, from the Balfour Declaration of 1917, through the establishment of Israel in 1948 and the following aggression, until these days. All that had been decided upon some 70-80 years ago. I am not ready to elaborate on my strategy in public. Unfortunately there is no one I could talk to about it, except for our Arab brothers who understand the logic, the importance and the value of this problem."[59]

But whatever Sadat's grand strategy was, it was directly responsible for the tremendous qualitative changes in the military balance of power in the Arab-Israeli conflict. The Arab side had lost in Egypt its most important military power while Israel had significantly enhanced its own military might. By 1977, the Israeli army had, by Israeli leaders' own admission, doubled its size, with more tanks than Britain and France combined, its air force, one of the largest and most technologically advanced in the world "exceeded only by the airfleets of the two superpowers" and equipped with the U.S.-made F-15s, the most advanced planes in the world.[60] At the same time, Sinai II started unravelling the web of Arab unity painfully woven to put an end to Israeli occupation of Arab territories. Syria, Iraq and the Palestinians accused Sadat of selling out to the enemy, and even "moderate" Arab regimes expressed reservations about the wisdom of the Egyptian President's strategic decisions.

The Relevant Positions and the Relative Forces of the American-Israeli Parties.

Shortly after coming to power in Washington the new Carter administration seemed interested in a comprehensive settlement of the Arab-Israeli conflict which it believed could be best achieved at an international peace conference to be convened in Geneva. With this in mind, Secretary of State Cyrus Vance undertook a tour of the Middle East in February 1977. The Arab countries agreed that for the purpose of negotiating a comprehensive peace with Israel, they should be represented by a unified delegation at Geneva with one voice speaking for all. Egypt agreed to this position because, as the Egyptian Foreign Minister put it, "it had no intention of betraying the other Arab countries."[61]

In Israel, the election of May 1977 brought to the Knesset a majority of Likud members composed of right wing politicians led by Menahem Begin, a former terrorist chief whom Ben-Gurion had once described as a Hitlerite type. The new Prime Minister was mostly known for what was usually publicly dismissed by Labour leaders as preposterous and irresponsible ideology. On the Palestinian-Israeli conflict there were, to be sure, only minor differences between Labour and Likud since both had always agreed on the basic goal of denial of Palestinian national rights. They differed on tactical matters with the Likud openly flaunting its messianic ideology and using it to justify permanent occupation of all of Palestine while the Labour had been using the concept of security to legitimize Israeli occupation of the Arab territories captured in 1967. Moreover, the Likud leaders showed little respect for Labour's calculations of public relations and sensitivity to Israel's image in the United States. Begin's ideological commitment to "a wholly redeemed land of Israel" was repeatedly reaffirmed in speeches and rallies when he was a marginal politician. As an aspiring prime minister he saw no reason to modify his ideas. The foreign policy platform of the Likud party, Begin's Herut and some other factions put together for the 1977 election, was uncompromising. It stated: "The right of the Jewish people to the Land of Israel is eternal and inalienable and is an integral part of its right to security and peace. Judea and Sumaria shall therefore not be relinquished for foreign rule; between the sea and the Jordan, there will be Jewish sovereignty alone."[62] As prime minister, Menahem Begin quickly modified Israeli political discourse and contemptuously rejected any reference to the occupied territories as either occupied or "West Bank." He referred to them as "liberated" territories for which he only used the biblical names of Judea and Samaria.

Begin chose Moshe Dayan for the post of Foreign Minister. Dayan was known to advocate a partial Israeli pullout from the Sinai in return for an end to the state of belligerency between Egypt and Israel. He had argued that such a withdrawal from the entrenched position along the Suez Canal would accrue military and political advantages to Israel. By reducing the burden of extended supply lines and costly fortifications, a partial withdrawal would actually enhance Israel's strategic position in the Sinai. Dayan also believed that a partial withdrawal would strengthen Israel's negotiating position because it would make more credible the threat of holding on the Sinai. In their secret talks of 1976, Henry Kissinger and then Israeli Prime Minister Yitzhak Rabin had discussed a plan for Israeli withdrawal to al-Arish-Ras Mohamed line in return for an Egyptian political agreement putting an end to belligerency. When the Likud came to power, Begin accepted the plan's basis of a trade off. But what he had in mind was not to trade off the Sinai for an end of belligerency from Egypt, but to trade off the Sinai for the West Bank and "for the Greater Land of Israel."[63] Begin believed that the most powerful Arab country could be isolated by offering her the Sinai back in return for an agreement that would remove Egypt from the military equation and leave Israel free to pursue its military options against the Palestinians. Accordingly, Dayan sent to Washington an Israeli draft of a possible Egyptian-Israeli treaty. The plan received the support of Secretary of State Cyrus Vance and President Jimmy Carter who forwarded it to Sadat, and urged him to consider it seriously.

In his first meeting with Israeli Prime Minister Yitzhak Rabin in Washington, President Carter presented him with an American position based on the need for a comprehensive settlement negotiated among the parties, including the PLO. "We see a possibility," he told Rabin, "that Palestinian leaders can be absorbed in an Arab delegation. And we don't know any Palestinian leaders other than the PLO."[64] Washington was interested in implementing Resolution 242 and shortly before newly-elected Israeli Prime Minister Begin arrived in Washington, the State Department issued a statement affirming that resolution 242 "means withdrawal from all three fronts in the Middle East dispute — that is Sinai, Golan, West Bank and Gaza."[65] When Begin met Carter in Washington, on July 19, the new Israeli prime minister forcefully presented his usual intransigent and uncompromising position: "he would accept no 'foreign sovereignty' over Judea and Samaria"[66] and was not interested in putting a halt to Jewish settlement activities. Shortly after, July 26, the PLO informed the White House that it was prepared to live in peace with Israel and was willing to make a public statement and give a private commitment to that effect to Carter if he were prepared to support an independent Palestinian "state unit entity" linked to Jordan.[67] In a memo to Secretary of State Vance prior to the latter's departure for the Middle East, Carter had written that if the parties did not accept American proposals "we need enough public support so that, with the U.S.S.R, we can marshall world opinions against recalcitrant nations," and informed Vance about the "need to make arrangements for Geneva," and "arrange for the PLO to attend together with Arab nations on the basis of UN Resolutions 242 and 338."[68]

Sadat Moves Closer to Israel

Fearful of the domestic political risk inherent in pressuring Israel, Carter preferred to use a strategy whereby the combined pressure of Arab, Soviet and American positions at the international conference would expose the recalcitrance of the Israeli leaders to the world and to American public opinion. Although Sadat had publicly stated on many occasions that he was following a similar strategy aimed at achieving common Arab goals or, failing that, at exposing Israeli intransigence, he proceeded to undermine Carter's plans by adopting a strategy more in line with Israeli thinking. Thus, while the Americans pushed for a single Arab delegation at Geneva, Sadat agreed with the Israeli position of "adamantly" opposing it. Whereas Carter and Vance seemed prepared for some PLO representation at Geneva, Sadat again agreed with the Israeli position of rejecting PLO representation. While Vance and his party were under instruction from Carter to push for the reconvening of a Geneva Conference, Sadat surprised Vance by telling him that there was no rush with respect to Geneva.[69] In effect, Sadat was moving closer to the Israeli position than the Americans thought would be possible for Egypt.

When Vance returned to Egypt after visiting Israel and other Arab countries during his Mideast tour, he was received by Sadat in Alexandria. It was a memorable meeting in which Sadat presented the American delegation with an Egyptian position that astonished and dismayed Ismail Fahmy, the Egyptian Foreign Minister who was present at the meeting. Fahmy gave the following account: "Discussing the outcome of his tour, Vance informed us in particular of the Israelis' interpretation of Security Council Resolution 242. In their view, Vance explained, the resolution did not require total Israeli withdrawal from the territories occupied in the 1967 War; it does require, on the other hand, not only the end of belligerency between Israel and the Arab States, but also full "normalization" of relations. It was a very biased interpretation, diametrically opposite to the Egyptian one. To my complete surprise, when Vance finished, President Sadat said in no uncertain terms that *he was in full agreement with that interpretation.* I had no option but to intervene and disagree most firmly. I sensed immediately Sadat was going to insist on his position and in fact he did so."[70] (emphasis added) An American official who attended the meeting noted that "Sadat was putting his cards almost face up," and seemed more interested in "ingratiating himself with the American side."[71]

Suddenly, and without the knowledge of his Foreign Minister, Sadat entered into secret talks with the Israelis, arranged through the Moroccans and aimed at exploring a separate track of direct Egyptian-Israeli negotiations which would naturally undermine American preparations for Geneva. The immediate object of the secret talks was to pursue the idea of a meeting between Sadat and Begin. A secret meeting for Egyptian and Israeli emissaries was arranged in Rabbat, Morocco.

Begin sent Dayan and Sadat sent his Deputy Prime Minister Hassan al-Tuhamy, a colourful and intriguing character who had been close to Sadat since the days of the Free Officers' revolt against the Egyptian monarchy. Dayan's account of the meeting shows that the Egyptian negotiator was interested in a bilateral Egyptian-Israeli agreement and some sort of Palestinian arrangement linking the West Bank and Gaza with Jordan. There was no Egyptian demand for the recognition of Palestinians' right to self-determination, nor did Dayan leave any doubt about Israel's determination to continue to occupy Arab Jerusalem and the West Bank.[72] Al Tuhamy's own account of the meeting was significant in that while it differed in important respects from Dayan's, it still confirmed Dayan's claim about Egypt's opening position regarding Palestinian rights. Sadat's special envoy said that he repeated to Dayan that Egypt demanded the return of "every inch of Arab territories your forces occupied in the 1967 aggression starting with Arab Jerusalem and the Golan Heights before the Sinai. The West Bank and Gaza to be returned to King Hussein as it was (sic) before the aggression."[73] Thus, Sadat's envoy seems to have presented to Dayan a negotiating position unlike the one Sadat claimed in public to be pursuing. In effect, the Egyptian opening negotiating position did not include a demand for the recognition of the Palestinians' right to self-determination, nor did it press for the inclusion of the PLO in the future negotiations as agreed upon by the Arab States at the Rabat Summit of 1974. And that despite the fact that Dayan had reportedly hinted that "Israel would be prepared to include the PLO in the peace process."[74]

U.S.-Israeli Showdown

In March 1977, Carter publicly called for the establishment of "a homeland" for the Palestinians. His remarks caused consternation among Jewish American leaders and were given an unwarranted enthusiastic reception by many in the Arab world. In fact, the full context of Carter's remarks clearly establishes that a "homeland" for the Palestinians did not mean self-determination and much less a

Palestinian State. Speaking at a town meeting in Clinton, Massachusetts, on March 18, Carter articulated three conditions for peace in the Middle East. "The first pre-requisite of a lasting peace," he stated, "is the recognition of Israel by her neigh-bors...The second one is very important and very, very difficult: that is, the establishment of permanent borders for Israel...And the third ultimate require-ment for peace is to deal with the Palestinian problem...There has to be a homeland provided for the Palestinian refugees who have suffered for many, many years. And the exact way to solve the Palestinian problem is one that first of all addresses itself right now to the Arab countries and then, secondly, to the Arab countries negotiating with Israel."[75]

It is important to note that Carter called for a "homeland" for the refugees and not for the Palestinian people, thus implying that the Palestinian problem is a humanitarian problem not a political problem. Moreover, it is also clear that Carter believed that finding such a homeland is an Arab problem and that the solution of the Palestinian problem is therefore the responsibility of the Arabs, a position which has been advocated by Israel all along. Still, the mere mention of "a homeland" for the Palestinians infuriated American Zionists and Carter had to water down subsequent public statements that might be construed as favourable to the Palestinians. He remained, however, committed to the general formula of "territories for peace."

Thus, with Begin's ideological commitment to a greater Israel precluding withdrawal from the West Bank and Gaza, and undermining Washington's efforts for a U.S.-mediated peace acceptable to "moderate" Arab States, Carter seemed to be heading for a confrontation with Israel. In an interview with *Time* magazine shortly after Vance left for the Middle East, Carter stated: "I think if a particular leader of one of the countries should find that his position is in direct contravention to the position of all the other parties involved, including oursel-ves and the Soviet Union, and was narrowly defined in his own country, there would be a great impetus on that leader to conform to the overwhelming opinion."[76]

Carter's meeting with Begin on July 19, confirmed the intransigence of the Is-raeli position and confronted Carter with the choice of taking forceful actions to pressure Israel, whose reliance on American economic and military aid was total, or admitting helplessness and fear of political damage to his presidency. He chose the latter course of action. On September 21, 1977, He told the visiting Egyptian Foreign Minister: "President Sadat repeatedly asks me to exercise major pressure on Israel, but I want you to know that I simply cannot do it because it would be a personal political suicide for me." The Egyptian Foreign Minister reported this dramatic confession to Sadat and urged him to reevaluate his total reliance on Washington but "Sadat was unresponsive."[77]

At the same time, Carter was realizing that Begin had meant what he had been saying about wanting to keep the occupied Arab territories. He was build-ing more Jewish settlements in the occupied territories, and, in violation of his commitment to Carter, was sending his army into Lebanon. The latter action prompted an angry response from the White House. On September 24, Carter wrote to Begin warning that "current Israeli military actions in Lebanon are a violation of our agreement covering the provision of American military equip-ment...If these actions are not immediately halted...further deliveries will have to be terminated."[78] But, when the American-Israeli showdown did materialize Carter was decidedly less firm. He failed to stand up to Israel and to American Zionists. The Carter-Begin confrontation was triggered by an apparently innocuous Soviet-American statement on peace in the Middle East.

On October 1, 1977, the U.S. and the U.S.S.R. issued a joint communiqué which called for the reconvening of a Geneva conference "as soon as possible" to work out a peace settlement that would be "comprehensive, incorporating all parties concerned and all questions" and should resolve all issues including such issues as "withdrawal of Israeli armed forces from territories occupied in the 1967 conflict; the resolution of the Palestinian question, including ensuring the legitimate rights of the Palestinian people, termination of the state of belligerency and establishment of normal peaceful relations."[79] The PLO welcomed the declaration saying that it contained "positive indications toward a just settlement of the Middle East conflict,"[80] even though it contained no reference to the PLO, to the Palestinians' right to self-determination, or to a return to the pre-1967 lines. Significantly, Sadat seems to have been concerned that the Soviet-American entente might hinder his preparations for separate negotiations with Israel, and he instructed Fahmy to urge Carter "that nothing be done to prevent Israel and Egypt from negotiating directly."[81]

The communiqué's reference to "the legitimate rights of the Palestinian people" infuriated Israel and the Israeli lobby in the United States. When Israeli Prime Minister Begin was presented with a copy of the statement by U.S. ambassador to Israel Samuel Lewis, "an angry meeting ensued."[82] Israel insisted that the basis for convening the Geneva conference were U.N. resolutions 242 and 338 because they "do not contain any specific reference to the Palestinians, thereby excluding their presence at the talks."[83] On October 4, Moshe Dayan met with Carter and Vance in New York to express Israel's total opposition to the Soviet-American communiqué. Dayan reportedly blackmailed Carter, threatening to publicly state that the American President refused to give Israel reassurances that the U.S. would not pressure Israel to accept a Palestinian State, even in federation with Jordan, or to withdraw from all occupied Arab territories.[84] Carter quickly gave in and retreated from his position and by the end of the meeting the American President had all but repudiated the joint Soviet-American statement. When he returned to Israel, Dayan divulged to the Israeli Knesset the content of the secret working paper of his New York meeting with Carter and Vance. It showed the extent of Carter's retreat. Carter gave in to four substantive Israeli demands: a) no participation of PLO members in the negotiations; b) removal of the question of Palestinian entity from the conference agenda; c) the opening plenary session at Geneva with the unified Arab delegation not to be permitted to remain in session during the conference; and d) no "negotiations" regarding the occupied Arab territories, the word "negotiate" to be replaced with "discuss."[85]

Carter's own warnings to Egyptian Foreign Minister Fahmy that he could not pressure the Israelis, was dramatically borne out by the October confrontation. Sadat should have heeded Carter's warnings about his own vulnerability and his demonstrated weakness vis-à-vis Israel and its lobby in the United States, of which the Carter-Dayan meeting gave a dramatic illustration. But Sadat failed to draw any conclusions that could warrant a reassessment of his strategy of total reliance upon Washington. In fact, Carter's retreat in the face of Dayan's threats may have strengthened Sadat's own beliefs in his ability to succeed where Carter failed, and reinforced his resolve to go it all alone.

Bread Riots and the Decision to Go to Israel

It has been suggested that Sadat's peace initiatives and his visit to Israel in particular, which he presented as a "sacred mission," were primarily motivated by economic considerations. In light of Sadat's strategy, which looked forward to an ever-hoped-for but never-materializing windfall prosperity from the American connection, and in light of the economic difficulties that Sadat's open door economic policy in fact exacerbated, it seems clear enough that Sadat's difficulties at home played a role in some of his grand and dramatic decisions such as the reopening of the Suez Canal in 1975 and the decision to go to Israel two years later. These decisions were no doubt partly a function of a desire to divert attention from domestic problems by keeping the "peace process" and Sadat's initiatives the focus of attention, partly a function of Sadat's own impatience with the slow pace of normal diplomacy, and partly a reflection of a genuine belief that he was on the right track to achieving his twin goal of peace and prosperity.

At the same time, Sadat's economic policies were part of an overall ideological reorientation aimed at weakening the twin foundations of Nasserism: Arab nationalism and Arab socialism. The assumption was that such a reorientation was necessary to get Egypt out of the Arab-Soviet camp and accelerate its acceptance and insertion into the American camp. The visit to Israel and the concessions made in earlier and later negotiations with Israelis and Americans were also part of the same strategy. The domestic opposition and internal difficulties which Sadat's economic policies aroused may have accelerated his strategy but they were not the driving force behind it. And that is because the ideological orientation was already underway in 1971 when Sadat moved against the old guards and purged the so-called centres of power from Nasserites and pro-Moscow elements. Sadat also announced in 1971 that he was ready to sign a peace treaty with Israel, including diplomatic and economic relationships. The move away from the Soviet bloc was confirmed in 1972 with the expulsion of the Soviet military advisors. The policy of Infitah (Openness), now generally recognized as responsible for many of Egypt's economic problems in the late seventies, was officially introduced in 1974 as part of the general political and economic reorientation of Egyptian policy which Sadat described as "ideological openness." By the end of 1976 Sadat was losing patience with the step-by-step approach and with the failure of Washington to verify his predictions about a total shift in American foreign policy, as was obvious from his frustrations with the interim Presidency of Gerald Ford and his repeated pleas to Washington to adopt a position consistent with its official policy.

The bread riots of January 1977 dramatized two results of Sadat's strategies: the failure of the Infitah policy, and the failure of the step-by-step diplomacy sponsored by Washington to achieve the results Sadat hoped for and desperately counted on to vindicate his controversial strategies. The failure of the one helped push the other out of the way. The failure of Sadat's economic policies increased his desperate need for fast results which the step-by-step diplomacy was unable to produce. Sadat decided that even the Geneva Conference, which the Carter administration was working to convene in 1977, may not bring the breakthrough that he hoped for. And even if did, it would not vindicate his controversial strategies; on the contrary it would vindicate the wisdom of having a common Arab negotiating strategies and goals. The bread riots of January 1977 did not, therefore, cause Sadat to modify the course of his ideological orientation. Nor did they bring about a serious reappraisal of Sadat's overall strategy. They simply accelerated a process already in march.

Sadat's economic policy of Infitah extolled the virtues of free enterprise and modernization, construed by Sadat to mean Westernization. He assumed that a liberalized economic system and a measure of political freedom would encourage Arab and American capital and technology to pour into Egypt. With an American superintended peace Sadat looked forward to a new Marshall Plan which was supposed to bring to Egypt, in his words, "prosperity that defies the imagination."[86] The policy of Infitah, officially launched by Law number 34 in 1974, was, according to one observer, initially welcomed by most Egyptians. But it quickly became apparent that the open door policy was "nothing less than a total retreat from Nasser's socialism and a wholehearted endorsement of a new capitalist orientation."[87]

The new policies succeeded principally in rearranging the economic priorities of the country, encouraging construction and urbanization at the expense of shrinking arable land, emphasizing consumerism and imports of luxury goods to the detriment of agricultural and industrial output. At the same time, this policy of virtually uncontrolled "openness" accelerated a process of disintegration and collapse of the country's balance of payments. It made possible "in all sectors of the society a social mobility the scope of which had no precedents since the end of World War I," observed Mahmoud Abdel-Fadil and Alain Roussillon, "at the price of vertiginous deepening of inequalities."[88] The exacerbated economic disparities inevitably fomented social discontent as "the contrast between the growing misery of the people and the enrichment of a small group of business operators grew apace."[89] The press, including semi-official news magazines such as *Rooz-al-Yussuf* began publishing accounts of bribery, corruption, profiteering and pointed accusing fingers at the growing army of "fact cats" and parasites. "Corruption," wrote Ghali Shoukri, "the highest stage of parasitic action, has become the central feature of the new Egyptian economic formula."[90]

Social discontent intensified and workers took to the streets chanting *Ya Batle al-Ubuur, Feen al-futuur*, "O Hero of the Crossing, Where is our Breakfast?"[91] When in January 1977 the government gave in to "commands" from the International Monetary Fund (IMF) to end its subsidies of basic commodities, "Tens of thousands of men and women poured into the streets" in spontaneous "bread riots" which quickly spread from Alexandria to Cairo to upper Egypt where Sadat was staying. The mob made for the rest house of the president who was obliged to make a hurried exit "leaving all his possessions and papers behind."[92] Sadat called the riots a "criminal ploy" by the communists, an "uprising of thieves," and responded by introducing more of the same policies. Later when the full extent of the corruption of members of Sadat's family was exposed, an Egyptian critic described Sadat's policy of Infitah as "the real uprising of thieves."[93]

In short, far from leading Sadat to rethink his overall strategy, economic difficulties reinforced him in his conviction that he must move even faster on the same track. But it was a track he embarked on because of ideological convictions and political considerations related to his overall assessment of his operational environment. Economic difficulties, and more importantly the prospect of economic prosperity, were certainly a factor behind the ideological reorientation initiated by Sadat in the early seventies; they were also a factor, but by no means the most important one, in decisions which reinforced Sadat's inclination for dramatic gestures and for a faster, if separate, strategy.

Sadat's Decision to go to Israel

The confrontation between Carter and the Israelis following the Soviet-American communiqué of October 1977 and the demonstrated weakness of the American president in dealing with Israel, seem to have had little impact on Sadat's secret preparations to deal directly, and alone, with Israel. This again might have been a function of Sadat's unrealistic assessment of the forces at play, and particularly of his belief in the power of his own "strategic thinking." The decision to go to Israel seems to have been taken without consultation with his Cabinet, his Arab allies, or even his American friends. American Secretary of State Cyrus Vance said that Sadat's decision came "with surprising suddenness." Sadat said that he was indirectly influenced by some reference Carter made in a letter to him about the need for some bold initiative. In September 1977, Sadat had received a personal letter from President Carter about which he wrote: "I cannot divulge the contents of Carters' letter to me, because of its personal nature, but…(it) directed my thinking for the first time toward the Initiative I was to take two months later."[94]

And this at a time, as mentioned earlier, when the American administration was moving closer toward reconvening the Geneva Conference. On October 28, 1977 Carter had written to Sadat: "I believe it will be possible for Palestinian representatives to be chosen by the Arab side who will be acceptable to all and who will faithfully represent Palestinian views…I propose to now proceed to work out with the Soviet Union co-chairman a call for reconvening the Geneva Conference."[95] On November 9, only 10 days before Sadat's sudden visit to Israel, Egyptian Foreign Minister Ismail Fahmy received a letter from Vance indicating that President Carter had already formally proposed to all Arab States the reconvening of the Geneva Conference.

It was during a visit to Romania on October 28, 1977, that Sadat told his Foreign Minister Ismail Fahmy for the first time that he was thinking about going to Jerusalem to speak before the Knesset. Fahmy opposed the idea on the ground that it would deprive Egypt of whatever negotiating leverage it still had. Back in Cairo, Sadat instructed Fahmy, who was preparing to go to Tunis for an Arab Foreign Ministers Conference scheduled for November 12, to insist on the importance of a unified Arab position before Geneva and to confirm that Egypt was fully committed to the PLO. He also told Fahmy to tell the Arab Foreign Ministers that the settlement of the Palestinian problem was the core of a just and comprehensive peace and said that he wanted the Tunis meeting to be "a historic one under Egypt's leadership."[96] Meanwhile, Sadat was engaged, without the knowledge of his Foreign Minister, in secret talks with the Israelis in preparations for his trip to Jerusalem.

On November 9, Sadat delivered a major speech to the People's Assembly of Egypt. During the speech, he suddenly departed from his text and emotionally declared that he was "ready to go anywhere in the world, even to Jerusalem, to deliver a speech and address the Knesset if this would help save the blood" of his sons.[97] Egypt's Foreign Minister, many of his colleagues in the Foreign Ministry elites and members of the Egyptian Cabinet were taken aback. Sadat had not told Fahmy that he was going to make such an announcement. After the speech, Sadat told Fahmy that his phrase about going to Jerusalem was "a slip of the tongue," and added: "Please Ismail, censor it completely."[98] Fahmy gave instructions to delete from President Sadat's speech the phrase dealing with the trip to Jerusalem. But when Sadat saw the first edition of the Cairo papers "he was extremely angry, and gave orders that the front pages should be remade, giving the 'end of the earth's offer fullest prominence."[99] The Foreign Minister objected to Sadat's decision and to the way it seems to have been made without consultation with, or the approval of the Cabinet. Fahmy wrote: "Sadat never explained the reasons behind his initiative. The National Security Council did not debate the initiative and did not approve it."[100] On November 17, Both the Egyptian Foreign Minister and Deputy Foreign Minister resigned in protest against Sadat's planned visit to Israel.

Fahmy also wrote that he was unable to explain the reasons that motivated Sadat to undertake the Jerusalem trip. In particular, he dismisses the economic explanation:

> While Egypt's economic problems were acute, they could not be solved by empty dramatic steps. Financially there was no problem. The Suez Canal and oil revenues were increasing fast. The remittances of Egyptians working abroad, particularly in the Arab world, were flowing back in unprecedented amounts. In 1977, the oil-producing Arab countries had agreed to form a consortium in order to boost the Egyptian economy. Moreover, Sadat's new policy to equip his army with the latest and most sophisticated Western weapons was fully supported by the Gulf Arab States, especially Saudi Arabia. They paid in cash and in full for these weapons, whether they were American or French. American economic aid to Egypt had already reached high levels before the trip. The major increase had taken place in fiscal 1976, when American economic assistance jumped to US$986.6 million from $371.9 million the previous year....Relations with the Arab countries could not have been better. The Arab Foreign Ministers' meeting in Tunis had been a triumph for Egypt. Diplomatic relations with Libya had been established. Even Sinai was not a problem. The American draft treaty between Israel and Egypt called for the complete withdrawal of the Israeli forces stationed in Sinai to the international borders of Egypt....The only party which benefited from Sadat's initiative was Israel. This is not a conclusion reached with the benefit of hindsight. It was perfectly clear from the very beginning.[101]

Sadat, however, made public statements based, once more, on a highly optimistic assessment of the psychological impact of his "sacred mission." On his return from Israel, he gave such an inflated assessment to the prominent Egyptian journalist Ahmad Baha Eddin: "Now everything has been solved. It's all over." The Egyptian newspaper editor inquired about the Palestinian issue, the West Bank and Gaza, Sadat replied: "Oh-that's all finished too." "What about Arab Jerusalem, Mr. President?," asked the Egyptian writer, Sadat responded: "In my pocket."[102] In his eagerness to convince sceptical Arab leaders of the validity of his assessment and of the alleged achievements of his visit to Israel, Sadat dispatched his Deputy Prime Minister Hassan al-Tuhami to Geneva where he told Saudi leaders: "We have been given a written pledge from the Israelis about the return of Arab Jerusalem to Arab sovereignty."[103] There was of-course no such letter and no such commitments from the Israelis as later events clearly demonstrated. In reality, then Egyptian Minister of State for Foreign Affairs Boutros Ghali, who accompanied Sadat to Jerusalem, recently told me that Sadat was extremely disappointed after his trip to Israel. He was, according to Ghali, under the impression that things would go as in traditional disputes between families in Upper Egypt. Once the head of one family paid a visit to the other family and ate at their house, then it automatically meant reconciliation between the two feuding families. Ghali said that he had long conversations with Sadat during that period and Sadat confided in him that he had believed that his visit to Israel would solve everything and that the psychological impact of the visit would wipe the slate clean. Sadat was hurt and puzzled when his expectations did not materialize.

As a result of Sadat's trip, the collective bargaining and multilateral negotiations leading to the Geneva Conference were first interrupted then shelved indefinitely. The Soviet role in the peace process practically came to an end, leaving the United States the only great power involved. Without the participation of all Arab countries united on a single position, "Israel was left free to manipulate the Palestinian issue as it saw fit."[104]

Egyptian-Israeli Negotiations

After his trip to Israel, Sadat became the focus of the world media which followed his every move and attempted to place his utterances within some sort of a coherent strategy. When he was specifically asked about his so-called grand strategy he was unable to articulate a plan or a coherent vision. On November 25, 1977, Walter Cronkite of CBS television interviewed Sadat and asked him to clarify the contradictory statements he had made the previous days; on the one hand, Sadat had repeatedly stated that he would never make a separate peace with Israel, on the other hand, he kept affirming that even if all the Arab countries boycotted his forthcoming Cairo conference he would go alone to Geneva. Unable to sort out Sadat's contradictory and evasive answers, Cronkite told Sadat "You have left me in confusion."[105]

From the outset, it was the Israelis who established the context for negotiations between Egypt and Israel the general principles of which were contained in an Israeli plan presented by Israeli Prime Minister Begin to President Carter in Washington on December 16, 1977. Begin told Carter that Israel would withdraw to the 1967 international lines between Egypt and Israel in return for a peace treaty and normalization of relations with Egypt. He cleverly stipulated that Israel intended to leave its Jewish settlements in the Sinai, thus presenting a negotiating position that he knew could not be acceptable to Egypt. He would thus exact a price from Egypt by appearing to make the significant "concession" of removing the Jewish settlers from the Egyptian Sinai. With regard to the other fronts, Begin presented to Carter a plan which he called "Home Rule, for Palestinian Arabs, Residents of Judea, Samaria and the Gaza District." It mentioned no Israeli withdrawal from the occupied Arab territories, recognized no political rights to the Palestinians, made no reference to the Palestinian refugees, and left with Israel the ultimate military control of the territories. Carter's national security advisor Zbigniew Brezezinski compared the plan to the South-African-controlled black enclaves, the Bantustans. Yet, President Carter told Begin that his proposals were "constructive," represented "a fair basis for negotiations"[106] and marked "a long step forward."[107]

Begin and his party went to Ismailiya, Egypt, on December 25, to present the Israeli plan to Sadat who had just appointed Mohamed Ibrahim Kamel as his new Foreign Minister. Kamel later told me that he accepted the appointment on one condition: that the peace Sadat was seeking to achieve be a comprehensive peace leading to the liberation of all the occupied Arab territories, not a separate peace just between Egypt and Israel. Sadat agreed. At the joint meeting of the Egyptian and Israeli delegations in Ismailiya, Begin read his lengthy proposals, often to the visible boredom and restlessness of the Egyptian delegation. On the Sinai front he made proposals that would impose severe military and political limitations on Egyptian sovereignty. "When the peace agreement is signed," he said, "the Egyptian army may be established on a line which will not reach beyond the Milta and Giddi passes,"[108] and the remaining three quarters of the Sinai were to be demilitarized with Israel keeping its military airports and early warning stations in the Sinai. In addition, Begin said that the Jewish settlements between Rafah and El-Arish and those between Eilat and Sharm el-Shaykh would remain in place. Undisturbed by the impact of his extraordinary proposals on his audience and to the incredulity of his hosts, Begin made the following remarkable claim: "Mr. President," he said (ignoring the rising tension), "the settlements will not infringe upon Egyptian sovereignty," and then, carried away by his own momentum, he calmly added "I should point out that we cannot leave our settlements and our citizens without a means of self-defence."[109] By proposing that Israel keep its Jewish settlements and military posts in an Egyptian Sinai three quarters of which will be demilitarized, Begin effectively denied Egypt's sovereignty over its own territories. In so doing he gave the Egyptians fundamental values to negotiate for: the recovery of their territory and the recovery of their sovereignty over the Sinai. At the same time, this strategy placed hierarchical values on the conflict in which the recovery of Egyptian territory became more important and more urgent than the question of a comprehensive settlement. Arab demands were to be divided and Egypt would have to worry about its own territories. One Israeli account of the meeting did not fail to observe that the Begin strategy implied that Sadat would have no option but to negotiate a separate peace.[110]

This seems to have escaped Sadat's attention, or, if it did not, seems to have made no difference to his own strategic planning for his negotiations with Israel.

Begin then proceeded to read his autonomy plan article by article, pausing after each paragraph "to praise its virtues, and pay tribute to his own great generosity and his excessive humanity."[111] The plan was, according to President Carter, "substantially" different from the one Begin had presented to him in Washington.[112] Still, Begin concluded his lengthy presentation by claiming that his plan had been supported and praised by the American president as well as by the British prime minister and "by everyone who saw it."[113] The meeting was a great failure because of the clash between Sadat's public position and Begin's; it was not even possible to agree on a final communiqué.[114] The failure of the meeting was acutely felt by Sadat whereas Begin could rightly consider the meeting a success from his point of view. Out of the Ismailiya conference the Israelis came with some significant advantages. First, they staked a negotiating position that required Egypt to concentrate on the recovery of its own territory and the re-establishment of its sovereignty over that territory. This would remain the Israeli strategy throughout the negotiations with Egypt until its final triumph at Camp David. Second, they were reinforced in their knowledge that Sadat was interested in a separate agreement and cared little for Arab or Palestinian demands. Sadat reportedly told the Israelis that it was his advisors who were insisting on a comprehensive approach. According to an Israeli account of the meeting, Sadat met with Begin privately and told him "half apologetically...that it was his advisors from the Foreign Ministry who had insisted that he not yield an inch on the matter of self-determination for the Palestinian people."[115] This naturally played into the hands of the Israelis who proceeded to exploit the confessed vulnerabilities of the Egyptian President by isolating him from his advisors to better extract commitments and concessions. "From Ismailiya on," observed one American official, "the Israelis repeatedly sought to deal with Sadat without the presence of his advisors; in due course the side followed suite. Ismailiya convinced Begin that progress could be made by isolating Sadat from the influences that surrounded him."[116] This conclusion was also recently confirmed to me personally in Cairo by Minister Mohamed Ibrahim Kamel.

Shortly after the Ismailiya meeting, the Israelis decided to move to the second phase of their game plan which consisted in increasing Sadat's worries about his ability to recover the Sinai and re-establish Egyptian sovereignty there. Thus, as the world was hailing the Egyptian-Israeli "peace negotiations" the Israeli cabinet authorized four more Jewish settlements in the Sinai. Ezer Weizman, then Israel's Defence Minister, explained that the decision was based on the calculation that "if the Egyptians acquiesced to our 'colonization' we would have pulled it off; if they refused to countenance the new 'settlements,' Israel could make a gesture and give them up in return for the right to retain the existing settlements."[117] The Israeli decision made sense and was consistent with the Israeli game plan of trade off: trading the Sinai for the West Bank. By building more settlements in Egyptian territory, Israel would be raising the stakes and increasing the value of recovering the Sinai, a core value to Egypt; it would thus put more pressure on Egypt to worry about the recovery of its own territory and the re-establishment of Egyptian sovereignty on it. And when Israel eventually agrees to dismantle the settlements, as surely it knew it would have to as a price for isolating Egypt, the action could be presented as a major "concession." The *quid pro quo* expected of Egypt would have to be on the Arab and Palestinian fronts. Weizman recognized that such was the basis of the Begin strategy: "He (Begin) must have decided to reach a compromise with the Egyptians in the South as a way of perpetuating some form of Israeli rule over Judea and Samaria. Whereas the Egyptians saw the Sinai agreement as a model for similar understandings with Jordan and Syria over the West Bank and the Golan Heights, Begin saw it as the precise opposite. As far as he was concerned, the withdrawal from the Sinai would be the end of story."[118]

Carter went to the Middle East in January 1978, to try to win Arab support for the Sadat initiative. The extent of Sadat's isolation had been dramatized a few days earlier when the Cairo conference he organized was attended only by the Egyptians, the Americans, the Israelis and UN observers, with no Arab or Palestinian representatives. On January 4, President Carter made a brief stopover in Aswan, Upper Egypt, to see Sadat. Carter made a statement which came to be known as the "Aswan Declaration." It contained a call for "the resolution of the Palestinian problem in all its aspects," and for a solution that enables the Palestinians to "participate," presumably with other participants, in the determination of their future. The statement did not mention the PLO and did not endorse the Palestinians' right to self-determination. Begin saw "benefits" in the Aswan statement but was opposed to its reference to a solution to the Palestinian problem "in all its aspects."

The next Egyptian-Israeli meeting was scheduled to take place in January, in Jerusalem. Sadat had agreed with the Israelis in Ismailiyia, without the knowledge or consent of his Foreign Minister Mohamed Ibrahim Kamel, to form two committees: a political committee and a military committee. The political committee was scheduled to meet in Jerusalem, and Kamel, who was upset that Sadat had not consulted him, was told by Sadat to get ready to leave for Jerusalem at the head of the Egyptian delegation. Sadat did not have any specific instructions or game plan to give to his delegation which was simply instructed to work from the American ideas presented to Sadat. Kamel later said: "Sadat did not send the American agenda to me, nor did he talk to me about it. However, I was surprised early the following morning, 15 January, by an invitation to attend a meeting of the national security council...presenting me to the members, he announced the purpose of the meeting, namely the departure of the Egyptian delegation to start on the meetings of the Political Committee. The Egyptian delegation was to leave the same afternoon for Jerusalem. I was taken aback and asked Sadat on what basis was I to leave. He replied that it would be on the basis of the American agenda he had received from the American Ambassador the previous day. I said I had not seen it and must make an adequate study of it before I left. Sadat flew into a rage and shouted, 'Are you afraid of going to Jerusalem?'"[119] Meanwhile, the Israelis were busy implementing their carefully-prepared game plan of increasing pressure on Sadat by raising the stakes in order to force him to concentrate on Egyptian issues to the exclusion of Arab or Palestinian issues. Thus, Mohamed Kamel reported that "while preparations were diligently underway for the meetings of the Political Committee in Jerusalem, grave reports, which were soon confirmed, came in. Israel was establishing new settlements in Sinai. The atmosphere became electrified, tension rose and Sadat awoke from his beautiful dream."[120]

Kamel told me that upon their arrival in Jerusalem the Egyptians were surprised by regular Israeli radio broadcasts claiming that Sadat had told Begin that the PLO was a terrorist organization and had no place in peace negotiations. Kamel protested to Begin, but the psychological climate of a negotiation context in which Egypt separated itself from the Arabs was already set. When the Political Committee eventually met, Kamel stated that Egypt was interested in "a comprehensive — rather than a separate — peace, based on complete withdrawal from all Arab territories occupied since 1967, including Jerusalem, and guaranteeing the basic rights of the Palestinian people including their right to self-determination."[121] Dayan stated that the task of the committee was to lay down the principles for a just solution with regard to the "Palestinian Arabs" and securing a peace agreement between Egypt and Israel. American Secretary of State Vance repeated the American position stated by Carter in his Aswan Declaration. At a dinner banquet the following evening, Begin repeated the claim that Israel was entitled to keep the occupied territories and gave a lengthy review of Jewish history from his perspective, concluding that Israel was perfectly entitled to keep its conquests and nobody could tell him otherwise. He ridiculed and castigated Kamel for calling for Israeli withdrawal from Jerusalem and referred to him as a young man, suggesting inexperience and lack of historical perspective. It was a most demoralizing and sobering experience for Kamel who had difficulty maintaining his diplomatic composure. After informing Cairo of the gulf between the publicly stated Egyptian position requiring a comprehensive Israeli withdrawal from the occupied Arab territories and the intransigent Israeli position interested only in a separate peace with Egypt, Kamel came to believe that Cairo had become convinced that Israel was interested only in a separate agreement with Egypt and that there was no chance of agreeing even to the general declaration of principles for a comprehensive settlement which Egypt demanded as a minimum. Sadat decided to recall the Egyptian delegation from Israel. Boutros Ghali was unable to explain to me the specific reasons that prompted Sadat to recall the Egyptian delegation. Ghali thought that Sadat's decision might have been intended to place pressure on the Israelis whose intransigent position had infuriated Sadat. Mohamed Kamel, however, told me that he was surprized by the decision which Sadat had made alone and, again, without any consultation or discussion with his Foreign Minister. Kamel believed that it was a bad decision which benefited only the Israelis. According to his analysis, the timing of Sadat's decision could not have been worse. Kamel had given American Secretary of State Vance a number of crucial questions to give the Israelis, whose answers would have indicated to Kamel whether there was any hope of continuing the negotiations or not. Given the positions stated by Begin and Dayan, Kamel was convinced that the Israelis would have told Vance that there was no change in their positions and that therefore their answers would have been negative, discouraging and frustrating. Kamel said that this would have been the appropriate time to withdraw from the negotiations and return to Cairo, letting the Americans and the world blame Israeli intransigence for the failure of the Jerusalem meetings. Kamel told me that instead of this politically-calculated withdrawal, Sadat ordered the Egyptian delegation to return to Cairo for reasons which he explained to no one, probably in a fit of anger.

With the failure of the Ismailiya, Cairo, and Jerusalem meetings Sadat was reluctantly beginning to concede that his "sacred mission" to Israel had not produced the miracles he expected and that the Israeli position had undergone no substantive modifications as a result of his breaking "the psychological barrier." He had decided to negotiate directly with the Israelis in the unfounded belief that this would produce faster results than the multilateral negotiations of Geneva favoured by the Soviet-American initiative. Three months after his visit to Israel, Sadat was unable even to get a declaration of principles for a comprehensive settlement from the Israelis. Admitting the precariousness of his position in the direct negotiations with Israel, he turned to the United States to plead for help to rescue his faltering initiative. Herman Eilts, the American ambassador to Egypt, conveyed Sadat's growing doubts and frustrations to Carter in an important cable under the heading: "Sadat and the USG: An Incipient Crisis of Confidence."[122] Eilts explained that Sadat was disappointed for not receiving enough support from the U.S. on the question of Jewish settlements in the Sinai, and was increasingly doubtful about the seriousness of American commitment to the Sadat initiative. Carter and his advisors decided to invite Sadat to come to Washington.

The U.S. As a Full Partner

Carter met with Sadat alone on February 4, 1978, at Camp David. When the Egyptian and American delegations met later, the Americans urged the Egyptians to submit a proposal for the West Bank and Gaza, but Sadat was by now anxious that he might not even be able to re-establish Egyptian sovereignty over the Sinai. He was, therefore, more interested in the possibility of an Egyptian-Israeli agreement and at thier first private meeting, he and Carter may have agreed upon what a member of the American delegation referred to as, "the importance of moving quickly toward a bilateral Egyptian-Israeli agreement;"[123] in other words, the separate agreement that Sadat had been publicly saying he would never sign. Moreover, Sadat seemed uninterested in the American strategy of attempting to put combined pressure on Begin on the question of Resolution 242 and the issue of the Jewish settlements. "Carter was therefore left in the awkward position of appearing to be more pro-Arab than Sadat,"[124] wrote a surprised American official.

The Americans and the Egyptians were pleased with the results of their talks. The Americans obtained from Sadat not to end the negotiations with Israel, which would have had negative domestic implications for President Carter. The Panama treaty was pending before the Senate and Carter needed the votes of senators who were strong supporters of Israel, and failure of the negotiations would reflect negatively on his Middle East policy. Carter and his advisors also seem to have convinced the Egyptians to accept an approach whereby the Americans would seem to be playing the role of honest brokers, which was Carter's way of avoiding the uncomfortable position of having to pressure Israel. And this is something he repeatedly said he could not do. Thus, it was agreed that the Egyptians would present a proposal for the West Bank and Gaza that included maximum Arab demands to counterbalance Begin's autonomy plan. The United States would then step in and submit a compromise plan based on the applicability of resolution 242 on all fronts and on the necessity of finding a solution to the Palestinian problem that took into account the legitimate rights of the Palestinians and permitted them "to participate" in the determination of their own future. Sadat was very pleased because he believed that this meant that the United States was ready to assume some responsibilities and finally play "the role of a full partner."[125]

A few days later, on February 16, Vance received Dayan in Washington. The Israeli Foreign Minister told the American Secretary of State that Israel would not accept withdrawal on all fronts, and would not evacuate the West Bank. "Israel," he said, "wanted peace with peace agreement with Jordan but without withdrawal."[126] In his meeting with Carter the same day, Dayan repeated the Israeli position. Carter explained that Sadat could not proceed without Hussein and that the King of Jordan could not join the negotiations without an Israeli agreement to the language of Resolution 242 as it applied to all fronts. Dayan asked "if Sadat would be content with words alone or if King Hussein actually had to join the negotiations." Carter replied that Sadat might be satisfied with a simple declaration of principles, thus confirming that he and Sadat had reached some understanding about Sadat's readiness to move separately for a bilateral agreement with Israel. The declaration of principles of the so-called framework for a comprehensive settlement would in effect be nothing more than what Dayan accurately understood it to be: words serving as a cover to enable Sadat to conclude a separate agreement with Israel.

A few days before Begin was scheduled to come to Washington, Israel launched a full scale invasion of Lebanon with 30,000 troops in a combined air, sea and land attack. The ostensible excuse was a Palestinian guerrilla raid on March 11, 1978. The Palestinian commandos had seized a bus north of Tel-Aviv and soon found themselves in a gun battle with the Israeli forces which had forced the bus to stop; the shoot-out turned into a death trap and 36 people were killed. The real objective of the Israeli invasion of Lebanon, however, was to carve up a portion of Lebanese territory and place it under the military command of a Lebanese renegade officer on the Israeli pay. That objective was accomplished after "Israel attacked and destroyed the villages used by the guerillas without regard to the presence of civilians," killing 2,000 Arab civilians and causing the flight of 200,000 Lebanese and Palestinian civilians. And "once again the Israelis had inflicted far more suffering than they had endured. The disproportion in hardship and death bore every sign of calculation."[127] Carter sent Begin a message requesting that Israel withdraw its forces and allow United Nations forces to enter Southern Lebanon. Begin responded by expanding the operations of his army and by refusing to allow the United Nations forces to control Southern Lebanon. Although the United States had voted in the Security Council for Resolution 425, which it had introduced, calling for withdrawal of the Israeli forces and establishment of UN forces in Southern Lebanon, the American President was unable to persuade Israel to comply with the demand of the international organization. And thus a confrontation had developed as a result of the Israeli invasion of Lebanon, and once more the outcome was a public spectacle of the helplessness of the American President vis-à-vis the recalcitrant Israeli ally.

Mahmoud Riad, former Egyptian Foreign Minister and Secretary General of the Arab League, bitterly observed that "Washington was being rebuffed at every turn. Not only did it fail to persuade Israel not to attack Lebanon; it also failed to implement the Security Council resolution to which it had subscribed, and finally it failed to follow through a suggestion it itself made, namely stationing a Lebanese battalion in a part of Lebanese territory."[128]

Begin arrived in Washington, on March 21, 1978 to find Carter "in a fighting mood." After fruitless discussions between the Americans and the Israelis, Carter summarized to Begin the "six noes" of the Israeli position: "Carter said that even if Israel was not required to withdraw completely from the West Bank, and even if there were no Palestinian State, Begin would still not show flexibility. He would not stop settlement activity; he would not give up the settlements in the Sinai; he would not allow the Sinai settlements to remain under UN or Egyptian protection; he would not agree to withdraw politically from the West Bank even if Israel could retain military outposts; he would not recognize that Resolution 242 applied to all fronts; and he would not give the Palestinians the right to choose, at the end of the interim period, whether they wanted to be affiliated with Jordan or Israel, or to continue the self-rule arrangements. Begin agreed that Carter had accurately described his views, but claimed that the six points had all been put in the negative. There was a way they could be stated in the positive."[129]

A few days later, on March 30, Sadat revealed to the Israelis his intentions, his ultimate goals and what he was prepared to settle for, thus exposing all his cards, undermining his own position and further restricting his negotiating power. He confided in Ezer Weizman, as he had done to Begin at the Ismailiya meeting of December 1977, his own limitations and the thrust of his "strategic thinking." The episode shows the extent to which Sadat was willing to trust his enemies, sometimes to the exclusion of his closest Egyptian advisors. In a remarkable passage in his memoir *The Battle for Peace* then Israeli Defense Minister Ezer Weizman revealed that at the March 30, 1978 meeting in Ismailiya between Sadat and himself, Sadat made some incredible confessions which Weizman himself found hard to believe. Weizman wrote that Sadat told him:

> The test for both of us is the Palestinian problem. I must tell my people that I have induced the Israelis to withdraw from the West Bank. I have excluded the PLO from my lexicon. By their own behaviour, they have excluded themselves from the negotiations. But I can say this only to you — not to Begin because the next day Begin would announce: 'Sadat has excluded the PLO!' I have to be able to tell the Arabs: 'The Arabs of the West Bank and Gaza will be able to shape their future, and the Israelis will leave! I don't care whether Hussein comes in or not. The West Bank and Gaza should be demilitarized. Any solution must guarantee your security. We shall try to find a suitable formula.

Weizman asked, "From your point of view — who is to take charge of Judea, Samaria, and Gaza? Who will rule there?

Sadat answered: "If Jordan enters the negotiations — Jordan, the representatives of the local population, and you."

"From that I understand that there won't be a Palestinian State," said Weizman.

Sadat replied: "Right! But if I say so to Begin, he will proclaim it from the rooftops the following day. But I can tell you: No State! And a small number of military strong points for Israel."

Weizman added: "Summarizing my conversations with Sadat put me into a better mood. Like us, the Egyptian President was not interested in a Palestinian State; he was willing to leave our West Bank settlements in place; he would substitute for Hussein should the king refuse to take part in negotiations. I was gratified to have Aharon Barak listening in on our conversations; without his testimony, no one in Israel would believe me."[130]

The U.S. Moves to Publicly Support the Israeli Position

After the Carter-Sadat meeting and the probable agreement of the two presidents to move toward a separate treaty, and with Carter unable to exert pressure on Israel for withdrawal from the occupied Arab territories, Washington moved to support Israel's demand for an agreement that separated Egypt from Arab and Palestinian interests. In a background briefing American Assistant-Secretary of State for Middle Eastern Affairs Harold Saunders told reporters that Washington did not intend to pressure Israel, and said that Vance would not be "playing into anybody's hands, particularly Sadat's hands." Saunders also recognized that Israel was not prepared to modify its position and "insisted that the issue regarding the sovereignty of the West Bank should be shelved...The United States government, for its part, considered the Israeli attitude...more in line with the American way of handling things." Saunders also stated: "It is common knowledge that the Israelis are looking for a separate settlement, and we have not sought to impose our views in this matter." When asked whether Sadat was ready to go back to the Arab fold, Saunders replied: "Just technically, the point at which that happens is when they arrange and agree on an Arab summit. And I am hopeful the Secretary can give him enough to work with, to suggest enough that we might work with together, so that decision won't be made."[131]

Clearly, the American objective was to keep the negotiations going and try to reach a separate agreement on the basis of a common American-Israeli-Egyptian entente before the Egyptians pressured Sadat to go back to the Arab fold. Kamel became suspicious of American motives and observed that:

> The American stand — whichever way you looked at it — was to keep negotiations going until a compromise was reached, which itself depended on concessions from both sides, not, however, in connection with security measures or the normalization of relationships — areas where compromise was possible — but on the very substance of the issue, land and sovereignty, which Sadat has asserted were not negotiable. The United States had, to all intents and purposes, set aside Resolution 242, upon whose implementation any settlement should be based, which had been agreed internationally and to which both Egypt and Israel had subscribed...Thus the resumption of the negotiations had become, for the United States, an end in itself, not only in the hope that Egypt might, at last, concede some of the territory on the West Bank which did not belong to it, but to prevent the alternative — a halt to the negotiations coupled with Egypt's return to the Arab ranks, followed by an Arab summit and a return to the Geneva Conference, where the Soviet Union would co-chair the meeting, which was precisely what both Israel and the United States did not want.[132]

Within this context, Carter issued his invitations for the Camp David Summit. When Vance arrived in Alexandria to invite Sadat to Camp David, Sadat and Vance met alone for several hours. After the meeting, it was Vance who told the Egyptian

Foreign Minister that Sadat had accepted to come to Camp David. The decision was once more taken without consultation with anyone in Egypt.[133]

On August 30, The Egyptian National Security Council met in Ismailiya to plot strategy for Camp David. The meeting was chaired by Sadat. He repeated his public position, increasingly difficult to believe, of rejecting any separate solutions with Israel. With regard to the occupied Arab territories and the Palestine question, he presented a position substantially different from his public positions on these issues but which clearly reflected the changing balance of power and the diminishing maneuverability Sadat's strategy imposed on him: "Gaza will be restored to Egypt and the West Bank to Jordan," Sadat told the members of the National Security Council, "This is approved by everyone. [!?] Were King Hussein to refuse…I shall not hesitate to pursue the negotiations and will pay no heed to their allegations that I am not entitled to speak on behalf of the Palestinians…With respect to the question of a Palestinian State, our project maintains the stand we adopted three years ago namely that *the Palestinians have their right to self-determination, with a tie to Jordan. I want to go to the limit. I shall object to the PLO even if it is accepted by Israel.*"[134] (emphasis added.) Sadat's statement contains obvious contradictions: on the one hand Sadat claimed to support the Palestinians' right to self-determination, on the other hand, he opposed the participation of the Palestinian people's representatives in negotiations dealing with their own future. Perhaps more significantly, the statement seems to confirm the position Sadat reportedly confidentially shared with Weizman at their March 30 Ismailiya meeting.

At Camp David

In coming to Camp David Sadat was bringing to its logical conclusion a strategy which gradually sacrificed allies and supporters and systematically worked from isolated and unrealistic assumptions. After signing the second disengagement agreement (Sinai II), breaking up with the Arabs (the sixth power in the world), severing all ties with the Soviet Union, and acquiescing in American secret commitments to significantly enhance Israeli strategic and military superiority, Sadat was as isolated as he was deprived of negotiating leverage, but he still believed that he could substantially affect the American-Israeli special relationship so as to achieve stated goals. It was yet another excessively optimistic assumption wholly unrelated to the reality of the balance of power between the parties. Sadat brought with him an Egyptian position which suffered from the weakness inherent in the fact that Israel was still in occupation of Egyptian territory. He relied on an American President who confessed his impotence vis-à-vis his recalcitrant Israeli ally. Sadat came to face an Israel militarily and strategically more powerful than ever, still in physical occupation of an important part of the Egyptian territory, and demonstrably able to influence American foreign policy. Sadat also brought with him a somewhat shaken but still genuine faith in Washington in spite of clear indications that the American-Israeli strategic and political relationship was too powerful a force to defeat by an Arab negotiator, let alone one who was isolated and wielding little leverage outside the removal of his country from the conflict. Sadat was in a precarious position.

It is not clear how Sadat and his delegation, including the Foreign Ministry professionals who had a good grasp of the issues and of the relative power of the parties, intended to accomplish their stated goals. Egyptian Foreign Minister Mohamed Kamel made a remarkable observation that gave a hint of the frame of mind of the Egyptian negotiators at Camp David. He confessed: "the Egyptian 'Framework for Peace' project was not intended as the basis for a negotiating position subject to bargaining. Had we had bargaining in mind, the project would have been based, for instance, on the partition resolution. In that case Israel would have been required to return all the territories it had annexed by force from the territories allocated to the Palestinian State by the terms of the said resolution from 1949 to 1967. Rather, the project depended on the strict implementation of Resolution 242, which contained the basic elements for a settlement of the conflict."[135]

It is not clear what the Egyptians had in mind if not bargaining and negotiations. Nor is it clear why their project was not based on the 1947 UN Partition Resolution on which Israel bases its own juridical existence. If the 1947 resolution is juridically valid for Israel, then surely it is at least equally valid for Palestine. It represents a juridical basis already accepted by the international community. Further, the partition resolution recognizes the legitimacy of the Palestinians' right to self-determination and national independence, whereas Resolution 242 treats the Palestinian question as a humanitarian rather than a political issue. In addition, by requiring Israel to withdraw only to territories occupied since 1967 and requiring the Arab States to recognize Israel's sovereignty and territorial integrity, Resolution 242 was in fact legalizing the Israeli occupation of the territories of Palestine seized by Israel in 1948-49 in excess of the area of the Jewish State as defined by the UN Partition Resolution. This clearly violates the principle of the inadmissibility of the acquisition of territories by force which Resolution 242 reaffirmed in its own preamble. That is precisely why the Israelis insisted that any negotiations be based on Resolution 242 and not on anything else. If the Egyptian delegation did not have bargaining in mind, as Kamel said, what did it have in mind exactly and how did it think it would achieve whatever goals were agreed upon? While Resolution 242 might have been appropriate for ending the Egyptian-Israeli bilateral negotiations it certainly was not adequate as the only basis for the Israeli-Palestinian conflict. And surely the Egyptian delegation must have known it. When I put these questions and observations to Deputy Prime Minister Boutros Ghali and Minister Mohamed Ibrahim Kamel, the leading Egyptian Foreign Ministry officials at Camp David, they were not able to recall any specific Egyptian strategy. Kamel told me that it was clear to the Egyptians that the Israelis would have rejected any Egyptian project based on the 1947 Partition Resolution. When I asked why the Egyptians conceded that fundamental point in advance and why they did not let the Israelis reject such a project, then the Egyptians could modify it in exchange for equally fundamental concessions from the Israelis, Kamel was unable to recall any specific rationale other than Sadat's eagerness to move fast and to raise as few obstacles to the negotiations as possible. This naturally meant that he was willing in advance to settle for much less than what his public declarations led the Egyptian people and the Arab world to believe. It also bespoke the fragility of his negotiating style and the vulnerability of his position. "Things would not have moved at all," Kamel told me, "had we presented an Egyptian project based on the 1947 UN Partition Resolution. But you are right, you are absolutely right. We should have presented a maximalist position and negotiated from there. But this was not the spirit in which Sadat operated at all. Sadat was very keen to get the Sinai back and that is all. If it were possible to get the West Bank and Gaza back for the Palestinians that would be very good, if not, that would be too bad. Sadat could not be bothered with this issue anyway, even though I and the Egyptian delegation were naturally pushing for a comprehensive settlement. The 1947 UN Partition Resolution was not considered at all as a basis for the negotiations."[136] The Egyptian delegation simply placed its faith in Sadat, who had little tolerance for those who challenged his views, and seems to have hoped that his reliance on Carter might pay off in the end. But this, to say the least, was an unrealistic expectation given Carter's own warnings to the Egyptians about his inability to pressure the Israelis.

The negotiations at Camp David confirmed Carter's candid admissions about his limitations in dealing with the Israelis. He did make some unconvincing attempts at getting Begin to agree at least to the officially stated American position on the conflict, but to no avail. According to a member of the Israeli delegation, Carter said at a meeting of the American and Israeli delegations at Camp David that he intended to bring up the issue of the national rights of the Palestinians. "Out of the question," Begin replied. Carter raised the question of a freeze on new settlements, the Israelis objected immediately. When the discussion came to Resolution 242's clause about the "non-acquisition of territory by force" Begin strongly affirmed: "We will not accept that (clause)." "Mr. Prime Minister," Carter replied, "that is not only the view of Sadat, it is also the American view — and you will have to accept it…" "Mr. President," Begin said tersely, "No threats, please."[137] In fact, it seems that it was Begin who was able to use threats against Carter. Thus, towards the end of the conference, Dayan warned the Americans that if President Carter insisted on "setting out in detail the American position on East Jerusalem, Begin would simply pack his bags and go home," American Secretary of State Vance recorded the outrage of the American delegation at being blackmailed by the Israelis: "We were very angry. Carter furiously demanded to know if Israel meant to tell the United States it could not even publicly state its own national position."[138] That is precisely what happened. The United States was not able, because of Israeli threats, to explicitly state its own official position in the letter dealing with Jerusalem.

It is surprising that the Egyptians were astonished when Carter told them that he would submit an American project for a settlement based on the Israeli self-rule plan. To make it acceptable to the Egyptian Foreign Minister whom Carter knew to be sceptical and far less sanguine about the prospect of an agreement than Sadat, the American President hinted to Kamel at the benefits that would flow to Egypt from the strategic alliance between the U.S., Israel and Egypt: "were Egypt, Israel and the United States on the same side, then no power outside or inside the area would dare oppose them."[139] It also should not have surprised Foreign Minister Kamel when the Americans stated that they could not treat the Egyptians and the Israelis as equally as the Egyptians, and particulary Sadat, seem to have expected. Ambassador Eilts told Mohamed Kamel, who was expecting the American project for consideration: "I am sorry, Mohamed, but something unexpected has happened: Begin has produced a written pledge to the Israeli government, signed by Kissinger in 1975. This commits the United States to abstain from presenting any project on the settlement of the Arab-Israeli conflict without prior consultation with Israel. Consequently, we shall be unable to give you a copy of the project we have prepared."[140] In effect, the Americans were admitting that every "American project" presented to Egypt would in reality be an "American" project marked by "consultations" with Israel. The fact that this came as a surprise to the Egyptian delegation suggests that some members of the delegation may have shared Sadat's optimistic assessment that the United States had embarked on a totally different policy and that its commitment to be "a full partner" in the peace process necessarily meant that it would be able to adopt a more even-handed approach to the Arab-Israeli conflict. Kamel told me that during the negotiations it was clear that the Americans were totally biased in favour of the Israelis "out of sheer weakness." And this was because in addition to the leverage Israel enjoys in and over American politics, President "Carter was anxious to produce any kind of success at the conference." And the Israelis knew it, and proceeded to astutely and ruthlessly exploit it.

After the American "consultations" with the Israelis took place, the "American" project was no longer American. According to Secretary Vance who participated in the Camp David negotiations: "The Israelis had crossed out all the language in the preamble drawn from Resolution 242, in particular the language dealing with the inadmissibility of the acquisition of territory by war. They also deleted references to the 'Palestinian people'…They eliminated reference to a peace treaty to settle the final status of the West Bank and Gaza…[and they] flatly refused to discuss our proposed language calling for a freeze on settlements while negotiations were in progress."[141] The Israeli Foreign Minister recognized that "there were many Israeli amendments to the American proposal that it was changed beyond recognition."[142]

When the Egyptians met to discuss the "American" project it soon became apparent that Sadat was anxious to accept it and forge ahead with the negotiations in spite of the opposition of his entourage. The Egyptian Foreign Minister expressed his opposition to the "American" project and pointed out that among other things it referred to Egypt taking over Jordan's responsibility should Jordan refuse to take part in the negotiations. Sadat became tense and shot back: "That is correct: I cannot have the initiative depend upon the humor of King Hussein." Then, in a fit of anger and mounting frustrations he made a surprising admission of his real views and said that if Jordan refused to participate he would take over that role and if the PLO objected, "I shall send Egyptian troops to the West Bank. I am aware that we shall lose some men, but they will kill ten men of the organization (PLO) for every Egyptian who is killed."[143] This thinking partly explains why some American officials had complained that Sadat's positions made Carter look more pro-Arab than Sadat. Kamel sensed that they were heading for a "disaster" and whenever he pointed his grave reservations to Sadat about the direction in which Sadat was taking the delegation, Sadat curtly dismissed his concerns. Eventually, Sadat gradually and systematically excluded Kamel from discussions, meetings and decision-making.

Throughout the Camp David negotiations Sadat followed his usual habit of having private meetings with Israeli and American leaders and making unilateral decisions, often without consultation with or even the knowledge of his entourage. Boutros Ghali, who participated in the Camp David negotiations as Sadat's Minister of State for Foreign Affairs, told me that Sadat not only often made decisions alone but on certain occasions would say to his Foreign Ministry officials something and would then proceed to do the opposite. Thus, despite reservations about his private meetings with Israeli leaders and against the advice of his delegation, Sadat asked to see Weizman alone shortly after the beginning of the Camp David conference. Typically, Sadat did not disclose to his Foreign Minister Kamel what transpired or what was decided at that meeting.[144] Weizman reported that Sadat frankly confided in him what he could settle for and what were his limits, thus giving away whatever negotiating cards were left for him to play. He gave away the threat of allowing the negotiations to fail and blaming Israeli intransigence and American helplessness for it when he told Weizman that whatever happened he (Sadat) was entitled to reach a separate agreement with the Israelis: "I will be frank with you. I am fully entitled to conclude a separate agreement with you, particularly after the attacks on me from various Arab leaders. But we have a traditional saying that a father cannot neglect any of his children. If Jordan doesn't come to the negotiation table, then I will be prepared to continue the talks and take the responsibility." Weizman made the following revealing comment: "This was an encouraging sign of things to come. Even if he remained alone he would not sabotage the conference." Understanding the importance of isolating Sadat from his advisors, Weizman added that after his meeting with Sadat: "I realized that Sadat remained determined to continue the peace process even though his patience was fraying, but I was also concerned over the fact that his entourage at Camp David was largely comprised of his 'ideological' aides: Deputy Prime Minister Tohamy, the Foreign Ministry group — Boutros Ghali, Osama el-Baz, and others — who had always adopted hard-line positions throughout the negotiations. Their ideological convictions did not permit them to accommodate new ways of thinking."[145] It was of course the Egyptians whom Weizman wanted to display new ways of thinking. There was no question that the Zionist ideological convictions underlying the Israeli positions could accommodate any "new ways of thinking" regarding Palestinian national rights or the end of Israeli occupation of the Arab territories. At any rate, Weizman's admission underlined once more the importance the Israelis attached to isolating Sadat from his delegation to better extract concessions and commitments from him.

On the eighth day of the Camp David Conference, Carter tried to get Sadat to agree to the deletion of the crucial sentence about the non-acquisition of territory by force, while Weizman was still pursuing the Israeli strategy of making Sadat believe that the stumbling block was really the question of Jewish settlements in the Sinai. Said Weizman: "I made one more effort to soften him up with regard to our Sinai settlements."[146] Carter also seems to have accepted the assumptions of the Israeli game plan as evidenced by his assessment of the situation which he shared with Dayan and Weizman. He told them that "Israel could no longer avoid the harsh choice: settlements or peace."[147] The principle of non-acquisition of territories by war, the principle of withdrawal from the occupied Arab territories, and the recognition of Palestinians' right to self-determination did not figure in this "harsh choice" as defined by Carter who seems to have accepted the perimeters of permissible negotiations, astutely laid down by the Israeli game plan, as confined to a "harsh choice" between a peace treaty with Egypt or Jewish settlements on Egyptian territory. A separate Egyptian-Israeli agreement was necessarily implied in this definition of "harsh choice."

Still, it was to Sadat that Carter turned to ask for more concessions and more "new ways of thinking." He explained to him that the present impasse was endangering his political career and urged him to accept the deletion of the reference to the non-acquisition of territory by war, the basis on which Resolution 242 established its formula "land for peace." The Israeli Minister of Defense recalled with satisfaction that Carter's pleas with the Egyptian President were successful and that "finally Sadat gave way and agreed to give up mention of the non-acquisition principle."[148] Sadat thus seriously compromised the foundations of Resolution 242 and its applicability to all fronts, at least during the Camp David negotiations. At the same time, the Israelis agreed to a verbal concession devoid of any real binding commitments with regard to the Palestinians. Weizman reported that as a concession Begin agreed to the inclusion of the term "legitimate rights" of the Palestinians and explained to the Israeli delegation that it was irrelevant because "If it is a right — that means it is legitimate. Can a right be illegitimate?"[149]

The Israelis, who had already, as mentioned above, understood the importance of isolating Sadat from his entourage in order to better extract concessions from him, actively sought to arrange private meetings with him. On at least two reported occasions, Weizman, who had privileged access to Sadat, urged him to meet with Dayan alone. According to Kamel, Sadat was also urged by Carter and Vance to meet with Dayan alone. Sadat agreed. Given the documented record, it seems likely that Sadat's meeting with Dayan was the *coup de grâce* which finished Sadat by taking the Israeli game plan to its logical conclusion of insisting that the real problem lay, not in whether or not Israel agreed to withdraw from all the occupied Arab territories but in the question of Jewish settlements in the Sinai and the Israeli determination to keep them. If Sadat refused to come around to the Israeli way of thinking, the helplessness of his position could be made clear to him and he would be left with no choice but to capitulate or go back to Cairo emptyhanded and humbled by the colossal failure of his "strategic thinking."

Sadat met with Dayan alone. Dayan reportedly said to Sadat that "he was courageous and forthright, and so he (Dayan) would be blunt with him. It was Sadat's belief that the problem centered around the solution to the Palestinian question, whereas the solution to this was easy when compared with the problem of the Israeli settlements and airfields in Sinai. He must know that neither Begin, Perez nor any other leader could under any circumstances relinquish them. It was not that they wished to expand by retaining them, but that it was a security matter, since the settlements formed a safety-belt for Israel, and had been designed and built for that purpose. The Israeli people feared no Arab State except Egypt...He must understand that even if Begin agreed, for the sake of argument, to evacuate the settlements in principle, he would be unable to do so until five or six years after the signing of a peace agreement between Egypt and Israel...Sadat had asked him...'Do you imagine (Sadat had reported) that it is possible for me to conclude any peace treaty with you which did not include the removal of the settlements and airfields and the restitution of Sinai with full sovereignty?' Dayan had informed him that, in that case, 'We shall continue to occupy Sinai and pump oil,' Whereupon Sadat wanted to know why he had not said so from the beginning, instead of wasting Carters', Dayan's and his (Sadat's) time. Dayan had answered: 'We did say so from the start, but you chose not to believe us'."[150] (emphasis added).

And indeed, the Israelis had stuck by that position from the very beginning. But Sadat, with no tangible indications to the contrary and every sign pointing to the Israeli game plan, chose not to include this fundamental factor into his "strategic thinking." In fact, Sadat was fully aware and fearful of this nightmare scenario but for some reason disregarded the possibility of its materialization. At a Press Conference in London on November 8, 1975, he had shown his full grasp of the risks inherent in entering negotiations with an enemy still in control of the fundamental object of negotiations: the territories. He explained that it was impossible for him to meet with Israeli leaders while Israel still occupied Egyptian territory: "How could I meet with the Prime Minister of Israel, while he is occupying part of my land? This would mean that I would come to the negotiating table to sign a capitulation; for, he would say that if we do not agree to this or that condition, they would not budge from their positions. This has always been their way of doing things."[151] Sadat may have feared this scenario but seems to have hoped that it would not materialize or that if it did, the American President would save him from this terrible predicament. His hopes proved unfounded on both counts.

After the meeting with Dayan, Sadat decided that he had made a mistake and ordered his delegation to prepare to return home. At this point, Vance came to convince him to stay. Sadat complained about the many concessions he had made and, to the surprise of his Foreign Minister who seemed to have been unaware of the concessions Sadat was talking about, Sadat made the following revelation: "There is a tendency to put our signatures to what has already been agreed, but to do so would oblige me to sign away concessions I would never have agreed to were it not that I wished to help Carter by ensuring that the failure of the Conference would not be attributed to him...It should be understood that the concessions I have made were for the sake of the United States and President Carter personally." [152] (emphasis added).

When Sadat prepared to leave the conference after it became clear that the Israeli proposal still reflected a determination to keep the Jewish settlements in Sinai, Carter went to see Weizman. On the basis of the military information provided by Weizman, Carter drew up a withdrawal plan which reflected Weizman's and Israeli general Tamir's ideas. Once more, Sadat agreed to meet alone with Carter. The American President presented Sadat with the Weizman plan and according to the account of the Israeli Defense Minister: "astonishingly enough, the Egyptian President accepted it almost in its entirety, making no more than a few minor modifications."[153] After the meeting, Sadat surprised his delegation with a *volte-face*. He told Kamel that he had changed his mind about packing up and returning to Egypt. He said that after his meeting with Carter he had decided to stay and sign the Camp David accords after all. When Kamel objected, Sadat replied: "I shall sign anything proposed by President Carter without reading it..." Kamel retorted, "Why, Rais, sign without reading? If it pleases us, we sign; otherwise we do not." Sadat insisted: "No. I shall sign it without reading it." Kamel exclaimed: "Could he possibly be as naive as he seemed? Or had he lost his senses? And why does he become so amenable to any request from Carter?"[154]

Kamel tried one last time to dissuade Sadat from signing and urged him to return to the Arab fold and come back with a new initiative for a comprehensive peace which will have the backing of the Arab world. Sadat rejected his Minister's plea and told him that he placed complete faith in assurances given to him by Carter: "President Carter has affirmed to me that when he is re-elected for another term, he will be in a very strong position and will be able to put pressure on Israel."[155] Sadat had all along placed greater faith in President Carter than in his own Ministers and advisors and this led him to accept concessions and make commitments on the basis of his personal admiration for and faith in the American President, despite objections from his Ministers. This assessment is corroborated by Vance who recorded that: "Right to the last moment, some of Sadat's advisers were still arguing that the agreements were slanted toward Israel's positions. But Sadat trusted President Carter and gave his consent."[156]

Sadat agreed to make one more concession as the Camp David conference came to an end. Weizman recounts that he went to see Sadat and told him that he wanted to enlarge the Israeli force stationed in the small demilitarized zone on the Israeli side of the border. "How many battalions do you want?" Sadat demanded. "Three battalions of our border guard," I replied. "All right, Ezer," Sadat said grandly. "For you — four battalions."[157]

Disappointed and reportedly dejected, Sadat recognized the limitations of his achievements, and responded to criticisms from the Egyptian delegation by indirectly admitting the helplessness of his position in the first place and by pointing to the vague assurances provided by Carter. When a member of the Egyptian delegation said that the agreement did not guarantee self-determination for the Palestinians, Sadat angrily replied: "It was not possible to do otherwise. President Carter confided to me that this phrase would, in his words, 'cost me my job'"[156] When Nabil El Araby, Director of the Legal Department and a member of the Egyptian delegation at Camp David, explained to Sadat that the letters Sadat accepted on Jerusalem were of no legal value, Sadat lost his temper and shouted: "You people in the Foreign Ministry are under the impression that you understand politics. In reality, however, you understand absolutely nothing. Henceforth I shall not pay the least attention to either your words or your memos. I am a man whose actions are governed by a higher strategy which you are incapable of either perceiving or understanding. I do not need your insignificant and misleading reports…Now be so good as to leave and do not come back to waste my time with futile legal arguments!"[159]

After Sadat's last private meeting with Carter "Every hour brought reports of further concessions."[160] The Egyptian Foreign Minister concluded that "the real problem was to be found neither in Israeli intransigence nor in America's spineless surrender to Israel. The real problem, I said, was President Sadat himself. He had capitulated unconditionally to President Carter who, in turn, had capitulated unconditionally to Menahem Begin."[161] Kamel could not endorse the concessions to which Sadat had agreed and preferred to resign his post as Minister of Foreign Affairs. He handed his resignation to Sadat at Camp David and refused to attend the signing ceremonies at the White House.

The guiding principles for "a just, comprehensive, and durable settlement of the Middle East conflict," and for the resolution of the Palestinian problem "in all its aspects" as formulated in the first Camp David document were essentially based on Begin's home-rule plan. They excluded both Palestinian self-representation and self-determination, bypassed the principle of non-acquisition of territory by force and spoke of "redeploying" the Israeli forces, thus jettisoning the principle of withdrawal from the West Bank and Gaza. The other document negotiated at Camp David provided a framework for a peace treaty between Egypt and Israel. It led to the Blair House talks which started in October 1978.

Blair House and the Egyptian-Israeli Treaty

At the Blair House talks the Egyptians demanded but were unable to obtain linkage between the implementation of the Egyptian-Israeli treaty and progress on arrangements for the West Bank and Gaza. The Israelis insisted on and obtained a separate peace treaty with Egypt. The Israelis also demanded and received that Egypt's treaty with Israel be given priority over Egypt's prior commitments to the Arab States.

During the Blair House negotiations, Begin started reneging on the Camp David agreements and announced plans for expanding the Jewish settlements in the West Bank. The American Secretary of State Cyrus Vance recorded American outrage at the Israeli violations of the U.S.-brokered accords: "While Cairo and Jerusalem were still considering the preliminary texts developed at Blair House, however, Begin announced plans for expansion of West Bank settlements. This step was contrary even to Begin's version of the Camp David accords. We were very angry, and I at once issued a public statement of regret." Vance described Begin as "immovable" and "adamant" and adopted positions which made it difficult to make progress in the talks at Blair House. Vance added: "the Israelis denied that there would ever be a referendum in which the Palestinians would participate, even though the Camp David accords explicitly provided that the agreement on the final status of the West Bank-Gaza would be submitted 'to a vote by the elected representatives of the inhabitants of the West Bank and Gaza'…Similarly, Begin now denied that there need be any withdrawal of the Israeli Defense Forces from the West Bank, although the Camp David accords specified that some Israeli forces would be withdrawn and the rest redeployed into a limited number of security locations."[162]

Although the Israeli actions should have raised doubts in Sadat's mind about the wisdom of making more concessions, Sadat gave in to American entreaties for more concessions. On December 10, 1978, Cyrus Vance went to Egypt to present to Sadat some Israeli demands with regard to the Blair House Talks and to urge Sadat to make more concesssions. "Sadat and his senior cabinet advisors believed that they had already gone beyond what was politically wise in meeting Israel's concerns…," Vance recorded, "and it was extremely difficult to get them to compromise once again. I stressed that we must find a way to close off the issues quickly…Finally, Sadat said he would accept the treaty text as written, thus overruling his cabinet. Further, he agreed to our interpretive statements and the letter on the priority of obligations. On the West Bank and Gaza side letter, Sadat again reversed a previous cabinet decision and dropped his demand for a fixed date for the elections, agreeing that the target date would be not later than the end of 1979."[163]

Sadat also agreed to formally terminate the state of belligerency between Egypt and Israel and to establish peace while Israeli troops were still occupying Egyptian territory. He accepted the Israeli demand that the process of normalization between the two countries get underway while Israel was still in occupation of Egyptian territory. He gave in to demands to severely limit Egyptian forces in all of the Sinai, even in the zone closest to the Canal. Former Egyptian Foreign Minister Ismail Fahmy noted that: "All provisions concerning the creation of demilitarized zones and the thinning of forces in the area between the two countries were implemented almost exclusively on Egyptian soil...The deployment of the Egyptian army was even limited in the zone closest to the Suez Canal. Nowhere in Sinai was Egypt free to exercise its full sovereignty...In effect the treaty surrendered Sinai's vital strategic value to Egypt and our first line of defence has been transferred from our frontier to the Suez Canal."[164]

Sadat also agreed to other limitations on Egyptian sovereignty by permitting the multilateral forces patrolling the demilitarized zone to be stationed on the Egyptian side of the border where Egypt itself can keep no troops. Israel refused such limitations on its side of the border. Sadat also agreed "as a favour" to his American friends to construct a new road through Sinai linking Jordan, Israel, and Egypt near Eilat. The road was intended for future use by the American Rapid Deployment Force and may have been of invaluable strategic usefulness during the Gulf crisis and the American-led war against Iraq.

Most significantly, Sadat agreed, as reported by Vance above, to the American interpretive statement and the letter on the priority of obligations. Begin had insisted that the Camp David treaty between Egypt and Israel be given priority over Egypt's treaty obligations to the Arab countries. Specifically, he demanded that Egypt repudiate its prior commitments and historic solidarity with the Arab world by agreeing to the priority of obligations clause in article VI, deleted from the text of the treaty published in Egypt. When the Foreign Ministry group in the Egyptian delegation objected, the Americans came up with a letter of interpretation designed to break the deadlock. The American letter was an exercise in contradictions and vagueness designed to gloss over Egyptian objections and meet Begin's demands. The interpretive minute which would be annexed to the treaty read as follows:

> It is agreed by the Parties that there is no assertion that this Treaty prevails over other Treaties or agreements or that other Treaties or agreements prevail over this Treaty. The foregoing is not to be construed as contravening the provisions of Article VI (5) of the Treaty, which reads as follows: 'Subject to Article 103 of the United Nations Charter, in the event of a conflict between the obligations of the Parties under the present Treaty and any other obligations, the obligation under this Treaty will be binding and implemented.'[165]

In other words, the American construction sought to assuage Egyptian anxiety by saying that there was no "assertion" that the treaty was being given priority over previous Egyptian commitments to the Arab States. But, it immediately gave in to Begin's demand by reaffirming the binding character of the obligation imposed by clause 5 of article 6, giving Egypt's commitment to Israel priority over its previous treaty obligations to the Arab States. A remarkably intriguing linguistic *tour de force* which, stripped of its adornments and obfuscations, essentially reads: there is no assertion that the Egyptian-Israeli treaty has priority over other Egyptian-Arab treaties, but in reality it does. By agreeing to this, Sadat may have essentially agreed to compromise Egypt's ability to abide by its prior commitments to the Arab countries, and accepted an implied contractual commitment to remove Egypt militarily from future conflicts involving Israel and the Arab countries even though Arab territories were still occupied by Israel. Then Minister of State for Foreign Affairs Boutros Ghali chose a different interpretation. He told me that the formula meant that "Egypt's obligations to the Arab world by virtue of its common defense commitments contracted in the collective Arab defense treaty of 1950 were more important than the Egyptian-Israeli treaty. And that is because the obligations under article 103 of the Charter of the United Nations were more important than any obligations under bilateral treaties."[166] However, in the most extensive legal study of the Egyptian-Israeli treaty and its contractual commitments, Guyora Binder identified a number of conflicts which the treaty posed for Egypt:

> First, Egypt may have violated its obligations to cooperate with its Arab partners in matters of foreign policy merely by pursuing peace unilaterally. Second, through its commitment not to use force against Israel, Egypt has compromised its ability to engage in joint military planning in anticipation of such hostilities. Third, Israel and the Arab League participants may already be belligerent. Egypt aside, none of the Arab League participants in the many Arab-Israeli wars have ever formally recognized an end to hostilities between themselves and Israel. In addition, the Israeli occupation of the West Bank and the Golan Heights may be considered continuing acts of aggression against Jordan and Syria, respectively. Thus Egypt may be considered to be under a continuing obligation to join in hostilities against Israel at the request of Jordan or Syrian or pursuant to an appropriate decision of the Arab League.[167]

In addition, the United States provided Israel, but not Egypt, with political and military commitments for upholding the treaty with Egypt. It signed with Israel a Memorandum of Agreement at Camp David which stated: "The United States will provide support it deems appropriate for proper actions taken by Israel in response to such demonstrated violations of the Treaty of Peace."[168] Mustapha Khalil, then Egypt's Prime Minister and Foreign Minister, launched an immediate protest when he received a copy of the agreement only twenty-four hours before the signing ceremony of the peace treaty. Khalil wrote to Secretary Vance on March 26, complaining that: "The American-Israeli Memorandum assumes that Egypt is the side liable to violate its obligations. The United States is supposed to be a partner in a tripartite effort to achieve peace and not to support the allegations of one side against the other."[169] Khalil sent two protest letters to Vance who must have informed Sadat who apparently "dismissed (the letters) as unimportant, reflecting Khalil's personal views rather than the stand of the Egyptian leadership."[170] Vance never answered the letters. Boutros Ghali, however, told me that Vance did offer to provide Egypt with a similar commitment but that the Egyptians refused for fear of appearing to be too closely associated with the United States. The basis for the alleged Egyptian refusal, however, is difficult to understand given that Sadat made no secret of the fact that his entire strategy relied on a closer association between Washington and Cairo and clearly accepted a subordinate role in the new strategic triangular relationship between the United States, Israel and Egypt.

At any rate, the peace treaty was signed on March 26, 1979, and so was the Memorandum of Agreement. The rest of the Egyptian delegation were reportedly "extremely unhappy about Sadat's attitude and his willingness to make concessions to the Israelis" and angered by his tendency to ignore the opinions of his delegation and take decisions single-handedly.[171]

Conclusion

The outcome of the Egyptian-American and Egyptian-Israeli negotiations reflected the balance of power between the negotiators in 1979. Israel was not only in physical control of vast Arab territories and virtually in control of a weakened American president unable to even publicly state official American positions on the conflict, it was also in control of the negotiation process, the substance of which it carefully manipulated and fundamentally influenced and controlled. Sadat had not only separated Egypt from the Arab world, he disdainfully ignored Egypt's traditional superpower ally, adopted contradictory positions which he easily modified, and naively believed in Kissinger's impartiality. He had, most significantly, practically disarmed Egypt, thus ensuring that even the mere thought of a military option as a negotiating chip could not be credibly entertained. Thus, whereas between 1970 and 1973 Egypt had spent $2,400 billion on armaments compared to Israel's $1,020 billion, the period of Egyptian-American and Egyptian-Israeli negotiations between 1974 and 1979 saw Sadat practically unilaterally reverse the strong position of the Egyptian army. Thus, for this five-year period of negotiations Egypt spent $1,730 billion compared to $5,200 billion spent by Israel which thus confirmed, by 1979, its determination to strengthen its undisputed military domination of the region.[172]

Still, a realistic assessment of the forces at play at the beginning of negotiations in late 1973 could have facilitated a far more effective utilization of the coalition power successfully marshalled by the Arab countries for the 1973 military operation and for the brief political battle which ensued. Although Sadat understood the significance of Arab unity and its potential as "the sixth world power" he took Egypt's leadership role for granted. And when his assessments and the strategic decisions that flowed from them elicited little support among the Arabs, he decided to sacrifice the tangible assets of Arab power for the uncertain hope that the perspicacity of his strategy would be vindicated. His strategy was based on a highly subjective assessment of the relevant policies of Israel and the United States and of their relative power. He made widely optimistic calculations of the impact of his so-called "strategic thinking" which essentially consisted of de-Nasserizing Egypt internally and externally and realigning its foreign policy along American objectives in the region. These objectives gave primacy to guaranteeing Israeli military superiority over all its Arab adversaries combined, and to having access to the region's strategic resources. In enthusiastically espousing these objectives, Sadat hoped that Washington would reward him by implementing its declared official policy of a comprehensive settlement in the region on the basis of Israeli withdrawal from the occupied Arab territories. But he overestimated Washington's ability and willingness to pressure Israel and underestimated the tenacity of Israel's commitment to hang on to its conquests. Most surprisingly, he entered his new alliances bereft of regional and international allies, thus ensuring that the weakness of his position would be used exploitatively. Most significantly, Sadat's decision-making and therefore his ability to make concessions undisturbed by the opposition of his Ministers, was facilitated by the authoritarian character of his rule. Had he been accountable to Egypt's political institutions or to the professional and bureaucratic elites who supported him, it is likely that he would have been unable to separate Egypt from the Arab camp and pursue a course of action that facilitated Israel's consolidation of the occupied Arab territories and left free to attempt military solutions to the Palestinian problem.

One of those Egyptian foreign policy officials who supported Camp David and was involved in its preparations made the following assessment of Sadat's negotiating techniques and strategies:

> I was heavily involved in its preparations that led to the successful conclusion of treaty negotiations...Sadat did not conduct himself in an appropriate manner (in the negotiations). He needed a better negotiating team. We were always surprised by the Israelis. The provisions of the treaty concerning the West Bank and Gaza were not clearly written. If we had a better negotiating team this would not have happened. The Israelis usually achieved their goals. We should have pressured the U.S. to take a more definitive stand on Israeli destruction of Palestinian homes. This was not even mentioned in the treaty. We should have worked harder to involve Western Europe and Japan in the peace process. These people cheered but did not kick in any money. Egypt took a great risk for peace. We could have done with less praise and more financial support. Sadat and his team should have tried to more effectively activate the Israeli peace wing. Such groups as the Labour Party and Peace Now would have supported us. We should not have alienated the Russians to such a degree. Their co-operation is necessary if any Middle East peace agreements are to hold. They have also been very supportive of Egypt in the past. It was a great mistake to cut ourselves off from them. Sadat should have avoided the severe confrontation with other Arab States. Sadat was too arrogant in the way he treated other Arab countries. He even toyed with the idea of selling other Arabs down the river...His sloppy negotiating techniques caused many problems for Egypt. They prevented us from taking maximum advantage of the opportunities presented by the treaty.[173]

In contrast to Begin and his negotiating team who showed firm commitments to positions from which they generally did not budge, Sadat adopted positions which were elastic, highly flexible, and often contradictory. His decision-making and negotiating strategies involved deceptions and manipulation, but generally vis-à-vis his own Ministers and Arab allies. Whereas Begin, Dayan and Weizman avoided making commitments by saying they had to have cabinet approvals, Sadat often made decisions alone without consultations and sometimes even without the knowledge of his advisors and Ministers; his unilateral decisions were made on the spot and in private meetings with Israeli and American negotiators. When his

Ministers were not kept in the dark and objected to a particular decision he ignored them. When the Americans asked for more concessions he obliged "as a favour" to his friend Carter and unilaterally reversed previously established policy decisions agreed upon by Cabinet. Certainly, the operational environment in 1978-79 had placed considerable constraints on the kind of agreements Sadat could get. But the documentary record leaves little doubt that Egyptian decisions and negotiating strategies from Sinai to Camp David and Blair House fundamentally reflected the preponderance of President Sadat's own psycho-political perceptions. These were largely based on a highly subjective and unrealistic assessment of the forces at play, unwarranted faith in a distant ally, a mistaken analysis of the relative power of the negotiating parties, ill-conceived negotiating strategies, naively generous concessions, and a political culture which allowed an authoritarian approach to decision-making.

Notes

1. *The Camp David Summit*, September 1978. Department of State. The United States Government, p. 3.
2. Anwar el-Sadat, *In Search of Identity: An Autobiography* (New York, Harper and Row, 1978), p. 290.
3. Michael Brecher, *The Foreign Policy System of Israel* (London, Oxford University Press, 1972), pp. 11-12.
4. Sprout, H., and M. Sprout, *The Ecological Perspective on Human Affairs* (Princeton, N.J., Princeton University Press, 1965); see also Ross Stagner, *Psychological Aspects of International Conflict* (Belmont, California, Brooks-Cole, 1967) and Joseph H. de Rivera, *The Psychological Dimension of Foreign Policy* (Columbus, Ohio, Charles E. Merrill, 1968).
5. Richard C. Synder; H. W. Bruck, and Burton Sapin, (eds.) *Foreign Policy Decision-Making* (New York, Free Press of Glencoe, 1963), see also Joseph Frankel, *The Making of Foreign Policy: An Analysis of Decision-Making* (New York, Oxford University Press, 1963).
6. Bahgat Korany, *How Foreign Policy Decisions are Made in the Third World* (Boulder, Colorado, Westview Press, 1986), pp. 39-60.
7. Ibid, p. 92.
8. Bahgat Korany and Ali E. Hillal Dessouki, *The Foreign Policies of Arab States*, (Boulder, Colorado, Westview Press, 1984), pp. 5-18.
9. Ibid, pp. 119-146.
10. Ibid, p. 124.
11. Andrew J. R. Mack, "Why Big Nations Lose Small Wars: The Politics of Asymmetric Conflict," *World Politics*, 27 (January, 1975), pp. 175-200.
12. Charles Lockhart, *Bargaining in International Conflicts* (New York, Columbia University Press, 1979), p.93. See also Glenn Snyder and Paul Diesing, *Conflict Among Nations* (Princeton, Princeton University Press, 1977).
13. Thomas C. Schelling, *The Strategy of Conflict* (New York, Oxford University Press, 1963).

14. Jeffrey Z. Rubin and Bert R. Brown, *The Social Psychology of Bargaining and Negotiations* (New York, Academic Press, 1975), p. 199.

15. Charles O. Lerche, Jr., and Abdul Said, *Concepts of International Politics* (Englewood Cliffs, New Jersey, Prentice Hall, 1963), p. 32. See also Robert Jervis, *Perceptions and Misperceptions in International Politics* (Princeton, Princeton University Press, 1976).

16. See Eqbal Ahmad, "What Washington Wants," in Nasser Aruri, (ed.) *Middle East Crucible: Studies on the Arab-Israeli Confrontations of 1973* (Belmont, MA, Association of Arab-American University Graduates, 1978), pp. 227-263, quotation from p. 258.

17. Raphael Israeli, *The Public Diary of President Sadat. Part Two. The Road to Diplomacy* (E. J. Brill, Leiden, The Netherlands, 1979), p. 460.

18. Ibid, p. 466.

19. Ibid, p. 657.

20. Naguib Mahfouz, *Al-Karnak* (Cairo, 1974), p. 57.

21. *Al-Ahram* (in Arabic) (Cairo), March 3, 1978.

22. Media attacks against the Palestinians and the Arabs were frequent and reached a peak, not coincidentally, in 1978 — the year the Camp David accords were signed. See Karem Yehia, "The Image of the Palestinians in Egypt: 1982-1985," *Journal of Palestine Studies*, vol. XVI, no. 62, (Winter, 1987), pp. 45-63. See also Ibrahim Karawan, "Egypt and the Western Alliance: the Politics of Westomania?," in Steven Spiegel, (ed.) *The Middle East and the Western Alliance* (London, George Allen and Unwin, 1982), pp. 163-181.

23. See the series of articles put together by Saad Eddin Ibrahim, (ed.) *Egypt's Arabism* (in Arabic) (Cairo, Al-Ahram Center for Political and Strategic Studies, 1978); see also *Al-Ahali* (in Arabic) (Cairo), March 22, 1978.

24. *The Public Diary of President Sadat*, vol.III, op. cit., p. 926.

25. Ibid, interview on January 25, 1975. p. 773.

26. Ibid, pp. 830-831.

27. Ibid, p. 912.

28. Ibid, p. 925.

29. Ibid, p. 513.

30. Ibid, pp. 462-465.

31. Ibid, p. 912.

32. Ibid, p. 917.

33. Ibid, p. 903.

34. Ibid, vol. III. op. cit., p.903.

35. Raphael Israeli, *Man of Defiance: A Political Biography of Anwar Sadat* (London, Weidenfeld and Nicolson, 1985), p. 157.

36. Mohamed Heikal, *Autumn of Fury: The Assassination of Sadat* (London, Andr Deutsch, 1983), p. 63.

37. *The Public Diary of President Sadat*, op. cit. pp. 514-515.

38. Eqbal Ahmad, "What Washington wants," op. cit., p. 229.

39. Henry A. Kissinger, *World Restored* (New York, Grosset and Dunlap, 1964), p. 322.

40. Tad Szulc, "How Kissinger did it: Behind the Vietnamese Cease-Fire Agreement," *Foreign Policy*, no. 15, (Summer, 1974), pp. 21-69.

41. Ismail Fahmy, *Negotiating for Peace in the Middle East* (London, Croom Helm, 1983), p. 167.

42. Heikal, *Autumn of Fury*, op. cit., p. 67.

43. Anwar el-Sadat, *In Search of Identity: An Autobiography*, op. cit., p. 291.

44. William B. Quandt, *Decade of Decision* (Berkeley, University of California Press, 1977), pp. 216-226.

45. Henry Kissinger, *The Years of Upheaval* (Boston, Little Brown, 1982), pp. 638-41.

46. Heikal, *Autumn of Fury*, op. cit., pp. 67-68.

47. Abba Eban, *An Autobiography* (New York, Random House, 1977), p. 561.
48. Israeli, *Man of Defiance*, op. cit., p. 145.
49. Heikal, *Autumn of Fury*, op. cit., p. 71.
50. Fahmy, *Negotiating for Peace in the Middle East*, op. cit., p. 74.
51. Israeli, *The Public Diary of President Sadat*, volume II, op. cit., p. 446.
52. Ibid, p. 562.
53. Fahmy, pp. 164-165.
54. Israeli, *The Public Diary of President Sadat*, volume III, op. cit., p. 1015.
55. Ibid, p. 1049.
56. Ibid, p. 1158.
57. Howard M. Sachar, *Egypt and Israel* (New York, Richard Marek, 1981), p. 240.
58. Mohamed Ibrahim Kamel, *The Camp David accords: A Testimony* (London, Routledge and Keagan Paul, 1986), p. 116.
59. Israeli, *The Public Diary of President Sadat*, vol. III, op. cit., p. 1177.
60. Ezer Weizman, *The Battle for Peace* (New York, Bantam Books, 1981), p. 156.
61. Fahmy, p. 193.
62. Sachar, *Egypt and Israel*, op. cit., p. 257.
63. Ibid, p. 258.
64. William B. Quandt, *Camp David: Peace Making and Politics* (Washington, D.C., The Brookings Institution, 1986), p.46.
65. Quoted in ibid, p. 73.
66. Ibid, p. 84.
67. Ibid, p. 85.
68. Quoted in ibid, p. 86. See also President Carter's interview with *Time*, August 8, 1977.
69. Ibid, pp. 87-94.
70. Fahmy, pp. 216-17.
71. Quandt, *Camp David*, p. 90.
72. Moshe Dayan, *Breakthrough: A Personal Account of the Egypt-Israel Peace Negotiations* (New York, Alfred A. Knopf, 1981), pp. 45-52.
73. Hassan al-Tuhamy, "Now I Can Speak About the Exchange," *October*, (in Arabic) (Cairo), no. 317, (November 21, 1982), quoted in Muhsen Awad, *Egypt and Israel, Five Years of Normalization* (in Arabic), (Cairo, Dar al-Mustaqbal al-Arabi, 1984), pp. 14-15.
74. Eitan Haber, Zeev Schiff, and Ehud Yaari, *The Year of the Dove* (New York, Bantam Books, 1979), pp. 11-12.
75. *The New York Times*, March 19, 1977.
76. *Time*, August 8, 1977.
77. Fahmy, pp. 196-197.
78. Quoted in Quandt, *Camp David*, op. cit., p. 103.
79. *The New York Times*, October 2, 1977.
80. Ibid.
81. Jimmy Carter, *Keeping Faith: Memoirs of a President* (New York, Bantam Books, 1982), p. 294.
82. *The New York Times*, October 2, 1977.
83. Ibid.
84. Zbigniew Brezezinski, *Power and Principle: Memoirs of the National Security Advisor, 1977-1981* (New York, Farrar, Strauss, Giroux, 1983), p. 108.
85. *The New York Times*, October 14, 1977.
86. Raphael Israeli, *Egypt: Aspects of President Anwar Al-Sadat's Political Thought* (Jerusalem, The Magnes Press, The Hebrew University), p. 55.
87. Saad Eddin Ibrahim, "Domestic Development in Egypt," in William Quandt, (ed.) *Ten Years After Camp David*, pp. 19-62. The quote comes from p. 23. See also Esmail Hosseinzadeh, "How Egyptian State Capitalism Reverted to Market Capitalism,"

Arab Studies Quarterly, vol. 10, no.3, 1988, pp. 299-318. Hosseinzadeh argues that "the turn to market forces to revitalize the stalled economy began not after but before Nasir left the scene." p. 317.

88. Mahmoud Abdel-Fadil and Alain Roussillon in a preface to "Egypte: années 80," a special issue of *Revue tiers-monde*, Paris, (January-March, 1990). See also Adel Hussein, *The Egyptian Economy from Independence to Dependency: 1974-79* (in Arabic), (Cairo, 1982), pp. 631-643; and Umima Kamel, "An investigation of Egypt's debts and the borders of security and danger," *Al-Ahram Al-Eqtesadi* (in Arabic) (Cairo), no. 838, (March 7, 1983).

89. Samir Amin, *The Arab Nation*, (London, Zed, 1978), p. 75.

90. Ghali Shoukri, *Egypt: Portrait Of A President* (London, Zed Press, 1981), p. 395; see also David Hirst and Irene Beeson, *Sadat*, (London, Faber and Faber, 1981), pp. 202-254; Mohamed Heikal, *Autumn of Fury*, op. cit., pp. 90-91; see also the impact of the policy of openness on the Egyptian economy analyzed by Mahmoud Abdel Fadil, "La chute des revenus extérieurs frappe une économie sans ressort," *Le Monde Diplomatique*, (April, 1986), p. 23.

91. David Hirst and Irene Besson, *Sadat*, op. cit., p. 231.

92. Heikal, *Autumn of Fury*, op. cit., p. 91.

93. Quoted in Muhsen Awad, *Egypt and Israel, Five Years of Normalization*, op. cit., p. 149.

94. Sadat, *In Search of Identity*, op. cit., p. 302.

95. Cited in Fahmy, pp. 247-248.

96. Ibid, p. 265.

97. Ibid, p. 265.

98. Ibid, p. 267.

99. Heikal, *Autumn of Fury*, op. cit., p. 97.

100. Ibid, p. 267.

101. Ibid, p. 282.

102. Heikal, *Autumn of Fury*, op. cit., p. 104.

103. Ibid, p. 104

104. Fahmy, p. 282.

105. Cited in ibid, p. 288.

106. Quandt, *Camp David*, op. cit., pp. 156-157.

107. Seth P. Tillman, *The United States in the Middle East* (Bloomington, Indiana University Press, 1982), p. 24.

108. Kamel, op. cit., p. 24.

109. Weizman, *The Battle for Peace*, op. cit., p. 129.

110. See Eitan Haber, Zeev Schiff, and Ehud Yaari, *The Year of the Dove, op. cit., p. 126.*

111. Kamel, p. 25.

112. Carter, *Keeping Faith*, op. cit., p. 300.

113. Weizman, p. 131.

114. Personal meetings with Dr. Boutros Ghali, Egypt's Deputy Prime Minister for Foreign Affairs, and Minister of State for Foreign Affairs at the time of the Ismailiya meeting. Cairo, 1991.

115. Haber, Schiff, and Yaari, *The Year of the Dove*, op. cit., p. 137.

116. Quandt, *Camp David*, op. cit., p. 159.

117. Weizman, p. 142.

118. Ibid, pp. 190-91.

119. Kamel, pp. 48-49.

120. Ibid, p. 50.

121. Ibid, p. 56.

122. Quandt, *Camp David*, op. cit., p. 166.

123. Ibid, p. 176.

124. Ibid, p. 177.
125. Kamel, p. 86.
126. Quandt, *Camp David*, op. cit., p. 180.
127. See Lewis W. Snider, P. Edward Haley, Abraham R. Wagner, and Nicki J. Cohen, in P. Edward Haley and Lewis W. Snider, (eds.) *Lebanon in Crisis* (Syracruse, New York, Syracuse University Press, 1979) pp, 91-111, the two quotes come from pp. 101-102.
128. Mahmoud Riad, *The Struggle for Peace in the Middle East* (London, Quartet Books, 1981), p. 311.
129. Quandt, *Camp David*, op. cit., p. 186.
130. Weizman, pp. 296- 299.
131. Cited by Kamel, p. 257.
132. Ibid, pp. 258-261.
133. Ibid, p. 268.
134. Ibid, p. 284.
135. Ibid, p. 327. When I asked him to comment on this, Boutros Ghali could not remember why it was decided to base the Egyptian project on Resolution 242 and not on the 1947 UN resolution partitioning Palestine. He said that Sadat often met alone with his personal advisor and Under-Secretary of State Oussama al-Baze without the presence of either Kamel or himself. Oussama al-Baze's office scheduled a number of meetings for me but al-Baze's travel schedule with President Mubarak made it difficult for him to accommodate me during the time I was in Egypt.
136. Personal meetings with Minister Mohamed Ibrahim Kamel in Cairo, 1990.
137. Weizman, pp. 364-366.
138. Cyrus Vance, *Hard Choices: Critical Years in America's Foreign Policy* (New York, Simon and Schuster, 1983), p. 226.
139. Kamel, p. 312.
140. Ibid, p. 325.
141. Vance, p. 220-21.
142. Weizman, pp. 364-366.
143. Kamel, pp. 334-335.
144. Ibid. p. 321.
145. Weizman, pp. 349-350.
146. Ibid, p.369.
147. Ibid, p. 369.
148. Ibid, p. 372.
149. Ibid, p. 373.
150. Kamel, p. 351.
151. Israeli, *The Public Diary of President Sadat*, op. cit., volume III, p. 1227.
152. Kamel, pp. 355-356.
153. Weizman, p. 368.
154. Kamel, p. 357.
155. Ibid, p. 365.
156. Vance, p. 226.
157. Weizman, p. 374.
158. Kamel, p. 351.
159. Ibid, pp. 374-75.
160. Ibid, p. 372.
161. Ibid, p. 358.
162. Vance, pp. 235- 238.
163. Ibid, p. 241.
164. Fahmy, pp. 294-295.
165. Vance, p. 244.

166. Personal meetings with Boutros Ghali in Cairo, 1991.
167. See Guyora Binder, *Treaty Conflict and Political Contradiction* (New York, Praeger, 1988), p. 11.
168. Fahmy, pp. 294-95.
169. For the full text of the Egyptian response see Fahmy, p. 297.
170. Ibid, p. 298.
171. Fahmy, p. 299.
172. Stephen Green, *Living by the Sword* p. 103.
173. "Conversations in Cairo: An Interview with Dr. Thaseen Basheer." Interview conducted by Norman Frankel. *Middle East Focus* (Summer, 1990), pp. 8-13, p. 8.

CHAPTER THREE

The Camp David Order: Reactions and Consequences

Traditional American foreign policy pursued two principal objectives in the Middle East: ready and cheap access to Arab oil and, from the Johnson administration on, guaranteeing Israel's military superiority over all Arab countries combined. It was possible to pursue these two contradictory goals as long as the Arabs were divided between pro-American conservative regimes led by Saudi Arabia and Soviet-supported "revolutionary" regimes led by Egypt. With superpower encouragement a mini-Arab cold war developed and ensured that the enormous Arab human and material resources could not be effectively harnessed to bring about a resolution of the Arab-Israeli conflict and of the question of Palestinian refugees on the basis of UN resolutions.

After the 1967 war and the conquest and occupation by Israel of large Arab territories, the challenge of reversing the consequences of defeat and ending Israeli occupation became more urgent than inter-Arab rivalries and disputes. Nasser began the process of healing almost immediately after the 1967 debacle and was able, before his premature death in 1970, to close the chapter on what Malcolm Kerr called the Arab Cold War. Egyptian President Anwar Sadat managed, and this may be his greatest achievement, to forge an unusual alliance between the conservative Arab order and Egypt, the chastised and sobered leader of the former "revolutionary" order. It was more than an alliance of temporary convenience, it was a unity based both on practical considerations and ideological affinity. Saudi Arabia and the rich Gulf countries were to provide the money, Egypt and Syria the manpower needed for the inevitable military attempt to liberate occupied Arab territories that Israel refused to return in exchange for peace treaties.

Meanwhile, the Nixon-Kissinger team had focused American foreign policy on China and South-East Asia; the challenges came from the Third World. Kissinger accepted the Israeli thesis that the status quo of occupation of Arab territories was an acceptable and manageable *modus vivendi* for the region; the Egyptian-Syrian military offensive in 1973 proved the fallacy of Kissinger's and Israeli leaders' calculations. The Organization of Petrolum Exporting Countries' (OPEC) declaration of economic independence after the 1973 Arab-Israeli war led to greater Third World control of oil production and pricing policy. Increased American military aid to Latin-American dictators failed to stop the Nicaraguan revolution. The Carter presidency seemed overtaken by events it was unable to control and sometimes incapable of understanding. In December 1977 President

Carter visited Iran and, at a reception banquet, toasted the new year with the Shah whom he congratulated for having transformed his country into "an island of stability." A year later, popular upheavals swept the Shah out of power and Iran out of the American strategic system in the region.

After fighting the 1973 war and scoring some military and psychological victories, the Arab coalition effectively coordinated political and economic activities and, for a brief period, displayed serious potentials for becoming, as Sadat repeatedly and proudly stated, the sixth power in the world. This would have meant bargaining with the United States, the ultimate arbiter of regional power, from a position of relative strength. Arab unity therefore threatened American ability to pursue its twin policy of contradictions: to have ready and cheap access to Arab oil and at the same time effectively help Israel consolidate its occupation of Arab land. The threat of Arab unity was short-lived. It was pre-empted by Sadat's strategic vision. By offering Egypt as a guardian of American interests in the region, he ensured that the potential of Arab economic power would not be used to persuade Washington to modify its effective support for Israeli occupation of Arab territories. Sadat fancied himself as a world leader ready to play the game of balance of power as a partner of the United States whom he repeatedly urged to forget the Vietnam syndrome, overcome its fears of military involvement and to project more power around the world. This thinking fitted well with the Nixon-Kissinger approach to international relations and enabled Kissinger to take Sadat down the road of separation from the Arab camp. The contradictions in American foreign policy for the region were protected and by the time the Camp David order was established, they became even more flagrant as Egypt and the Arabs helplessly watched the Americans support the Israeli invasion of Lebanon, the bloody attempt at liquidating the Palestine question, and the besieging of an Arab capital.

The Nixon Doctrine had relied on regional allies such as the Shah of Iran to protect American interests by force if necessary, without committing American boys to the ungrateful, bloody and costly task of actually doing the fighting as had been the case in Vietnam; after the Iranian revolution, Washington lost in the Shah the major pillar of its Middle East strategic system. Pro-American conservative Arab regimes, particularly those with oil resources and strategic access to the Indian ocean where a superpower nuclear submarine arms race was underway, became exposed to the threat of radical revolutionary Islam which the new Iran proposed to export. Further, the perception of threat increased when in late 1979 CIA support to the Muslim rebels fighting the Marxist regime in Afghanistan finally provoked the Soviet Union into that great game of empire Britain once played in Afghanistan: in December 1979, the Soviet Union invaded Afghanistan and Soviet troops found themselves close to vital American interests in the Middle East.

President Carter responded by enunciating his own doctrine: instead of relying on regional allies to protect its own interests, the United States will have to rely on its own military forces and actively intervene to defend its interests and the regimes guarding those interests. The Rapid Deployment Force was created for that purpose. Traditionally, the threat to American Middle East strategic, economic and political interests was perceived to come from the Soviet Union, but in reality it most frequently came from nationalist forces and revolutionary upheavals. The Rapid Deployment Force was therefore theoretically directed against Soviet threats to American interests in the Middle East, but more practically it was to be the principal instrument of support for the new American-based strategic and political order that resulted from the Camp David agreements. The chief objective of this Camp David order was to ensure, as Carter tantalizingly suggested to Mohamed Ibrahim Kamel at Camp David, that no power outside or inside the region could stand up to the American-Israeli-Egyptian strategic cooperation. The Camp David order was therefore to be theoretically directed against outside powers, meaning the Soviet Union, but more realistically against powers from inside the region, whence the real threat to American interests most frequently came. In short, the Camp David order was to deter both Soviet and regional challenges to the American-supported economic, political, and military order in the region. In this mission, it relied on American might impressively displayed in the Rapid Deployment Force.

Instead of a general framework for a comprehensive resolution of the Arab-Israeli-Palestinian conflict in all its aspects, Camp David turned out to be a framework for a new geostrategic and political order in the Middle East. By separating Egypt from the Arab camp and incorporating it into the American strategic system, where it filled the vacuum created by the defection of Iran after the overthrow of the Shah, Camp David managed to bring under some control the upheavals and turmoils threatening American interests in the region in the late seventies. With Egypt neutralized and a Reagan administration reducing Middle East problems to communism and terrorism, and encouraging Israel's role as an American strategic asset, Israel warred against its neighbours, consolidated its occupation of the Arab territories, invaded Lebanon and attempted a bloody final solution to the Palestine question.

But this view of Camp David and the implied role expected of Egypt in it necessitated a radical realignment of traditional Egyptian foreign policy priorities along lines compatible with the American vision for the region; an almost total separation of Egypt not only from its Arab alliances but, more importantly, from its own Arab environment, its own Arab nationalist sentiments, and its traditional bonds of solidarity with the Palestinian cause. Nasser had believed and repeatedly affirmed that the basis of his policy was the realization that Egypt was an inseparable part of its Arab environment. In his *Philosophy of the Revolution,* he had rhetorically asked: "Is it possible for us to overlook that, around us, lies an Arab circle, and that this circle is as much a part of us as we are a part of it, that our history has been merged with it and that its interests are linked with ours?" Sadat thought it was. He confidently embarked upon the task of separating Egypt from its Arabism as a necessary prerequisite for insertion into the American strategic system. After Camp David, he was pressured to continue the process of de-Arabizing Egypt, of taking it away from its Arab character and closer to the new American-Israeli partnership. Thus, Washington subordinated its economic and military aid to Egyptian acquiescence in Israeli actions; Israel insisted, and with American help, pushed for a process called "normalization" of relations with Egypt; normalization was supposed to achieve the separation of Egypt from its Arabism enough to politically, culturally, and ideologically subordinate Egyptian solidarity with the Palestinian cause to an understanding acceptance of the Zionist ideological foundations of Israel; this in turn was meant to facilitate acceptance of the necessity of continued Israeli occupation of Palestinian land and the subjugation of its people.

These dynamics pulled Egypt in different directions as the tension inherent in their conflictual forces increased. There was tension and conflict: conflict between Egypt the leader of the Arab world, and Egypt the junior partner in the American-Israeli-Egyptian alliance; Egypt the defender of the Arab cause and Egypt the player in a balance of power game favourable to the Israeli cause; an Egypt unable to wage any more wars and anxious for a necessary peace for the whole region and Egypt the helpless spectator of Israeli-triggered violence and war against the Arabs; Egypt the promoter of Arab interests and Egypt the guardian of American strategic designs. The growing tension of these conflicts culminated in Sadat's dramatic end. Throughout the 1980s Egypt was rent by contradictions which often erupted in turmoils, upheavals, and insurrections which nearly led to popular uprisings. Egyptian reactions to Camp David were therefore necessarily divided. On the one hand, most Egyptians accepted Camp David as the first stage of a comprehensive peace agreement to be followed by Israeli withdrawal from the West Bank, Gaza, and the Golan Heights and similar peace treaties with Syria and an independent Palestine. Most Egyptians assumed that Camp David would bring about "a just and comprehensive" resolution of the Arab-Israeli conflict, and looked forward to an end to all wars and occupation in the region. On the other hand, when it quickly became clear that Camp David was used to separate Egypt from its Arab responsibilities and neutralize its military power to serve the interest of an imperial Israel bent on continued occupation and faster dispossession of the Palestinian people, Egyptians were almost unanimous in rejecting this vision of Camp David. The Egyptian government itself opposed this application of Camp David but was unable to do little beyond verbal protestations. Although Israeli leaders violated their own commitments to Camp David and proceeded along the path of conquest and destruction as the Israeli invasion of Lebanon dramatically demonstrated, official Egypt remained divided: on the one hand its commitment to the treaty with Israel remained unshaken, and on the other hand, it quickly became obvious that it would be impossible to totally separate Egypt from its Arab environment and acquiesce in the Israeli military solutions to the Palestine question. Hosni Mubarak, who succeeded Sadat as president of Egypt, quickly came to that realization and found it to be his lot to walk a delicate balancing act as he brought Egypt back to the Arab world. It is likely that had he lived to witness how Israeli leaders used Camp David to try to liquidate once and for all the Palestine question, even Sadat would have seen the necessity of an Egyptian return to the Arab fold.

Camp David Exposed

The gulf between Sadat's declared objectives in entering the Camp David negotiations and what he was able to accomplish at the end of the negotiations was most cogently summed up in a memorandum sent to Sadat by his former comrades from the Free Officers group which overthrew the Faruk monarchy in 1952. Zakaria Muhyi Eddin, Abdel-Latif al-Baghdadi, Hussein al-Shafii, and Kamal Eddin Hussein, the only surviving members of the July 23 Revolutionary Command Council, reminded Sadat of the public commitments he made and presented him with an analysis of the Camp David accords which showed them to be woefully incompatible with Sadat's publicly proclaimed principles and negotiating objectives. The document gives an excellent and succinct exposition of the views of the Egyptian opposition to Sadat's separate agreement with Israel, and it is, therefore, worth quoting at length:

> In order to be fair to ourselves and to everyone else, we must remind you of your public statements and the solemn commitments which you have undertaken at every national and international forum both at home and abroad...Your statements and commitments can be summarized under the following:
> 1. The necessity of recovering every single inch of Arab territory occupied in June 1967 after complete Israeli withdrawal from all the territory, namely Jerusalem, the West Bank, Gaza, the Golan and Sinai.
> 2. In order to achieve a permanent peace, the Palestinian problem must be solved on the basis of the legal rights of the Palestinian Arabs, including their right to self-determination, and on finding a just solution to the refugees problem.
> 3. It is unacceptable to sign a separate peace treaty with Israel.
> 4. Insistence on the unity of the Arab position as a primary principle for dealing with Israel and for regaining our rights now and in the future.
>
> The Camp David accords have struck us a shocking blow because of their total incompatibility with the preceding principles...The first agreement surprised us because it is analogous to the Begin plan concerning the Palestinian problem.
>
> 1. It makes no mention and offers no assurance of an Israeli military withdrawal from the West Bank, Gaza or Jerusalem.
> 2. It offers no recognition of the rights of the Palestinian people to self-determination.
> 3. It deletes any reference to the operations underway for the establishment of Israeli settlements which are totally illegal.
> 4. It leaves the position of Jerusalem uncertain.
> 5. (It) corresponds with Israel's policy of dividing the case and dealing with each of the parties separately.
> 6. By signing the Camp David accords, a false legitimacy would be bestowed upon the existing illegal conditions which in turn would lead to the continued occupation and the Judaization of the West Bank and Gaza.
>
> As for the second agreement, it is also surprisingly similar in its objectives to the Begin plan, as the following points will elucidate:
>
> 1. It represents a separate agreement between Egypt and Israel...(It) represents an abandonment by Egypt of its historic duties toward the Arab nation in its struggle for existence, at a time when Egypt is naturally and constitutionally an inseparable part of the Arab nation where both sides are inter-

dependent...The isolation of Egypt from the Arab nation has always been an objective of European imperialism.

2. The first article of this agreement states that Egyptian sovereignty over Sinai will be completely re-established after Israeli withdrawal. Several provisions of the agreement contradicts this assertion. Sinai, which runs 250 kilometers from east to west, would be disarmed for the most part. Only one company of Egyptian soldiers can patrol the 50 kilometers east of Suez, a force insufficient to protect itself or Egypt. This would also mean that the eastern frontier, which is feebly protected, had been shrunk by 150 kilometers from the western frontier. Israel, on the other hand, would have no territories disarmed. The area of limited armament on the Israeli side (in the Sinai) is three kilometers and would be manned by four battalions and protected by whatever forces Israel deems necessary. Some areas of Sinai, Sharm al-Shaykh and the vicinity of Rafah, are to be internationalized. It denies the major part of Sinai protection making its inhabitants and resources eternally subject to Israeli exploitation and greed. Egypt has committed itself to Israeli security, but has overlooked its own present and future security. This is contrary to all logic. The issue, therefore, is not the security of Israel, but the provision of an easy path for Israel to reconquer the Sinai without incurring losses.

3. It is clear that Israel's long-range aim is economic domination as a prelude to political control. What is taking place will facilitate this task.

4. The terms of this agreement violate the Arab League Covenant, mutual defense agreements, as well as cultural and economic accords, leaving many unanswered questions. First, what will Egypt's attitude be in the face of an Israeli attack on any of the other Arab States. Second, what would be the common ideology between Egypt and the Arab nation since the former has reconciled itself to the precepts of Zionist thought which are being disseminated while Israel occupies our lands. How can we reconcile ourselves with the Arab nation?

...Having analyzed the Accords, we feel that the matter is extremely serious and that we face a most dangerous situation...In our view, a summary of the Accords reveals:

1. Splintering of the Arab nation, which denies that entity its most important weapon.

2. Isolating Egypt from the Arab nation in order to weaken both, thus permitting both to fall victim to Israeli imperialism in the area.

3. Conferring legitimacy on the various illegal conditions and plans of Israel.
4. Maintaining Egypt in a state of insecurity and an absence of sovereignty in the face of growing Israeli power aided and abetted by the United States of America.
5. Liquidating the Palestinian problem and the Palestinian people to the benefit of Israel.[2]

The failure of Camp David as a framework for a comprehensive and just peace in the Arab-Israeli conflict was quickly exposed by the use Israel made of it. It was obvious from the beginning that the agreements were inadequate as a basis for a resolution of the Arab-Israeli conflict in all its aspects; indeed the Camp David promise of a comprehensive settlement never materialized because it was a false promise from the start. Even the Americans readily recognized that the accords were a triumph of Israeli strategy and a vindication of Israeli power politics approach to the conflict. William Quandt, member of the National Security Council in the Carter Administration and member of the American negotiating team at Camp David, readily admitted that the Camp David accords gave Israeli Prime Minister Menachem Begin "every reason to believe that...his vision of a powerful Israel, in permanent control of Jerusalem, the West Bank, and Gaza, would be the historical legacy of Camp David."[3] This vision of an imperial Israel in permanent control of occupied Arab territories may still materialize; but its realization was rendered difficult by the opposition to Camp David inside and outside of Egypt and, more significantly, by the refusal of the Palestinians, particularly those under occupation, to acquiesce in what Egypt, Israel and the United States had decided for them.

But the Camp David accords themselves had indeed laid the ground for the possibility of permanent Israeli control of the occupied Palestinian territories. Notwithstanding Egyptian and American claims to the contrary, the Accords were understood by Israel, whose actions mattered the most since it was in occupation of the Arab territories, as sealing Egypt's fate and paving the way for Israel's bloody attempts to liquidate the Palestinian problem. Rafael Eitan, then Israel's Chief-of-Staff General, candidly admitted that the Camp David Treaty "will enable the IDF (The Israeli Defense Forces)...to free forces for the Eastern front."[4]

Indeed, there was no doubt that the Israeli military and political establishment, including those who had opposed Camp David such as Yitzhak Shamir, agreed at the time on one thing: that the separate treaty significantly enhanced Israel's strategic and political position by separating Egypt from the Arab camp and dividing the Arabs.[5] This strengthened the position and encouraged those within the Israeli establishment who favoured repressive solutions to the Palestinian problem. Although the arrest, deportation, and detention of nationalist Palestinian leaders and the establishment of Israeli-controlled "village leagues" as so-called Palestinian representatives continued to be a feature of Israeli-Palestinian relations, the Camp David accords gave a boost to right-wing Israeli elements who favoured an even more repressive and drastic measures for the liquidation of the Palestinian question. It was only a matter of time before various forms of Israeli violence would culminate into and naturally lead to the invasion of Lebanon and the bloody attempt at a final solution for the Palestinian problem.

The negotiators at Camp David claimed to have based the Accords on Resolution 242; but the fundamental basis of that resolution — Israeli withdrawal from occupied Arab territories in return for peace — was discarded. The Camp David document mentioned withdrawal only in connection with "a redeployment" of the Israeli forces in the occupied Arab territories. When pressed by reporters to be specific about withdrawal, an American official said that the Israelis intended to leave about 6,000 troops in the West Bank and Gaza. But, exclaimed a reporter, "That's what the Israelis have now."[6] The embarrassment of American administration officials only highlighted the contradiction between political rhetoric and the reality to which Camp David was giving its seal of official approval. Another significant victory for the Israeli negotiators was their ability to ban from the Camp David accords any reference to Palestinian national rights. President Carter claimed in his book *The Blood of Abraham* that he and President Sadat were convinced that the Camp David accords had protected the Palestinians' right to self-determination. This claim was later confirmed to me by a deputy minister at the Egyptian Ministry of Foreign Affairs. But nowhere in the Accords was the word self-determination mentioned. Nor did Israeli Prime Minister Menachem Begin leave any doubt about how he interpreted the accords' reference to the "legitimate rights" of the Palestinians which he described as "an emphasis devoid of any real content."[7] A rhetorical concession to which he assigned no importance and therefore saw no problem whatsoever in violating. The Camp David accords were in fact based on Begin's own plan of self-rule for the Palestinians about which the *New York Times*, not known for its pro-Arab positions, wrote that: "It does not take an Arab eye to read into it much 'rule' but little 'self.'"[8] Still, although largely based on his own autonomy plan, Menahem Begin quickly reneged on whatever concessions he made to get the agreement and contemptuously ignored Secretary Vance's and President Carter's protestations. Carter bitterly complained that Begin "proved unwilling to carry out the more difficult commitments" of Camp David.[9] But to no avail.

Israel continued to consolidate its hold on the occupied territories and to build new settlements at a brisker pace than it did before the Camp David accords. Between 1967 and 1977 Israel built 47 Jewish settlements in the occupied Palestinian territories. Between 1977 and 1982 the number of settlements in the West Bank and Gaza increased from 47 to 149, in addition to the 16 settlements in and around Jerusalem.[10] Moreover, the Israeli government adopted the position that it intended to raise its claim to sovereignty over the West Bank and Gaza in clear violation of Camp David which provided for autonomy for the Palestinians under occupation without prejudice to the final status of the occupied Arab territories which was to be decided upon through negotiations with elected representatives of the Palestinians. Even non-Likud Israeli leaders were embarrassed by the duplicity and deception of an Israeli government which affixed its signature to an international document only to promptly violate its provisions. "It is clear," commented former Israeli foreign Minister Abba Eban, "that the Israeli government policy is so distant from Camp David that when Likud spokesmen invoke the agreement, they are rather like Casanova invoking the Seventh Commandment."[11]

Egypt's New Alliances: The American Connection

The Egyptians were shocked by the Arab reactions to the Egyptian-Israeli treaty and by the extent of Egypt's isolation in the Arab world. Arab economic aid to Egypt was discontinued, diplomatic relations were severed, and Egypt, the leader of the Arab world, was expelled from the Arab League. In addition, Egypt's membership in the Islamic Conference Organization was suspended and its relations with the socialist countries deteriorated; in the case of Bulgaria, diplomatic relations were completely severed. Sadat found little or no support in the Organization of African States or within the Non-Alignment Movement. Even the European countries expressed only cautious support, tempered by some reservations. In fact, Sadat found himself with little or no support outside the Egyptian social class which constituted the basis of his power. He was determined, however, to forge ahead both with the implementation of the various provisions of the Camp David accords, and his vision of an Egypt firmly entrenched in the American camp. To that effect, he never tired of attempting to convince the United States that Egypt could be a reliable strategic regional partner, more valuable because of its geography and political stability. In effect, Sadat wanted to compete with Israel for Washington's favours by casting Egypt in the role of another American strategic asset in the region.

Sadat's eagerness to belong to the American camp was made evident by the multiplicity of signals he had been sending to Washington long before the Camp David accords were signed. He had purged the Egyptian leadership from the pro-Soviet elements in 1971; he expelled Soviet military advisors from Egypt in 1972; he waged a limited war with decent military results for the Arabs after a show of unprecedented military and political coordination, only to allow Kissinger and Nixon to sow dissent and divisions between Sadat and his coalition partners. He shut out the Soviet Union from the diplomatic process that followed the 1973 war; he agreed to Nixon's demand to terminate the Arab oil embargo and initiate a strategy of separate agreements between Egypt and Israel (Sinai I and Sinai II), thus starting Egypt on the path of defection from the Arab camp. Sadat also responded to American and World Bank demands for new economic policies that were more in line with Washington's view of open door policies than with the specific needs of the Egyptian economy. Yet, Washington was slow in responding to Sadat's pleas for inclusion into the American strategic system. It carefully and skilfully used its military deliveries to affect Egyptian economic, political and military priorities. Thus, Egypt was "compensated" after signing the Sinai II accords with the delivery of six C-130 transport airplanes. In the summer of 1977, Washington agreed to sell Cairo fourteen additional C-130s "to enhance Egypt's logistical flexibility."[12] As secret preparations were underway for Sadat's visit to Israel and the pursuit of a separate path, Sadat gave further proof of his desire to firmly belong to the American camp by abrogating the Egypt-USSR friendship treaty and terminating the naval and air privileges enjoyed by the Soviets in Egypt.

To convince Washington of Egypt's strategic value and ability to act as a client State, Sadat enthusiastically supported American strategic designs in the region. Thus, in 1977, Egypt intervened to support the corrupt regime of President Mobutu of Zaire, America's and Israel's ally in Africa, against guerillas threatening his hold on power. In 1979, Sadat offered to intervene to help the pro-American monarchy of Morocco in its war with Algeria. Still, Washington seemed more interested in using its military aid to Egypt specifically for the purpose of getting Sadat to agree to more concessions to Israel that he otherwise might have found difficult to accept. Herman Eilts, former American Ambassador to Egypt, recognized that American promise of increased military aid to Egypt "was significant in persuading President Sadat to accept the Camp David accords and the peace treaty even though he knew that these documents were deficient in expressing Egypt's commitment to the overall Arab cause."[13] It was not until Sadat finally signed the Camp David accords that Washington agreed to compensate him by including Egypt in its Middle-East strategic system. After Camp David, American military sales to Egypt jumped from $68.4 million in 1976 to $937.3 million in 1978.

With the collapse of the Shah's regime in Iran, in January 1979, and the Soviet intervention in Afghanistan in December 1979, American planners set out to rebuild a new strategic consensus in the region. Egypt under Sadat was an eager and ready partner. The Carter administration elaborated and adopted what came to be known as the Carter Doctrine. It put in place a special American force called the Rapid Deployment Force to intervene in the Middle East to protect American interests in the region against threats so broadly defined that they could easily include everything from Soviet intervention to local nationalist revolts; it was another blanket authorization for the use of American power to intervene in distant regions, the Truman Doctrine revisited but in a vastly different international environment no longer as completely dominated by the United States as in the late forties. In conformity with the tenets of the Carter Doctrine, the Pentagon set up a Central Command specifically for the purpose of intervening in the Middle East; military cooperation between the United States and Egypt was enlarged and formalized; two airborne warning and control systems (AWACS) were deployed in Egypt in 1979-1980, and $1.5 billion in military credits was made available to Cairo. Agreements were signed between the two countries for co-production of arms, use of Egyptian military facilities and joint training and maneuvers. On January 1, 1980, U.S. Air force staged military exercises using airborne warning and control systems in Upper Egypt to practise contingency plans for the region. In November of the same year, the U.S. Rapid Deployment Force participated in a two-week long exercise called Operation Bright Star designed to give the American forces practical experience in the Middle Eastern desert. Egypt was being fully integrated into the American strategic system. In 1986, at a top level conference on low intensity conflict, the Rand Corporation proposed that the U.S. develop a multinational low-intensity warfare force to provide support for Third World countries fighting revolutionary movements. The troops for such a force were to be provided by friendly Third World countries which included Jordan, Morocco, Pakistan, Turkey and Egypt.[14] Under Nixon, Washington armed its local allies to defend American interests and do the fighting if necessary; under Reagan the formalization of the Nixon Doctrine with direct American military coordination was proposed; under Bush it all came together in Operation Desert Storm with direct and massive American involvement.

Egypt also cooperated with the French to facilitate their military operations in support of Hissein Habre in Chad against the Libyan-supported rebels.[15] Cairo also acted on behalf of the United States, providing military assistance to the Afghan Mujahideen in their war against the Soviet Union-supported communist regime of Afghanistan in the early 1980s. Sadat also offered the U.S. access to Egyptian military facilities such as the Rais Binas military base on the Red Sea for use for the failed American mission to rescue the American hostages held in Iran in 1980. He continuously urged Washington "to project more military power in the Middle East," and exhorted it to get rid of "the Vietnam complex."[16] In being more Catholic than the Pope, Sadat was basically ignoring the growing domestic opposition to his domestic and foreign policies and scornfully dismissing the unpopularity of his eagerly-assumed role as an American gendarme in the region. He was running a serious risk of meeting the Shah's fate but he foolhardily dismissed the advice to be circumspect in his eager sponsorship of American projections of power. An American observer in Cairo at the time remarked that "American diplomats spoke occasionally of saving Sadat from himself by persuading him to restrain his enthusiastic pro-Americanism."[17] But neither entry into the American strategic system for the region nor the important military sales Washington made to Cairo were significant enough to alter a regional balance of power which, as a result of Sadat's strategies and policies, had become more decisively dominated by Israeli military might.

Hosni Mubarak, who became president of Egypt after Sadat was assassinated in 1981, proved weary of too public an embrace of American goals in the region. Thus, he was reluctant to carry out a joint Egyptian-American plan to attack Libya in 1985. In September of that year, Admiral John Poindexter, President Reagan's National Security Advisor, arrived in Cairo. He met with President Mubarak and urged him to set in motion the previously established Rose Plan for a joint American-Egyptian attack on Libya. Poindexter offered assurances that Egypt would be provided "direct U.S. combat support." The Egyptian President replied: "look, Admiral, when we decide to attack Libya it will be our decision and on our timetable."[18] The American-Egyptian strategic cooperation, however, continued, and joint Egyptian-American military exercises were held more or less regularly.

In August 1986, Egypt participated with American and Israeli naval teams in a search operation for an Israeli submarine allegedly lost off the coast of Alexandria in 1968. American P-3 surveillance aircrafts and S-3 submarine hunting aircrafts were used in the operation. Because of the extreme sensitivity of the operation Egyptian Foreign Ministry sources stated that the search would be conducted by Egyptians with the help of "American equipment." No reference to Israeli involvement was published by the Egyptian press.[19]

By 1987 there were 2,500 American soldiers based in Egypt.[20] By the end of the same year Egypt had received American military equipment and training worth $9.5 billion. The United States sold to Egypt a variety of weapon systems which included Tanks, F-4 and F-16 aircrafts, armoured personnel carriers, artillery, and air defense missiles.

The arming of Egypt was both a compensation for agreeing to Camp David and an inducement to continue the ideological orientation Sadat started. It served two specific functions: it rewarded and strengthened the Egyptian army, the power base of the Sadat regime, and it directed its energy into a subordinate role of useful support for American strategic interests. Both functions carefully fed the process of separating Egypt from its Arabism and ensuring that rearming Egypt would not upset the Israeli-dominated military balance of power in the region. As a result, the underlying principle in the American military deliveries to Egypt remained clearly articulated, unambiguous in its intentions and obvious in its implications: Egyptian inclusion into the American strategic system changed nothing, and could not change anything, in the special American-Israeli strategic relationship. American and Israeli strategic interests, not Egyptian interests, defined the relationship in the tripartite American-Israeli-Egyptian strategic axis. The American ambassador to Egypt frankly stated that "there could be no absolute Egyptian military parity with Israel."[21]

The Israeli Connection: "Normalization" of Israeli-Egyptian Relations

The Israelis wanted more than diplomatic recognition and political and economic relations with Egypt; they sought an acceptance of the ideological underpinnings of their State. This was clearly the goal of the process which came to be most inappropriately called normalization. One would have expected that full diplomatic, political and economic relations would have ushered in as normal a relation as could be expected between former enemies. But Egypt and Israel were no normal enemies. Their disputes did not solely arise from bilateral inter-state conflicts; they encompassed questions about the very legitimacy of the existence of Israel and its responsibilities for the destruction of the Palestinian society which it displaced.

A peace treaty between Egypt and Israel may have ended the belligerency between the two countries and settled their bilateral disputes with regard to Israeli occupation of Egyptian territories. But Israel wanted from its treaty with Egypt more than peaceful bilateral relations. Knowing the central place Egypt occupied in the Arab culture and the Arab world, it wanted a change in the Egyptian view of Israel, its history, and the political ideology underpinning its national existence. This implied that Egypt should engage in a process the end result of which should be ideological acceptance of the Zionist-Israeli enterprise in Palestine. This in turn required renouncing the long-held views about and sympathy for the Palestinian people. Sadat had already put in motion a process whereby Egypt was dissociated from its Arab character. And thus the de-Arabization of Egypt served as a prelude for weakening Egyptian sympathy for the Palestinians on the basis of Arab and Muslim solidarity. The process of normalization the Israelis demanded was supposed to accelerate the separation of Egypt from its support for the Palestinian nation. In short, the Israelis insisted on a systematic process of normalization because, as a Western observer put it, they "expected Egyptians and Arabs to accept the Zionist foundations of their state"[22] And this in turn was expected to deal a serious blow to the Palestinian cause and possibly terminally weaken the Palestinian people's rival claim to Palestine, a longtime goal of political Zionism.

Ismail Fahmy, the Egyptian Foreign Minister who resigned in 1977 in protest against Sadat's visit to Israel, suggested that Israel's insistence on a variety of agreements of normalization between Egypt and Israel was also motivated by a desire to make the separation of Egypt from its Arab environment irreversible even after Sadat's departure. "It was not enough for the Israelis to push Sadat into a situation from which he could not back out," observed Fahmy, "They wanted additional guarantees...probably knowing that the peace agreement was only between Israel and Sadat, but not between Israel and Egypt."[23]

In addition to giving the Egyptian-Israeli contractual commitments priority over other and prior Egyptian contractual obligations to the Arab States, the Egyptian-Israeli treaty also specifically obligated Egypt to separate itself from the Palestinian resistance. Any Palestinian activities directed against Israel may be described as "hostile acts" and Egypt was made legally obligated to consider such acts as criminal offenses and to take the necessary measures against their perpetrators. Article 3 of the treaty provided for the normalization of relations between the two countries including "full recognition, diplomatic, economic and cultural relations," and obligated the signatories to ensure that the perpetrators of acts of "hostility" against either party be brought to justice. The general intent of this provision was clearly to forbid Egypt from providing assistance to the Palestinian resistance which, after being *de facto* banned from Jordan and Syria, has now been legally proscribed from the most important Arab country. Palestinian resistance had nowhere to go except retrench in Lebanon, its last refuge where Israeli leaders will hunt it down and try to militarily wipe it out in 1982.

This legal separation of Egypt from active Palestinian resistance to Israeli occupation was strengthened by a series of agreements on additional measures of normalization designed to bring about a psychological separation of Egypt from the Arab camp generally and from the Palestinian cause specifically. Sadat implicitly and possibly unwittingly accepted these assumptions and acceded to American demands for normalization of relations with Israel without linkage to the progress of the autonomy talks which were going nowhere. Moreover, cognizant of the fact that there was significant opposition in Egypt to the assumptions underpinning normalization, he introduced a number of changes to Egyptian laws to stifle criticisms and outlaw opposition to normalization. In a study of the process of normalization and its impact on Egyptian legislations published in the Egyptian magazine *Al-Dawa* (July, 1981), Egyptian lawyer Adel Aid cited the following decrees and amendments intended to outlaw opposition to normalization with Israel:

a) Presidential decree no. 33 issued on May 3, 1979 during the parliamentary election campaign, to amend section 11 of the People's Assembly Law. The amended text made it a criminal offense to oppose the peace treaty. It stipulated that all political parties and all candidates to the Peoples' Assembly must abide by the principles approved by the Egyptian people in the April 20, 1979 plebiscite. Defiance of that law to be considered an election crime punishable by imprisonment up to 3 years and a maximum fine of three thousand Egyptian pounds. In addition, the offense of opposing the treaty was to automatically result in the loss of the right to run for political office;

b) Law no. 36, 1979, which modified section 4 of the existing law on political parties in Egypt. The changes denied the right to form, or to continue to be leaders of political parties, to any individual with links, connections, or collaboration with any organizations or political parties which opposed the basic principles which Sadat had approved by the 1979 plebiscite. In that referendum, Sadat had asked the Egyptian people to say yes or no to peace and yes or no to the dissolution of the Assembly two years ahead of schedule. According to the official count, 92.2 percent of the electorate turned out for the exercise and of those, the government advanced the usual claim, 99.9 percent approved Sadat's decisions.

c) Law no. 95, of 1980, the so-called Law of Shame. In addition to imposing severe limitations on individual freedoms, the law spelled out more punishments for opposing the peace treaty with Israel. Under this law, a person found guilty of such an offense was to be barred from running for political office, from nominations for a judicial office, and from any administrative office in the public sector or in professional associations. The offender was also to be removed from any job related to information, education, or any position of influence on public opinion.

d) Law 148, of 1980. Section 18 of that law deprived of the right to publish or own newspapers anyone deprived of the right to run for office and the right to belong to political parties and anyone who had been convicted under the previously mentioned laws.

Adel Aid pointed out that these laws had given the treaty with Israel more autonomy and protection in Egypt than the Egyptian constitution itself since there is nothing in the constitution which limits the individual's freedom to criticize it and to call for changes in it. Needless to say nothing of the sort happened in Israel where many Israeli politicians, including Yitzhak Shamir, who would succeed Menahem Begin as Prime Minister, opposed the Camp David treaty.[24]

Article 6 (section 5) of the Egyptian-Israeli peace treaty imposed on Egypt the obligation to give its treaty commitments to Israel priority over its previous defence treaty commitments to the Arab States. Opponents did not fail to point out the serious implications of such encroachment upon Egyptian sovereignty and Egypt's obligations to the Arab nation. Muhsin Awad observed that the treaty meant that "Israel and the United States exchanged the occupation of part of Egyptian territory with the occupation of part of the Egyptian will. Israel will withdraw to the international borders of mandated Palestine, and the United States and Israel will advance to the heart of Cairo to participate in the formulation of its political and economic orientations and the reshaping of its mind and existence to conform with the logic of the American-Israeli peace."[25]

Implementation of "Normalization"

To make normalization a practical reality, high-level standing committees of normalization were established in Israel and Egypt and were placed under the joint authority of the Ministry of Defence and the Ministry of External Affairs. The two central committees established normalization committees in the fields of culture, commerce, tourism, air and land transportation, irrigation, and agriculture. Between 1979 and 1982, Egypt was persuaded to sign more than fifty agreements outlining cooperation in these areas. Agreement was reached on May 8, 1980 for the implementation of additional specific measures of normalization of relations and authority for supervision was transferred to the Ministry of External Affairs in both countries.

Although Sadat accepted and supported normalization and decreed its implementation, he was able to convince few Egyptians of the wisdom of his actions. The major professional associations of doctors, journalists, university professors and lawyers all voted to boycott normalization, with the Egyptian Lawyers Association adopting a particularly active stand and remaining in the forefront of the Egyptian intelligentsia's opposition to normalization. The reactions of most ordinary Egyptians to the implementation of the specific agreements of normalization could be gauged from popular manifestations of protest and opposition which sometimes took the form of violent attacks on Israelis. Thus, when the Israeli embassy was opened in Cairo, on February 8, 1980, while Israeli forces still occupied Egyptian territories, sadness and anger marked the event. The characteristic wailing of Arab women at funerals was heard near the building of the Israeli embassy. Lawyers at the Egyptian Lawyers Association burned two Israeli flags from the top of their building in protest against this "act of betrayal" and "sell out to the Americans," and raised the Palestinian flag on their building.[26] Khalid Muhyi Eddin, one of the original members of the group of Free Officers, who carried out the 1952 revolt, and chairman of the left wing Progressive Unionist Party, told a demonstration of angry Egyptians protesting the event: "The establishment of relations with Tel-Aviv at a time when the Arab territories are still occupied does not represent a new phase of the peace process, it represents a new form of occupation."[27]

The demonstrations of protest and anger against the opening of the Israeli embassy and the arrival of Israel's first ambassador fuelled more anti-Israeli and anti-normalization sentiments in Egypt. Protests spread to the countryside and seem to have touched the peasantry. As Sadat was receiving the diplomatic credentials of Israel's first ambassador to Egypt, an Egyptian farmer named Saad Halawa held two municipal employees in the village of Aghouri, near Cairo, in what might have been the first politically motivated hostage-taking incident in contemporary Egypt. During the 19-hour police siege, Halawa seems to have used a public-address system to broadcast his feelings and his demands. These were expressed in the slogan "No Reconciliation, No Recognition, No Negotiations." He broadcast patriotic speeches of Egyptian President Gamal Abdel Nasser and patriotic songs of the popular singer the late Abdel Halim Hafez. Halawa urged the people to "go out in the streets and demand the fall of Khedive Sadat (in reference to Khedive Ismail whose policies ruined Egypt financially and led to the British invasion and occupation of Egypt in 1882) and his entourage. He (Sadat) must, along with the dogs to whom he sold himself, and the whole world know that struggling Egypt says 'No' to collaboration, betrayal and humiliation."[28] The security forces stormed the building where Halawa was holding up his hostages and shot and killed him. It seems that the incident might have gone unreported had it not been for the fact that a foreign correspondent had filed a story on it which had already been broadcast. The official newspapers Al-Ahkbar and Al-Ahram reported, on February 28, two days after the incident, the official version of what happened and one of these read: "A demented peasant suffering from depression because of his failure at school and his inability to interest the village's young girls in him as a future husband, stormed into the village's council office of Aghouri, in the Kalioubia province, and took two of its employees as hostages. He demanded that his family give him some land, and that the Agricultural Cooperative give him some machinery and fertilizers. He also demanded...the removal of Israel's ambassador from Egypt. But the police force, thank God, intervened, and arrested him after he was wounded."[29]

Continued hostile demonstrations in front of the Israeli embassy raised fears of violent attacks on embassy personnel and the Israeli embassy had to be moved to what was considered a more secure sight: the top floors of a 20-story building at 6 Ibn al-Malik Street near the Nile in Giza. Tight security measures were taken; the street to the embassy was blocked from traffic and a helicopter pad was reportedly placed on the roof. Still, late one night in early 1985, a rocket was fired at the embassy from a car travelling on the adjacent University Bridge; it missed the embassy floor and landed in an apartment in the adjacent building, causing no injuries. The Egyptian government denied that there had been an attempted attack against the Israeli embassy and claimed that the damage had been caused by an air-conditioner that had exploded inside the apartment.[30]

In other areas of normalization, popular boycott seemed to be the order of the day. Thus, on December 17, 1981, Egypt and Israel signed a memorandum of understanding on Tourism after direct travel between the two countries had been established in 1980. The Israeli airline *El-Al* flew three times a week between the two countries, but because of security reasons the departure times of its flights were not posted and its planes did not remain overnight in Egypt. Few Egyptians seemed interested in supporting normalization in tourism between the two countries. And the Egyptian government did not seem anxious to go out of its way to encourage a different behaviour. The result was that the Israelis took advantage of normalization in tourism while Egyptians largely boycotted it. For instance, the number of Israelis visiting Egypt constantly increased from 14,000 in 1980, to 38,000 in 1981, to 45,000 in 1982, and 63,000 in each of 1983 and 1984.[31] Egyptians, however, largely ignored the possibility of visiting Israel. A year after it opened its offices in Cairo, in June 1982, the Israeli Government Tourist Bureau closed for lack of business. The number of Egyptians who visited Israel has remained extremely low. According to some sources up to 90 percent of travellers from Egypt who visit Israel are Palestinians carrying Egyptian travel documents and going to Gaza to visit relatives. Tourism in Israel by Egyptian nationals was described as "virtually nonexistent."[32]

In the area of trade, normalization was not more successful. A bilateral trade protocol between Egypt and Israel was signed in April 1980. But trade between the two countries remained very low with most trade deals arranged through third parties. Outside Egyptian oil, which Sadat undertook to sell to Israel, Egyptian exports to Israel remained insignificant, usually less than $1 million yearly. Israel mainly exported to Egypt agricultural machinery and petrochemical products, often through a third party in Europe. The Egyptian public sector, where nationalist feelings are strong, remained opposed to trade with Israel, and outside the Suez Canal Bank, then controlled by a contractor friend of Sadat's, Egyptian banks were unwilling to handle Israeli accounts.

"Normalization" and Ideological Penetration

Israel expected normalization, as suggested earlier, to bring about some fundamental changes in the Egyptian way of thinking about Israel and by extension about the Israeli-Palestinian conflict. Such was the message clearly delivered to the Egyptian people by Israeli President Yitzhak Navon who, during his visit to Egypt in late October 1980, told his Egyptian hosts: "Cultural exchange is no less important than military and political arrangements; what is depicted about us in your literature and your mass media has no basis whatsoever in reality." Navon urged the Egyptians to work to "keep religion away from Arabic thought, and work for the establishment of a joint Egyptian-Israeli committee composed of intellectuals, writers and scientists...because those who cannot change their ways of thinking cannot change their conditions."[33]

This was also the message which Shimon Shamir, the director of the Israeli Academic Center in Cairo, sought to drive home to the Egyptian intellectuals whom he persistently, and vainly, attempted to bring around to accepting the process of normalization. Shamir was unable to establish any institutional contacts with Egyptian universities. He was also unable to receive lecture invitations at any of the Egyptian universities he contacted to offer his services. Upon his departure in 1984 he expressed regrets that his mission was less successful than he had hoped, and affirmed that in the long run the nature of the peace between Egypt and Israel would be determined by the kind of cultural relations the two countries would develop. In reaction to Shamir's comments, an Egyptian diplomat said: "How can we talk about sending musical bands and artists to Israel when they are massacring people?"[34]

The emphasis the Israelis placed on normalization and its attendant cultural penetration of Egypt bespeaks the importance they attach to the acceptance by Egypt of the tenets of ideological Zionist thought as a means of transforming the nature of the Arab-Israeli conflict. The Camp David peace treaty seriously modified the balance of power in the region and rendered unlikely a repeat of the 1973 successful Arab military, political and economic coordination. Israel expected the process of normalization to undermine any possible Egyptian contributions to Arab ideological opposition to political Zionism. An Egyptian intellectual observed that "Egyptians are expected to accept the ideological foundations of Israel and in this context the series of allegations about Israel's defensive wars; Egypt's unconscious involvement in a conflict that did not concern her; Palestinians' selling their land to the Israelis; the falsity of the calls for Arab union and Arab solidarity; and the inversion of the whole edifice of historical and political truths on which the struggle of the Egyptian and Arab people was built over the past half a century."[35]

Official Egypt, however, proved more responsive than Egyptian intellectuals and professional associations to Israeli demands for normalization in a number of areas including, most significantly, the Egyptian educational system. Thus, the Egyptian school curriculum was modified to reflect "the era of peace," and significant changes were introduced for the indoctrination of Egyptian students into the new realities, Egypt's identity and its place in the world, and the nature of the Arab-Israeli conflict. For instance, an account of the "the Ramadan Crossing" (the 1973 October War) in the Grade Six curriculum was replaced with a story about Rifaah al-Tahtawi — a nineteenth century Egyptian translator of European works; the change is meant to emphasize Egypt's character as a nation looking toward the West. A book called *Arab Nationalism* was removed from the curriculum of the third year of preparatory school and replaced with another book called *The Arab Republic of Egypt and the Modern World.* An Egyptian intellectual described the new book as containing references to Zionism as "a political movement which aims at gathering all the Jews from all over the world and bringing them to Palestine without reference to the racial exclusionist dimensions of the movement, the illegitimacy of its claim on Palestine or the nature of its occupation."[36] The following paragraph was withdrawn from a grade-six geography book: "In 1948, Zionist Jews, assisted by the imperialist powers, succeeded in taking over the land of Palestine. They drove out most of the Arab inhabitants and usurped their land. However, the Palestinians and the Arabs worked toward the liberation of Palestine and the return of the Palestinian people to their homeland."[37] New chapters were added to the history books prescribed for the preparatory and secondary schools in Egypt. The new additions praised the Camp David accords and denigrated the Arabs who were described as "incapable of understanding the international changes."[38]

By 1981, the Egyptian school system reflected the prevalent ideology and the drive to separate Egypt from its Arab milieu. A study of the political education Egyptian children were receiving through their textbooks in history and civic education found that "only 16 percent of instruction was aimed at promoting the sense of belonging to the Arab nation, whereas 54 percent was devoted to Pharaonic Egypt and 30 percent to the Egyptian identity per se...considered independently of the Arabic or Islamic nation."[39] Egypt extracted no similar normalization in the Israeli educational system with regard to the denigrating, reductive and racist representations of Arabs in Israeli school books.[40]

Israel also placed a special emphasis on psychology within the context of normalization of relations. A series of conferences sponsored by the United States was organized around the themes of psychology and conflict in the Middle East and psychology in the Arab-Israeli conflict. The first of these conferences was held in January 1980 at the Watergate hotel in Washington D.C., and focused on internal psychological factors inhibiting negotiations. A second meeting was held in Lausanne, Switzerland and focused on "assault on humanity and its cruelty and how to have peace in the end." A third conference was held in Alexandria, Egypt, in May 1982 and was surrounded with secrecy following the negative reactions to the publicity generated by the Watergate conference. Joint research projects presented at the conference investigated various sources and forms of resistance to normalization and participation in the peace process and appropriate methods of overcoming them. Critics of normalization pointed out that it was a gross oversimplification to reduce the Arab-Israeli conflict to a question of psychological barriers as Sadat mistakenly persisted in doing, and as many of the American, Israeli, and Egyptian conference participants implied in their presentations. Such a reductive context for the analysis of the conflict establishes a wholly inappropriate and unconvincing symmetry between the victim and the victimizer, the oppressed and the oppressor, and is at odds with the existential conditions of the mighty Israelis and subjugated Palestinians. Critics pointed out that Israel was using the symptoms of an ideological conflict to try to pass it off as the roots of the conflict thereby avoiding the indefensible realities of its occupation of Arab lands and its oppression of the Palestinian people. Within this context, normalization and the emphasis it placed on psychology become in fact a vehicle of social engineering for the creation of psychological excuses for Israeli behaviour.[41]

Egyptian Opposition to "Normalization"

Most professional associations as mentioned above were strongly opposed to normalization. The Lawyers Association, the Medical Professions Association, the Association of Egyptian Film Critics, the Association of Egyptian Journalists, and the Federation of Egyptian Artists all publicly stated their opposition to normalization with Israel. The National Federation of University Students, The National Federation of University Professors, The Egyptian Society of Writers and Composers and The Association of Chemical and Nuclear Engineers also publicly declared their opposition to normalization.[42] Typical of the position of the Egyptian professional associations was the statement made by the Association of Egyptian Dentists in the October-November (1983) issue of *Al-Hekma* magazine. It denounced "Israel's attack against Iraq's nuclear plants, its continued occupation of Arab territories in Golan, the West Bank and Gaza, its wanton aggression against brotherly Lebanon, the atrocious massacres in Sabra and Shatila; and Israel's continued policy of building settlements in occupied Arab territories and its attempts to change the character of Arab Jerusalem."[43]

Egyptian intellectuals' opposition to normalization also took the form of individual and institutional boycott of Israeli institutions. Other than Dr. Muhammad Shaalan, of the Al-Azhar University, Professor Abdel-Azim Ramadan, from Menufiyya University, and Ambassador Tahsin Bashir — all three of whom had participated in the Watergate conference on psychology in the Arab-Israeli conflict — very few Egyptian academics agreed to cultivate any relations with visiting Israeli academics. Shaalan, who visited some Israeli academic institutions in October 1980, wrote an article describing his views in the *Jerusalem Post*. He argued that Egypt had made a gesture by recognizing Israel and called on the Israelis to make a similar gesture by recognizing the Palestinian nation, otherwise, he warned, Israel would remain isolated and drag Egypt with it in an Egyptian-Israeli ghetto. Shaalan's views received some support from some Israelis but the Israeli government itself, as a Western observer noted, "was bent on a diametrically opposed policy."[44] Shaalan's visit to Israel was strongly condemned by fellow academics and other Egyptian intellectuals opposed to normalization. Dr. Said al-Nishaii, a professor at Cairo University, wrote an article entitled "The Zionist Penetration Under the American Umbrella." In it al-Nishaii warned against Israeli attempts to circumvent Egyptian intellectuals' opposition to normalization: "The Israelis are following some indirect means of circumventing the almost unanimous popular Egyptian boycott. They are resorting to the American umbrella for help with this problem, just as they used and continue to use the American economic, military and political aid. The current plan consists in getting Zionist professors who have dual Israeli-American citizenship to contact from their American universities Egyptian professors and intellectuals." Al-Nishaii urged continued boycott of Israeli institutions and academics.[45]

Opposition to normalization also took the form of boycotting Israel's representatives in Egypt. Israeli diplomats were unsuccessful in getting the Egyptian intelligentsia to accept them and integrate them into Egyptian cultural life. This may have been due, on the one hand, to the hostility most intellectuals expressed towards normalization and, on the other hand, to the very unpopular personality of Israel's first ambassador to Cairo, Eliahu Ben-Elissar. When a year after his arrival in Egypt, Eliahu Ben-Elissar announced his intention to go back to Israel, the semi-official Egyptian magazine *Rooz El-Yussif* may have expressed the sentiments of most Egyptians who knew the Israeli ambassador when it wrote: "In going back to his country Eliahu Ben-Elissar leaves behind him in Egypt not a single friend. Even those who volunteered to befriend him had to withdraw because the extreme arrogance of Ben-Elissar's behaviour was unique in the diplomatic corps and had not been seen in Egypt since the days of the British occupation."[46]

A majority of Egyptian intellectuals and of the Egyptian educated classes seemed constant in their opposition to normalization and in their belief that real peace with Israel might not be possible. At any rate these were the findings of an opinion poll conducted in 1984 to find out what Egyptian intellectuals thought of Israel and of normalization. The poll surveyed the views of university professors, professionals, journalists and university students. The results showed that 78.5 percent of the participants thought that Israel was organically linked to the United States much like any one of its fifty states; 46 percent of respondents thought that normalization with Israel was impossible whereas only 6 percent thought it possible. On the question of Arab-Israeli relations and Israel's ability to have peaceful relations with the Arabs, 75.5 percent responded negatively and only 24.5 percent thought it was possible.[47]

In March 1984, the Committee for the Defense of the National Culture issued an appeal in *Al-Muwajaha*, published by the leftist opposition, The Progressive Unionist Party. The appeal was entitled "An Appeal to Every Nationalist Egyptian: Boycotting any Scientific and Cultural Activities with Israel is a National and Human Duty." It read in part: "Any participation in any activity in Israel or in Egypt is a violation of the most elementary nationalist principles which impose the obligation of not dealing with the Israeli enemy...which continues to threaten Egypt with reoccupation of Sinai if Egypt departed from the line of behaviour imposed by Israel. Any participation in 'normalization' activities with Israel also violates the principles of Arab solidarity, since the Israeli forces which occupied and destroyed Lebanon, killed thousands of its sons and of the Palestinian people, are still in occupation of Lebanon. Israeli record of crimes keeps growing, from the destruction of the Iraqi nuclear plants to the annexation of Jerusalem which Israel declared to be its unified capital, to the annexation of the Golan Heights...and the oppression by every means of the Arabs in the occupied Palestinian territories."[48] A number of Egyptian intellectuals who opposed normalization with Israel reportedly received death threats in letters mailed in Cairo and attributed by the Israeli newspaper *Ma'ariv* to an extremist right wing Israeli organization headed by Meir Khane[49] (an American citizen who migrated to Israel where he openly advocated the expulsion of the Palestinians en masse and who was subsequently assassinated in New York, in 1990, by an Egyptian immigrant).

Strong opposition to normalization may have been spearheaded by Egyptian intellectuals, but it seems to have had the support of ordinary Egyptians. This was evident from popular demonstrations of protest every time Sadat's zeal for normalization, which often went beyond contractual obligations and political prudence, was advertised. Thus, when it became known that Sadat had promised the Israelis he would alleviate their chronic water supply problems by diverting the much-needed Nile water to Israel, the news was greeted with a storm of popular opposition. The Egyptian Ministry of Foreign Affairs denied that such a project was contemplated. On January 17, 1980, Egyptian Prime Minister Mustapha Khalil strenuously denied that the Egyptian government had any intention of doing such a thing and asserted that Egyptian waters would only serve Egyptian lands. Khalil tried to rationalize Sadat's statements by explaining that President Sadat was only trying to show goodwill but that no such project was ever seriously considered. But official denials were discredited with the publication in August 1980 of letters exchanged between Sadat and Begin and letters exchanged between Sadat and King Mohammad II of Morocco verifying the commitments Sadat had made.[50]

Sadat's gestures of "goodwill" led him to more erratic behaviour. He seems to have become particularly sensitive to the ideological beliefs of the Israeli leaders he hosted in Egypt and went out of his way to avoid criticizing or even confronting them, often to the furious indignation of his Foreign Ministry officials. Thus, while Sadat was meeting alone with Begin at his winter house in Aswan in January 1980, Egypt's Minister of State for Foreign Affairs Boutros Ghali issued a statement to the press saying that there can be no progress in achieving peace between Egypt and Israel unless the Palestinian question was seriously addressed. Begin was furious when he found out about Ghali's statement and reportedly asked Sadat to sack his Minister. Boutros Ghali told me that when he heard about Begin's request to Sadat from the journalists accompanying the two leaders, he took it seriously enough, knowing how sensitive Sadat was to Israeli demands. Reasoning that he was on his way out anyway, Ghali decided to speak his mind and tell Sadat what he really thought of his negotiating style with the Israelis. Ghali said to Sadat: "Mr. President, we agreed at the working session before your meeting with Begin that you would make no concessions to the Israelis concerning the normalization process such as the date of opening the border, the inauguration of air flights between the two countries, unless the Israelis made concessions on the Palestinian issue, and they have made no concessions to you on the Palestinian issue." Sadat flew into a rage and screamed at Ghali: "I made these concessions to Begin to calm him after your silly declarations to the press had angered him. You messed everything up and caused great pain to Begin who could not sleep and was very upset. All this because of you. Who told you to issue a statement saying that there would be no progress in the peace between Egypt and Israel unless there was progress on the Palestinian question?"[51]

When Sadat hosted Israeli President Yitzhak Navon and a group of Labour Party leaders in Cairo, in November 1980, strong criticism from opposition leaders and overt hostility by many Egyptian intellectuals forced the cancellation of Navon's address to the People's Assembly. Similarly, Navon's scheduled visit to the Helwan iron and steel factory was called off because workers threatened massive demonstrations in protest against the visit. Sadat decided to back off this time.

But Sadat felt confident enough, a few months later, to force normalization measures. Thus, when in 1981 the organizers of the Cairo International Bookfair refused an Israeli request to participate with the pretext that the application was made after the deadline, Sadat intervened and imposed Israeli representation at the Fair. When the Fair opened, widespread popular protests forced the Israeli exhibitors to remove the Israeli flag from above their stand; Egyptian protesters distributed leaflets and small decals of Palestinian flags and shouted anti-normalization slogans. Demonstrators clashed with riot police and many Egyptian students and intellectuals were arrested. Among those arrested was the Egyptian writer Nabil al-Hilali who was interrogated by officers of the national security forces. Al-Hilali was reportedly asked: "What is your position on publishing Israeli books in Egypt?" Al-Hilali replied: "I am against any dealings with Israel which remains an enemy as long as it continues to occupy an inch of Egyptian territory, and as long as it remains at war with brotherly Arab countries. This makes it an enemy of the Egyptian people under our constitution, the first article of which stipulates that the Egyptian people are part of the Arab nation, and therefore the enemy of the Arab nation is an enemy of the Egyptian people."[52]

Despite popular protest against Israeli representation at international fairs in Cairo, the Egyptian government proved more sensitive to pressure from Washington and Israel. It decided to exclude Palestinian representation at the fourteenth annual Book Fair in January 1982. However, after the Israeli invasion of Lebanon with its horrifying daily images of massive and indiscriminate Israeli bombardment of civilian areas and of the humiliating siege of an Arab capital, Egyptian opposition to normalization grew fiercer and led the Mubarak government to freeze all bilateral agreements on normalization between Egypt and Israel. Accordingly, the government excluded Israeli representation at the Book Fairs of 1983 and 1984.

When Cairo permitted Israeli participation at the International Fair of January 1985, the decision provoked a storm of protest from Egyptian intellectuals. The Egyptian government placed the Israeli booth on the second floor of Pavillion 3, whereas all the other exhibitors were represented on the first floor. The government also decided that there would be no national flags either outside the Fair compound or in front of individual booths. When the Egyptian Prime Minister arrived for the official opening of the Fair he was greeted, as he entered the Palestinian booth, with shouts of "Palestine is Arab" from the crowds. The shouts intensified as the Prime Minister headed for the Israeli section on the second floor. The commotions and hostile shouts finally forced him to cut short his visit to the Israeli section of the pavilion. When shortly after, the government learned that a large demonstration was being organized for Friday, when the Fair was to open its doors to the general public, it decided to close the exhibition hall of the Fair on Thursday, only three days after its official opening. This meant that the Israeli booth, located in the exhibition hall, would not remain for the rest of the duration of the International event. The American embassy protested to the Egyptian government within 24 hours of the publication by the Egyptian press of the government decision. The Egyptian government gave in and decided to keep the exhibition hall open for 5 more days. On the day of the opening, Friday, January 25, Egyptian demonstrators carrying banners proclaiming Egypt's and Palestine's Arabism and shouting anti-Camp David and anti-normalization slogans, gathered in front of the building where the Israeli booth was located and burned the Israeli flag. On Sunday, another and much larger demonstration took place. After shouting anti-Israel and anti-Camp David slogans the demonstrators held a public meeting in front of the building housing the Israeli section. The speakers included representatives of the political opposition as well as representatives of Egyptian intellectuals opposed to normalization. These included Dr. Said al-Nishaii who spoke against it on behalf of the Faculty Association of the University of Cairo.

On January 22, the Egyptian Lawyers Association held a press conference which was attended by Egyptian intellectuals and representatives of the local, Arab and international media. Mohamed Fahim Amin, the Secretary General of the Association told the Conference: "Our association has from the very beginning adopted clear and frank positions against the Camp David accords and the 'normalization' of relations between Egypt and Israel. We have raised the Palestinian flag since 1978 and it will remain there on top of our building until it returns to its original place in its own country. The Egyptian Lawyers Association shall continue to oppose imperialism and Zionism and shall remain a place of refuge to all freedom-lovers and a citadel for freedom and democracy. If the enemy continues to insist on forced 'normalization' we shall oppose it forever."[53]

The Egyptian press, both opposition and government newspapers, devoted a great deal of attention to Israeli presence at the 1985 Cairo Bookfair. Following the news that Israel would be permitted to participate in the Fair, the Egyptian newspaper *Ahkbar al-Yum* (a government paper) published a caricature showing Israeli leader Yitzhak Shamir displaying five Israeli books bearing the following titles "Sabra and Shatila," "Invasion of Lebanon," "Bombardment of Iraqi Nuclear Reactor," "Annexation of Golan," and "Annexation of Jerusalem." The caption underneath read: "Israel at the Cairo Bookfair" and underneath it: "A free advertisement published by *Ahkbar al-Yum* for the Israeli booth at the Bookfair." Another caricature published by the opposition paper *Al-Ahali* on January 16, mocked the Egyptian government cooperation with normalization measures and its role in spreading Israeli ideas and ideological beliefs. It showed a policeman and a peasant engaged in a heated debate about Israeli books at the Fair. The policeman is shown protesting and saying: "Not at all, these are not imported ideas, they are now being made right here locally."[54] In addition to critical articles in the opposition papers, government newspapers also published articles criticizing Israeli participation at the Cairo Bookfair. In an article entitled "From the Heart" Muhsin Mohamed wrote in the government-supported *Al-Jumhouria*: "There is a clear precedent for all of this. And that is the refusal to travel to Israel of Egyptian businessmen, popular and professional organizations, and Egyptian tourists, even though Israeli tourists have been coming to Egypt...There is nothing in this Egyptian position to suggest religious fanaticism, on the contrary Egyptians welcomed (Sadat's) visit to Jerusalem and the various peace initiatives in the hope that they would lead to peace and prevent another war between the two countries. This Egyptian position was in reality an expression of the hope that Israel would withdraw from the occupied Arab territories and return Jerusalem, and when this did not happen, the Egyptians realized that Israel had never changed."[55]

On Friday, February 1, about 3,000 demonstrators held another public meeting at the International Bookfair. In addition to members of the political opposition, representatives of professional associations, the Egyptian Lawyers Association, the Egyptian Federation of University Professors, the Egyptian Federation of University students and members of the Committee for the Defense of the National Culture participated and spoke at the demonstration. All condemned normalization with Israel and promised that the struggle against it shall continue.[56] At the 1986 Cairo International Book Fair, Egyptian protests against normalization took a violent turn when three Israelis were shot, one was killed by members of the organization "Egypt Revolution."

Egypt Isolated and Israel Freed

At the regional level the most significant consequence of Camp David has been the neutralization of Egypt as a force in the Arab-Israeli conflict and the removal of the threat of another 1973-like coordinated Arab military effort. This left Israeli leaders free for the first time since the establishment of the State of Israel in 1948 to pursue the destruction of whatever is left of the Palestinian society and the dispersal of its people, largely unconcerned by Arab reactions. The Israeli invasion of Lebanon, encouraged by the United States,[57] and launched precisely for the purpose of liquidating the Palestinian resistance once and for all, would ultimately fail to achieve its goal of "final solution" for the Palestine question. But the invasion did serve to illustrate the success of Camp David in neutralizing Egypt and consecrating the hegemonic militaristic domination of Israel over the region, an inevitable result given the nature of Egyptian-American relations, on the one hand, and the "special relationship" between Israel and the United States, on the other.

No sooner had Sadat signed Camp David that he realized that in the triangular relationship between the U.S., Israel and Egypt, American aid was subordinated to Egypt's acquiescence in Israeli actions. He could hardly fail to understand Washington's intentions; they were often bluntly articulated to him and to Egyptian officials. Egypt was in effect, as the American ambassador to Egypt pointed out, "judged by Washington on how it conducted itself toward Israel."[58] U.S. Aid imposed guidelines on Egypt that subordinated Egyptian internal needs to peace with Israel and oriented programmes and researchers in the direction of normalization of relations between Egypt and Israel. The guidelines clearly stipulated that to be eligible for American aid, Egyptian projects had to "involve both Arab and Israeli participation, with clear evidence of support and participation from both sides...and have development focus or *make substantive contributions to normalization of relations.*"[59] (emphasis added). One hardly needs to add that no similar restrictions were imposed on American aid to Israel for the purpose of "normalizing" its coercive and abnormal relations with the Palestinians.

Although effective in using its aid to pressure Egypt into greater normalization of relations with Israel, the United States was unable to restrain Israeli behaviours in the region and protect Sadat from the humiliating spectacle of moving closer to Israel even as its leaders were lashing out against Arabs and Palestinians. Both Israel and the United States seemed little concerned about how the Egyptian people would perceive their leader or what consequences growing opposition to his policy could ultimately produce. Thus, shortly after Egypt signed a protocol for cultural cooperation with Israel, thereby making it a criminal offense in Egypt to oppose Camp David, Israel completed its annexation of Arab Jerusalem by extending its judiciary system to the old Arab city, infuriating many Egyptians and strengthening opposition to Camp David. In February 1981, The Socialist Labour Party, then the major opposition party in Egypt, withdrew its support of Camp David and raised the Palestinian flag on its headquarters. There were more dramatic instances of public humiliation for Sadat. On June 7, 1981, only two days after his meeting with President Sadat, Israeli Prime Minister Begin sent his air force to bombard Iraqi nuclear plants. Seymour Hersh reported in his recent book *The Samson Option* that the raid could not have been made without the help of the ultra-secret satellite intelligence pictures the United States pledged in 1979 to share with Israel, the only country to benefit from this intelligence gathering. In July of the same year, Israel launched a massive air strike against residential West Beirut, in which 300 civilians were killed and 800 wounded. Egyptians were stunned; the few supporters of Camp David were speechless and anger and frustration swept across the spectrum of political ideologies. Sadat was shocked and unable to explain not only what happened to Lebanon but increasingly what had happened to his enthusiastic support for Camp David and for normalization. Humiliated Egyptians blamed it all on their president and many Egyptians, as one Egyptian professor put it, "perceived their president either as a fool or as a traitor."[60]

Sadat desperately looked to Washington to extricate him out of this humiliating and increasingly dangerous predicament. But once more he was forced to confront the failure of his "strategic thinking" which had led him to gamble that he could substantively affect the special relationship between the United States and Israel. In 1981, Ronald Reagan had come to the White House unabashedly committed to Israel as a strategic asset in the Middle East whose problems he simplistically and conveniently reduced to communism and Kremlin-backed terrorism. As a result, Reagan was reportedly astonished by Sadat's public interest in the Palestinian question which, in Reagan's view, had already been settled by the Camp David accords. When Sadat came to Washington in August 1981, he received a warm welcome but no commitment from the American President to exert any pressure on Israel to modify its behaviour, to change its policy of repression and dispossession, or to make any commitments to withdrawing from the occupied Arab territories. Sadat returned to Egypt empty-handed, humiliated, feeling lonely and extremely dejected at being let down by his American friends whom he expected to be "full partners," willing to save him from the humiliation Israeli actions were inflicting on him. Unable to translate peace with Israel into stability in the region and prosperity in Egypt, wielding no influence with his American allies and Israeli friends, and isolated in the Arab world, Sadat faced mounting opposition at home after his failed trip to Washington. He responded in his usual dramatic style with what he called "a purge." In September 1981, he arrested and threw in jail 1,500 opposition leaders, intellectuals, writers and religious leaders, sparing no one, not even the seventy-year old Supreme Guide of the Muslim Brotherhood, Omar al-Telmissany.

Nawal al-Sadawi, a leading Egyptian feminist, was among those intellectuals Sadat arrested. She wrote from her prison: "I had been looking for a satisfactory reason for my arrest and the arrest of this enormous number of people of such different persuasions, tendencies and ideas. Those people whom Sadat arrested had nothing in common except their opposition to the peace with Israel."[61] On October 6, 1981, Sadat was assassinated by army officers belonging to a militant Islamic group.

Sadat's vice-President, Hosni Mubarak, succeeded him as president. Mubarak lost no time in reassuring the American ally that "the policy of Sadat is going on."[62] The new Egyptian president respected the substance of Sadat's policy while adopting a less confrontational attitude vis-à-vis the opposition which Sadat had usually silenced or rounded up and threw in jail. He released almost 50 percent of those arrested by Sadat in his latest purge and allowed the republication of opposition newspapers. But Mubarak also reaffirmed his commitment to the two pillars of Sadatism: open-door economic policy at home, on the one hand, and, on the other hand, continued support for the Egyptian-Israeli treaty and for the strategic partnership between Washington, Tel-Aviv and Cairo.

This commitment was soon to be put to the test and to prove unwavering. As the final Israeli withdrawal from the Sinai was about to be completed, the Egyptian Ambassador in Israel gave this remarkable interview to the Jerusalem Post (April, 25, 1982). The ambassador made statements which bespoke clearly the Mubarak government's commitment to Camp David, and to the process of normalization and its ideological implications:

> Q. Do you think that the Egyptian-Israeli treaty is strong enough to withstand the absence of progress in the autonomy talks after the Sinai is returned next week?
>
> A. It is not subject to cancellation
>
> Q. Regardless of what happens to the autonomy talks?
>
> A. Regardless of anything
>
> Q. Even if Israel annexed the West Bank?
>
> A. Even if it annexed the West Bank.

The Jerusalem Post reporter added that the Egyptian ambassador believed that the peace treaty could withstand "not only the continuing impasse on the autonomy talk, but the shock of Israeli invasion of Lebanon."[63] The subsequent events were to prove that the Egyptian ambassador's remarks faithfully reflected the Mubarak government's position on Camp David.

A few weeks after the interview of the Egyptian Ambassador was published, Israel launched, on June 6, 1982, a full-scale invasion of Lebanon. There may have been no connections between the two events, but it is reasonable to assume that whatever doubts may have existed within the Israeli leadership regarding Egypt's reactions to the invasion were put to rest by the assurances provided by the Egyptian government and publicly confirmed by its ambassador in Israel. Still, the Israeli action shocked the Egyptian supporters of Camp David and left them deeply embarrassed. At the same time, it strengthened the position of the Camp David critics and of those who had argued that it was impossible to live in peace with Israel because its very existence was predicated on the destruction of the Palestinian nation, and this no Egyptian could accept. Israeli leaders claimed that their invasion of Lebanon would be limited to southern Lebanon, much like their previous invasion of that country in 1978. But in Egypt very few people were prepared to believe anything from Israeli leaders; and sure enough Egyptian cynicism was confirmed when Israeli leaders' claims turned out to be yet another deceptive strategy; Israeli troops carried their war machine all the way to Beirut, encircling, besieging and starving the Arab capital as Israeli air force mercilessly reduced it to rubble in a frenzy of indiscriminate bombings that spared no one. It was impossible to find anyone in Egypt to speak in support of Camp David and those who had supported it in the past either kept an embarrassed silence or spoke out and admitted that they had clearly been fooled. Egyptian intellectuals who had believed that Camp David could bring peace to the region argued that Israel saw in Camp David nothing more than an effective means of removing Egypt from the Arab-Israeli and Israeli-Palestinian conflicts. Even supporters of Sadat's initiatives and of the separate peace treaty with Israel argued that had Sadat lived he would have changed his mind about Israel. Saad Eddin Ibrahim, writing in the government-supported newspaper *Al-Jumhouria* gave the following typical analysis:

> What Israel aims to achieve from the peace treaty with Egypt:
> ...the peace treaty with Egypt was meant to accomplish one thing, and only one thing from Israel's point of view: and that is the neutralization of Egypt and its removal from the Arab-Israeli conflict. It then becomes possible for Israel to realize all its strategic plans for the region which are the following:
>
> 1. The elimination of the Palestinian resistance and the dispersal of the rest of the Palestinian people from the occupied territories.
> 2. The annexation of the West Bank and Gaza to Israel once and for all.
> 3. The consolidation in fact and in law of the annexation of the Golan Heights.
> 4. The annexation of part of southern Lebanon and the control of the sources and the water of the Litani river.
> 5. The elimination of any emerging Arab military power at an early stage.
> 6. The elimination of any Arab or Islamic nuclear potentials in the region extending from Pakistan to Morocco, a region which (Israeli general) Ariel Sharon considers to be Israel's legitimate security zone in which it is entitled to intervene.
> 7. The establishment of confessional and sectarian mini-states in the Middle East which will be controlled by Israel militarily and politically, on the one hand, and, on the other hand, will help add to Israel's racial existence a form of "legitimacy."
> 8. The Menahem Begin government has been busy implementing these seven strategic goals since it came to power in Israel in 1977, and has not allowed the peace treaty with Egypt to delay by one minute the execution of these plans. On the contrary, the security provided by Egypt's removal from the struggle has hastened their implementation. Thus, in the past four years Israel has built twice as many settlements as it had built in the previous ten years. It completed the annexation of Arab Jerusalem, annexed the Golan Heights, destroyed Iraq's nuclear reactors, violated Saudi Arabia's and Jordan's air space several times, intensified its campaign

of oppression against the Palestinian people in the West Bank and Gaza, and dropped tons of bombs on civilians in Beirut and in the Palestinian refugee camps.

...It is a mistake to think that the Reagan administration has no clear policy in the region. Maybe it does not have a publicly stated policy. But as a superpower, it cannot afford not to have a policy in this vital region of the world. And how else can one explain the American decision to increase its economic aid to Israel only two weeks before the Israeli invasion of Lebanon? And how else can one explain the American decision to sell 75 new F-16 combat aircrafts to Israel only ten days before the Israeli invasion of Lebanon? And what is the significance of the statement made in Washington that the strategic cooperation between the two countries (frozen by Washington after Israel annexed the Golan Heights) has been revived only a week before the invasion? And how can we explain the American decision to use its veto every time the UN Security Council agrees to a resolution to condemn or impose sanctions on Israel? There may be no American public policy but the total sum of American behaviour leaves no doubt about the undeclared American policy: giving Israel all it needs for its existence, aggression, and domination...so that it may impose an order in the Middle East compatible with their interests. There is no other explanation...We believe that had Sadat survived the assassination he would have changed his views about many of the statements he made with good intentions, particularly those related to Israel. That is why we say to the decision makers in Egypt that Egyptian regional policy must be totally reviewed. Egypt cannot deceive itself and content itself with verbal condemnations of the Israeli aggression against Lebanon...Israel must not be allowed to interpret Egypt's commitment to the peace treaty as a license to sow destruction in the Arab Middle East.[63]

As the Israeli invasion of Lebanon began to take the full dimensions it finally acquired, the pressure grew on President Mubarak to take some actions. He resisted calls for the repudiation of Camp David and allowed the flow of Egyptian oil to Israel to continue uninterrupted. Washington was assured that "Camp David is a fact." Still, the Israeli siege of Beirut and the daily images of indiscriminate Israeli bombardments of an Arab capital led to massive angry demonstrations in Egypt. The day the PLO fighters left Beirut, wrote Saad Eddin Ibrahim, was a moment of "profound sadness all over Egypt...mixed with an amorphous collective sense of guilt and impotence."[65] Had it not been for Camp David, which removed Egypt from the Arab camp, it was frequently argued, it is unlikely that the Israelis would have wreaked so much destruction on the Lebanese and Palestinian peoples, and inflicted great humiliation on the Arabs by besieging and mercilessly bombing an Arab capital. The massacre of Palestinians in Sabra and Shatila by the

Phalangists, armed, protected and aided by the Israeli army, finally made Mubarak decide that he could no longer ignore the Egyptian people's demands for actions. He responded to Egyptian anger by recalling Egypt's ambassador from Tel-Aviv.

Ironically enough, the year 1982 witnessed "the consolidation of the 'normalization' programs with Israel."[66] Thus, trade with Israel during the year 1982 actually increased, with the greatest portion of the increase taking place as the Israeli army stormed the capital of Lebanon and drove the Palestinians out of Beirut. Israel exported to Egypt $48 million worth of goods, with $7.5 million during the first quarter of 1982, jumping to $40 million during the last four months of the year. President Mubarak also allowed the flow of Egyptian oil to Israel to continue uninterrupted during the height of the Israeli invasion of Lebanon, despite rising demands for stopping Egyptian oil deliveries to Israel. Typical of Egyptian opposition in this regard was Egyptian parliamentarian Tawfiq Zaghlul's protest to the government against the policy of providing Egyptian oil "to the Israeli tanks that are killing the Palestinian and the Lebanese peoples."[67]

Violence, Turmoil and Reassessment

After the Israeli invasion of Lebanon, it was no longer possible to publicly associate Camp David with the so-called peace process. Camp David was now perceived by most Egyptians and Arabs as responsible for the killing of thousands of innocent Palestinian and Lebanese civilians. It became synonymous with a process more related to war and destruction than to genuine peaceful co-existence. Camp David's remaining few supporters in Egypt had nothing to say while its critics charged on the attack. Egypt had been duped, it was frequently argued, into abandoning its traditional Arab leadership role in a "peace process" that gave Israel the strategic advantage of dividing the Arabs and enabled it to wage war against the Palestinians and the Lebanese. The perceived complicity of the United States in the Israeli invasion of Lebanon embarrassed the pro-American Egyptian elements of the government and fuelled anti-American sentiments.

The few Egyptian intellectuals who had championed Camp David and the normalization of relations with Israel admitted having been deluded by Israel and the United States. Tawfiq al-Hakim, Egypt's dean of letters and champion of the Egypt-first thesis, concluded that he "had been deceived in his search for peace with Israel."[68] Anis Mansour, one of the most prominent Egyptian writers who had become chief advocate of normalization with Israel, wrote: "There is not a single voice in Egypt that has not disavowed its previous faith in the possibility of total peace with Israel...We had reconciled with Israel looking forward to the possibility of comprehensive peace...It turned out to be a mistake."[69] Mounting Egyptian anger against Israeli actions in the region led to more violent attacks on Israelis in Egypt. The "Revolution of Egypt" headed by civilian and military men who included Khalid Abdel Nasser, son of the late President, engineered several armed attacks against Israeli diplomatic and military personnel in Cairo. The Israeli military attaché was shot and wounded on June 4, 1984, and an Israeli diplomat was shot and killed on August 20, 1985. Many of the members of the revolutionary group were hunted down and eventually arrested in 1987. Significantly, it was reported that many of the changes that took place in the high ranks of the Egyptian army shortly thereafter came after the government realized the extent of support the "Revolution of Egypt" had acquired within the Egyptian army where disaffection was gaining ground.[70]

In response to mounting popular anger in Egypt, the government suspended the normalization process with Israel. In addition, President Mubarak took, in December 1983, the first step toward Egypt's return to the Arab fold without repudiating the separate treaty with Israel. He received PLO chairman Yasser Arafat and emphasized Egypt's support for the Palestinians' right to self-determination.[71]

But the Mubarak government's rapprochement with the Palestinians brought Cairo in conflict with Washington in an incident which was as humiliating as it was revealing of the nature and the limits of the Egyptian alliance with the U.S. When on October 7, 1985 four Palestinian guerrillas high-jacked the Italian liner Achille Lauro, the Egyptian leaders successfully convinced them, after an American hostage had been killed, to surrender and to release the rest of the hostages. President Mubarak arranged for an Egyptian civilian plane to fly the four Palestinians to stand trial in Tunis by the PLO, who had condemned the highjacking. But the CIA, which according to the well-informed Bob Woodward "had the Egyptian government wired electronically and had agents from top to bottom"[72] intercepted Mubarak's phone conversations and learned the top secret details of the Egyptian flight arrangements. The Egyptian plane carrying the four Palestinians was intercepted by U.S. Navy F.14 fighters over the Mediterranean, and forced to land at a NATO base in Sicily, Italy, where the four Palestinians were abducted by Italian authorities.[73] Enraged Egyptians denounced the American action as an act of air piracy. To the Egyptian people the incident offered a dramatic illustration of the subordinate nature of Egypt's role within the American strategic alliance. To President Mubarak, in addition to his public humiliation, the incident revealed the extent of American spying inside Egypt. It was a sobering realization of the limits of Egypt's power vis—à-vis the United States, the "full partner" in the peace process.

Another Israeli strike against an Arab country further eroded the already weakened Camp David constituency in Egypt. The Israeli bombing of the PLO headquarters in Tunis on October 1, 1985 provoked in Egypt widespread anger which exploded into a popular demonstration during the funeral of two Egyptians who had been killed during the Israeli raid. The Israeli action was universally seen as an outrageous act of State terrorism and Egyptian opposition calls for the repudiation of Camp David became more strident. Israel was clearly taking full advantage of the military neutralization of Egypt in the Arab-Israeli conflict, not only to impose its hegemony on the Middle East but also to extend its militarism to the zone defined by General Ariel Sharon as representing Israel's legitimate security area: from Pakistan to Morocco. Many Egyptians perceived their country as having been relegated to an irrelevant role in the Arab-Israeli conflict. An atmosphere of rising tension enveloped the country with many people in the capital expecting upheavals and calamities in the region and even in Egypt itself. Events seemed to be getting out of control, acquiring their own unstoppable momentum of chaos driven by anger and frustrations. And once more Egyptians felt helpless.

On October 5, 1985, Suleiman Khater, an Egyptian military conscript serving in Ras Burka (Sinai), shot a group of Israeli tourists who had started to climb toward his post, killing seven of them. The government claimed that Khater had gone berserk, and President Mubarak tried to minimize the shooting by calling it "a small incident." Egyptian intellectuals, students, and opposition leaders turned the incident into a *cause célèbre*, claiming that Khater's act was fair revenge for the Israeli bombardment of the PLO Headquarters in Tunis five days earlier. The most prominent lawyers in Egypt volunteered to defend Khater whose actions were compared to the patriotic acts of members of the Egyptian resistance to the British occupation. Khater was tried in camera and sentenced to life imprisonment by a martial court. Shortly thereafter, the government announced that he had committed suicide, a claim many people were unwilling to believe.

Coming at a time when anti-American and anti-Israeli sentiments were fuelled by the Israeli bombardment in Tunisia and the humiliation suffered at the hands of the Americans, the Khater trial and the announcement that he had committed suicide touched off massive demonstrations. In their frustrations and sense of impotence, many Egyptians saw Khater as a sort of folk hero who had the courage to respond to Israel's outrageous actions in the region. Demonstrators and opposition papers called for the abrogation of the Camp David Treaty. In an article entitled "Suleiman Khater's War and Israel's Peace" Muhsin Awad summed up the feelings of many of those Egyptian intellectuals whose opposition to normalization seemed vindicated by Israeli and American behaviours in the region:

> There hasn't been in Egypt since the 1919 revolution as many signatures as there were for Suleiman Khater…There hasn't been a trial which became a trial of public opinion as much as that of Suleiman Khater. And although what this young soldier did may have been subject to differences of opinion; and although some may disagree that what he did was a national duty, the man has become a sort of a great referendum in which the Egyptian people expressed their feelings loudly and clearly on the most important issue it has dealt with in the past few years: the issue of the relations with Israel, or more exactly the issue of Egypt's orientation.
>
> Israel's leaders demanded his head…And quickly he was transferred to a military tribunal and just as quickly he was tried under the provisions of martial law — which the government had previously promised not to use except in case of outside aggression or terrorist attacks — ignoring the request of the defense counsellors to refer the trial to the judiciary system. The government also ignored the protestations of the defense counsellors who were denied access to the documents related to the charges. The authorities also refused to take into account medical opinions about the psychological condition of Khater who was deemed sane and responsible for his actions. He was accordingly sentenced to life in prison. On the day following his death the newspaper *Al-Ahram* treated us to the opinions of three professors of psychology about the instability of Khater's mental health. In a

commentary unique in its absence of logic, the respectable newspaper deduced that Khater's psychological condition led to his suicide. Thus the man was sane enough to assume the responsibility of the accident and be sentenced to life in prison, but unstable enough to choose suicide. This is one of the miracles of the Egyptian media.[74]

An American academic who was in Cairo at the time and witnessed first hand the extent of popular frustrations, anger, and the upheavals which swept Egypt in opposition to normalization commented: "Given the growing Egyptian anger at Israeli actions in Lebanon, and at the failure of all efforts to obtain concessions for the Palestinians, it is striking that there were no known attacks on Israeli diplomats or tourists for more than five years"[75] after the signing of the Egyptian-Israeli treaty.

In February 25, 1986 the serious riots many Egyptians had feared and predicted began to materialize. Major units of the Central Security Forces, stationed in Giza across the Nile from Cairo, mutinied against the State. Their revolt spread quickly to other units in Upper Egypt but most of the damage and violence took place in Cairo where several thousands looted, burned, and destroyed hotels, stores, cars, and nightclubs in the pyramid district — Egypt's main tourist area. Clashes with riot troops and the repression of the mutiny left 700 dead and 716 wounded.[76] Many reasons were advanced to explain the underlying causes of the mutiny, some were cast in economic terms, others were related to the collective psychology of the rioters. They had been engaged in quelling demonstrations of angry students and popular riots of protest against Israeli actions, and many of them basically sympathized with the underlying causes of the riots they were called upon to repress; their mounting anger was increasingly directed at the State apparatus. This repressed anger exploded into open revolt after the dramatic fate meted out to Suleiman Khater seems to have personally touched many members of the Central Security Forces to whom Khater was a comrade and a sort of a hero. Significantly, many Egyptian observers agreed that had the rioters not resorted to violence and destruction many more Egyptians, angered by rumours of bribery and corruption in high circles, would have joined the revolt and transformed it into a mass uprising with wholly unpredictable consequences.

Reorientation

President Mubarak inherited Camp David and its contractual obligations. He accepted the legality of the Egyptian-Israeli treaty but showed none of the exuberance and zeal his predecessor had for the process of normalization. He carried out contractual commitments under Camp David, such as oil deliveries to Israel even during its invasion of Lebanon and the opening of the Israeli Academic Center in Cairo. He reacted with restraint to the Israeli invasion of Lebanon and resisted calls for the severance of diplomatic relationship with Tel-Aviv. He allowed medical relief supplies from Egypt to Lebanon but refused to heed calls for sending Egyptian volunteers to fight in Beirut. On the other hand, following the Israeli invasion of Lebanon, Mubarak stopped any pressure on Egyptian intellectuals to meet with Israelis and reportedly conveyed the new orientation to the presidents

of the Egyptian universities which had come under pressure from Sadat to host Israeli visitors and to promote normalization.

At the same time, Mubarak set out to repair the damage done to Egypt's
reputation in the Arab world in an attempt to restore a measure of respectability to
its role in the Islamic and non-aligned organizations. To that end, he refused to visit
Israel because of Israeli insistence that he go to Jerusalem, a visit he deemed incon-
sistent with Israeli actions designed to eradicate the Arab character of the city and
defy the international community's position on Jerusalem. Mubarak did, however,
return the Egyptian Ambassador to Tel-Aviv when Israel accepted arbitration on
the disputed Taba strip (eventually settled in Egypt's favour) and withdrew from
most of Lebanon in 1985.

Mubarak was interested in and worked towards restoring Egypt's credentials in the Arab world. He received Arafat in Cairo in 1983 and stressed Egypt's
support for Palestinian self-determination. In cooperation with France, the
Mubarak government developed a Franco-Egyptian peace plan for the Middle
East which was put forward at the United Nations Security Council in 1983 but
never came to a vote because of opposition from the United States. Mubarak
personally attended the Non-Aligned Countries Summit in New Delhi in 1983. A
year later he managed to get Egypt's membership in the Islamic Conference
Organization restored. He also played an active role in brokering the Palestinian-Jordanian accord of 1985 in preparation for peace negotiations with Israel
which never materialized. During Shimon Peres' trip to Alexandria in 1986,
Egyptian Prime Minister Dr. Ali Lutfi reportedly went so far as to state to Peres
that the Palestinian question was a question of domestic and national security
for Egypt.[77] A position which tended to negate normalization's chief objective of
legally and psychologically separating Egypt from the Palestinian cause. In his
Arabic review of Egyptian foreign policy from 1983 to 1990 *Al-Seyassa al-
Kharighia al-Meisria*, Boutros Ghali reported that at their Alexandria meetings,
September 11-12, Mubarak persuaded Peres to accept the idea of an international peace conference.

Mubarak also personally attended the Islamic Conference Summit in Kuwait
in 1987 where he affirmed Egypt's appurtenance to the Islamic world and its
responsibility to contribute to its development. Furthermore, the Mubarak
government also worked to improve Egypt's damaged relations with the Soviet
Union and by 1984 full diplomatic relations between the two countries were restored. Soviet-Egyptian trade improved and by 1986 Egypt had become the largest
trading partner of the Soviet Union in the Arab world. In March 1987, Moscow
agreed to re-schedule Egypt's debt, estimated at $3 billion and, in April, an agree-
ment was reached to resupply Egypt with spare parts for Soviet weapons used by
the Egyptian army.[78]

At home Mubarak allowed a greater measure of liberalization and
democratization than his predecessor was willing to contemplate. As a result, the
opposition Wafd Party contested in court, in 1984, and won a decision invalidating
the law enacted under Sadat which had prevented the party from participating in
Egypt's political life. All opposition papers, with the exception of those of the Muslim Brotherhood, were allowed to resume publication. Most professors and journalists fired by Sadat from their positions for having opposed normalization and/or
Camp David were reinstated in their former positions. In his attempts to stifle op-

position to normalization Sadat had also passed a law allowing him to personally chose the leadership of the Egyptian Lawyers Association which had been most active and vocal in its opposition to normalization with Israel. Under the Mubarak regime, the Lawyers Association challenged the law in court and won.

Government papers were allowed to join opposition papers in denouncing Israeli actions in the region and American support for Israeli hegemony. As a result, articles critical of Camp David and of Israeli and American policies began appearing in government papers where it was frequently argued that inclusion of Egypt in the American-Israeli strategic alliance was meant to serve the interests of the United States and Israel at the expense of Egypt and the Arabs. "The United States policy," wrote an Egyptian academic in *Al-Ahram*, "supports the Israeli offensive power to enable Israel either to impose the continuation of the status quo and the occupation of Arab territories, or to negotiate from a position of overwhelming strength…The American-Egyptian military cooperation was based on the fundamental imperative of always keeping Egypt militarily inferior to Israel."[79] The imperative of subordinating Egyptian interests to American-Israeli strategic interests was indeed a constant of the Egyptian-American-Israeli strategic alliance. Increasingly, it was becoming a source of exasperation to the military in Egypt who are woefully aware of the growing inferiority of the Egyptian army vis-à-vis the Israeli army. A longtime Western observer of the Middle East noted: "It is a grievance of the Egyptian military that since it has become Egypt's main arms supplier, the U.S. makes sure that, in quantity and quality, the Egyptians fall further and further behind the Israelis." Field Marshal Abu Ghazala, then Egypt's Defence Minister, told a parliamentary committee that "the basic danger" to Egypt still came from Israel. He invoked the Arab Defence Pact of 1950 claiming that "our commitment to the Arabs overrides any other commitment, including Camp David."[80]

At the same time, the huge technological advance of the Israeli army over all the Arab armies combined was made more dramatic by public revelations about Israel's nuclear capabilities and by the launch, in September 1988, of Israel's first satellite, Offeq I. Although the Egyptian media played down the event, the military in Egypt could not avoid coming to terms with its obvious significance and implications. "The danger lies not so much in the satellite," said Former Defence Minster Lieutenant General Mohammed Fawzi, "but in the rocket which blasted it off. It means that Israel can hit any target in the Arab world,"[81] using a chemical, nuclear, or conventional bomb.

In the 1987 parliamentary election, the Islamic Alliance displaced the New Wafd Party and emerged as the main opposition party in Egypt. The platform of the Islamic Alliance, a coalition composed of the Socialist Labour Party, the Liberal Party and the Muslim Brotherhood, stated: "Egyptian security requires Arab integration, support for the Palestinian struggle, and cooperation with the Islamic countries in all spheres. This definitely calls for the freezing of Camp David in preparation for its abrogation."[82] The election results and the composition of the new opposition coalition have given the politicized Muslim organizations political clout which cannot be easily dismissed.[83]

The Iran-Iraq war provided Egypt with a unique opportunity to accelerate its return to the Arab fold. At the Arab summit conference in Amman in December 1987, Egypt was pardoned and a new inter-Arab compact was struck: the Gulf countries would provide cash to finance Egypt's arms manufacturing industries, and Egypt would use its military power to deter and, in case of need, actively defend the petro-monarchies of the Gulf against military attacks from revolutionary Iran. The Amman Summit reversed the decisions of the Baghdad Summit of 1978 which had led to the economic and political isolation of Egypt in the Arab world. By 1988, the Mubarak government had restored diplomatic relations with most of the Arab countries which had ostracized Egypt following Camp David. In December 1988, Iraqi President Saddam Hussein visited Egypt and discussed plans for formally inviting Egypt to attend the 1989 Arab Summit where he played a leading role in facilitating Egypt's return to the Arab fold.[84] Egypt was also credited with playing an active role in bringing about the American decision to formally open talks with the Palestine Liberation Organization.[85] In 1989, Egypt was formally welcomed back to the Arab fold and, once more, looked forward to playing an active leadership role.

By 1990, the shortcomings of Sadat's strategies and of the Camp David accords were commonly recognized as responsible for many of the upheavals which engulfed the region. Although the Egyptian-Israeli treaty is viewed by the Camp David supporters as a positive achievement, the Camp David accords themselves were considered long dead and buried as a credible framework for a comprehensive solution to the Arab-Israeli and the Israeli-Palestinian conflicts. An Egyptian official who was directly involved in the preparations that led to the conclusion of the Camp David accords made the following instructive assessment in 1990: "The Camp David process is dead. Israel refused to implement Part Two of the treaty. This section deals with the Palestinian question. The treaty is alive and has withstood many challenges. It serves the interests of Israel and Egypt. There is peace between Israel and Egypt so that means the treaty is alive. The procedure for implementing Palestinian autonomy has not worked because the Israelis violated the treaty. Therefore that section of the treaty dealing with the Palestinians is inoperative. The Israelis accuse us of abrogating the treaty because of our recognition of the Palestinian State. However, Israel had already broken the treaty by extending her system of justice to the Golan Heights and East Jerusalem." In answer to a question about normalization the same former Egyptian official replied: "Egypt is over-normalizing. As long as Israel occupies part of the land of the Palestinians Egypt will not be able to have normal relations. I will not visit Israel. I know many others who feel as I do. Normalization does not mean one should put aside the norms of accepted civilized behaviour. The Israelis cannot expect normal relations with any Arab country as long as they continue to occupy Palestinian land. There is nothing in the Camp David treaty that says that Israel can occupy and swallow Arab land and that Egypt should have normal relations with her while this condition persists."[86]

Conclusion

The official position of the Israeli government has been one of disappointment at Egypt's failure to transform normalization into a special relation between Israel and Egypt. Israel also criticized Mubarak's rapprochement with the Palestinians and Egypt's various peace plans in 1983 and in 1989 as violations of the spirit of Camp David (another indication, if one were needed, that Israeli leaders considered that the Camp David spirit negated Palestinian national rights and implied permanent Israeli control over the occupied Arab territories). There were, however, Israeli establishment figures who had the courage and intellectual honesty to admit the responsibility of their government for the failure of the Camp David framework. Noting the flagrant violation of Camp David by the Israeli leaders, former Israeli Minister of Foreign Affairs Abba Eban wrote that the Israeli government's decision to raise its claim to sovereignty over the occupied territories had no precedence in the jurisprudence of any government "for such a total contradiction between an international agreement and a national statement of policy."[87]

Shimon Shamir, former director of the Israeli Academic Center in Cairo and later Israeli ambassador to Cairo, wrote after he returned to Israel: "Seeing my own country from Egypt through the eyes of Egyptians was not a very pleasant experience...Jewish terrorism, racism, and...expansionism"[88] were disturbingly evident. Ezer Weizman, Israeli Minister of Defense and member of the Israeli delegation that negotiated the Camp David agreement, recognized the responsibility of his government for the failure of Camp David. He candidly wrote in 1984: "We didn't take the autonomy issue seriously; we said 'no more war' and went ahead and made war; we went into Lebanon...and we killed and bombed-and then we have the effrontery to complain that Egypt is returning to the Arab world!"[89]

Sadat may have genuinely believed that he was pursuing the best interests of Egypt, the Arab States and the Palestinian people. His dramatic fate, however, demonstrated the risk inherent in pursuing policies that ignored domestic opposition, denied Egypt's geographical and historical regional ties, relied on the good will and the power of distant allies to solve domestic economic problems and regional conflicts, and adopted negotiating strategies with no contingency plans, should the grand design collapse. Egypt's enormous economic problems, with seemingly uncontrollable demographic explosion (one million Egyptians are added to Egypt's population every nine months), staggering national debt, crippling bureaucracy, and shrinking ability to produce enough food for its people required the end of Egypt's isolation.[90] Mubarak seems to have understood the inescapable necessity of putting an end to Egypt's isolation in the Arab world. He managed to bring Egypt back to the Arab fold without repudiating its basic commitment to the principle of peace with Israel and a negotiated settlement of the Arab-Israeli and the Israeli-Palestinian conflicts. He was also aware of the importance of building a domestic consensus behind his policies. The leaders of the ruling National Democratic Party do not miss an opportunity to suggest the government's need for a stable domestic front.[91] Political stability in the domestic front will no doubt continue to be influenced by the economic and political priorities of the government, including its position on the Arab-Israeli conflict and the Palestinian question.

There are few people in Egypt who publicly defend Camp David, and opposition to normalization seems undiminished. Before the 1991 war against Iraq shattered Arab consensus and further divided the Arab world, most Egyptians were welcoming Egypt's reintegration into the Arab fold. Looking back at the decade of turmoil and upheaval following Camp David, an Egyptian historian said: "Camp David was the triumph of a strategy always employed by imperial and colonial powers, to sever us from our Arabic and Islamic environment."[92] Today all legalized opposition parties in Egypt, not to mention the powerful various professional associations, are publicly on record against Camp David. "An observer of the Egyptian scene," wrote an Egyptian professor, "would be hard pressed to point to prominent voices that still publicly hail peace with Israel. Most Egyptians are resigned to the status quo generated by Sadat's initiatives. A few justify it, a few apologize for it, and a significant but growing minority are actively working against it."[93]

In fact, opposition to normalization remains as strong in Egypt as popular support for the Palestinian cause is solid. This was evidenced by the strong criticisms directed at Israel for its repression of the Palestinian uprising and by the massive anti-Israeli and pro-Palestinian demonstrations of January 1988. In addition, there was a public outcry when the members of the organization "Revolution of Egypt," responsible for the attacks against Israelis between 1985 and 1987, were brought to trial in February 1988. Opposition papers defended the accused and justified their actions in the context of patriotic motives similar to those that animated Egyptian resistance to British occupation.[94] Boutros Ghali told me that Israel could not hope to have fully normalized relations with Egypt as long as it continues to occupy Palestinian lands.[95] "Egypt's peace with Israel is cold," an Egyptian intellectual opposed to normalization told me, "and will get colder if Israel refuses to recognize the Palestinian people's rights to independence and self-determination."[96] The unanimity on this issue in Egypt transcends political differences, ideological lines and personal loyalties.

At the time of the 1917 Balfour Declaration, Egypt was too preoccupied with its own struggle for independence from British occupation to take an active interest in the Zionist-Palestinian confrontation. In fact, many Egyptians initially accepted and even welcomed the Zionists' claims that they were only interested in contributing to the economic development of Palestine. But as the process of Zionist infiltration and political, economic and demographic transformation of Palestine grew under the protective umbrella of British occupation authorities, the process of dispossessing the Palestinians inevitably led to riots, violence, and growing confrontations. These eventually culminated into the Palestinian revolt of 1936-39 which, although violently repressed by the British, touched the Egyptian people and crystallized for Egypt its identity as a leading Arab country and its responsibility for the defense of helpless Palestinians fighting to preserve their society. On the occasion of Egypt's admission to the League of Nations, the Egyptian Foreign Minister devoted the bulk of his address to the defence of the rights of the Palestinians. "There is in every Arab and Muslim soul," wrote the Egyptian writer Abd al-Munim Khallaf in September 1938, "a bit of the spirit of Palestinian fighters."[97] Egypt's Arabism became ever since entwined with the fate of Palestine and experienced with it the defeat of 1948, the growth of expansionist Israeli power in 1956, and the humiliation and loss of national territories in 1967.

For the sake of recovering Israeli-occupied Egyptian territory, Sadat played up the Egypt-first thesis and succeeded in separating Egypt from its Arab milieu throughout the second half of the seventies, enough time to allow him to conclude the Camp David separate agreement. But strong opposition to normalization and its expected assumptions about the Palestinian-Israeli conflict and Egypt's separation from the Palestinian cause, dramatized the difficulties inherent in trying to shape Egyptian destiny on one's own image and will. The Palestinian uprising, which started in December 1987, helped strengthen Egyptian opposition to accommodation with Israel at the expense of the rights of the Palestinian people. After initially expressing cautious support for the American proposals put forward by Secretary George Shultz in March 1988, which were a continuation of the discredited autonomy talks of the Camp David accords, President Mubarak moved to support the proclamation by the Palestine National Council, in Algiers in November 1988, of an independent Palestinian State in the West Bank and Gaza. In extending diplomatic recognition to the new Palestinian State, Egypt under Mubarak established the political link Camp David failed to make under Sadat between the Israeli-Egyptian treaty and the Palestinians' right to independence and self-determination in their own country. And by the end of 1989 Egypt was fully reintegrated into the Arab world and, as Boutros Ghali put it in his review of the Egyptian foreign policy mentioned above, one unshakable truth about Egypt was reconfirmed, namely, that the Egyptian people are an inseparable part of the Arab nation.

But these developments and their implications for an Egyptian-led Arab front united in its commitment to a negotiated settlement of the Arab-Israeli-Palestinian conflict on the basis of justice and international legitimacy, were cut short by the consequences of the Iraqi invasion of Kuwait in August 1990, and the confrontation with the United States which ensued. Arab consensus, and to a lesser degree Egyptian consensus under Mubarak, that Camp David did not go far enough in recognizing Palestinians' rights to self-determination and in establishing a framework for a just and enduring peace in the region would be destroyed by the Arabs' divided response to the crisis precipitated by the Iraqi action. The balance of power which will result from the American-led war against Iraq will further weaken the Arab and Palestinian bargaining position and ability to improve on Camp David. Indeed, with the elimination of Iraq as a significant Arab military power to contend with in any Arab-Israeli equation, the realignment of Egypt along stricter American policy orientations, and the collapse of the Soviet Union as a superpower, the ascendency of Israel and the United States in the region became both entrenched and unchallenged. The Shamir government's view that Camp David may in fact have gone too far would become even more difficult to challenge in view of the weakened bargaining power of the Arab and Palestinian parties. The new Israeli Labour government would take a less intransigent approach to Camp David but still grounds its peace position within the rejectionist context of denying Palestinian rights to self-determined national existence.

The chapters on the war against Iraq explore the process of confrontation which further modified the balance of power at the expense of the Arabs. But before we examine the dynamics of confrontation in the war against Iraq, it is important to understand that both the scale and the objectives of the war may not have been possible had it not been for a well-managed North-American public opinion which continued to see the Arab-Israeli and Israeli-Palestinian conflicts largely through the dominant Zionist perspective. The chapter on language and propaganda and the linguistic management of challenges to media interpretations of the Palestine question critically analyses the reconstitution of a dominant ideology which was shattered by the horrific images of the siege of Beirut and without which occupation and continued dispossession of the Palestinians would be more effectively opposed in the West. It examines how despite growing sympathy for the

Palestinian cause and incontrovertible evidence of Arab readiness for a negotiated settlement of the Arab-Israeli conflict on the basis of UN resolutions, it is still possible to dehumanize the Arabs, and therefore make them more acceptable victims of massive and mechanized warfare.

Notes

1. Gamal Abdel Nasser, *The Philosophy of the Revolution* (Cairo, Government Printing Office, nd), p. 59.
2. The full text was published in ALF BA(Baghdad) November, 25, 1978, and reproduced in Faith Zeadey, (ed.) *Camp David: A New Balfour Declaration.* Special Report, no. 3, (Detroit, Michigan, AAUG, February, 1979) pp. 55-57.
3. William B. Quandt, "Camp David and Peace Making in the Middle East," *Political Science Quarterly,* vol. 101, no. 3, 1986, pp.357-77, the quote comes from p. 358.
4. See *Contemporary Middle East Survey,* 1981-1982, p. 127.
5. See Avi Shlaim and Avner Yaniv, "Domestic Politics and Foreign Policy in Israel," *International Affairs,* vol. 56 (Spring, 1980), pp. 242-62.
6. Quoted in Alexander Cockburn and James Ridgeway, Who Won at Camp David? *The Village Voice,* September 25, 1978.
7. *Ma arrive,* September 20, 1978.
8. Editorial of *The New York Times,* January 2, 1978.
9. Jimmy Carter, *The Blood of Abraham* (Boston, Houghton Mifflin, 1985), p. 44.
10. *The Middle East* (in Arabic), quoting Jordanian sources, January 3, 1984.
11. Quoted in Carter, *Blood of Abraham,* p. 57.
12. See Ibrahim Karawan, "Egypt and the Western Alliance: the Politics of Westomania?," in Steven Spiegel, (ed.) *The Middle East and the Western Alliance* (London, George Allen and Unwin, 1982), pp. 163-181.
13. Hermann Frederick Eilts, "The United States and Egypt," in William B. Quandt, (ed.) *The Middle East: Ten Years After Camp David* (Washington, D.C., The Brookings Institution, 1988), pp. 111-149. The quote comes from pages 142-43.
14. See *MERIP,* "The Middle East Living by the Sword," January-February, 1987, no. 144, p. 35.
15. See Michael Weir, "External Relations," in Lillian Graig Harris, (ed.) *Egypt: Internal Challenges and Regional Stability* (London, Routledge and Kegan Paul, 1988), p. 79-99.
16. *The New York Times,* December 9, 1980.
17. See Alan W. Horton, "Egypt: Sadat and After," *UFSI Reports* (Indianapolis, Indiana, University Field Staff International), no. 5, 1983. p. 5.
18. See Bob Woodward, *Veil: The Secret Wars of the CIA, 1981-1987* (New York, Simon and Schuster, 1987), p. 414.
19. Ann Mosely Lesch, "Irritants in the Egyptian-Israeli Relations," *UFSI Reports* (Indianapolis, Indiana, Universities Field Staff International), 1986, no. 34. pp. 1-7, p. 4.
20. See *MERIP,* "The Middle East Living By the Sword," (January-February, 1987), no. 144, p. 24.
21. Hermann Eilts, "The United States and Egypt," in Quandt, *The Middle East,* op. cit., p. 143.
22. See Barbara Harlow, "Egyptian Intellectuals and the Debate on the 'normalization' of Cultural Relations," *Cultural Critique,* no. 4, (Fall, 1986), pp. 33-58. The quote comes

from p.37. See also the report published by the Committee for the Defence of the National Culture, published in the first issue of *Al-Muwajaha*, (in Arabic) (Cairo, July, 1981), pp. 12-13.

23. Ismail Fahmy, *Negotiating For Peace in the Middle East* (London, Croom Helm), 1983, p. 296.

24. Adel Aid, "'Normalization' and its impact on Egyptian Legislations," *Al-Dawa* (in Arabic), no. 63, (July, 1981), pp. 28-9, quoted in Muhsin Awad, *Egypt and Israel: Five Years of 'normalization'* (in Arabic) (Cairo, Dar al-Mustaqbal al-Arabi, 1984), pp. 50-53.

25. Ibid., pp. 57-58.

26. See "Egypt Burnt the Zionist Flag and Raised the Palestinian Flag," in *Al-Hadaf*,(in Arabic), March 1, 1980, no. 477, vol. 11. p. 2 5.

27. Ibid., p. 24.

28. The story is told in Shafiq Ahmad Ali, "When Insanity Becomes Associated with the Fatherland: From the Secret File on Sadat and 'normalization': The Assassination of Saad Halawa," reviewed by Mohamed Hakem in *Al-Muwajaha* (in Arabic) (Cairo, May, 1986), no. 6, pp. 146-148.

29. Cited in Ibid., p. 146.

30. Ann Mosely Lesch, "Irritants in the Egyptian-Israeli Relations," *UFSI Reports*, op. cit., pp. 1-7.

31. Anne Mosely Lesch, "Egyptian-Israeli Relations: 'normalization' or Special Ties?," *UFSI* (Indianapolis, Indiana, University Field Staff International), 1986, no. 35, p. 3; see also Saad Eddin Ibrahim, "Domestic Development in Egypt," in Quandt, (ed.) *The Middle East*, op. cit., pp. 19-62.

32. See Anne Mosely Lesch, "Egyptian-Israeli Relations: 'normalization' or Special Ties?" in Lesch, Ann Mosely and Mark Tessler, *Israel, Egypt, and the Palestinians: From Camp David to Intifada* (Bloomington, Indiana University Press, 1989), pp. 61-85.

33. Quoted in Hazim Hashim, *The Israeli Conspiracy against the Egyptian Mind: Secrets and Documents* (in Arabic) (Cairo, Dar al-Mustaqbal al-Arabi, 1986), p. 188.

34. See Anne Mosely Lesch, "Egyptian-Israeli Relations: 'normalization' or Special Ties?" in Lesch, Ann Mosely and Mark Tessler, *Israel, Egypt, and the Palestinians: From Camp David to Intifada*, op. cit., pp. 61-85.

35. Muhsin Awad, op. cit., p. 198.

36. Ibid., pp. 184-85.

37. Muhsin Awad and Said al-Bahrawi, "Four Years of Cultural 'normalization' Between Egypt and Israel," *Al-Muwajaha*, (Cairo, June, 1983), p. 19.

38. Ibid., p. 19.

39. Nadia Hassan Salim, "Political Education of Egyptian Children Through an Analysis of Their School Textbooks," in *Proceedings of the Seventh International Congress of Statistics and Research in the Political Sciences and Demography*, March 27 to April 1, 1982 (Cairo, Ain Shams University, 1982), p. 12) (in Arabic), cited in Karem Yehia in "The Image of the Palestinians in Egypt 1982-1985," *Journal of Palestine Studies*, vol. XVI, no.2, (Winter, 1987), pp. 45-63. The quote comes from page 48; see also Abdul-Monem al-Mashat, "Egyptian Attitudes toward the Peace Process: Views of An Alert Elite," *Middle East Journal*, vol. 37 (Summer, 1983); and Abdul-Monem al-Mashat, "The Egyptian-Israeli Settlement," *Journal of Arab Affairs*, vol. 5 (January, 1986), pp. 81-110.

40. See for instance Sami Khalil Marri, "Arab Education in Israel," (Syracuse, Syracuse University Press, 1978); Sarah Graham-Brown, *Education, Repression, Liberation: Palestinians* (London, World University Service, 1984); Yerach Gover, "Were You There, Or Was It a Dream?: Ideological Imposition on Israeli Literature," *Journal of Palestine Studies*, vol. XVI, no. 61, (Autumn, 1986), and Fouzi El-Aswar, The Portrayal of Arabs in Hebrew Children's Literature, in the same issue of *Journal of Palestine Studies*; see also the poll published by *The Jerusalem Post* on September 9, 1988 showing that 40

percent of Israeli high school students hate the Arabs. For anti-Arab racism in Israel see the testimony of an Israeli journalist who disguised as an Arab in Yoram Binur, *Brebis galeuse, (Paris, Presses de la Cité, 1990).*

41. See Muhsin Awad, "Psychology in the Arab-Israeli Struggle: Illusions of Treatment...or Treatment of Illusions?," *Al-Muwajaha* (in Arabic) (Cairo, February, 1984), no. 2, pp. 38-58.

42. Muhsin Awad and Said al-Bahrawi, "Four Years of Cultural 'normalization' Between Egypt and Israel," *Al-Muwajaha* (Cairo, June, 1983), p. 30.

43. Hazim Hashim, *The Israeli Conspiracy against the Egyptian Mind*, op. cit., pp. 285-286.

44. See Ann Mosely Lesch and Mark Tessler, *Israel, Egypt, and the Palestinians: From Camp David to Intifada*, op. cit., pp. 61-85. The quote comes from page 73.

45. *Al-Shaab*, (Cairo), March 17, 1981.

46. *Rooz El-Yussif*, (Cairo), February 23, 1981, in Muhsin Awad, op. cit., p. 61.

47. Hazim Hashim, op. cit., p. 290.

48. *Al-Muwajaha*, (Cairo, November, 1984), no. 3, p. 142.

49. Hazim Hashim, op. cit., p. 290-291.

50. See Muhsin Awad, *The Israeli Strategy for "normalization" With the Arab Countries* (in Arabic) (Beirut, The Center for Studies in Arab Unity, 1988), pp. 72-73.

51. Personal meetings with Dr. Boutros Ghali, Egypt's Deputy Prime Minister for Foreign Affairs, in Cairo, 1991.

52. See the full text of the interrogation reproduced in *Al-Muwajaha* (Cairo, April, 1985), no. 4, pp.137-139.

53. Ibid., pp. 52-56.

54. Ibid., pp. 57-61.

55. Reproduced in ibid., p. 80.

56. Ibid., pp. 8-22.

57. See Zeev Schiff and Ehud Yaari, *Israel's Lebanon War* (New York, Simon and Schuster, 1984), p. 71.

58. Herman Fredrick Eilts, "The United States and Egypt," in Quandt, (ed.) *The Middle East*, p. 127.

59. "Regional Cooperation, Criteria That Aid Applies in Considering Proposals For Regional Activities," reproduced in *Al-Muwajaha*, (Cairo, June, 1983), no. 1, p. 83.

60. Saad Eddin Ibrahim, "Domestic Development in Egypt," in Quandt, *The Middle East*, pp. 19-62. The quote comes from p. 28.

61. Nawal al-Sadawi, *Memoirs from the Women's Prison* (in Arabic), (Cairo, Dar al-Mustaqbal al Arabi, 1984), p. 214.

62. *The New York Times Magazine*, January 31, 1982, p. 26.

63. Quoted in Muhsin Awad, *Egypt and Israel*, op. cit., pp. 83-84.

64. Saad Eddin Ibrahim, "Egypt Needs to Take a Stand Against the State of Oppression and Aggression," *Al Joumhouria* (in Arabic) (Cairo), June, 10, 1982.

65. Saad Eddin Ibrahim, "Domestic Development in Egypt," in Quandt, *The Middle East*, pp. 19-62, op. cit., p. 34.

66. Muhsin Awad, *Egypt and Israel*, op. cit., p.113.

67. Ibid., p.119.

68. Quoted in Ibrahim, "Domestic Developments in Egypt," in Quandt, *The Middle East*, p. 33.

69. Anis Mansour, *Al-Ahram*, (Cairo), July 17, 1982.

70. See Muhsin Awad, *The Israeli Strategy of "normalization" with the Arab Countries*, (Beirut, The Center for Studies in Arab Unity), (in Arabic), 1988. p. 263.

71. See Mohamed Sid-Ahmed, "L'Egypte et l'OLP," *Le Monde Diplomatique* (Paris), February, 1984.

72. Bob Woodward, *Veil: The Secret Wars of the CIA* (New York, Simon and Schuster, 1987), p. 87.
73. Ibid., pp. 414-416.
74. See the full article in Muhsin Awad, "Suleiman Khater's War and Israel's Peace" in *Al-Muwajaha* (Cairo, May, 1986), no. 6, pp. 69-82.
75. See Ann Mosely Lesch, "Irritants in the Egyptian-Israeli Relations," *IJFSI*, op. cit., p. 2.
76. See Jean Gueyras, "Egyptian Conscripts' Revolt Widely Seen as a Cry Against Injustice," *Le Monde*, April 5, 1986, reproduced in the *Manchester Guardian Weekly*, April 12, 1986.
77. The statement was reported in an editorial entitled "Do Not Weaken Or Be Saddened," published in *Al-Shaab* (in Arabic) (Cairo, September 16, 1986). The editorial read in part: "Despite the statement by Prime Minister Dr. Ali Lutfi to Peres that the Palestinian question is a question of domestic and national security for Egypt, this statement was not repeated in the subsequent meetings or in the official statement." It was published in *FBIS* on September 25, 1986.
78. See Abdel Monem Said Ali, "Egypt: A Decade after Camp David," in Quandt, *The Middle East*, pp. 63-93.
79. *Al-Ahram*, (Cairo), July 15, 1988.
80. See David Hirst, "Egypt as the Heart of the Arab Nation," the *Manchester Guardian Weekly*, January 10, 1988.
81. *Middle East Times*, (London), October 1-7, 1988.
82. See *Al-Shaab*, (Cairo), March 24, 1987; see also Jean Gueyras, "Democracy and Islam on the March in Egypt," *Le Monde*, reprinted in the *Manchester Guardian Weekly*, May 13, 1984.
83. See Alexander Buccianti, "Egypt Faced with Rising Tide of Fundamentalist Violence," *Le Monde*, May 13, 1986, reprinted in the *Manchester Guardian Weekly*, May 25, 1986, p. 12.
84. *October Weekly Magazine*, (Cairo), 1988.
85. See the story in *Akher Saa* (Cairo), December 21, 1988.
86. Conversations in Cairo: An Interview with Dr. Tahseen Basheer. *Middle East Focus*, (Summer, 1990), pp. 8-13, p. 9.
87. Abba Eban, "Obstacles to Autonomy," *New Outlook*, (Tel-Aviv), June-July, 1984.
88. Quoted in Anne Mosely Lesch, JPI, November 24, 1984, p.10.
89. Yediot Ahronot, 2 November 1984, quoted in Anne Mosely Lesch, in Ibid., p.10.
90. See Lilian Graig Harris, (ed.) *Egypt: Internal Challenges and Regional Stability*, op. cit.; see also "L'Egypte en Fermentation," *Le Monde*, (Paris), August 21, 22, 23, 1984.
91. See Usama al-Ghazali Harb, "Political Stability and the Future of the Democratic System," *Al-Ahram*, June 24, 1988.
92. Cited in David Hirst, "Egypt as the Heart of the Arab Nation," the *Manchester Guardian Weekly* (England), January 10, 1988.
93. Ibrahim, in Quandt, *The Middle East*, op. cit., p. 20.
94. See *Al-Ahali* and *Sawt al-Arab* weeklies during February and March 1988.
95. Personal meetings with Dr. Boutros Ghali, Egypt's Deputy Prime Minister for Foreign Affairs. Cairo, 1991.
96. Personal meetings with Muhsin Awad, Secretary-General of the Organization of Human Rights in the Arab world, Cairo, 1989-90-91.
97. See James Jankowski, "Egyptian Response to the Palestine Problem in the Inter-War Period," *International Journal of Middle East Studies*, vol. 12 (1980), pp. 1-38, the quote comes from p. 20.

CHAPTER FOUR

Language and Propaganda: The Linguistic Management of Challenges to Media Interpretations of the Palestinian Question

The Power of Language and the Language of Power

Language has traditionally played a powerful and crucial role in the Zionist project for the seizure of Palestine, the establishment of a Jewish State, and in the propagation and unchallenged triumph in the West of the Zionist version of the Arab-Israeli-Palestinian conflict.

From the very beginning language was adroitly used to reconstruct realities which did not fit the Zionist vision, to modify facts which hampered its acceptance by the West, and to paint pictures which embellished Zionist intentions, denigrated its detractors, while remaining both disciplined and flexible, able to fit the context of its time and accommodate the needs of its audience. This led to the construction of a virtual system of interpretation, a school of representation framed by the ideas, aspirations, visions, and the political dreams of the Zionists. The rise of such a system created its own truths and an ideological consciousness about Palestine which admitted no dissension, allowed no competition, and was as attentive to details as it was self-contained and self-perpetuating.

In his *On Truth and Lie in an Extra-Moral Sense* Nietzsche observed that the truth of language resided in a mobile army of metaphors and anthropomorphisms and in a sum of human relations enhanced poetically and rhetorically which after long and repeated use seem firm, canonical and obligatory. Consider Arab leaders' use of the linguistic resources of their incomparably rich language with their flowery and poetic rhetoric, exaggerations, and elaborate metaphors. Poetically, such use of the language was majestic in its sweep, intoxicating in its sonority, and transporting in its beauty; politically, it was as inappropriately unrealistic as it was dangerously misleading: it swept the unpleasant realities of relative power and replaced them with wishful thinking; eliminated sober considerations of options and constraints with intoxicated fixations; replaced policy with grand rhetorical commitments, and created its own "truth": dictatorial, unforgiving, and absolute "truth." The Israelis made astute use of such colossal communicative failings and easily mobilized Western opinion for their 1967 war against the Arabs. During the confrontation with the United States which followed the Iraqi invasion of Kuwait in 1990, Saddam Hussein, ignorant of the West and of its political discourse, would fall into the same linguistic trap, one of many traps he went out of his way to unearth. The Bush administration, on the other hand, made astute use of an "army of metaphors." Saddam Hussein was cast as Hitler; Kuwait was "raped"; Bush was a hero, a good cop: "What we say goes" he said to the Third World. The ingredients of a "just war" were in place: a villain (Saddam Hussein); a victim (Kuwait and freedom) and a hero cop (Bush and the United States.) The metaphors created their own logic and their own "truth" which excluded negotiations and required confrontation.

Consider the early Zionist slogan about Palestine being "a land without a people for a people without a land": in one stroke it strips a people of its land, denies and annihilates its existence, rejects the assimilation of the Jews in their respective European societies, establishes the concept of the Jewish people as a distinct entity despite opposition from assimilated European Jewry, and creates in the collective consciousness of European audiences the image of Palestine as an empty heaven ready to receive a homeless people. The "truth" of this statement will be enhanced by countless poetic embellishments, endless passionate pleadings, and creative historical reconstructions supported by invocations of divinity, history, imperialism, civilizing missions, and will to power. Soon, the "truth" of the statement will be firmly established, become canonical and obligatory; its "official" character deeply entrenched, rejecting challenges and dismissing dissent as dangerous heresy.

Consider further the Balfour Declaration which was basically drafted by the Zionists in collaboration with British politicians who ensured that it included some safeguards to give Britain a way out should the Zionist enterprise backfire for some reason or another. Although volumes have been written on the period and on the Balfour Declaration, few people focused on the effective and crucial role played by language in facilitating the Zionist project. Still, we need only concern ourselves here with some creative and highly instructive linguistic masterstrokes which made the Balfour Declaration what it is: a linguistic masterpiece of manipulation, deception, and contradictions. Both Zionist leaders and the Llyod George Cabinet knew that over 90 percent of the people of Palestine were Muslim and Christian Palestinians and that less than 10 percent of its population were Palestinian Jews, many of whom were firmly opposed to Zionism. Now how could the British Cabinet facilitate the Zionist project of turning such a country into a Jewish State? How could a British government, ostensibly fighting a war in the name of peoples' right to self-determination, publicly promise to reduce the majority to a minority to accommodate the nationalist designs of European Zionists who enjoyed no support among British Jewry? How could it promise to help give credence to the concept of Jewish nationality and thus possibly undermine the political status of all the assimilated Jews who considered themselves British citizens? The answer lay in the language of obfuscation: find a construction which seemed to safeguard the rights of the Arab majority while in fact denying by implication that there was an Arab majority in Palestine at all. At the same time this construction should specifically safeguard the political rights of the assimilated Jews. Zionists and British efforts were crowned with success in this important safeguard clause in the Balfour Declaration: "it being clearly understood that nothing shall be done which may prejudice the civil and religious rights of *the non-Jewish communities in Palestine*, or the rights and political status enjoyed by Jews in any other country." (emphasis added). Thus, the Arab majority was creatively reduced to the status of *non-Jewish communities* and was thus linguistically subordinated to the Jewish minority, as if the Jews were the majority in Palestine and there were, dispersed here and there, some isolated Muslim and Christian communities. The construction offered protection to the Arab majority while at the same time reducing it to an invisible, scattered, and unimportant minority; and so there *seemed* to be no violation of rights involved here. It was a masterstroke of deception and manipulation, and it worked.

The Balfour Declaration contained another creative linguistic achievement. Since the Zionists and the British *knew* the reality of the Palestinian Arab majority in Palestine, they were weary lest the language of the Balfour Declaration betray Zionist intention of seizing Palestine from its inhabitants and transforming it into a Jewish State. Zionist leaders had to be circumspect and appear reassuring while at the same time getting Britain to endorse as much as possible their demands. Again the language of obfuscation was put to effective use. The Zionist drafters were ready with the appropriate linguistic term; they suggested that the British promise them a *homeland,* in Palestine, a term which could be construed to mean heaven for refugees, rather than a State which implied both Jewish nationality and Jewish majority. In a country whose Jewish population was around 8 percent the term "Jewish State" would have aroused fear, suspicion and violent opposition to the project of wresting Palestine from its inhabitants. Moreover, Britain would have found it difficult to publicly endorse such an explicit design at a time when it presented its entry into Palestine and other Arab lands as moved by the noble motive of liberating peoples from the shackles of Ottoman oppression and promoting the principle of self-determination. Max Nordau recounted with pride how he instructed the First Zionist Congress, which met in Basle in August 1897, in the art of linguistic deception already deemed necessary for the Zionist project: "I did my best to persuade the claimants of the Jewish State in Palestine that we might find a circumlocution that would express all that we meant by saying it in a way so as to avoid provoking the Turkish rulers of the coveted land. I suggested Heimstatte (homeland) as a synonym for 'state'…This is the history of the much commented upon expression. It was equivocal but we all understood what it meant. To us it signified Judenstaat (Jewish State) then and it signifies the same now."[1]

The Zionist use of the language reflected astute opportunism and genius manipulation which fitted the situation, suited its time and adapted to its context. Thus, Zionist leader Chaim Weizmann used the language of diplomacy and compromise with the British; when he talked to the Arabs he used the vocabulary of collaboration and common interests; when the confidentiality of his intimate relations with the British or with his wife allowed him to speak his mind, his language about the Arabs revealed an attitude of condescension and racial superiority. Occasionally, however, there were Zionist leaders who were much less disciplined in public and frankly stated their beliefs, their ideological convictions and their designs.

Dr. Eder, acting chairman of the Zionist Commission in Palestine, was ahead of his time, using the language of power long before the Zionists were powerful enough to impose their designs on the majority inhabitants of Palestine. The Haycraft Commissioners, who had come to Palestine to examine the causes of the Arab riots of 1921, wrote: "Until the Commission came to examine Dr. Eder, acting Chairman of the Zionist Commission, they were unaware to what extent such expressions of opinion as those we have quoted above were authorized by responsible Zionists. Dr. Eder was a most enlightening witness….In his opinion, there can only be one National Home in Palestine, and that a Jewish one, and no equality in the partnership between Jews and Arabs, but a Jewish predominance as soon as the numbers of that race are sufficiently increased…There is no sophistry about Dr. Eder; he was quite clear that the Jews should, and the Arabs should not, have the right to bear arms, and he stated his belief that this discrimination would tend to improve Arab-Jewish relations.."[2]

After the establishment of Israel, language continued to play a crucial role in the fabrication of necessary myths, authoritatively documented by the late Israeli writer Simha Flappan, to reconcile the forcible establishment of the Jewish State on the rubble of the destroyed Palestinian society with the proclaimed Zionist moral ideals. Thus, the Palestinians were not expelled, they "left" their country; Israeli military outposts in the demilitarized zones were "agricultural settlements," the Qibya massacre was "a punitive raid," the Egyptian Sinai was not conquered in an act of aggression in 1956 it was "liberated." Similarly, Menahem Begin insisted that international law did not apply to the Arab territories that Israel conquered and occupied in 1967, because these territories were not occupied territories but rather "liberated territories." The crucial role of language, its use and manipulations were clearly appreciated by Likud leaders who understood that their ideological convictions could be persuasively vehiced to the world through effective language education. On September 23, Menahem Begin's advisors announced a set of linguistic guidelines for public speaking about the Arab-Israeli conflict which gives insights into the crucial role Zionists traditionally attached to language use:

We must put an end to the term *West Bank*. These territories have names, and only these names may be used: *Judea and Samaria*. This usage must be strictly observed both vis-à-vis non-Israelis abroad and in Israel itself. The term 'annexation' as applied to the idea of including these territories in the State of Israel must be wiped out. One can annex land that belongs to someone else. The use of the term *annexation* only strengthens the false and mendacious claims of the Arabs and their friends regarding Arab ownership of Eretz Israel, and may even appear to grant legitimization to the Jordanian conquest.

When referring to the idea of including Judea, Samaria and Gaza in the State of Israel the terms to be used are *inclusion* or *the application of Israeli law*, according to the circumstances — but on no account *'annexation'*!

The very use of the term *return of territory* has helped the Arab argument that the territory in question *belongs to them*, since one obviously does not speak of *returning* something except to its *owners*. In any event, the idea that Judea, Samaria and Gaza (let alone Sinai and the Golan) belong to the Arabs has taken root among many people (even people of goodwill) in the world — the majority of whom, including journalists and politicians, are not professional historians or experts on Zionism. Since the peace negotiations (on their understanding) will be first about ter-

ritory...settlement in these territories appears to them unneces-
sary and provocative...It is clear to them that Israel will have to
return the territories in the end.

In short: the conflict is not a result of territorial conquest but
of the refusal of the Arabs to recognize our rights to our mother-
land...[3]

At the Camp David Conference Begin managed to manipulate Carter and
Sadat into believing that he made a concession to the validity of Palestinian claims
and rights in agreeing to the inclusion in the Camp David accords of the term Palestinian "legitimate rights." In reality, it was a rhetorical concession which Begin later
proceeded to ignore, claiming that it was void of any meaning since all rights were
by definition legitimate. He made sure that Carter was disabused and shortly after
the Camp David conference Begin suggested to Carter that his linguistic *tour de
force* in no way diminished Begin's position that the autonomy he was generously
granting to the Palestinians applied to the *residents* of Judea and Samaria but not to
the territories which Begin claimed belonged to Israel forever. Carter confirmed
that Begin told him: "The expression 'Palestinians' or 'Palestinian people' are being
and will be construed and understood as 'Palestinian Arabs', which, according to
official Israeli policy, means that the agreements only refer to the residents of the
territories which, for Prime Minister Begin, are part of the historic fatherland of the
Jews."[4]

Turning Points

It is reasonable to say that the Zionist-Israeli language and the ideological
values it reflected informed the dominant discourse used in the West to "cover,"
report on, and analyze the Arab-Israeli-Palestinian conflict. The Israeli invasion of
Lebanon in 1982 and the Palestinian uprising which erupted in 1987 represented
turning points in the history of the conflict over Palestine. In projecting to the West
powerful and irrefutable images of Israeli brutality and repression, and of
desperate but stubborn Palestinian resistance against overwhelming odds, they
directly and dramatically challenged the ideas, assumptions, contexts, political
agenda and view of history which informed the American media's discourse of
representation and interpretation of the Palestinian question since the beginning
of the conflict.

Although there exists no systematic study of the extent to which these two
events affected the recent developments in the conflict, it is safe to state that at the
very least they dramatized to Western and particularly American public consciousness the plight of a people struggling for national survival. At best they may have
sanctioned Palestinian nationalism to the extent of making possible the recognition by the United States, Israel's main supporter, of the impracticality of continued
Israeli occupation and of the inevitability of coming to terms with the long denied
Palestinian national rights.

The long-dominant Western discourse of interpretations and representations
of the Palestine conflict shows that the consensus of public opinion makers in the
United States has historically been based on denying the existence of the Palestinian people as a nation, absolving Israel of responsibility, and, to appropriate the

title of one of Edward Said's books, blaming the victim. The most influential public opinion makers are the so-called elite media, sophisticated newspapers such as the *New York Times* and the *Washington Post,* and prestige television news shows such as ABC *Nightline,* which target the educated and politically-conscious classes, shape their views, influence their perspectives, and inform their opinions on American foreign policy and international affairs. In showing a side of Israel persistently denied and carefully ignored in the West, the Israeli invasion of Lebanon and the Palestinian uprising gave rise to a dynamic and conflictive relationship between the inherently irrefutable realities of various images of Israeli brutalities in Lebanon and repression of Palestinian youths in revolt and their power to challenge the dominant discourse of interpretations, on the one hand, and, on the other hand, the elite media's interpretative and analytical approaches to the Palestinian conflict. The two clearly contradicted and conflicted with one another. They projected images and assumptions about the Palestine conflict which were informed by two different realities, one lived by the Palestinians, the other constructed and propagated for Western consumption by the Israelis. And the argument that the Israeli invasion of Lebanon and Israeli repression of the Palestinians in revolt were temporary aberrations is too simplistic and too obviously spurious to resolve the contradiction. It ignores both the historical record and the ideological context which made the invasion of Lebanon and the repression of the Palestinian uprising possible.

The dominant views about the Palestine conflict are so strongly entrenched and widely held by elite media, public opinion makers and policy planners in the United States that challenges to their supremacy were easily repelled in the past. The invasion of Lebanon, however, was no ordinary challenge and the daily televised images of Israeli merciless bombings of Lebanese cities evoked horror and disgust in a public opinion accustomed to different stories about Israel. The image problem, and it is instructive that Israeli leaders should think that it was all an image problem and nothing else, had to be systematically tackled. The siege of Beirut had shattered many an admiring image and conception about Israel in the West, and a whole process of ideological reconstruction had to be undertaken. It relied on a two-pronged attack: the first was directed against international and particularly American public opinion and was vehicled by a *Hasbara* project, an Israeli propaganda *blitzkrieg* in 1982 that blamed the negative stories about Israel on Western bias, pro-Palestinian media, and launched a sustained public relations campaign in the West to rehabilitate the traditional image of Israel. The other was directed against the White House where the Israelis found in Ronald Reagan a president who easily accepted their claims that all Middle Eastern problems were traceable to communist conspiracy and PLO terrorism. Both components of the process of ideological reconstruction were extremely successful. Thus, although the Begin government had contemptuously rejected the September 1982 Reagan peace plan and responded to the American President's call for a freeze on Jewish settlements by announcing an accelerated programme of additional Jewish settlements in the occupied Arab territories, the Reagan administration increased its military support for Israel. The strategic and ideological alliance which existed in fact between the United States and Israel was formalized and military cooperation strengthened.

The Palestinian uprising was the litmus test for the success or failure of the campaign for ideological reconstruction of the "official" views on Palestine which followed the siege of Beirut. Judging by how the media responded to the Palestinian uprising and by the language used to "cover" it and analyze it, one must unavoidably conclude that Israeli propaganda was remarkably successful in controlling the public relations damage of the Lebanon invasion. Elite media played a crucial role in this process of psychological and linguistic management of challenges to the established ideological canons on the Palestine question.

There exists a wealth of studies about information, the media, propaganda and politics. This chapter has been influenced by the classic and penetrating analyses provided by pioneers such as Walter Lippmann, Harold Lasswell, and Edward Bernays.[5] The labours of these men have served for years as indispensable sources of reference and analytical tools for many a work on the media. Lippmann's discussion of public opinion and the making of a common will has rarely been surpassed. Lasswell's analysis of the relationship of power that underpins the communication process in democratic as well as in totalitarian systems remains remarkably valid. Bernays' pioneering work on the engineering of consent has inspired many a radical critique of the role of the media. A mention should also be made of the valuable work carried out by the Glasgow University Media Group since 1974. Their detailed and systematic monitoring of media coverage of current affairs provides sustained evidence of the political partiality of the news organizations.[6] More recently, Edward Herman and Noam Chomsky put forward a carefully constructed propaganda model which they applied to media coverage of Central America, South East Asia, and the attempted assassination of the Pope. They argued that news coverage, selection of context, premises and general agenda were highly functional for the establishment as well as responsive to the needs of governments and major power groups.[7]

A number of less well-known but nonetheless valuable studies have been made on specific issues, and serve as useful signposts for further analysis. Edward Herman's examination of how the *New York Times* covered the 1984 Salvadoran and Nicaraguan elections illustrates the intimate relationship between the established power and the elite media.[8] Janice Terry's careful use of content analysis served to document the pro-Israeli bias of the editors of influential American papers, as well as the decrease in pro-Israeli and anti-Arab editorial coverage of the *New York Times*.[9] Michael Suleiman's work on public opinion and the Palestinian question reported invaluable data and continues to provide helpful insights into these issues.[10] Noam Chomsky's careful documentation of how the White House staged the American bombardment of Libya in 1986 is a dramatically cogent example of media's cooperative role in maintaining public ignorance of certain foreign policy issues.[11]

While indebted to all of the above, the following discussion is not based on systematic dissection of print or electronic media coverage of the Israeli invasion of Lebanon or of the Palestinian uprising. Rather, it presents an analysis of the resilience of the dominant discourse of interpretation used by elite media to report on and analyze the Palestine question despite easily documented evidence that its assumptions are not supported by the historical record and its normative interpretations not shared by the international community. It also reflects my interest in what Roslind Brunt and Martin Jordan called the media's "vocabulary of bias,"[12] used to inculcate and support the assumptions underpinning the dominant "official" frame of reference. The implicit and explicit use of language to convey beliefs, assumptions and ideological orientations wrapped in a context of "objectivity" may be called the language of political bias and propaganda. Such language has traditionally been used to reinterpret the Palestinian question, construct a useful system of beliefs and symbols, and deal effectively with the "bad news," i.e., information and images which creep past the constructed system and contradict or challenge the dominant beliefs and assumptions that inform the views of the public and decision makers about the Palestinian conflict.

The Israeli invasion of Lebanon produced images, raised questions and caused doubts about the validity of many of the assumptions underlying the elite media's representations and interpretations of the Palestinian conflict. Such a climate should have been favourable to the many highly relevant facts about the Palestinian conflict, the historical record and the surrounding mythologies; these facts were reported by Israeli writers drawing from recently declassified Israeli army and cabinet documents. Easily documented and occasionally reported by the media, these facts confirmed the already available evidence from Arab and other sources but were generally dismissed or ignored by Western media. Such revelations by Israeli writers undermine many of the central assumptions of the dominant media's interpretations, i.e., Israel's unwavering commitment to peace and the Arabs' dedication to rejectionism, or the Palestinians' responsibility for their own plight. Now, given the availability of these facts, and given their Israeli sources, and the damaging images of Israel's invasion of Lebanon, one could have expected some modification in the elite media's dominant interpretations of the Palestinian conflict. At least one could have expected some efforts at placing the Israeli invasion of Lebanon within the context of Zionist leaders' belligerent approach to the Palestinians and their society. Instead, the historical record was ignored and the Israeli invasion of Lebanon was placed within a context that presented it as an abominable aberration caused by the rebellious and deceptive mind of Israeli Defense Minister Ariel Sharon who lied to the Israeli cabinet about his real intentions in Lebanon. The result of such interpretation was that very little substantive modification of the underlying dominant assumptions about the Palestine question occurred.

The Palestine uprising represented even more dramatic challenges to the elite media's interpretative frame for and dominant assumptions about the Palestine question. The media responded by mobilizing all the "official" historical, political and interpretative contexts which traditionally informed their representations to their readers. An analysis of the language used to "cover" the Palestinian uprising shows that the media allowed some recognition of the unavoidable and persistent reality of Palestinian dispossession and oppression but never went so far as to question the basic assumptions of the dominant "official" interpretations of the conflict they have been routinely representing to their readers. This bespeaks the remarkable resilience of a propaganda system able to reinterpret and integrate inconvenient facts such as the Israeli invasion of Lebanon and the revelations made by Israeli scholars, and, at the same time, assure the continuing dominance of the same fallacious assumptions about the conflict. Reinterpreting inconvenient realities was necessary in order to justify the elite media's failure to question official governmental policies that deny the relevance of the victim's claims and rights despite overwhelming support by the international community. The partial admission of the reality of Palestinian victimization was unavoidable because the images of Israel's repression of the Palestinian uprising were both longer in duration and more dramatic in impact than previous images of Arab-Israeli interstate confrontations. Television played a significant role in accentuating these images because it gave them a sense of immediacy and finality which removed much of the interpretative latitude — so crucial to the language and the context of the system of interpretation — available to print media.

As it will become palpably patent below, the elite media have successfully managed to integrate and reinterpret the challenging realities without substantially modifying the dominant assumptions or questioning official policy values. I have used the framework of the propaganda model constructed by Edward Herman and Noam Chomsky to show how premises and claims put forward by Israel are treated uncritically because "friendly" Israel, by definition, tells the truth, opposes terrorism, loves democracy and seeks peace. Different criteria of evaluation are applied in treating "unfriendly" Palestinian and Arab views, beliefs, and victims. It will be possible therefore to see how the media's linguistic management of challenges to its "official" frame of reference serves a propagandistic function of symbolizing and supporting a discourse of interpretation which is both compatible with and subservient to the American government's official position of denying the Palestinians their right to self-determination.

The "Official" Frame of Reference

The propaganda model constructed by Herman and Chomsky is based on the following components: (a) the concentrated ownership and profit orientation of the mass media; (b) advertising as the mass media's primary source of income; (c) media reliance on information provided by the government and by "experts" funded and approved by agents of power; (d) the use of "flake strategy" as a means of disciplining the media; and (e) the slogan of anti-communism enlisted as a national "religion" and control mechanism, although this, given the collapse of the Soviet Union and the communist empire, will obviously have to be replaced by another useful slogan. (Israel's ambassador in Washington has been trying to draw the attention of American policy makers to the danger of Islam. Some media outlets have been responsive and anti-Islam stories have started to appear more regularly). Propaganda campaigns will be attuned to power and elite interests and mobilized when the themes, facts, and victim identification in a given story meet the test of usefulness to these interests. Definitions of value and dualistic attention to "worthy" and "unworthy" victims will be based on utility and will differ in quality.

Applying this propaganda model to explain why the elite media's frame of representation and interpretation is unfavourable to Arabs in general and Palestinian Arabs in particular, and biased in favour of Israel, requires consideration of seven unique elements: (a) the substantial role of the influential American Jewish community and its ability to use its considerable financial and organizational power to affect the American political process and set limits on acceptable public debate about the question of Palestine by the effective and systematic use of a wide range of strategies including invocation of the Holocaust and of anti-Semitism; (b) the success of Israel and its friends, led by Henry Kissinger, in selling to the American public and its security managers the notion of Israel as a strategic asset, an agent of the United States policy entrusted with deterring nationalist threats to American interests in the Middle East and ensuring continued access to strategic resources; (Boutros Ghali told me that in his opinion the Gulf crisis proved the irrelevance of that argument); (c) genuine American sympathy for the plight of the Jews after World War II and identification with Israel as a "Western" democracy claiming to share American ideals and political culture; (d) sophisticated knowledge by Israel and its friends of the inner workings of the Western and particularly American political system and media; (e) alliance with various domestic constituencies to promote American foreign policy orientations based on increased militarization in order to enhance the value of American-Israeli strategic cooperation; (f) historic lack of interest in public relations matters by Arabs and their chronic inability to present the Arab cause in terms comprehensible to Western audiences; and (g) ignorance and suspicion of Arabs and their history by the American public.

The present discussion, however, is primarily concerned with the results of the interactions of these factors in their totality vis-à-vis the Palestinian conflict as reflected in the elite media's language of interpretation and the assumptions it defends against inconvenient challenges.

The dramatic televised images of the Palestinian uprising revealed to Western audiences — possibly greater in number than ever before — the asymmetrical nature of the confrontation between exclusionist political Zionism and the Palestinian society it displaced. This asymmetry had always been at once the dominant characteristic of Palestinian encounter with political Zionism, and the most consistently "reinterpreted" feature of the Western media's representation of the conflict to Western audiences.

From the very beginning reinterpretation was of crucial importance in the construction of a propaganda system to cover Palestine. Thus, inconvenient facts such as Zionist displacement of Palestinian society was reinterpreted within a context that aroused sympathy for the displacer, not the displaced. Such a context was created through the American media's depiction of Israel as an outpost of Western civilization in the midst of an alien and inhospitable culture, as well as by systematic exploitation of human-interest themes that echoed the American political and cultural experience: the hardships faced by a society of immigrants, the idea of an underdog facing and triumphing over natural and human adversity, or the frontier mentality of bravery and conquest. In effect, Zionist political culture could count on sympathetic reactions in the West regardless of its actions against Palestine's original inhabitants of whose existence the media said little. The context thus established remained the dominant frame of reference within which the conflict over Palestine was covered and interpreted. A typical example appears in the conclusion of a study focusing on media analysis of Israel's responsibility in the Qibya massacre in 1953, in which troops led by Ariel Sharon forced the Arab inhabitants "to remain inside until their homes were blown up over them"[13] — an act which evoked harsh condemnation by the American Jewish community and which was censured by the UN Security Council. Ralph Crow, the author of the study, found that although "reported facts were overwhelmingly pro-Arab," the media's expression of opinion continued "to favour the Israeli cause irrespective of the merits of the particular case in question."[14] This conclusion was publicly corroborated recently by knowledgeable media insiders such as retired CBS *News* vice-president Ernest Leiser who admitted: "over the years I've detected — and it was certainly true of my own news judgements — that Israel is given the 'benefit of the doubt' whenever possible."[15] An Israeli government official also recently admitted that his government relies on a number of American Jews "from network executives to bookers...who are more loyal to Israel than to their employer....This translates," he added, "into 'favors' ranging from sympathetic coverage to getting negative stories about Israel killed."[16]

In addition to reinterpretation of inconvenient facts, the construction of an interpretative propaganda system also relied on neglecting and dehumanizing the victim. Thus, the traditional Western media image of the Arab underwent an instructive metamorphosis in order to cultivate the idea of a split between "worthy" and "unworthy" victims, with Arabs categorized as the latter. The old romantic stereotype of a horse-riding, desert-wandering, good-looking Arab popularized by Hollywood during the Valentino era, gradually gave way to a new and sinister stereotype of a dark, scheming, camel-riding, woman-collecting coward. The famous Zionist propaganda slogan claiming that Palestine was "a land without a people for a people without land" developed its own truth which, as mentioned above, defined the Western approach to Palestine and justified the neglect with which the media treated Palestine's Arab majority. With the establishment of the State of Israel in 1948, and the dispersion and expulsion of close to 800,000 Palestinians, the Western media noted the unavoidable reality of Palestinian presence and victimization, but reduced their status to that of refugees rather than stakeholders in a conflict the media presented as being Arab-Israeli, i.e., a conflict between States. The massive Arab defeat in 1967 underscored to the Palestinian people the imperative of self-reliance, and thus served to galvanize their energies into an assertive nationalism. In their first major military test, east of the Jordan in 1968, the Palestinians proved their ability to fight back and inflict serious losses on the attacking Israeli troops, emerging as an organized, albeit minor, military force. In 1974, the PLO gained Arab and then international recognition of its right to press for self-determination and to be the Palestinians' sole legitimate representative. Media coverage, however, tended to emphasize the misguided Palestinian acts of hijacking and of desperate, bloody and suicidal actions, placing them within a context which reinforced established stereotypes of the dominant frame of reference. Thus, the image of the Palestinians cultivated by Western media went from non-existent entity, to that of refugee, to that of terrorist, accompanied by little or no reference to historical context or causality.

With the Arab oil embargo following the 1973 war, the stereotype of the Arab received another refinement in the dominant ideological discourse on the conflict: the Arab became an oil vendor and blackmailer. In the collective Western, and particularly North American consciousness, the Palestinian "terrorist" and the Arab "blackmailer" became inherently capable of neither political accommodation nor peaceful intentions. Thus, in 1975, about 50 percent of the American public and about 75 percent of Jewish Americans thought of Arabs as backward, underdeveloped, greedy, arrogant, and even "barbaric."[17] A faithful reflection of the successful propagation of degrading and dehumanizing images and stereotypes.

In his review of American attitudes toward Arabs, Jews, Israelis, and Palestinians, as reflected in public opinion polls between 1939 and 1979, Michael Suleiman concluded that the most striking result of the study was the centrality of the Jewish question and Israel to the various agencies of public opinion assessment, and "the almost total ignorance, or deliberate negligence, of the fate of the Palestinian Arabs." He also noted that the most startling and clear conclusion that emerged from available public opinion data was that "while in the 1930s and 1940s existent anti-Semitism was directed against Jews, it is today directed mostly against the Arabs."[18] This was a logical extension and a vindication of the successful effort made by political Zionism in giving the West dehumanizing representations of the Palestinian Arabs; (it is a measure of the success of Zionism that *it* represented the Arabs to the West). Zionist leader Chaim Weizmann's lecturing to the British in 1918 about "the treacherous nature of the Arab…[who] screams as often as he can and blackmails as much as he can"[19] found natural echo and continuity in Israeli Prime Minister Menachem Begin's characterization of the Palestinians as "two-legged beasts," and in Prime Minister Yitzhak Shamir's more recent description of them as "grasshoppers." In internalizing, and acquiescing in the propagation of these racist images, Western public-opinion makers found themselves ignoring Palestinian and Arab humanity and the validity of their grievances. In 1986, *CBS* Television refused to air a Bill Moyers' commentary criticizing denial of representation to the Arab view even when it took the form of paid commercials. When Rick Kaplan, executive producer of ABC *Nightline* news show was asked in 1987 why Israeli representatives were virtually permanent fixtures on the programme, with no Palestinian representation to speak of, he said it was because there were not enough "credible Arab guests."[20] The circle was thus completed: the dominant, degrading and denigrating images and stereotypes of the Arabs propagated by the media have become so widely accepted they could now be invoked as valid excuse to justify refusal to recognize the credibility and the validity of Arab views and Arab humanity by the same media.

Thus, the "official" frame of reference, which played a significant role in American hostility to the Palestinian Arab cause, was built on the following premises: (a) basic sympathy for the subjugating political Zionist culture in Palestine with concomitant neglect, marginalization and dehumanization of its victims; (b) reinterpretation of the conflict as one between States: intransigent, powerful, and anti-American Arab States rejecting any compromise versus a flexible, weak, democratic and pro-American Israel eager to live in peace — the lightning 1967 Israeli attack and its military consequences so impressed the security managers in Washington that the notion of a weak Israel was replaced by that of the need for a strong Israel as a valuable strategic ally; similarly the postulate about Arab rejectionism was modified after Sadat's signing of a separate treaty and rejectionism was applied to the Palestinians and the "confrontation states"; (c) violent acts by the Arabs are "aggression" and "terrorism," while violent acts by Israel (regardless of the immeasurably greater number of victims produced) are understandable reprisals almost always directed at "guerilla bases"; and (d) Palestinian self-representation and self-determination are "illegitimate," through association with terrorism and reinterpretation of accepted legal and moral criteria applicable to the conflict over Palestine. It is no exaggeration to say that one would be hard pressed to find extensive media analysis of the Palestinian question which did not rely on one or several of these premises, often with some nuances but sometimes crudely, as basic assumptions and interpretative contexts for developments in and coverage of the conflict, thus justifying and perpetuating the dominant frame of reference.

Challenges to the "Official" Frame of Reference

There are two kinds of challenges which confront the dominant frame of reference. The first is what might be called factual and normative challenges: facts that raise doubt about the validity of the normative criteria by which aggression, blame, responsibility, legitimacy of claims and the historical record in the Palestinian conflict are determined. Factual and normative challenges would, for instance, include the real historical record as opposed to the propagandistic and "official" one about the positions of Israel, the Arab governments and the PLO with regard to a settlement of the conflict. If these facts were allowed into and absorbed by the dominant frame of reference they would undermine its foundations and obviate the validity of many of its assumptions and analytical perspectives. Since these factual and normative challenges reach only a small audience of researchers and professional students of the conflict, and have traditionally enjoyed no powerful constituency or institutional support to present them even minimally as competing, alternative versions of the historical record of the conflict, the elite media seem to have had no difficulty ignoring them, as will become evident from the analysis of the language of interpretation used to deal with the challenges of the Palestinian uprising.

The second kind of challenge confronting established canons is what might be called dramatic challenges: images too dramatic to be dismissed lightly or too protracted to have no impact on public opinion — the images, for example, of President Sadat addressing the Israeli Knesset, of the Israeli siege of Beirut as indiscriminate bombardments engulfed an Arab capital in flames, or the daily images of Palestinian youths defying and being shot and killed by the Israeli army of occupation. These dramatic challenges reached an immeasurably wider audiences than the normative challenges could ever hope to reach. They could not be easily dismissed and required therefore a more careful response. The media's response to the Palestinian uprising took the form of allowing for the unavoidable and undeniable reality of Palestinian oppression and struggle while at the same time placing that reality within a context which relied on the fundamental assumptions of the dominant frame of reference, i.e., absolving Israel of responsibility and requiring the victims to show reasonableness and realism in accepting the usurpation of their rights and land.

Factual and Normative Challenges

One of the most significant factual and normative challenges with which the historical record presents the propagandistic frame of reference is directed at the dominant representation of Israel as being committed to peace and the Arabs to rejectionism. Thus, while the public positions of the Arab regimes was traditionally one of commitment to a struggle to liberate Palestine, the private and real positions differed substantially.

I have already mentioned in chapter one some of the important facts recently confirmed for the first time by Israeli writers drawing from declassified Israeli cabinet documents. Given the importance of these facts for the "official" frame of reference, I think that they bear repeating. Thus, in his book *Nineteen Forty-nine: The First Israelis* Israeli writer Tom Segev documented how Israeli leaders rebuffed early Arab peace proposals in favour of reliance on Israeli might to enforce the status quo and perpetuate a state of dynamic tension and siege to be exploited for further territorial expansion. Segev wrote: "The Arabs 'recognized' Israel and were ready to discuss peace, but Israel did not accept the conditions" of allowing the Palestinian refugees to return and permitting the establishment of a Palestinian Arab State as provided for by the United Nations resolution.[21] In using declassified cabinet documents to systematically debunk the sacrosanct myths about the Palestine conflict carefully constructed by Israel, the late Israeli writer Simha Flapan wrote a book "in the hope of sweeping away the distortions and lies that have hardened into sacrosanct myth[s] and which had become accepted as historical truth."[22] With regard to the specific myth of Israel's undying commitment to peace and Arab dedication to rejectionism, Flappan wrote: "on the contrary, from the end of World War II to 1952, Israel turned down successive proposals made by Arab states..."[23] to reach a negotiated settlement of the conflict. Even Gamal Abdel Nasser, portrayed in the West as a dangerous radical, was ready as early as 1955, shortly after he consolidated his power in the new revolutionary regime, to negotiate a peaceful settlement with Israel so that he could turn his attention to the more pressing task of economic development and social programmes in Egypt. When asked by Jean Lacouture in 1955 if he was ready to recognize and make peace with Israel, Nasser replied: "It is now clear that the Israelis would like peace on the basis of the status quo, that is the Tripartite Declaration of 1950; whereas certain Arabs, including the Egyptian government, want it to be on the basis of the partition of 1947."[24]

In November 1967, King Hussein made it clear to western Europe and the United States that he and Nasser were prepared to recognize Israel and reach a negotiated settlement on the basis of UN resolution of withdrawal from the Arab territories occupied by Israel in the 1967 war. Nasser also accepted American Secretary of State William Rogers' 1969 peace plan providing for Israeli withdrawal and a negotiated settlement of the Arab-Israeli conflict. Israeli leaders, supported by Kissinger, were angered by the call for withdrawal from occupied Arab territories and refused any serious cooperation with Rogers. Kissinger's manipulations eventually eliminated Rogers from Middle East policy making and shelved his plan. In February, 1970, Nasser told Eric Rouleau of the prestigious French newspaper *Le Monde,* that "it will be possible to institute a durable peace between Israel and the Arab States if Israel evacuates the occupied Arab territories and accepts a settlement of the Palestinian refugees.... If Israel had accepted to apply UN resolution on the Palestinians' right to repatriation when it was adopted [1949] we would have established a definitive peace twenty years ago."[25] Similar peace offers were made by Egypt in 1971 and by Jordan in 1972, and turned down by Israel.[26] In 1976, the United States vetoed a UN Security Council resolution calling for a negotiated settlement "with appropriate arrangements to guarantee the sovereignty...of all states in the area and their right to live in peace within secure and recognized boundaries," including Israel and a new, reduced Palestinian State to be established in the West Bank and Gaza. The resolution was supported by the PLO, Egypt, the USSR, Jordan and Syria.[27] Subsequent Arab peace proposals such as the Fahd plan of 1981 and the Fez plan of 1982, based on security guarantees for all States in the region — including Israel — and self-determination for the Palestinians, were opposed by the United States and Israel. These Arab peace offers, now confirmed by Israeli scholars, had little impact on the dominant media's ideological discourse which continued to rely on the propagandistic assumptions of the "official" frame of reference and their dualistic attention to "worthy" and "unworthy" victims, friendly and unfriendly "peace processes." Consequently, the media's discourse continued to conveniently reject, deny, and when admission was inevitable, to marginalize the peace offers made by the Arabs and the Palestinians.

Israeli leaders have repeatedly rejected any possibility of a negotiated settlement which recognized Palestinian national existence or diminished Israeli territorial expansion. In any rational context, Israeli leaders would be described as rejectionist of peace in the Middle East on the basis of international legitimacy. Yet, this inconvenient fact is routinely dismissed and has not been allowed to modify the usual distribution of blame and assignment of responsibility for the failure to reach a negotiated settlement of the Palestine conflict. The Begin government, for example, adopted the position that, following the transition period of the Camp David accords, "Israel will raise its claim and will act to fulfil its rights to sovereignty over Judea, Samaria, and the Gaza district."[28] Although former Israeli Foreign Minister Abba Eban stated that he was unable to find any precedent "in the jurisprudence of any government for such a total contradiction between an international agreement and a national statement of policy,"[29] the implications of such a flagrant violation of the Camp David accords did not have a substantive impact on the dominant assumptions relating to Israel's commitment to peace — even to the Camp David peace agreement which denied Palestinian national rights altogether. Further, in angrily rejecting the Reagan peace plan of September, 1982, and the American President's appeal for a freeze on Jewish settlements in the occupied Arab territories, the Israeli cabinet unanimously decided to "continue a Jewish program of establishing a Jewish population there to consolidate Israel's hold on the areas....Israel," the cabinet declared, "will reserve the right to apply sovereignty over the territories at the end of the five year transition period of Palestinian 'autonomy' envisioned by the Camp David accords."[30] The reaction of the *New York Times* to this Israeli vision of peace consisted in simply reiterating support for Camp David: "Far from betraying the Camp David accords Mr. Reagan aims to restore the promise that Mr. Begin drained from them."[31] Given its disapproval of Israeli violation of the Camp David accords and rejection of the Reagan plan, the *New York Times* could have logically raised some pertinent questions about the Israeli government's real commitment to a negotiated settlement. It did not. It was not possible for instance to question whether the Israeli government was really committed to peace or whether it was using the so-called peace process to mask expansionist tendencies. The displeasure with Israel had to remain within the permissible limits of criticism and therefore revolved around the superficial differences between Camp David and the Reagan plan, both of which, it should be recalled, reflected the real rejectionist positions: rejection of the Palestinians' right to self-determination, rejection of the representativity of the PLO, and rejection of international legitimacy as embodied in all UN resolutions to serve as the basis of a peaceful settlement of the conflict. In the tone-setting "official" discourse of the editors of the *New York Times,* the dominant assumptions about the relative roles and commitment to peace, rejectionism and denial of national existence remained unchallenged and unchanged.

In addition, the Zionist role in displacing and dispossessing the indigenous Palestinian people has been corroborated recently by Israeli writers. Meron Benvenisti, for example, described the systematic dispossession of the Palestinians in his 1985 study *Land Alienation in the West Bank* in which he highlighted the hitherto hardly-publicized fact that "in 1947, the Jews possessed less than 10 percent of the total land of mandatory Palestine [with the rest in Arab hands]...Now the Arabs (including the Arab citizens of Israel) are left in possession of 15 percent of that land." He argued that with respect to the occupied Arab territories, the process of dispossession is so advanced and "Jewish presence is so extensive that it precludes the possibility of a peace settlement based on a return of the West Bank to Arab sovereignty."[32] In his book *The Birth of the Palestinian Refugee Problem: 1947-49* Israeli historian Benny Morris "shatter[ed] [the] Palestinian exodus myth"[33] by demonstrating the responsibility of the Zionist leaders and Jewish army for the expulsion of Palestine's native inhabitants, with the help of an occasional massacre, between 1947 and 1949. Walid Khalidi and Erskine Childers had independently and separately exposed, in the late 1950s and early 1960s, the fallacy of the Israeli-fabricated propagandistic story about Palestinian exodus. But this was the first time that an Israeli scholar, drawing from previously unpublished army and cabinet documents, established Zionist responsibility for the expulsion of hundreds of thousands of Palestinians. Referring to the long-dominant Israeli version of the events, uncritically accepted in the West where it became a basic article of faith of the dominant frame of reference, Morris said in an interview on Israeli television that "people's minds have been warped by 40 years of nonsense."[34] Morris also described how after the "carnage" and "slaughter" of Palestinians in Lydda and Ramle in 1948, Ben-Gurion gave instructions to expel those Palestinians who survived.[35] None of these Israeli-documented inconvenient facts were allowed to disturb another basic assumption and analytical tool in the dominant frame of reference, namely, the propagandistic notion that the Palestinians are responsible for their own plight because they "left" their country in response to Arab appeals. As we shall see below, this basic fabrication will be reaffirmed in the course of the media's confrontation with the Palestinian uprising, thus suggesting that the inconvenient facts have been conveniently suppressed or ignored.

Other inconvenient facts were reported but were not used in any way to modify or introduce nuances into the usual assumptions of the "official" frame of reference. For instance, the media carried stories about "Jewish extremists" and "religious zealots" slinging army-issued submachine guns and carrying a Bible as they passionately invoked a divine right to dispossess and expel the Palestinians for the sake of "a Jewish renaissance [in] all of the Holy land."[36] The media also partially publicized the solution that these "extremists" advocate for the Israeli-Palestinian conflict. It should be noted here that media's discourse does not use "extremist" to describe mainstream Israeli leaders who are systematically and vigorously engaged in dispossessing the Palestinians, but reserve it only for those few, and therefore exceptional, cases of "extremist" leaders who advocate dispossession by vulgar and crudely violent methods such as massive expulsion of the Palestinians. These few "extremists" include for instance the usual suspects such as Ariel Sharon who supports the establishment of a Palestinian State even by force...in Jordan, and Rabbi Meir Khane who preached that the only way to deal with Arabs in Israel was to expel them "for the long term ultimate answer must not be to place a few amateurish bombs at Arab doors, but the expulsion of the Arabs of Eretz Yisrael."[37] Other media reports detailed the "torture campaign [and] the routine use of physical means and pressure" against Palestinians held prisoners in Israel.[38] In addition, some exposure was given, more in Canada than in the United States, to FBI reports about "Jewish terrorism" in North America. An internal 1986 FBI memo noted that several key Jewish suspects have fled to Israel where they sought asylum in Kiryat Arba, a Jewish settlement in the West Bank described by the FBI as a "haven for right-wing Jewish extremist elements."[39] Other FBI documents revealed that "from 1981 through 1986, 24 terrorist incidents in the United States have been attributed to Jewish extremist groups."[40]

It is also important to note that the terrorist past of Prime Ministers Begin and Shamir had been public knowledge and openly debated for years in Israel. After the June 1992 election in Israel, the *Globe and Mail* reported (July 4) that the Israeli paper *Haaretz* featured a story about the terrorist past of Prime Minister Shamir and his involvement in murders and assassinations. In particular, the paper reported that the defeated Prime Minister had been chosen for the terrorist Stern Gang because of he had "a lot of experience in murder, assassinations, planting bombs, threats and harassment." The media's dominant frame of reference, however, almost never referred to Begin or Shamir as terrorists and almost always reserved its self-righteous condemnations for the Palestinians, to the point where most Palestinians entered the collective North-American subconsciousness as either refugees or terrorists. It is also an incontrovertible fact that in sheer morbid number of victims, organized Israeli State terror, both in scale and sophistication, makes Palestinian acts of random violence look pathetically amateurish. For example, the total number of Israeli civilians killed in all acts of terrorism between 1967 and 1982 was 282 persons.[41] Yet, in one single raid, the bombardment of residential West Beirut on July 17, 1981, Israel killed 300 civilians and seriously wounded 800. In 1988 alone, there were more than twenty-five Israeli raids on Lebanese villages and Palestinian refugee camps with scores of civilian victims, routinely described by the dominant media discourse as "Palestinian guerrilla targets." Yet, the concept of "Israeli terrorism," a reality lived tragically by the Palestinians for as long as its roots and consequences have been ignored in the West, was inadmissible into the "official" frame of reference because it would be incompatible with yet another article of faith of the propaganda system: violent acts by enemies are aggression and terrorism, whereas violence committed by friends and allies, regardless of its immeasurably greater number of victims, is understandable reprisal. From this disconcerting conformity in the elite media's discourse, the British newspaper the *Manchester Guardian*, which once played a crucial role in publicizing Zionist propaganda to British public and politicians from 1916 onward, occasionally stands out as a unique exception. Thus, it recently gave an exceptional front-page prominence to Israeli State terrorism. In its February 23, 1992 weekly edition and under a leader entitled: "Israel goes back to politics by assassination," the paper reported the Israeli assassination of the Hezbollah leader in Lebanon, Sheikh Abbas Musawi and concluded with a bang: "Israel has a history of political assassination going back to before independence, with the Stern Gang and the murder of the UN negotiator, Count Folk Bernadotte. The leader of the gang, Mr. Yitzhak Shamir, is now Prime Minister." On rare occasions, when some of the more intellectually honest elite media get impatient with Israel, the facts are allowed to speak for themselves. This was one of these occasions. Israeli human rights activist Israel Shahak duly noted that these occasions were rare indeed even in the most respected liberal papers, and castigated the *Guardian* for its more frequent silence. Commenting on the paper's breaking of silence about Shamir's terrorist past, Shahak wrote to the *Guardian* (March 22, 1992):

> It would perhaps interest your readers more that Shamir's Stern Gang offered an alliance to Adolf Hitler whom it addressed with great respect in early 1941. They noted in their letter to 'Herr Chancellor Hitler' that the proposed alliance is to be based on close ideological similarities.
>
> I am noting this fact, widely discussed in Israel for years, also because it points to a long-standing negligence of the 'Guardian Weekly', namely its meticulous avoidance of description of any aspect of Jewish chauvinism or Jewish racism, and especially Jewish religious fanaticism. The corresponding traits among Arabs, are, however, reported by your paper.
>
> This inevitably causes you, quite often, to mislead your readers. For instance, you often discuss 'Israeli settlements' in the Territories. However, this term is misleading. The settlements, and all the land which was taken over by the State of Israel, are legally intended solely for Jews. Israeli Arab citizens, even if they rose to a high rank in the army and became military governors in the Territories, cannot settle in those settlements. Equally so, only those of Her Majesty's subjects who happen to be Jewish can settle there, all the others cannot, even if they are keen supporters of Shamir. This means that the settlements are one aspect of an Apartheid regime prevailing there in all aspects of life, but never mentioned by you, solely because this Apartheid favors Jews.
>
> It has been often said that those who are silent bear part of the blame for the crimes which are being encouraged by their silence. I think that this can apply to the policies of your paper, even if caused by good intentions.

Dramatic Challenges

Eric Hooglund has presented evidence of a "consistent pro-Israeli bias"[42] in press coverage of the Israeli invasion of Lebanon. Noam Chomsky has exposed American media's "overwhelming tendency, from the first day [of the Israeli invasion of Lebanon], to adopt the point of view and the general interpretations provided by the aggressor."[43] I shall make only brief reference to the Israeli invasion of Lebanon, particularly insofar as its images represented dramatic challenges to the ideas and assumptions informing elite media interpretations of the Palestinian conflict.

In clearly pitting Israelis against Palestinians, the invasion gave back to the conflict the duality of its roots, showing millions of viewers the asymmetry of a confrontation between a powerful, militarized Israel supported by a superpower against a weak, dispossessed people struggling for national survival. These dramatic images helped rescue the Palestinians from the confinement of the reductive images of refugees and terrorists, and rehabilitated them as a people fighting for their "'legitimate rights'…and…yearning 'for a just solution'…"[44] Significantly, the Palestinians also managed in the process to impress upon the enemy and Western public consciousness the extent of their resolve and determination. For instance, the idea of "heroism," reserved in the dominant frame of reference for Israeli military prowess, was grudgingly conceded to the Palestinians by observers and Israeli generals. The Palestinians' stubborn resistance and, as Chris Drake of the *BBC* put it, "tremendous battle against overwhelming military odds," led Mordechai Bar-On, former Israeli army chief education officer, to observe that "the PLO's desperate and heroic fight has, in addition to its other accomplishments, brought it glory in the eyes of the Palestinians."[45] Veteran Israeli army commander General Ehud Mizrachi, who participated in the Israeli invasion of Lebanon, lamented the fact that "every Palestinian position had a price tag and that price, regrettably, was excessively high," and said that he was "compelled to salute and respect"[46] the Palestinian fighters. In their book *Israel's Lebanon War*, respected Israeli analysts Zeev Schiff and Ehud Yaari reported how the Palestinians fought like tigers against the enormous Israeli firepower arrayed against them.

Other fundamental assumptions from the dominant frame of reference were also challenged. For instance, the misconception popularized by the media that the much-talked about balance of power in the Middle East meant some sort of delicately-preserved equilibrium between competing powers was shattered by the images of staggering military power unleashed by Israel on the grossly outnumbered Palestinians. Thus, the *Jerusalem Post* (June 7, 1982) reported that by Israeli intelligence estimates, the Palestinians had between 10,000 and 12,000 troops in Lebanon, about 35 T-34 Soviet tanks, of World War II vantage, a number of artillery pieces, anti-aircraft guns, and ground-to air-Sam 7 missiles. The Palestinians had no air or navy forces. Against these Palestinian forces and a few thousand soldiers from the decimated Lebanese army along with some anti-Israeli private militia, the Israelis launched a formidable force of 90,000 soldiers, 1,300 tanks including 650 M-48s and 810 of the latest M-60 American tanks, 1,300 armoured personnel carriers, 634 combat aircraft including 120 of the latest American F-15s and F-16 fighters, an unchallenged navy, and a multitude of terror weapons including cluster bombs, phosphorus bombs and shells, and airbust bombs and shells.[47] The relentless bombing of an Arab capital, without fear of intervention from other Arab States prompted NBC's John Chancellor, reporting from Beirut under Israeli bombardment, to speak of "an imperial Israel" bent on imposing a *Pax Hebraica* on the region. Immediately the following day Zionist demonstrators gathered in front of the NBC building to protest Chancellor's unusually audacious criticism. How could Chancellor depart from the "official" line, report what he saw, and make independent deductions incompatible with the established assumptions about peace-loving Israel?

In addition, the convenient media representation of a Palestinian threat to Israel was briefly but dramatically pre-empted by the reality of victimization — graphically illustrated by the images of massacred Palestinians in Sabra and Shatila. The reality of the conflict between a clearly powerful and aggressive Israel and a weak and helpless Palestinian people resisting exile and continued dispossession while trying to preserve whatever is left of its national existence, was reconstructed and came to life for millions of viewers. The dramatic challenge these images and those of the siege of Beirut represented to the "official" frame of reference could have triggered a process of reappraisal and intellectually honest re-examination of the dominant canons. They did not. They were interpreted by Israeli leaders as representing no more than a public relations problem, unlikely to modify the entrenched consensus of the elite media or the nature of the relationship between Israel and the United States. This assessment was vindicated by the resurfacing, practically unscathed, of the major assumptions informing the dominant frame of reference during the confrontation which pitted the elite media against the challenges of the Palestinian uprising.

Palestinian Uprising and Media's Language of Interpretation

Jan-Ola Östman's discussion of pragmatics draws attention to the relationship between language and language users whose culture, psychological make-up and sociological background determine the context in which their communicative acts are performed.[48]

Östman also draws an important distinction between explicit and implicit aspects of language. In responding to the dramatic challenges of the images of the Palestinian uprising, the elite media used implicit and explicit language to establish a context in which dominant interpretative assumptions were reiterated and confirmed. The ease with which this process of linguistic management of the unwelcome challenges was accomplished suggests that the damaging images of Israeli-Palestinian confrontation in Lebanon and the inconvenient facts that have since emerged have been reinterpreted to fit unthreateningly into the "official" frame of reference.

The language used to interview, analyze and report on the Palestinian uprising set a context which contradicted and negated the one established by the offensive asymmetrical realities communicated to the American public by the damaging images of the Palestinian uprising. In defense of the "official" frame of reference both the pragmatics (context) and the semantics (meanings) of the language used by elite media relied on the following techniques: (a) reinterpreting the reality to reverse the respective roles of oppressor and oppressed; (b) ignoring and reinterpreting inconvenient facts to neutralize their challenging impact; (c) denying the historical record and reiterating assumptions that inform the dominant frame of reference and its "official" historical record; (d) marginalizing inconvenient facts that have become too overwhelming to ignore; and (e) allowing for the unavoidable reality of Palestinian subjugation while presenting it within a context informed by the dominant assumptions, placing the blame on the victim and supporting official policy positions.

One of the first reactions to the Palestinian uprising was what Herman and Chomsky call the flake strategy: extremely negative reactions to media coverage of an issue that make it difficult to deviate from "official" assumptions and canonical beliefs. I have already mentioned the strong protests against NBC reporter John Chancellor's coverage of Lebanon in 1982. Similarly, from the very beginning of the Palestinian uprising, a Zionist writer accused the media of coverage she claimed was pro-Arab, reflecting "historical illiteracy" and indulging in "deliberate disinformation" orchestrated by "left wing forces."[49] It was a faithful reproduction of the strategy and the discourse embodied in the *Hasbra* project launched by Israel to deal with the image problem caused by the invasion of Lebanon. This flake strategy notified the media that deviation from the "official" frame of reference would be subjected to violent attacks. The flake strategy also serves another useful function: it is used by the media to claim that if they are being accused by both sides of being partial, then they must be objectively impartial.

Equally unsubtle was the vocabulary used by the media from the very beginning of the Palestinian uprising. Thus, demonstrations in Eastern Europe throughout 1988-1989 were regularly described by the media as pro-freedom and pro-democracy movements. And in a rational world, lives sacrificed by young Palestinians for their independence would be just as precious and worthy of support as those sacrificed by Chinese students for democracy or South African Blacks for freedom, as a group of American Jewish professors affirmed in newspaper advertisements in the United States. Yet, Palestinian demonstrations were frequently described with a vocabulary borrowed directly from official Israeli discourse. The media reported that the Palestinian "residents" of the occupied territories (official Israeli terminology, as if Palestinians living in their own country were simple guest workers) were engaged in acts of "violence," causing "unrest" and "disturbances."

There were also some intriguing and implicitly revealing linguistic constructions. For instance, anchors and radio announcers sometimes referred to the West Bank and Gaza as "*Israel's* occupied territories." In a *Newsweek* piece presenting Israel as "besieged," the reporters wrote: "something tragic is happening in Israel and *its* occupied territories."[50] The *Washington Post* referred to the Palestinian uprising in bold letters as "riots *in Israel.*"[51] In effect, these linguistic constructions may be suggestive of the extent to which the elite media have internalized the logical consequences of their dominant interpretations: the subjugation of the Palestinian people historically, geographically, ideologically, and even discursively to Israeli representations of the conflict.

Television played a crucial role in the dramatic challenges produced, inter alia, by the televised images of the Israeli invasion of Lebanon and the Palestinian uprising. It also played a role in the elite media's response to these challenges, by the documentaries it showed and those it failed to show, by the choice of "experts" and power agents it interviewed, and by the differences in the questions addressed to the interviewees, depending on which side they represented. Of particular significance to my interest in the pragmatics and semantics of the language of propaganda and its role in the elite media's response to the challenges of the Palestinian uprising were the two interviews PLO Chairman Yasser Arafat gave to the American Television Network ABC and to its Canadian Counterpart CBC shortly after the outbreak of the Palestinian uprising.[52]

Arafat was confronted with a forceful display of some of the fundamental assumptions informing the "official" frame of reference and was constantly forced to be on the defensive, particularly since both interviewers focused on the "violence" of the Palestinians and on their responsibility for their own plight. Both the ABC and CBC interviewers set their questions within the dominant *reinterpreted* asymmetry of the conflict in which the victim was blamed and asked to be reasonable and make more concessions. They thus focused on the question of unconditional Palestinian recognition of Israel and avoided asking Israeli officials, whom they frequently interviewed, about Israeli recognition of the Palestinian people. Further, the ABC *Nightline* interviewer inquired if the Palestinians should not accept responsibility for their fate because, after all, they "left" Palestine when Israel was established in 1948. This construction implying voluntary departure sought, in effect, to negate the inconvenient facts about Palestinian expulsion, and to reaffirm a principal pillar of the dominant frame of reference which denies Israel's responsibility and blames the victim. (Confronted with a similar approach that questioned his support for the PLO during the ABC interview with Nelson Mendela on June 21, 1990, the South-African leader dealt the *Nightline* interviewer some intellectual knock-outs, exposing the duality of criteria by which freedom and oppression are defined by the dominant media's frame of reference. The interviewer was literally speechless for a few seconds before he recovered his composure).

The CBC interviewer made more extensive, and often more aggressively creative, use of the implicit language of propaganda. For example, throughout the interview with Arafat she repeatedly used the construction "the whole world," putting it in linguistic contrast (and therefore ideological opposition) to Arafat's position, in such leaders as: "the whole world is waiting for you, why wouldn't you....; the whole world is watching you, why can't you...; Israel is waiting for you to make a move, when will you...?"[53] The vocabulary, the constructions and their context made Arafat seem responsible for obstructing peace and for holding up what "the whole world is waiting for." At the same time, this use of the language put the whole world behind Israel — since the whole world and Israel are anxiously waiting together in one camp, the good and patient one — for an Arafat isolated in another camp, the recalcitrant and obstructionist one. This created peculiarly unique images that boldly contradicted and sought to negate the actuality of the real world's condemnation of Israeli oppression, and the real world's expression of sympathy and support for the Palestinians. At one point, the interviewer seemed to have decided subconsciously that propagandistic linguistic constructions were not enough, and resorted to cognitive dissonance: the replacement of unpleasant realities by one's own perceptions of things more attuned to one's liking. This resulted in the following remarkable request: the CBC interviewer told Arafat to go on radio and tell the young Palestinians in revolt "to lay down their arms" as a goodwill gesture. This creative linguistic construction proposed nothing less than the complete reversal of the inconvenient and readily ascertainable reality, brought to millions of viewers by daily televised images, of overarmed Israeli soldiers shooting and killing unarmed Palestinian youths. That such a reversal of roles was easily accomplished, that there was no uproar from the viewers about what the interviewer was saying, bespeaks the strength of the entrenched perceptions of media and public, trained to instinctively blame the victim.

The print media also engaged in linguistic constructions that relied on some dominant assumptions to achieve role reversal. Thus, Glenn Frankel of the *Washington Post* devoted a good portion of his analyses and coverage of the Palestinian uprising to the impact of Israel's iron fist policy, not on the Palestinians as one might naturally expect given that the policy was directed against them after all, but on the Israeli soldiers and on "the soul-searching inside the army"[54] which, it was reportedly feared, might "have lost its way." It was inevitable therefore, Frankel suggested, not to see the Israeli army as a victim of "a complicated chain of circumstances," and as an army that saw itself "caught in the middle between radical forces."[55] This was a remarkable *tour de force* whereby the reporter managed to discretely equate, on the same moral plane, the Palestinians' action of resisting occupation with the Zionist settlers' action of implanting themselves among the Palestinians with the protection of the Israeli army. By depicting both Palestinians and Zionist settlers as radical forces, the reporter seemed to be striking a balance, establishing a context of moral neutrality and objective validity for his discerning analysis. In reality, Frankel's construction effectively accomplished two objectives: portray the Palestinians once more as radical, dangerous and therefore deserving subjugation while absolving Israel from responsibility since only the Zionist settlers are depicted as radical forces. It is as if the Zionist settlers had parachuted from the moon with no help from the Israeli State ideological and military apparatus to subjugate the inhospitable Palestinians and make their dispossession possible; it is as if in all of this the Israeli army were acting as a neutral United Nations-like peace-keeping force caught between these two radical communities.

Corollary to the implicit objective of absolving Israel from responsibility was the less subtle objective of portraying the Israeli army of occupation as the the "victim" in this unfortunate "chain of circumstances." To strengthen the case he was making for this unremarkably usual theme, the *Washington Post* reporter relied on a central assumption of the "official" frame of reference that could be counted on every time Israeli actions evoked horror and dismay in a public taken aback by a reality incompatible with the media-propagated image of the Israeli army. Within the context of "soul searching" and "victim of circumstances," Frankel was able to seriously assert that the Israeli army was "a fighting force that once prided itself on its sensitivity to human suffering."[56] This remarkable statement included no historical point of reference and therefore the reader was invited to construe the use of the adverb "once" as referring to what preceded the Palestinian uprising. In other words, the Israeli army prided itself on its sensitivity to human suffering until November 1987, just prior to the outbreak of the Palestinian uprising which forced the army into "unfortunate circumstances" and agonizing "soul-searching." As if the various massacres from Deir Yassein in 1948, Qibya in 1953, Kafr Qassem in 1956, to the routine collective punishment of Palestinians, the eradication of entire Palestinian villages, the blowing up of houses, the razing of refugee camps, the bombing of civilian areas and the use of prohibited lethal weapons during the invasion of Lebanon had not taken place. You would think that there had been enough "soul-searching" by now.

In effect, Frankel was making a mockery of the memory of his readers; or perhaps he knew better; his readers had already forgotten the Israeli invasion of Lebanon and the public relations damage caused by it had been contained and brought under control; the reconstruction of ideology had been successful and the management of consent both subtle and effective. In short, Frankel proposed nothing less than the complete obliteration from the collective public consciousness of whatever might have been left of these horrifying images of the Israeli invasion of Lebanon and the siege of Beirut, and of whatever doubt they might have raised about the validity of the traditional theme of the Israeli army's "sensitivity to human suffering" and the equally dominant assumption about Israel being "truly a moral state, as the original Zionist dreamers intended."[57] In the process, he used one of the reliable techniques of the dominant frame of reference: role reversal in which the Palestinians became "radical" and the Israeli army became a victim of "unfortunate circumstances." A remarkable and audacious achievement considering that daily televised images were showing to millions of viewers Israeli soldiers shooting and killing unarmed Palestinian teenagers.

The accidental killing of an Israeli girl (whose story and name were given qualitatively different coverage from that given to Palestinian victims) by an Israeli settler who had fired at Palestinian stone-throwers, gave the same *Washington Post* reporter another opportunity to set a context defined by dominant interpretations. Although the Israeli army report stated that "as far as the investigators could determine no weapon was fired by the Arabs in the village,"[58] and that the Israeli children recognized, as did the army, that Palestinian villagers actually came to help and "escort the group out of the area...toward their settlement,"[59] the American reporter was more successful than the Israeli army at establishing and insinuating at Arab guilt. He wrote: "Each side viewed her death through its own dark prism. Jewish West Bank settlers saw it as the final outrage. *Arabs as just another battle in a war.*"[60] (emphasis added) This last construction is remarkable considering the facts established by the Israeli army itself. But the intent here is not to be concerned with facts but rather with dramatizing a confrontation set in a useful ideological context: that of two radical forces. Thus, the statement that the Arabs saw the incident as "just another battle in a war" not only implied Arab guilt and absence of remorse for an incident in which Palestinians actually tried to save the Jewish victim shot by a Jewish settler, but also, once more, set a context in which the conflict was presented as, not between Israel and the Palestinians, but between Palestinians and Zionist settlers — two extremes between which the Israeli army is once more being victimized.

The elite media also reported and commented on the Palestinian uprising within a context that denied the historical record and absolved Israel of responsibility. Thus, the editors of the *Washington Post* conceded that the Palestinians had a legitimate grievance (the images sent by the uprising made such a recognition unavoidable), but confined its origins to "the 20-year occupation" which they described as being "more liberal to Palestinians than most Arab regimes are to their own citizens," and traced its cause to a war "generated by Arabs in 1967," blaming the conflict on "a continuing Arab refusal to sit down and make peace."[61] The official historical record kept by the *Washington Post* seems to have started only in 1967 as if the pre-1967 Palestinian refugees did not exist. Referring to a war "generated by the Arabs in 1967," clearly blames the Arabs without going so far as to crudely falsify the historical record about a war started by Israel. Had the paper used terms such as the war 'initiated' or 'began' or 'started' or even 'triggered' by Arabs in 1967, such constructions would be a blatant falsification of what many educated readers knew to be the reality of a *blitzkrieg* attack launched by Israel with the complicity of the Johnson administration. But the use of "generated" is brilliantly suited for the purpose: it is vague enough to obscure the real historical record while clearly blaming the Arabs for a war Israel actually started.

Israeli leaders justified their 1967 war on two grounds: First, Egyptian President Gawal Abdel Nasser had closed the Gulf of Aqaba to Israeli shipping and this allegedly threatened Israel with economic strangulation; and second, the Arabs were allegedly preparing to launch a war of destruction against Israel. Neither claim stands up to an intellectually honest examination of the real historical record. The *New York Times* (June 4, 1967) revealed that Israel received less than 10 percent

of its imports through the Gulf of Aqaba and reported American officials as saying
(June 5) that "only one Israeli vessel had passed through the straits in the last two
years," and that therefore accepting the closure of the Gulf of Aqaba was "a practical concession Israel could make without much sacrifice." At the end of the war,
the *New York Times* published a statement from Harvard University International
law professor Roger Fisher in which he said:

> United States press reports about the Gulf of Aqaba situation were
> grossly one-sided. The United Arab Republic (Egypt) had a good
> legal case for restricting traffic through the straits of Tiran...a right
> of innocent passage is not a right of free passage for any cargo any
> time. In the words of the Convention on the Territorial Sea:
> 'Passage is innocent so long as it is not prejudicial to the peace,
> good order or security of the coastal state.' In April, Israel con-
> ducted a major retaliatory raid on Syria and threatened raids of
> still greater size. In this situation was Egypt required by interna-
> tional law to continue to allow Israel to bring in oil and other
> strategic supplies through the Egyptian territory — supplies
> which Israel could use to conduct further military raids? That was
> the critical question of law. The exercise by Israel of the belligerent
> right of retaliation on Syria in April may have been morally
> justified (although the United Nations found that it was not and
> censured Israel). Even so, it provided a fair basis for the UAR to
> assert the right to exercise a comparable (and less bloody) bel-
> ligerent right — namely to close the Straits of Tiran to strategic
> cargo for Israel...taking the facts as they are I, as an international
> lawyer, would rather defend the legality of the UAR's action in
> closing the Straits of Tiran...than defend the legality of the preven-
> tive war which Israel launched this week.

Professor Fisher then regretted, before enumerating examples of American
double standards with the Arabs and the Israelis, that "one can see that it may be
difficult to convince the Arabs that the United States does not decide issues on
grounds of race or religion but on the grounds of principles."[62]

If we put aside the bombastic statements made by Arab and Egyptian leaders
more out of fear and wishful thinking than out of real power to act, the real, as opposed to the rhetorical intentions of the Egyptian leadership were made clear to
Western media and politicians, namely that Egypt had no offensive intentions
against Israel. The Egyptian troops dispatched to the Sinai were more a symbolic
gesture of solidarity with Syria in the face of Israeli threat of invasion. General
Yitzhak Rabin admitted that much in a statement published in February 1968 by
the French newspaper *Le Monde*. Rabin said that he "did not think Nasser wanted
war. The two divisions he sent to Sinai on May 14 would not have been sufficient
to launch an offensive against Israel. He knew it and we knew it."[63] Moreover,
Nasser told officials of the Johnson administration that he would be prepared to
submit the dispute to the International Court of Justice for a ruling on whether or
not Egypt acted legally in closing the Gulf of Aqaba. Israeli leaders refused. They
also turned down other offers to reach a negotiated settlement of the crisis and

adamantly refused to allow UN forces to be stationed on Israel's side of the armistice lines as Egypt had done on its side for years. The Americans were increasingly finding Egyptian proposals for a negotiated solution to the crisis difficult to refuse; the Israelis were finding them impossible to accept.[64] The war option held out the attractive prospect of achieving what the invasion of Egypt in 1956 failed to accomplish: the elimination of Nasser and his regime as symbol of pan-Arabism and Arab nationalist opposition to the destruction of the Palestinian society.

Nasser, on the other hand, welcomed the opportunity to send to Washington Egyptian Vice-President Zakaria Muhyi Eddin to negotiate a compromise settlement. On June 1, 1967, State Department official Charles Yost arrived in Cairo to prepare the way for Mohieddin's visit to Washington. He discussed with Foreign Minister Mahmoud Riad possible compromise settlements. Riad indicated that Egypt was prepared to make a major concession by accepting to live with Israeli ships passing through the Gulf of Aqaba and suggested that Egypt was even prepared to allow the flow of oil to Israel through the Gulf of Aqaba to continue. Mohieddin was expected to arrive in Washington on June 7. Israel launched the war on June 5.

Dominant Western discourse on the Arab-Israeli conflict refers to the 1967 Israeli attack as a preventive war, thus implying acceptance of the Israeli propaganda claim that Israel had to go to war to prevent the Arabs from launching a war of destruction. In reality, at no time was Israel threatened with an Arab war of destruction and, as Israeli journalist Amnon Kapeliouk found out, "at no time was Israel's existence in danger..." General Ezer Weizman, Operation Bureau Chief in June 1967, was frank: "There has never been a danger of extermination."[65] The *New York Times* reported (August 21, 1982) another frank admission by Menahem Begin himself: "The Egyptian Army concentration in the Sinai approaches do not prove that Nasser was really about to attack us. We must be honest with ourselves. We decided to attack him." Israeli generals including Haim Bar-Lev and Mattityahu Peled were even more frank; they confirmed that the claim of a threat to Israel's existence was a fabrication for useful propaganda purposes: "All these stories about the danger of extermination had been invented word by word and were *a posteriori* justification for the annexation of new Arab territories."[66]

Zionist historian Jon Kimch candidly recognized that while in public American leaders were emphasizing the importance of a peaceful settlement and a role for the United Nations, the Johnson administration was encouraging Israel to launch its war and "take care" of the situation. It encouraged the Israelis not to give in to pressures for a peaceful settlement because even the Americans "might find it necessary to join in these pressures for they had to protect themselves at all cost against the suspicion of collusion...In effect, what happened during the last days of May was that the United States had reached an *understanding* with the Israeli defence forces which cleared the way for the 5 June *initiative...*"[67] (emphasis added).

These are refreshingly frank admissions by Israeli generals, writers and historians about Israeli leaders' responsibility for preferring war over a negotiated settlement and American encouragement of Israeli belligerent intentions. But the *Washington Post* seems to keep a different "official" historical record in which Arab warmongers are by definition responsible for all violence in the region.

Nor does the "official" historical record kept by the *Washington Post* seem to have room for such inconvenient facts as the documented Arab peace plans, the PLO's readiness to negotiate with Israel on the basis of UN resolutions, or Arab, international and even American peace initiatives which were consistently rejected by Israel. But in the ideological discourse and the language of propaganda of the "official" frame of reference, democratic and peace-loving Israel is always ready to make peace while backward Arabs and terrorist Palestinians are always rejecting Israeli peace offers. It was logical therefore for the editors of the *Washington Post* to blame the conflict on "a continuing Arab refusal to sit down and make peace." In fact, the symbolic concession to Palestinian grievances made by the editors of this prestigious paper may have served less as an expression of genuine sympathy than as an excuse to defend and reaffirm the tenets of a dominant frame of reference under assault from the damaging images of the Palestinian uprising.

The negation of inconvenient facts has traditionally represented an effective mechanism for denying the Palestinians and their views fair access to public opinion. Thus, although the PLO has repeatedly indicated its willingness to recognize Israel and live peacefully beside it long before the unilateral recognition of Israel offered by the Palestine National Council (PNC) in Algiers in November 1988, the dominant assumption that the PLO was incompetent to make peace offers remained operative. Thus, in an interview with Anthony Lewis and Youssef Ibrahim of the *New York Times*, Arafat was asked if he visualized a Palestinian State living in peace with an Israeli government next door. Arafat answered: "In our Palestine National Council, we said land for peace,"[68] when the PNC met in Amman in 1984. Lewis observed that "his comments represented, I believe, Arafat's most unambiguous commitments yet to a negotiated peace with Israel."[69] In fact, as early as November 1978 Arafat told American Congressman Paul Findley to tell President Carter that: "The PLO will accept an independent Palestinian state consisting of the West Bank and Gaza, with a connecting corridor, and in that circumstance will renounce any and all violent means to enlarge the territory of that state."[70] Findley wrote that Secretary of State Vance "took note" of the statement but no public announcement was made. In April 1981, the PNC unanimously endorsed the Brezhnev plan which, in February of the same year, called for a settlement based on the sovereignty of all States in the region, including Israel. Arafat made unambiguous commitments to a two-state solution in a series of public statements in Europe and Asia in 1984, and again more recently during his interviews with ABC and CBC in January 1988, repeating these commitments once more during the Arab summit meeting in Algiers in July 1988.

If the technique of ignoring and denying inconvenient facts proved ineffective because these facts had become too overwhelming and too public to be denied, the elite media, anxious that dominant interpretations not be undermined, would integrate these facts but marginalize them to the point of implying their irrelevance. When Arafat called for negotiations with and mutual recognition of Israel and Palestine in April-May 1984, "the *Times* refused — not failed, refused — to report the fact or even to run a letter referring to it. The *Times* also refused to report, or to accept letters, on Arafat's statement of January 14, 1988 that the PLO would [recognize Israel's right to exist if it and the United States accept a PLO participation in an international Middle East Peace Conference] based on all UN resolutions, including UN 242."[71] The "official" discourse simply denied the inconvenient record of PLO peace offers. Thus, the editors of the *New York Times* wrote, "until the PLO summons the courage and wisdom to accept peace with Israel in return for some kind of Palestinian homeland it would be folly for Israel to bargain"[72] The *New York Times* was aware of the PLO peace offers but considered the PLO, by definition, incompetent to make peace offers, particularly if these were based on some form of equality of treatment between Israelis and Palestinians in which both peoples recognized each other's national rights. This was precisely the difficulty the *New York Times* had with the PLO peace offers. All that the editors would concede to the Palestinians was "some kind of Palestinian homeland," which falls short of self-determination for the Palestinian people, a position which is both consistent with the official American position and rejectionist of the international consensus supporting Palestinian rights to self-determination.

When denial could no longer be maintained and the *New York Times* finally reported the PLO position as outlined in the interview Arafat gave to its reporters Lewis and Ibrahim,[73] the story was presented in a lower front page section under the headline: "Shamir and Arafat both Scornful of U.S. Moves for Mideast Peace." This set a negative tone for what was theoretically, given the record of denying the real PLO peace offers, a most significant statement of the position of the Palestinian leadership. Still, given the *New York Times* admonitions to the PLO, one would expect that what Lewis described as "Arafat's most unambiguous commitment yet to a negotiated peace with Israel," would satisfy the editors of the influential newspaper. Judging by how it was reported, and the linguistic context within which it was presented "Arafat's most unambiguous commitment" must have fallen short of what the editors wanted. And this because by reporting the news under a negative headline saying that Arafat and Shamir were both scornful of U.S. peace initiatives, the *New York Times* was accomplishing two objectives at the same time: playing down the importance of the PLO's peace offer and therefore facilitating its rejection by the real rejectionist camp, and associating Arafat with the rejectionist Israeli camp by lumping him with Shamir and implying that both were adopting negative and ungrateful attitudes. In effect, the distinguished paper was suggesting to its educated readers that Arafat's call for negotiations with Israel was as much an obstacle to peace as Shamir's opposition to the American peace initiative. A not too subtle linguistic management of an inconvenient fact that could no longer be ignored but which had to be subordinated to the imperatives of the "official" record and its interpretation techniques.

The marginalization and reinterpretation of inconvenient facts were also evident in ABC *Nightline* anchorman Ted Koppel's interview with then Israeli Foreign Minister Shimon Peres.[74] Koppel raised the issue of the Israeli assassination in Tunis of Palestinian leader Abu Jihad, widely reported by the media as having been ordered by the Israeli cabinet with Shamir, Peres and Rabin voting in favour.[75] Instead of exploring the implications for the conflict, and indeed for international relations, of statesmen being directly implicated in acts of assassination, the ABC interviewer asked the Israeli Minister for his analysis of the assassination's impact on Palestinian-Syrian relations. This was an astonishing angle to pursue considering the information available to the interviewer about a statesman implicated in an act of murder. The approach was, however, consistent with the requirement of the dominant frame of reference and its propaganda techniques in which friends' acts of terrorism become understandable reprisals to be played down, marginalized and rendered irrelevant.

Two French writers used linguistic constructions which were at once supportive of the dominant interpretations and suggestive of the influence of the condescending Orientalist approach, popular in Europe, to the Middle East. Jean-Marie Domenach, writing in the French newspaper of record *Le Monde*, identified Israel's dilemma as how "to get rid of 1,700,000 Arabs whom no one, not even so-called 'friendly' Arab countries wish to take in." And then he added: "They can hardly be expected to be left to their own devices."[76] These constructions managed to pervert the essence of Palestinian resistance to occupation and dispossession, sidestep the significance of the Palestinian uprising, reduce the Palestinian people to a bunch of refugees who have to be "taken in" by somebody to look after — all in a context of nineteenth-century paternalistic colonialism in which the backward people are presumed to be unable to look after themselves and could not possibly be "left to their own devices." Commenting on the uprising, André Fontaine, of the same prestigious French newspaper wrote that recent events in the Middle East and "the new turn taken by the Palestinian resistance" authorized him to conclude that "this liking for the collective death has not disappeared in the East."[77] One can easily imagine the Western reaction to an "Eastern" analyst's description of the American Civil War, World War I and World War II, and French resistance to German occupation as clear signs of "Western liking for collective death." As Edward Said has shown in *Orientalism*, the Orientalist tradition, which grew around, served and was fed by colonial institutions in Europe, produced Orientalists dedicated to observing, evaluating, and condescendingly judging the East, a perennial object of both fascination and domination. By "covering" the Palestinian uprising with an Orientalist tradition as a backdrop for all analytical and interpretative contexts, these distinguished French writers used linguistic constructions which in effect supported and reinforced many of the usual assumptions of the "official" frame of reference dominant in the West.

Occasionally, the persistent and popular character of the Palestinian uprising elicited dissident, empathetic reactions. Anthony Lewis, the leading media liberal in the United States, described the uprising as the latest chapter in "the Palestinian struggle"[78] — a sympathetic term connoting determined effort to achieve legitimate aspirations. CBS News anchorman Dan Rather introduced a report about the Palestinian uprising as coming from "occupied Palestine,"[79] an image-rich expression whose evocative power briefly but poignantly restored to the Palestinians their continuous and emotional association with their country and its plight — a reality negated by the vagueness of the dominant term "occupied territories." But Rather dropped that reference rather quickly in subsequent broadcasts, presumably after its significance and import were brought to his attention. Mary McGrory, one of the very few writers who dared to criticize Israel in the elite media, wrote about Palestinians "living under apartheid," and remarked that "if those killed and wounded were Israelis, you can imagine the outcry. But the casualties were Palestinians...and the silence on Capitol Hill was awful."[80]

The local print media, less sophisticated and less pretentious, were less disciplined in adhering to the assumptions of the dominant frame of reference. The language of these papers in their news coverage and expressions of opinion reflected more closely the reality of the Israeli-Palestinian confrontation and ignored the traditional limits which circumscribe all debates and discussions about the Palestine conflict. Israeli repression of Palestinian nationalism was condemned for its "grotesque" and "vicious" character. The Israeli policy of systematically "uprooting [the Palestinians] from their homeland" was denounced. Headlines and news stories recognized the existence of "the Palestinian people" and referred to "occupied Palestinian territories."[81] Revelations by Israeli scholar Benny Morris about the responsibility of Zionist leaders for the expulsion of Palestinians from Palestine, along with a critical article I wrote for a local newspaper were printed under a screaming headline that read: "Palestine: The Brutal Truth."[82] Editorials hinted at the Nazi-like character of Israeli actions as they condemned "the shootings, the deportations, the house burnings...and the makeshift gas chamber."[83]

When the media's dominant interpretations and underlying assumptions were challenged by the support for Palestinian self-determination articulated by the highly visible black presidential candidate Jesse Jackson, apologists of the "official" frame of reference responded aggressively. For instance, following Super Tuesday's remarkable showing, in March 1988, by Jesse Jackson in his bid for the Democratic Party's nomination, CBS anchorman Dan Rather invited William Safire of the *New York Times* to analyze the results. Safire chose to focus on what he called "the danger" of the Jackson candidacy, which he traced to his position on the Israeli-Palestinian conflict — a position which essentially called for mutual recognition of Palestinian and Israeli rights. Safire also ridiculed Jackson's proposal for the internationalization of Jerusalem, saying that it would be like calling for the internationalization of Washington D.C. Safire and Rather laughed, but Rather preferred to keep silent about, unless he was unaware of, the fact that while the international community recognized Washington as the capital of the United States, it rejected Israel's claim on Jerusalem as its capital which is recognized only by two States: Costa Rica and El Salvador, both recipients of special Israeli military assistance. The rest of the international community, including the United States, rejects Israel's illegal annexation of East Jerusalem. But this fact did not keep this highly influential media personality from making an inappropriate and misleading analogy before millions of American viewers, and get away with it.

While more critical of Israeli actions than the American elite media, the *Globe and Mail,* Canada's only national newspaper and counterpart to the *New York Times*, also relied on the dominant frame of reference and its various techniques to construct a context for some of its stories about the Palestinian uprising. Thus, it presented Israeli labour leader Shimon Peres as a man dedicated to a negotiated settlement and whose efforts for peace are hampered by "his own Prime Minister Yitzhak Shamir, or *outright refusal...(of) the Palestinians and the Arab states.*"[84] In another piece about Israel, this influential Canadian paper gave respectability to one of the central assumptions of the elite media's interpretative frame: Israeli innocence and Arab guilt. One of its reporters opined: "After all, in forty years there have been five wars —*and all began as a result of aggression against the new state.*"[85] (emphasis added). The reality is quite different from this crass propagandistic statement. The 1948 war was initiated by the Zionist leaders in March for expansionist purposes and the Arab armies' belated intervention in May barely managed to stop the fall of all of Palestine under Zionist control. The 1956 and 1967 wars were initiated by Israel for political and largely expansionist purposes, as can easily be documented from Israeli sources. The 1973 war was initiated by Egypt and Syria after Israeli leaders refused all UN and Egyptian entreaties for a negotiated withdrawal from the occupied Arab territories. The 1973 Arab military offensive was directed at Israeli troops, not at Israel, occupying Egyptian and Syrian territories. The 1982 Israeli invasion of Lebanon was launched by Israel not because of Palestinian aggression but precisely because the PLO's respect of the 11-month cease-fire along the Lebanese borders threatened to enhance the international credibility of the Palestinian leadership as the inevitable peace interlocutor at a time Israeli leaders were planning war to liquidate the Palestinian resistance once and for all. The remarkable *Globe and Mail* statement was either the product of unusual ignorance or crude falsification of the historical record or both. At any rate, it was perfectly compatible with the requirements of the "official" record and its propaganda discourse. One can easily imagine the uproar against the *Globe and Mail* if such ignorance and falsification were directed against the Zionists or even against a different party with less powerful political supporters. Consider for instance the possible repercussions of the publication in this respected paper of a statement such as: "World War II was started by an act of Polish aggression against Germany." But with regard to the Middle East and particularly the Palestine conflict, the *Globe and Mail* writer was able to ignore the historical record and prevent its easily documented facts from disturbing or even introducing some nuances into the ignorant, false, crude but convenient assumption of permanent Arab guilt and inherent Israeli innocence.

The November 1988 meeting in Algiers of the PNC and the adoption of some historic and far-reaching decisions, which included the proclamation of an independent Palestinian State, represented dramatic and normative challenges that could not be ignored. The PNC specifically accepted the 1947 UN Resolution partitioning Palestine into a Jewish State and an Arab Palestinian State, and thus officially renounced all legal claims to the major part of Palestine on which Israel was established. The *New York Times* responded to these decisions by using the marginalization of inconvenient facts and role reversal strategies. It dismissed the Palestinian peace offer because it "amounted to the same old fudge that Arafat had offered up for years."[86] (Note the indirect recognition of the existence of previous Palestinian peace offers and the implication that the problem was not that the PLO did not make peace offers, but rather it was that the *New York Times* did not like the offers). The editors of the *New York Times* found that "the Algiers meeting, regrettably, became another wasted opportunity." This made it easy to blame the Palestinian leadership for not being responsive to the anguish of the Palestinians in revolt who "are clamoring for a new approach." In effect, the PLO's peace offer was being rejected by the influential paper because it was incompatible with the rejectionist assumptions of the dominant frame of reference. The elite media are unaccustomed to associating Palestinians with the concept of "peace plans" (media language of interpretation does not use constructions such as " Palestinian peace plan") which, by definition, is reserved for American and Israeli plans. The strategy of marginalization was used again when the PLO chairman finally used the very language demanded by Washington to unequivocally recognize Israel and renounce terrorism before the United States could begin dialogue with the Palestinian leadership. The *New York Times* was reluctant to recognize the significance and implications of the PLO statements. It recognized that the opening of contact between the Americans and the Palestinians was "a stunning breakthrough" but attributed it, not to the unusual concessions made by the PLO, but to "the be-wildering Middle East diplomatic gyrations."[87] It seemed at the time that nothing the Palestinians could do or say would win them the favour of the editors of the prestigious paper.

The challenges of the Palestinian uprising, on the other hand, may have been responsible for forcing government officials to concede the brutality of Israel's repression and the impracticality of continued occupation, which the American government had been effectively, if not officially, supporting. When then Canadian Minister for External Affairs, Joe Clark, criticized before an Israeli lobby group Israeli actions which he qualified as "unacceptable," his Zionist audience of members of the Canada-Israel Committee, jeered, booed, and many walked out in protest. The incident was indicative both of the privileged treatment Zionist sup-porters of Israeli policies have been accustomed to receiving — hence the rage at criticisms of Israeli repression — and of the impact on the public that the damaging images of Israeli repression must have had. Indeed, the strong public support for the Minister's criticism of Israel vindicated his correct reading of the public mood.[88] A similar recognition seems to have taken place in the United States. Following the April 1988 Israeli assassination of Abu Jihad, Yasser Arafat's deputy and top military man of the PLO, former American Congressman Paul N. "Pete" Mc-Closkey said: "Israel is an ugly little nation that no longer deserves support," a statement broadcast by a major television network for it represented an unprece-dented level of criticism of Israel.[89] Furthermore, an American administration offi-cial described President Bush and Secretary of State James Baker as "working to rectify the impression which developed in Israel during the Reagan years that Is-rael is more important to the U.S. than the U.S. is to Israel."[90] Baker told the power-ful pro-Israeli lobby, the American Israel Public Affairs Committee (AIPAC), that they should urge Israel "to lay aside, once and for all, the unrealistic vision of the greater Israel."[91]

Yet, there is no evidence that a substantive change in American foreign policy or in the basic assumptions of the "official" frame of reference as reflected by the language, context and positions of public opinion makers, has taken place. The American government continued to finance the cost of Israeli occupation, and in 1989 Congress voted to give Israel $600 million in addition to the regular $3 billion in annual forgivable aid, with $25 million of the additional funds for settlement of Soviet Jews. In an interview Arafat gave to NBC *Meet the Press* before the Iraqi in-vasion of Kuwait and the vilification of the PLO because of its position on the crisis, the Palestinian leader complained about the exclusion of the PLO from the unfold-ing peace process; but he also expressed commitment to a negotiated settlement and to the continuation of the PLO-American dialogue. After the interview, the principal interviewer asked the two guest reporters for their assessment of Arafat's answers. Bob Novak dismissed Arafat's answers as "ranting and raving...and propaganda from the 1960s and the 1970s."[92] The inconvenient reality of Pales-tinian commitment to a negotiated peace with Israel was rejected and grossly reinterpreted to conform with the media's dominant representations and inter-pretations of the Palestinian conflict. Moreover, the current Middle East peace negotiations seem to largely reflect the ideas of the Israeli government, and con-tinues to be *the* "peace process." The Palestinian peace plan, presented at the 1988 PNC meeting in Algiers, remains excluded and ignored, as does the Palestinian leadership in exile. Absent from the current peace process are any references to the PLO, the principle of self-determination, the Palestinian right of return or a Palestinian State. Debate and discussions continue to be circumscribed by the "official" frame of reference and by its established canons.

Conclusion

For decades, the Western media, and particularly the elite media which inform and mould the perceptions of the educated and politically-conscious classes, have adopted the historical version and the normative views of the Zionists-Israelis with regard to the Arab-Israeli-Palestinian conflict. These views became so entrenched, so supremely dominant and unchallenged that they developed into canonical truths, an "official" frame of reference with unshakable assumptions, unquestioned interpretative contexts, and unrivalled linguistic management of all events, historical analyses, developments and confrontations in the conflict over Palestine.

Recently, there have been numerous challenges to the "official" frame of reference's hold on representations and interpretations of the Palestine question. These challenges included the publication in the West by Israeli writers of Israeli-documented evidence of the real historical record, largely at variance with the one propagated by the elite media. Other challenges came from sustained exposure in the West to the images of the Israeli invasion of Lebanon. Because of the power of the elite media, the nature of the relationships between media, interest groups and State apparatus, and a host of other reasons, the real historical record and the competing normative interpretations of the various aspects of the conflict were ignored. The Israeli invasion of Lebanon created an intellectual climate in which it was possible to raise questions about the validity of the media's uncontested frame of reference, its language of propaganda and its monopoly on representations and interpretations of the Palestine question. While indeed questions were asked, doubts were raised, and genuine anxiety expressed, not least by Jewish critics of Israeli policies, the ascendency of the "official" frame of reference, its assumptions, interpretative contexts and its language of propaganda were shaken but remained in control. This was made possible both by the inherent resilience of the strongly-entrenched pro-Israeli views and by the success of the campaign of ideological reconstruction, sweeping aside doubts and cynicism about Israeli policies and reaffirming the supremacy of the "official" views about the conflict.

The Palestinian uprising presented dramatic challenges that could not be ignored because of their power (if left unchallenged) to undermine, maybe more severely than the Israeli invasion of Lebanon, the basic assumptions of the "official" perspective. It was therefore necessary to manage these damaging images of overarmed Israeli troops shooting unarmed Palestinian youngsters. Inconvenient realities and facts were linguistically managed, reinterpreted, neutralized and integrated within contexts derived from the "official" record on the conflict; thus the reality of Palestinian subjugation and oppression was unavoidably conceded but without modifying dominant assumptions or questioning official policy values. On the contrary, reporters, analysts, editorial writers and interviewers — often reflecting unconscious bias but sometimes aware of what they were doing and saying — used a variety of techniques which included reinterpretation of reality to reverse respective roles of oppressor and oppressed, neutralization of inconvenient facts through denial or marginalization, denial of the historical record, repeated affirmation of dominant assumptions, and the use of different criteria to establish worth and credibility.

The analysis of the pragmatics and the semantics of the language used to interview, report on and analyze the events of the Palestinian uprising shows that it continued to reflect a resilient frame of reference that reinterprets and integrates the factual, normative, and dramatic challenges confronting its "official" record. Elite media's dominant interpretations remained compatible with official State policy and responsive to the needs of powerful interest groups. Thus, despite symbolic concessions made to the inescapable reality of Palestinian subjugation, the elite media's normative assumptions and interpretative contexts remained rejectionist of both the historical record and the international consensus on the legitimacy of Palestinian national rights.

Notes

1. Christopher Sykes, *Cross Roads to Israel: Palestine from Balfour to Begin* (London, 1965), quoted in Punyapriyta Dasgupta, *Cheated by the World: The Palestinian Experience* (New Delhi: Orient Longman, 1988), p. 43.
2. Yehoshua Porath, *The Emergence of the Palestine-Arab National Movement 1918-1929* (London, Frank Cass, 1974), p. 56-57.

3. *Israeleft* no. 132, September 1, 1978, quoted in Jan Metzger, Martin Orth and Christian Sterzling, *This Land is Our Land* (London, Zed Books, 1983), pp. 32-33.
4. *New Outlook* (November/December, 1978), p. 34.
5. See Walter Lippmann, *Public Opinion* (New York, Macmillan, 1961); Harold D. Lasswell, "The Theory of Political Propaganda," *American Political Science Review*, 21 (1927); and Edward L. Bernays, (ed.) *The Engineering of Consent* (Norman, University of Oklahoma Press, 1955).
6. See The Glasgow University Media Group (Peter Beharrel, Howard Davis, John Eldridge, John Hewitt, Jean Oddie, Greg Philo, Paul Walton, and Brian Winston), *Bad News* (London, Routledge & Kegan Paul, 1976); see also by the same authors, *More Bad News* (London, RKP, 1980); see also Greg Philo, John Hewitt, Peter Beharree, and Howard Davis, *Really Bad News* (London: RKP, 1980); see also Lucinda Broadbent, John Eldridge, Gordon Kimmett, Greg Philo, Malcolm Spaven, and Kevin Williams, *War and Peace News* (Milton Keynes, Open University, 1985).
7. Edward S. Herman and Noam Chomsky, *Manufacturing Consent: The Political Economy of the Mass Media* (New York, Pantheon Books, 1988).
8. See Edward S. Herman, "The New York Times on the 1984 Salvadoran and Nicaraguan Elections," in *Covert Action Information Bulletin*, no. 21 (Spring, 1984), reprinted in *Mesoamerica* (September, 1984), pp. 15-16.
9. See Janice Terry, "A Content Analysis of American Newspaper," in Abdeen Jabara and Janice Terry, (eds.) *The Arab World from Nationalism to Revolution* (Wilmette, Illinois, Medina University Press International, 1971).

10. See Michael W. Suleiman, "World Public Opinion and the Palestinian Question," in Glenn E. Perry (ed.) *Palestine: Continuing Dispossession* (Belmont, MA, Association of Arab-American University Graduates, 1986); see also Michael Suleiman, *American Images of Middle East Peoples: Impact of the High School* (New York, Middle East Studies Association of North America, 1977); see also the series on "Media and U.S. Perceptions of the Middle East," *American-Arab Affairs* (Fall, 1982); see also Edmund Ghareeb (ed.) *Split Vision: The Portrayal of Arabs in the American Media* (Washington, D. C., American-Arab Affairs Council, 1977); and Michael C. Hudson and Ronald G. Wolfe, (eds.) *The American Media and the Arabs* (Washington, D. C., Center for Contemporary Arab Studies, Georgetown University, 1980).

11. See Noam Chomsky, *Pirates and Emperors* (Montreal, Black Rose Books, 1987).

12. See Roslind Brunt and Martin Jordan, "The Politics of 'Bias': How Television Audiences View Current Affairs," in Jeremy Hawthorn (ed.), *Propaganda, Persuasion and Polemics* (London, Edward Arnold, 1987), pp. 141-155.

13. E. H. Hutchison (a UN observer from the United States), *Violent Truce* (New York, Devin-Adair, 1956), cited by David Hirst in *The Gun and the Olive Branch*, (London: Faber and Faber, 1984), pp. 181-182.

14. Ralph Crow, "Zionism and the American Press: Is there Bias?" *Middle East Forum*, vol. 32, no. 3, (957), pp. 78-82.

15. Robert I. Friedman, "Selling Israel to America: The Hasbara Project Targets the U.S. Media," *Mother Jones* (February/March 1987).

16. Ibid.

17. See Michael W. Suleiman, "American Public Support of Middle Eastern Countries: 1939-1979," in Michael C. Hudson and Roland G. Wolfe (ed.), *The American Media and the Arabs*, pp. 13-36. (Washington, D.C., Center for Contemporary Arab Studies, Georgetown University, 1980), p. 36.

18. Ibid., p. 14-24.

19. Doreen Ingrams, *"Palestine Papers 1917-1922: Seeds of Conflict* (London, John Murray, 1972), p. 31.

20. Robert I. Friedman, *Mother Jones*, op. cit.,

21. Tom Segev, *Nineteen Forty-nine: the First Israelis* (New York, The Free Press, 1986), p. 23.

22. Simha Flapan, *The Birth of Israel: Myths and Realities* (New York, Pantheon Books: New York, 1987), pp. 4- 8.

23. Ibid., 10.

24. Jean and Simone Lacouture, *Egypt in Transition*, translated by Frances Scarf (New York, Criterion Books, 1958), 462.

25. See *Le Monde*, February 19, 1970.

26. Noam Chomsky, *The Fateful Triangle: Israel, the United States, and the Palestinians* (Montreal, Black Rose Books, 1984), pp. 64-65.

27. Noam Chomsky, *The Chomsky Reader* (New York, Pantheon Books, 1987), p. 394.

28. Abba Eban, "Obstacles to Autonomy," *New Outlook* (Tel Aviv, June/July, 1984), cited in ibid., p. 390.

29. Ibid., p. 390.

30. Ibid., p. 390.

31. *New York Times*, September 3, 1982.

32. *Washington Post*, reprinted in the *Manchester Guardian Weekly*, April 7, 1985.

33. Ian Black in the *Manchester Guardian Weekly*, March 23, 1986.

34. Ibid.

35. Benny Morris, "Operation Dani and the Palestinian Exodus from Lydda and Ramale in 1948," *The Middle East Journal*, vol. 40, no. 1, (Winter 1986), pp. 81-109, the quote comes from p. 91.

36. *Newsweek*, April 5, 1982.
37. *The Globe and Mail* (Toronto), May 2, 1986.
38. Ian Black, *The Manchester Guardian Weekly*, November 8, 1987.
39. *Washington Post*, November 19, 1987.
40. Ibid.
41. B. Michael, *Haaretz*, July 16, 1982, cited in Chomsky, *The Fateful Triangle*, op. cit., p. 74.
42. *American Arab Anti-Discrimination Committee*, "U.S. Press Coverage of the Israeli Invasion of Lebanon," no. 10, (Washington, 1982), cited in ibid., 288.
43. Ibid., p. 288.
44. Ronald Reagan quoted by Clovis Maksoud in the *New York Times*, September 3, 1982.
45. Mordechai Bar-On, "The Palestinian Aspects of the War in Lebanon," *New Outlook* (October, 1982), cited by Chomsky in *The Fateful Triangle*, op. cit., p. 312.
46. In a statement broadcast by the Israeli army radio at 1:30 p.m. on June 12, 1982 and printed in *PCNA Newsletter* (August, 1983), pp. 7-9.
47. International Institute for Strategic Studies, *The Military Balance 1982-1983* (London, International Institute for Strategic Studies, 1982), *Financial Times*, June 23, 1982; *Jerusalem Post*, December 10, 1982.
48. See Jan-Ola Östman, "Pragmatic Markers of Persuasion," in Jeremy Hawthorn (ed.) *Propaganda, Persuasion and Polemic* (London, Edward Arnold, 1987), pp. 91-105.
49. Barbara Amiel, "The Message between the Lines," *Maclean's* (Toronto), April 4, 1988.
50. *Newsweek*, January 11, 1988.
51. *Washington Post*, January 11, 1988.
52. January 7, 1988 with ABC *Nightline*, and January 14, 1988 with CBC *Journal*.
53. CBC *Journal*, January 14, 1988.
54. *Washington Post*, reprinted in the *Manchester Guardian Weekly*, February 7, 1988.
55. *Washington Post*, reprinted in the *Manchester Guardian Weekly*, April 17, 1988.
56. Ibid.
57. Georgie-Anne Geyer, reprinted in the *Province* (Vancouver, Canada) January 6, 1988.
58. *Globe and Mail* (Toronto, Canada) April 8, 1988.
59. Ibid.
60. *Washington Post*, April 17, 1988.
61. *Washington Post*, reprinted in the *Manchester Guardian Weekly*, January 24, 1988.
62. The *New York Times*, June 11, 1967.
63. Anthony Nutting, *Nasser* (London, Constable and Company, 1972), p. 410.
64. William B. Quandt, *Decade of Decisions: American Policy Toward the Arab-Israeli Conflict, 1967-1976* (Berkeley, University of California Press, 1977), p. 57.
65. Amnon Kapeliouk, "Israïl était-il réellement menacé d'extermination?," *Le Monde*, June 3, 1972; and Amnon Kapeliouk, "Les occasions manquées du conflit de juin 1967," *Le Monde Diplomatique*, June 1992.
66. Ibid.
67. Jon Kimch, *There Could Have Been Peace* (New York, The Dial Press, 1973), p. 258.
68. *New York Times*, March 12, 1988.
69. *New York Times*, March 13, 1988.
70. Paul Findley, *They Dare to Speak Out: People and Institutions Confront Israel's Lobby* (Westport, Connecticut, Lawrence Hill & Company, 1985), p. 13.
71. *AP*, January 15, reported by Noam Chomsky in "The Palestinian Uprising: A Turning Point?" *Z*, May 1988. I am indebted to Professor Chomsky who was good enough to share this information with me.
72. *New York Times*, March 2, 1988.
73. *New York Times*, March 13, 1988.
74. ABC, April 28, 1988.

75. Jean-Pierre Langelier, *Le Monde*, April 20, 1988, reprinted in *Manchester Guardian Weekly*, May 1, 1988.
76. *Le Monde* (Paris), May 14, 1988.
77. *Le Monde* (Paris), February 10, 1988.
78. *New York Times*, reprinted in the *Globe and Mail* (Toronto), January 16, 1988.
79. *CBS News*, January 6, 1988.
80. *Washington Post*, reprinted in the *Manchester Guardian Weekly*, January 17, 1988.
81. *Vancouver Sun* (Vancouver), April 2, 1988.
82. *The Province*, (Vancouver), March 27, 1988.
83. *The Province*, April 17, 1988.
84. *The Globe and Mail* (Toronto), June 13, 1988.
85. *Globe and Mail*, (Toronto), June 18, 1988
86. *New York Times*, November 16, 1988.
87. *New York Times*, November 20, 1988.
88. *Globe and Mail* (Toronto), March 11, 1988.
89. *CBS News*, April 20, 1988.
90. Richard C. Hottelet, "Pushing U.S. Policy out of its Rut," *Christian Science Monitor*, August 10-16.
91. Ibid., 18.
92. NBC *Meet the Press*, December 10, 1989.

PART II

THE WAR AGAINST IRAQ

CHAPTER FIVE

The Making of a Crisis

The 1990 Iraqi invasion of Kuwait was a violation of international law which was vigorously and rightly condemned by the international community. Iraq's grievances against Kuwait may not have been groundless but resorting to aggression and invasion of a sovereign country is wholly unjustified as a means of resolving disputes. The code of morality is indivisible and trying to rationalize exceptions to it is an attempt to set up two parallel codes, one for friends and another for enemies.

In choosing to respond to the crisis precipitated by the Iraqi action with military confrontation and in waging war against Iraq, US President George Bush invoked the necessity of upholding the rule of law in a new world order.

The ideal of a new world order is praiseworthy. But the historical record shows that wars have not traditionally ushered in new world orders. American President Woodrow Wilson promised that World War I would bring about a new order no longer based on the discredited system of nineteenth century balance of power which led to war, but on the principle of self-determination. It didn't happen. The post-war settlement in the Middle East was imposed by force against the wishes of the people and based on the colonial interests of France and England who divided the region amongst themselves. World War II was followed by the establishment of the United Nations whose charter was based on the primacy of the principle of peaceful resolution of conflicts and the sanctity of the rule of law. But the necessary attempt to give the International Court of Justice compulsory jurisdiction was opposed by the United States. The Connally Amendment rejected the jurisdiction of the International Court of Justice in "disputes with regard to matters which are essentially within the domestic jurisdiction of the United States *as determined by the United States of America*."[1] This essentially placed the United States above international law, agreeing to abide by or reject its principles and universal applicability as it saw fit — a tenuous basis for building respect for the rule of law. The obsession with containing the Soviet Union and preventing it from exporting its system to the Third World led to a new world order which was very much like the old order — based, not on the rule of international law, but on the balance of power, and the new balance of terror. The result was a cold war between the two superpowers essentially fought in the Third World.

The Bush administration's professed concern for the sanctity of international law is also praiseworthy. But one can legitimately ask who entrusted Washington with the task of being the guardian at the gate. The historical record of its foreign policy could not be said to have done much to enhance respect for the rule of international law. In its obsessive policy of combatting Third World nationalism, Washington subverted democratically elected regimes (Iran 1952, Guatemala 1954, Chile 1973), invaded sovereign nations (Dominican Republic 1965, Grenada 1985, Panama 1989), and warred against neighbours (Nicaragua in the 1980s.), not to mention its long, fateful and ultimately losing intervention in Vietnam.

In the Middle East, the United States did make two constructive and admirable stands: the first was in 1919 when President Wilson sent an American commission (the King-Crane Commission) to ascertain the wishes of the people and help establish the post-War settlement in the Middle East on the basis of self-determination. The second was in 1956 when the United States strongly opposed the Anglo-French-Israeli invasion of Egypt following President Nasser's nationalization of the Suez Canal. President Eisenhower condemned the action and insisted on and obtained Israeli withdrawal from the occupied Sinai. He rightly described his diplomatic success as a triumph for the United Nations and for the rule of law. To most Arabs, however, these constructive American stands were dwarfed by the subsequent disappointing record of American foreign policy in the region after the disastrous 1956 invasion of Egypt put an end to the traditional Anglo-French imperial influence in the Middle East. During the 1960s and particularly after the 1967 Arab-Israeli war, American foreign policy showed a consistent proclivity to pursue inherently contradictory goals: to have ready and cheap access to strategic Arab resources yet continue to effectively, if not officially, support Israeli occupation of Arab territories and Israeli military domination of the region.

In its support of Israel, the United States often found itself alone against the whole world. Washington went so far as to threaten to destroy the United Nations organization by withdrawing from it completely if its members went ahead and used the sanctions provided for under the Charter for members who consistently defied the organization and the will of the international community, an area in which Israel holds a unique record. Thus, two attempts by the UN members to expel Israel, in 1975 and again in 1982, were foiled because of American threats. In addition, the United States almost consistently used its veto power to block at the Security Council resolutions condemning Israel's behaviour and continued defiance of earlier Security Council resolutions.

Thus, in May 1990, a 1,000-page report from the Swedish Save the Children Organization documented that the Israeli army "had systematically become child-killers. Between December 1987 and December 1989, 159 children under age 16 were killed by soldiers. The average age of the dead was 10. Between 50,000 and 63,000 children were beaten, gassed or wounded."[2] Yet, less than a month after the publication of that report, the Bush administration exercised its veto power to block a Security Council Resolution calling for sending UN observers to investigate Israeli violations of Palestinian human rights in the occupied Palestinian territories. More than 100 countries have now recognized the State of Palestine. Washington, however, continued to deny the unstoppable international support for the Palestinian national identity, threatening to cut off funds to UN agencies that accepted Palestine as a member State. And this at a time when a report by the Rand Corporation recently commissioned by the US Defense Department, concluded that sooner or later there will be a Palestinian State.

The war against Iraq in 1991 was fought in the name of the United Nations with the official aim of putting an end to Iraqi occupation of Kuwait. Yet, it started with the systematic destruction of the Iraqi industrial-military complex, hardly a United Nations aim. Washington's rejection during the war of several Soviet peace plans, accepted by Iraq and providing for unconditional withdrawal from Kuwait, confirmed American determination to eliminate Iraq as a regional power. As early as four days after the beginning of the war American officials were admitting that "Iraq must be destroyed militarily irrespective of whether it gets out of Kuwait or not."[3] This was more of an American-Israeli goal than a United Nations goal.

Having eliminated Iraq as a major Arab power with the potential of challenging Israeli domination of the region, the United States worked hard to eliminate the Palestinian leadership as a legitimate partner at the negotiating table. Washington claimed that the PLO backed Saddam Hussein in the war and therefore lost the right to be at the negotiating table. This is a spurious argument. While the PLO position did hurt its international stand and gave an opportunity to its detractors to question its credibility, the legitimacy of the PLO as representative of the Palestinians does not derive from its strategic calculations or miscalculations. It derives from the overwhelming support the organization enjoys among the Palestinians and from the recognition granted it by the international community. In eliminating the PLO as a negotiating partner and in giving in to Israeli demands that the Palestinian delegation at the Madrid peace conference, convened in October 1991, not include Palestinians from East Jerusalem, Washington reduced the Palestinian conflict to the only dimension that seemed acceptable to Israel, that of administrative arrangements for the occupied Arab territories which the Shamir government did not miss an opportunity to insist that it would never give up — all the while accelerating the pace of dispossessing the Palestinians under occupation, expropriating their land and erecting new Jewish settlements.

The war against Iraq may have kicked the Vietnam syndrome, said to be responsible for inhibiting American projections of power, preserved the petromonarchies of the Middle East, and enhanced Israeli domination of the region, but will UN Security Council resolutions which were good enough to wage total war against Iraq be good enough to get Israel to comply with the will of the international community and recognize the national rights of the Palestinian people? Will UN resolutions that justified ending Iraqi occupation of Kuwait by force be good enough to end Israeli occupation of Palestinian, Syrian, and Lebanese territories by peaceful means? The answer to these questions will surely provide an indication of the nature of the new world order as it applies to the Middle East. A critical analysis of the anatomy of crisis and confrontation and the war against Iraq leads to the perhaps cynical but eminently realistic conclusion that far from being based on the rule of law, the new world order looks more like the old one which existed at the end of World War II: a unipolar world dominated by only one military superpower determined to prevent challenges to its regional and global hegemony and intent upon using all necessary means including military intervention to defend its economic interests and all regional socio-political and military order capable of advancing those interests.

The Iran-Iraq Conflict Factor

In its drive to contain the Soviet Union and interdict its access to the Middle East, the United States sought to extend to the region a modern version of *cordon sanitaire* consisting of a chain of military alliances encircling the Soviet Union from all points and containing its dreaded communist influence. The Middle Eastern link in this military encirclement was the Baghdad Pact, directed at the so-called soft-belly of the Soviet Union. The pact was opposed by Israel which feared and opposed any rapprochement between the West and the Arabs, and by Egyptian President Gamal Abdel Nasser who argued that the threat to the Arabs came not from the Soviet Union but from Israel. The overthrow of the English-sponsored Hashemite monarchy in Iraq in 1958 took Baghdad out of the Western orbit and placed it in an Arab "revolutionary" camp dedicated to pan-Arabist ideals. This enhanced Iraq's profile as an opponent of the status quo and enemy of Israel and placed it on the American list of "radical revolutionary" forces opposed to American interests and al-lies in the area. American foreign policy makers responded by articulating an American Middle East foreign policy based on military interventions to support the status quo against revolutionary upheavals. The policy was embodied in the Eisen-hower Doctrine, first invoked to justify intervention in Lebanon to support a pro-American president against the rising tide of pro-Nasser nationalist forces. At the same time, Israel responded to the changes in Baghdad by launching a major opera-tion for the destabilisation of Iraq mainly through financial, military and logistical support to Iraq's Kurdish minority in the north.

When Britain announced, in 1968, its intention to withdraw from east of Suez by 1971, a struggle for power over the Gulf began between Iraq and Iran, a rivalry fuelled by Israeli and American support for the Shah's regime in Iran. When a new "revolutionary" Baath government came to power in Baghdad in 1969, tension be-tween Iraq and Iran steadily grew and was exacerbated to the point of crisis. Teheran abrogated the 1937 Iraqi-Iranian treaty which had established the borders between the two countries at Shatt al-Arab, and relations between Baghdad and Teheran deteriorated until they were completely severed in 1971. The Baghdad government, directing its attention to its conflict with Iran and turning away from its publicly-declared commitment to pan-Arabist ideals, sought and obtained weapons from the Soviet Union with whom it signed a Friendship Treaty. This was a strategic success for Israel whose periphery strategy aimed at diverting Arab at-tention from the Arab-Israeli conflict by supporting non-Arab nations on the edge of the Arab heartland, Iran, Turkey, and Ethiopia, in an ongoing effort to weaken all Arab States. Iraq's decision to turn its attention to the conflict with Iran was also a failure for pan-Arabism and a cause of a serious rift between the two sister Baathist governments in Baghdad and Damascus; the Syrians accused the Iraqis of shirking away from their Arab responsibilities in the battle against Israel and wast-ing their energy in the wrong direction.

Impressed by the Israeli lightening attack and military performance in the 1967 Arab-Israeli war, and by the Shah of Iran's megalomanic ambitions, the Nixon ad-ministration saw new opportunities for the defense of American interests in the Middle East without the direct involvement of American troops. The 1969 Nixon Doctrine envisaged reliance on regional surrogate powers to enforce respect for the status quo and defend American interests. In the Middle East, this role was fulfilled by Iran in the Gulf and Israel in the Fertile Crescent. The increase in oil prices which followed the 1973 Arab-Israeli war allowed the Shah of Iran to amass huge sums of money which Washington encouraged him to invest in the most massive armament programme in the history of his country. In a bid to turn his country into a regional superpower, the Shah went on a frenzied shopping spree, buying $20 billion worth of American arms during the period 1972-1978 alone. Although Iraq had turned to the Soviet Union, the Iranians were gaining the upper hand in military and strategic advantages with the help of the United States and Israel. In a typical *tour de force* of deception and manipulation, the Nixon-Kissinger team signed a solemn declaration of principles with the Soviet Union in Moscow, in May 1972, to "promote conditions in which all countries will live in peace and security and will not be subject to outside interference."[4] The solemn Nixon-Kissinger commitment not to interfere in other countries affairs lasted twenty four hours. The next day after signing the Moscow declaration they flew to Teheran where they secretly promised the Shah to clandestinely supply arms to the Kurdish rebels in Iraq as part of the campaign to destabilize and weaken Iraq in its rivalry with Iran and at the same time turn its attention away from the Arab-Israeli conflict. It was a "doubly Machiavellian" coup.[5] Kissinger prided himself in his accomplishment: "The benefit of the Nixon's Kurdish decision was apparent in just over a year: only one Iraqi division was available to participate in the October 1973 Middle East war."[6]

Washington was interested in using the Kurds to destabilize Iraq but not to overthrow its regime. The same principle would remain operative following the American-led war against Iraq in 1991. Turkey and Iran had important Kurdish minorities and a total Kurdish victory in Iraq could spill over and foment rebellion against their pro-American governments. As a result, American weapons and CIA funds for the Iraqi Kurdish minority had to be enough to destabilize the central government in Baghdad but not enough to bring about its collapse. An American congressional report, the Pike Report, noted the cynicism inherent in the American enterprise of subversion: "This apparent 'no win' policy of the United States and its ally [Iran] deeply disturbed this Committee. Documents in the Committee's possession clearly show that the president, Dr. Kissinger, and the foreign head of State [the Shah] hoped that our clients [the Kurds] would not prevail...Even in the context of covert action, ours was a cynical enterprise."[7]

On March 6, 1975, with the help of Algerian President Houari Boumedienne acting as host, intermediary and interpreter, the Shah of Iran and Saddam Hussein, not yet the president but already a dominant figure in Iraq, settled their differences over the Shatt al-Arab dispute in favour of Iran. In return for allowing Iran to play the role of guardian of the Gulf, a necessary role for the Shah's pretensions of regional superpower, the Shah agreed to stop all aid to Iraq's Kurdish rebels; Iraq was able to launch a major offensive against the Kurds and to put an end to their revolt. The Algiers accords upset American and Israeli calculations because it suddenly freed Iraq from having to worry about its conflict with Iran or about the internal challenge from the Kurds to its central regime. Iraq could now potentially redirect its energy toward the Arab world and the Arab-Israeli conflict. Israeli worries increased with each successful move Iraq made in the West where Saddam Hussein was able to conclude important trade agreements with Germany and Italy and significant economic and military deals with France including in particular the delivery of modern French weapons and the construction of Iraq's Osirak nuclear facility. When he officially became president of Iraq, in 1979, Saddam Hussein was presiding over a prosperous country enriched by growing oil sales profits, an expanding social and economic reform programme and a modernizing industrial-military complex. Having consolidated his own power base and eliminated his rivals at home, Saddam Hussein turned his ambition to a regional leadership role. Surveying the regional scene he could not resist the opportunities presented by the two momentous events of the year 1979: the overthrow of the Shah by an Iranian popular uprising, and the signing of the Egyptian-Israeli separate peace treaty. The first weakened American and Iranian hold on the Gulf and opened the way for an Iraqi challenge; the second alienated Egypt from the Arab world and left its traditional leadership position vacant. Power opportunities emerged in the Gulf and in the Arab world in the same year; Iraq was the only country capable of attempting to fill either. Saddam Hussein wanted to fill both. He led the Arab drive to expel Egypt from the Arab League in March 1979 leaving Iraq the most important military power in the League and ready to don the mantle of Arab leadership.

The fall of the Shah, a central pillar in American security planning for the region, and the consequent disintegration of the Northern Tier security system was followed by the Soviet invasion of Afghanistan. The Carter administration already in disarray over developments in Iran, was in a state of shock. It had been taken aback by the Iranian revolution because of a failure of intelligence which had allowed Carter to believe that under the Shah, Iran remained an island of stability. The Russian invasion of Afghanistan also seems to have come as an unexpected shock to the Carter administration. Now that Russian control of Afghanistan brought the Soviet Union dangerously close to the Persian Gulf and to the strategically-important Straits of Hormuz, and, given repeated past statements of policy about the vital strategic importance of the Gulf to American interests, a decisive American response was required. Less than a month after the Soviet invasion of Afghanistan, President Carter announced, on January 23, 1980, that his administration was committed to the defense of the Gulf region: "Let our position be absolutely clear: An attempt by any outside force to gain control of the Persian Gulf region will be regarded as an assault on the vital interests of the United States. It will be repelled by use of any means necessary, including military force."[8] Thus the Carter Doctrine was enunciated, a statement of policy making and yet another American commitment to military intervention in the Middle East. It was directed at the Soviet Union, but it might as well have served as a warning to ambitious regional leaders tempted to fill the power vacuum left by the collapse of the Shah regime. But then again, by the end of the Iran-Iraq war Saddam Hussein, although suspicious of American intentions, would have welcomed an Iran-like regional power role sanctioned by Washington. But given the Israeli regional strategy and the special Israeli-American relations, such a scenario was unacceptable to Israel.

Throughout 1980 and while Iran and Iraq engaged each other in sporadic border skirmishes, Iraq received intelligence information to the effect that Iran was on the verge of collapse, and that its army was demoralized, rent by internal divisions, and ready to overthrow the revolutionary government. The intelligence information suggested that an Iraqi military intervention could put an end to the conflict with Iran and result in a quick and decisive defeat of the Khomeini regime. The prospects of quick victory seemed tantalizing. In one quick Israeli-style attack and victory, Saddam Hussein could visualize himself as the successor to the Israeli strategist Moshe Dayan and realize his twin ambition of domination over the Gulf and leadership of the Arab nation where he could already see himself as the new Nasser of the Arabs.[9] On September 17, 1980, he denounced the 1975 Algiers accords with Iran, and a few days later sent his army into Iran for the expected quick operation. It turned into a death trap; he found himself caught in the moving sands of an eight-year trench warfare which resulted in the death of hundreds of thousands of Iraqis, and ruined the country's prosperous economy, costing Iraq an estimated $120 billion. The fateful intelligence information which encouraged Saddam Hussein into this bloody and ruinous venture was reportedly fabricated by the Israelis and passed on to the Americans to then pass on to the Iraqis.[10]

From the beginning of the Iran-Iraq war, Israel was ready to exploit the trap in which Saddam Hussein seems to have fallen. First, it took advantage of Iraqi preoccupation with the war with Iran and launched an unprovoked attack, on June 7, 1981, on the Iraqi Osirak nuclear facility. The *New York Times* described the attack as an act of "inexcusable and short-sighted aggression."[11] The attack only served to reinforce Saddam Hussein's argument that with the defection of Egypt, Iraq had to develop modern technology and a powerful army to act as the main Arab deterrent to unchallenged Israeli power. As a US Army War College Study noted: "Were Iraq to become a nuclear power, Israel's hegemony over the Middle East would be at an end."[12] Israeli leaders also took advantage of the Iran-Iraq war to establish a strategic axis of cooperation with the strongly anti-Zionist Islamic regime in Teheran, providing it with intelligence and military equipment.[13] Israeli agents purchased weapons from Europe and shipped them, with American blessings, to Iran. As late in the war as October 1987, Yitzhak Rabin, then Israel's Defense Minister, was publicly admitting the nature of the Israeli game: "Iran is Israel's best friend and we do not intend to change our position with regard to Teheran."[14] The Soviet Union, France and other Western countries provided Iraq with military aid; Washington readily cooperated militarily with Baghdad, hoping that the Iraqi military venture would put an end once and for all to the threat revolutionary Iran posed to the pro-American conservative petro-monarchies of the Gulf.

However, as American military cooperation with Iraq grew steadily during the first years of the war, Israel and its friends in Washington worked hard to convince the Reagan administration that the Khomeini regime was on the verge of collapse and unless the United States improved its relations with Iran, the field would be left open for Moscow to determine alone the nature and the orientation of the Khomeini regime's successor. Israeli Deputy Foreign Minister David Kimch proposed a secret scheme whereby the United States could deliver weapons through Israel to Iran in return for Iranian help in releasing American hostages held by pro-Iranian militia groups in Lebanon. The money raised from the arms sales would secretly fund the Contras — the mercenaries organized and supported by the Reagan administration and Israel to harass the Sandanista regime in Nicaragua. Accordingly, Washington entered secret negotiations with Teheran in 1985 and agreed to provide the Iranians with weapons and military intelligence. In January 1986, President Reagan authorized a programme of covert operations to strengthen ties with Iran, and soon the United States was providing military aid and intelligence information to both sides in the Iran-Iraq war simultaneously. Secretary of State George Shultz, a strong supporter of Israel, candidly recognized that the Iran-Contra secret game was "an Israeli scam from the very beginning."[15]

Unwittingly perhaps, Reagan was playing into Israel's hands and helping its goal of prolonging the war until Iran and Iraq bled each other out.

As a Democratic Senator from Missouri, Harry Truman had urged the Roosevelt administration to play the same game in World War II by helping both the Russians and the Germans so that they would "kill as many as possible."[16] As the Nazis drove deeper into the Soviet Union in 1942, the United States and Britain twice promised to open a second front to take the pressure off Russia and twice reneged; it wasn't until 1944 that a second front materialized, but by then the Red Army had driven out the Nazis at a cost of twenty million Russians killed. After the war, the Russian intransigent position reflected Moscow's suspicions of the United States intentions and of President Truman's new world order particularly as it applied to Eastern and Central Europe. Some forty five years later, the Iran-Contra scandal reflected the same *realpolitik* approach to international relations. When its objectives were exposed and the extent of duplicity measured, Saddam Hussein's sense of being targeted and besieged became even more acute. He was now convinced that the United States was secretly working with Israel to bring about the overthrow of his regime. This strengthened his resolve at the end of the Iran-Iraq war to turn his country into a major regional power.

The Iran-Iraq war also provided Egypt — ostracized from the Arab camp for signing a separate treaty with Israel — with an opportunity to accelerate its return to the Arab fold. In return for Saddam Hussein's support for an end to the Arab boycott of Egypt, President Sadat agreed in the summer of 1981 to let the Iraqi leader use thousands of Egyptian workers already in Iraq in the war against Iran. Egyptian military aid to Iraq continued to grow under Hosni Mubarak. Specifically, Cairo agreed to use the Egyptian military power to deter, and in case of need actively defend against any Iranian threat to the conservative monarchies of the Gulf.

Iraq and the US on a Collision Course

The end of the Iran-Iraq war, however, brought into conflict two competing visions: the acquiescence of the pro-American camp led by Egypt and the Gulf regimes in the economic, political and military order in the region, and Baghdad's ambitious challenge to its dominance. Whereas to the supporters of the dominant Camp David order the end of the East-West confrontation vindicated their belief that the alliance with Washington was the correct course to follow, to Saddam Hussein the end of the cold-war rivalry deprived the Arabs of their traditional Soviet support and made them even more vulnerable to the hegemonic designs of the United States. He argued that the end of the bipolar world had not been replaced by a multipolar world but rather by a unipolar world dominated by the United States. Such a world would not be characterized by interdependence, but rather by growing economic and military inequalities. It was therefore imperative to ensure that Washington's quest for the extension and affirmation of its domination be challenged. And this could be done only if regional powers such as Iraq were able to deal with Washington from a position of strength.[17]

In its quest to reconstruct its war-ravaged country, the Iraqi regime looked to the Gulf petromonarchies for the alleviation of its crippling debt of $80 billion, half of which it owed to Saudi Arabia and Kuwait. It expected Kuwait to write off the debt in recognition of Iraq's role in stopping the Khomeini regime from exporting its Islamic revolution to the Arabian peninsula. Baghdad also looked forward to building on the strategic relationships it developed with Washington during the Iran-Iraq war and hoped to receive technological aid from the United States and be able to raise the price of oil with American approval to pay for it. Neither expectation materialized. The end of the Iran-Iraq war ended Iraq's usefulness to Washington. The Iraqi regime's vision of balance of power and of a privileged role as defender of conservative Islam against Iranian revolutionary ambitions, as well as its determination to rebuild its economy and modernize its military, were seen as potential threats to American interests and American allies in the region.

This was largely the result of Israeli lobbying in Washington where Israel and its friends persuasively argued that the real threat to stability in the region did not come from Israeli repression of the Palestinian uprising, or occupation of Arab territories but from Iraq's challenge to the status quo and from Iraqi ambitions to be a regional power. An anti-Iraq campaign was initiated literally within days of the end of the Iran-Iraq war. The cease-fire intervened on August 20, 1988, and on September 8, Secretary of State George Shultz was unexpectedly and dramatically making a public statement in which he accused Iraq of using poison gas against the Kurds in August. He based his accusation on a report prepared by the Congress where Israel's friends had been actively denouncing the Iraqi regime, and calling on Reagan to stop dealing with it. The charge of Iraqi use of poison gas particularly in the Halabja incident was uncritically propagated by the media as a graphic example of the monstrosity of a regime that kills its own people. The charge, which became an article of faith in the anti-Iraq campaign before, during and after the Gulf crisis, seems to have been based on shaky evidence and dubious motives. A study commissioned by the US Army War College's Strategic Studies Institute found that: "Photographs of the Kurdish victims were widely disseminated in the international media. Iraq was blamed for the Halabja attack, even though it was subsequently brought out that Iran too had used chemicals in this operation, and it seemed likely that it was the Iranian bombardment that had actually killed the Kurds."[18] Indeed, Iraq protested its innocence and invited the foreign correspondents to come to the Kurdish areas and ascertain the facts for themselves; no conclusive evidence of poison gas use in August, as Shultz had charged, could be found.[19] After the war against Iraq, an official of the Bush administration readily conceded, now that the charges served some useful propaganda purposes, that hundreds rather than thousands of Kurds had died at Halabja, and that "there probably wasn't an attempt on either side to kill the villagers."[20]

The Shultz allegations were also dismissed by the US Army War College study cited above: "Having looked at all that was available to us, we find it impossible to confirm the State Department's claim that gas was used in this instance. To begin with there were never any victims produced. International relief Organizations who examined the Kurds — in Turkey where they had gone for asylum — failed to discover any. Nor were there ever any found inside Iraq. The claim rests solely on testimony of the Kurds who had crossed the border into Turkey, where they were interviewed by staffers of the Senate Foreign Relations Committee. We would have expected, in a matter as serious as this, that the Congress would have exercised some care. However, passage of the sanctions measure through Congress was unusually swift. "[21] Indeed, within 24 hours of the Shultz allegations, the Senate had voted unanimously to impose sweeping sanctions against Iraq. It would have been materially impossible for the Senate to move so swiftly had the groundwork not been adequately prepared irrespective of the merits of Shultz's accusations which were never seriously examined. Because of a bureaucratic technicality, however, the sanctions measures failed. But Shultz's allegations signalled that the US and Iraq were set on a confrontation course. Although the White House continued to claim that it wanted to improve relations with Baghdad, the anti-Iraqi campaign continued unabated. By November 1988, Iraq was accusing the United States of orchestrating with Israel a campaign to undermine its security. To draw attention to the deteriorating relations between the two countries, the Iraqi regime ordered an American diplomat expelled from Baghdad, to which the United States retaliated by expelling an Iraqi diplomat. A chain of actions-reactions was set in motion and in due course, given the forces at play, inexorably led to increasing confrontation.

The efforts of Israel and its lobby in the United States to whip up an anti-Iraq campaign in the Congress and to embark the United States on a confrontation course with Saddam Hussein, coincided with, and were facilitated by a revision of American strategic thinking. Indeed, the geostrategic analysis made by American military policy planners of the post cold-war geopolitical realities was not unlike that made by President Saddam Hussein. A 1988 U.S.-government document entitled "Discriminate Deterrence" identified the post cold-war military challenges for the US as coming no longer from the Soviet Union but from Third-World regional powers.[22] The document recommended that the US be prepared to militarily confront developing regional powers in what was called medium-intensity warfare. Although American forces would not use nuclear weapons in these confrontations, they would be expected to strike hard and in a massive way — as became obvious from the way Washington conducted the war against Iraq.

The strategy was reminiscent of the American military doctrine of the early fifties known as the Doctrine of Massive Retaliation. This doctrine was supposedly designed to deter communist aggression by threatening massive retaliation against the territories of the communist countries. But when the Soviet Union mastered the ballistic missile technology in the late fifties and became able to launch missiles with nuclear warheads against the territories of the United States, the strategy lost its credibility. It was inconceivable that the United States would risk nuclear retaliation against its own territories for the sake of a third party. The strategy was discarded and replaced by a new doctrine called Flexible Response whereby the American military would choose from a number of escalating options to respond to communist aggressions. But since the designated communist enemy now possessed the weapon of ultimate destruction and the means of visiting its devastations on the national territories of the United States, the new American strategy essentially meant the consecration of the doctrine of Mutual Assured Destruction (MAD). Peace between the superpowers was enforced by the terrifying certainty that war between them would assure their mutual destruction. As Pierre Gallois predicted in the 1960s in his important work *Paradox de la paix* and in his subsequent Sorbonne lectures, the United States was committed to avoiding nuclear confrontation with the Soviet Union but equally determined to continue to project power around the globe for the defense of its interests; for this reason it was bound to develop an interventionist conventional-weapon force essentially relying on air power and ready to be dispatched anywhere in the world to impose respect for *Pax Americana*.

The latest American military doctrine elaborated in 1988 in "Discriminate Deterrence" deals with challenges emanating from regional powers whose military capabilities did not pose a direct threat to the territories of the United States. In addition, given the elimination of the Soviet Union as a rival power, it was now possible for Washington to contemplate massive military operations without having to worry about the reaction of its former superpower rival. In short, the elimination of the Soviet Union as a competitor superpower removed the incentive for restraint in American projections of power. If Vietnam and mounting economic problems at home had led some people to predict the decline of the American empire, a massive attack against a regional power unable to retaliate against American territories and unlikely to involve superpower confrontation would assure the sort of victory that would restore faith in American might. It would also send a clear message to the economic giants in Europe and Japan that their economic prosperity, and their greater need for Mideast oil, are tributary of American power. The unfolding of such a scenario could help re-establish the US claim to the 20th century as the "American Century." Less than two weeks after the beginning of perhaps the most massive air campaign in history was unleashed against Iraq, President Bush appeared before the American congress to deliver the state of the union address: "If anyone tells you America's best days are behind her," he told the cheering audience, "they are looking the wrong way."[23]

In his first speech on national security on May 24, 1989 President Bush announced that the United States faced two challenges: one related to the political turmoils in the Soviet Union, the other concerned the security of the United States. He emphasized that the security challenges facing the United States did not come only from the East but also from the threat posed by the emergence of regional powers which were rapidly modifying the world strategic equation. The United States, Bush proclaimed in a key passage, must challenge "the aggressive ambitions of renegade regimes." Describing a regime as "renegade" would henceforth set the stage for confrontation with the United States. In October of the same year, President Bush signed National Security Directive #26 as the basis for American policy in the Persian Gulf. The directive stated that "Access to the Persian Gulf and the key friendly states in the area is vital to US national security...the United States remains committed to defend its national interests in the region, if necessary and appropriate through the use of US military force, against the Soviet Union and *any other regional power with interests inimical to our own*." (emphasis added). Iraq was specifically mentioned by name as a country with which the United States had significant differences over chemical, biological and nuclear weapons; but whose behaviour the United States government was trying to influence by political and economic means.[24] The fact that Iraq was singled out was no mere coincidence for illustrative purposes. Top level discussions on the Iraqi threat and how to confront it had been taking place in Washington. During the first week of October 1989 General Norman Schwarzkopf, Commander of the US Central Command (The Rapid Deployment Force for the Middle East, based in Florida) paid a special visit to Saudi Arabia. At a meeting with US Ambassador Charles Freeman in Riyadh, Shwartzkopf stated that an Iraqi invasion of Kuwait was "probable" and that such an action would represent a threat to the ruling Wahabite monarchy in Saudi

Arabia.[25] By the end of 1989, top American military officials had reached the consensus that the threat to regional stability and American access to Middle East strategic resources clearly came from Iraq.[26]

In February 1990, US Secretary of Defense Dick Cheney approved a secret document directing the American armed forces to de-emphasize the Soviet danger and focus on strategies for eventual military conflicts with Third-World regional powers like Syria and Iraq.[27] The document reportedly directed the military to modify their strategy from one based on the defense of Iran against possible Soviet invasion to one based on the defense of American access to oil resources against a number of other possible threats. These included the possibility of the Arab nations of the Gulf moving closer to some form of political and economic union which would strengthen the traditionally divided Arab countries and give them important leverage in their economic and political relationship with the West .[28]

American policy planners had traditionally feared that pan-Arab drives for consolidation of Arab economic resources and coordination of political priorities in an attempt to forge a common Arab front would strengthen Arab control of their own oil resources and enhance their bargaining power with the Western consumers. As early as 1964, John Badeau, American ambassador in Egypt, was already warning that the first Arab Summit could herald an era of a stronger and more united Arab world: "Granted we have, in past policy papers," he warned the Johnson administration, "almost routinely put inter-Arab harmony on the list of our objectives. But now that it seems as though it may be coming to pass are we really sure we like it?"[29] American opposition to Arab unity efforts necessarily implied a commitment to maintain the status quo of divisions, rivalries, and therefore collective weakness. Challenging such a status quo became a threat to "stability" and to vital American interests. The established balance of power between the energy-dependent but militarily powerful American-led industrial world and the oil-rich but militarily dependent Arab nations had therefore to be maintained against the threat of collective Arab economic and political actions of the type which produced the 1973-74 Arab oil embargo. For only a commitment to defend such a status quo can guarantee that Arab economic power would not be used to challenge the contradictions in American foreign policy priorities in the Middle East.

Another source of possible threat identified by American policy planners was the political awakening of the Muslim populations of the former Soviet Republics close to the Middle East oil fields. This could lead to some sort of spiritual and political solidarity between the Soviet Muslims and the Gulf Muslims, thus enhancing the political power of the Arab populations of the oil-rich Gulf. A third source of threat resided in the political aspirations of leaders like Saddam Hussein who wanted to break out of the dependency relationship by converting Arab economic power into industrial and military might. If allowed to succeed Saddam Hussein's challenge would have radical implications for the economic, political and military balance of power in the region and for the nature of the Arab-American relationship. Saddam Hussein's ambition had to be checked to preserve the "stability" of the status quo and its lopsided distribution of economic and military power. With help from obliging and cooperative media, the threat posed by ambitious regional leaders to the status quo seems to have been identified as having more immediacy and urgency. At any rate, the Israelis were already actively involved in confronting it: on March 22, 1990, Gerald Vincent Bull, the Canadian artillery expert who worked on Iraqi weapon programmes and widely reported to have been working on a supergun for Iraq, was gunned down outside his Brussels apartment by Israeli assassins.[30]

At about the same time American military strategy was being redirected to deal with potential threats from regional powers such as Iraq, the North-American media had already taken its cue from the American Congress where vocal friends of Israel were wiping up anti-Iraq sentiments. Media stories began playing up the Iraqi threat to "stability," i.e.; to the status quo and the established distribution of economic and military power in the Middle East. The following titles are illustrative and instructive: "Iraq, a state based upon butchery" (*Manchester Guardian*, March 25); "Iraq's Grisly Record" (*Washington Post*, March 25); "The horror in Baghdad" (*Manchester Guardian*, March 25); "Iraq Seeks To Be Arab Superpower" (*Washington Post*, April 1); Iraq and The Bomb" (*Washington Post*, April 8); "Chemical Arms threat by Iraq" (*Manchester Guardian*, April 8). And these were telling titles of stories and articles published by the "liberal" press during the months which preceded the Iraqi invasion of Kuwait.

Typical of these negative stories was an article published by the *Washington Post* entitled "Iraq's Arsenal of Horrors" written by Dan Raviv, an American, and Yossi Melman, an Israeli — hardly a disinterested writer. In it, the two writers catalogued for the readers events and arguments to support their opening proposition that: "The Iraqi dictator, Saddam Hussein, is emerging as the most dangerous man in a dangerous region."[31] The list included the predictable and by now familiar arguments: "Hussein threatened to destroy half of Israel, if the Jewish State attacked Iraqi facilities as it did in 1981." This argument implied of-course that the threat to retaliate against a possible Israeli attack made Iraq, the defender in this case, a dangerous State, but not Israel, the attacker; a logic consistent with the reversal of roles which characterized media interpretation of the Arab-Israeli and Israeli-Palestinian conflicts. The writers then explained the existence of an "Iraqi plot...to smuggle nuclear-warhead detonators from California to Iraq by way of Britain." The two writers admitted that, "these, incidentally, were krytons — the same devices that the Israelis managed to smuggle from California five years ago," but stopped short of applying to Israel the same criteria they applied to Iraq. The same surreptitious action committed by Israel did not make the Jewish State a dangerous State, but contemplated by Iraq five years later did make it a dangerous State. And that is because nuclear weapons in the hands of peace-loving Israelis are safe, but the same weapons are dangerous in the hands of warmongering and insane Arabs. Nothing new here. The writers also cited "Iraq's execution...of Farzad Bazoft, a British-based Iranian journalist, on espionage charges," and "Israeli and Western analysts," reporting "with near certainty" that Iraq was trying to develop "a chemical arsenal, biological agents, nuclear bombs, and the all-important delivery vehicles that could reach Hussein's two chief enemies, Iran and Israel."[32]

In Israel, talk of imminent war with Iraq was complimented with calls for action against it. The Iraqis claim that they learned in March 1990 that Israeli leaders were preparing another attack on Iraq similar to their 1981 strike against Iraqi nuclear facilities. Arab leaders were disturbed by the increasing crescendo of the anti-Iraq campaign. The Arab League sent a statement to the American government on May 30, expressing astonishment "at the attitude of the United States —

the first power to have used nuclear weapons during the Second World War — and its refusal of Iraq's right to declare that it could use the weapons it possesses to respond to any new attack by Israel — which has acquired all types of destructive weapons, thanks to the direct assistance extended by Western states."[33] But there was no letting up in the anti-Iraq campaign as the American Congress cut off Iraqi food purchase credits, the Department of Agriculture delayed Iraqi purchases of American commodities, and negative media stories about Iraq abounded. Sensing that the anti-Iraq campaign must be the necessary prelude to an already prepared attack against Iraq, King Hussein of Jordan warned the Arab Summit meeting in Baghdad, held in May, about the dangers of this "unholy campaign against Iraq." The final statement of the Baghdad Summit expressed serious concerns about "the hostile tendentious political and media campaigns, and the scientific and tech-nological ban against Iraq," and fear of the consequences of "the continuation of these campaigns against...[Iraq's] sovereignty and pan-Arab security and warns that there are preparations to facilitate aggression against it...The conference af-firms the right of Iraq and all the Arab states to reply to aggression by all means they deem fit to guarantee their security and sovereignty."[34]

The pieces were falling into place; the process of demonization and outlawing Iraq was inexorably moving toward its disastrous logical conclusion. Israel was reaping its benefits already: first demonizing Iraq helped the Israeli case of em-phasizing the "belligerent and treacherous nature of its radical neighbours." Second, it helped Israeli leaders direct world attention away from, as *Time* magazine observed, "Israel's intransigence and expansionism."[35] Washington also used the process of demonizing Iraq to prepare public opinion for what seemed like an inevitable confrontation with Baghdad. On July 27, the House and Senate voted to impose important economic sanctions and to withhold $700 million in com-modity loan guarantees from Iraq. Thus American sanctions against Iraq were al-ready in place *before* Iraq invaded Kuwait.

The double standard involved in demonizing Iraq because of its armament programmes while indirectly supporting the more massive and infinitely more sophisticated Israeli nuclear and biological weapon programmes did not go unchallenged by the more critically-minded and intellectually-honest observers: "American threats against the Libyan factory at Rabta are common," observed one European commentator, "President Bush has condemned the Iraqi nuclear programme, but we are still waiting for a reaction from the White House con-cerning the accumulation by Israel of atomic bombs and toxic gas. Reading the editorials of the North American press could lead one to think that only the Arabs, 'brutal and unscrupulous', are likely to use these arms. And yet, the United States, a democratic country, covered Vietnam with toxic weapons. And who can guarantee that Mr. Ariel Sharon, who could become Minister of Defense or even Prime Minister in Israel, will not use similar weapons?"[36]

Iraq and Kuwait on a Collision Course

As Iraq was being demonized in the North-American press and singled out for confrontation and punishment, Iraqi-Kuwaiti negotiations on a number of bilateral issues, which the Iraqis claimed to be of vital importance to their national security, were experiencing serious difficulties. The Iraqi economy depended heavily on the export of oil, which traditionally passed through Syria and Iran. Syria, which sided with Iran in its war with Iraq, had shut off the oil pipeline that gave Iraqi oil access to the Mediterranean. Iran had easily interdicted Iraqi access to the Gulf. The two new Iraqi pipelines passed through Saudi Arabia and Turkey, both close allies of Washington and therefore unreliable conduits from the Iraqi point of view. To reduce this vulnerability, Iraq was now proposing to build a naval facility at the Gulf village of Umm Qasr linking it to the Iraqi inland port of Basra. The two uninhabited Kuwaiti islands of Bubiyan and Warba were considered by Iraq to be important for the security of the new port and the Iraqis wanted Kuwait to give them guaranteed access to the two islands. Kuwait reportedly proved uncooperative.

Further, the rich Gulf monarchies claimed that economic difficulties made it impossible for them to continue to subsidize their less fortunate Arab neighbours which they had generously done in the past. The collapse of oil prices in the mid 1980s "wanted by Washington, orchestrated by Kuwait and the United Arab Emirates, and tolerated by Saudi Arabia," resulted in significant reductions of development aid the oil-producing Arab countries were giving to the Arab world.[37] Between 1976 and 1988 this aid fell from 4.23 percent to 0.86 percent of their gross national product, aggravating the already precarious economic situations and mounting foreign debt burden of the less fortunate Arab countries. The windfall profits realized from huge increases in the price of oil in the 1970s had led to greater economic inequalities among the Arabs by the end of the 1980s. Thus, less than 10 million Arabs (the citizens of the six Gulf States) enjoy the benefits of a surplus of $462 billion in Western banks whereas the other 190 million Arabs are burdened by the growing weight of $208 billion of debts representing 52 percent of the gross national products of all the Arab countries put together.[38]

The Iraqis, who depended on oil sale for 95 percent of their export revenues, were also angered by what they believed to be Kuwaiti cooperation with Washington to overproduce oil, driving its price down and undermining the already war-devasted Iraqi economy. Kuwait, on the other hand, reportedly held assets and investments in the West of between $120 and $200 billion from which it received interests which, starting in 1986, had began to generally exceed its oil revenues. In essence, cooperation with Washington to keep the price of oil between $18-$22 a barrel cost Kuwait little financial hardship but assured the political and military support of the United States, and at the same time complicated the Iraqi task of reconstructing its economy and rebuilding its army. It also infuriated the Iraqis who repeatedly argued that the survival of the Arab monarchies of the Gulf was made possible only through Iraqi blood sacrifices in the Iran-Iraq war. Khomeini had made no secret of his utter contempt for Arab monarches nor of his intention to bring down their regimes. There is little doubt that had Baghdad fallen, the way would have been opened for the Iranians to march to Saudi Arabia and, as they repeatedly threatened, liberate Mecca from the House of Saud. After the war with Iran, Saddam Hussein's favourite speech theme became the blood sacrifices paid by the Iraqis to stop the Iranian revolution from spreading to Saudi Arabia and the Gulf Emirates. Few Iraqis believed that Kuwait or Saudi Arabia expected their financial assistance to Iraq during the war to be repaid. So when the Kuwaitis demanded repayment of Iraqi debt with interests, Saddam Hussein was enraged and claimed that Kuwait owed Iraq $2.4 billion for oil allegedly stolen through slant Kuwaiti drilling into Iraq's Rumalia oil fields across the border.

Jordan, which traditionally enjoyed privileged relationships with the West but which had been displaced by Egypt's rise as the defender of the Western-based Camp David order, saw the crisis looming at the horizon. Jordanian officials were reportedly surprised by what they described as the Kuwaiti defiant attitude in Iraqi-Kuwait negotiations. They claimed to have been told by Kuwaiti officials that Kuwait had received assurances from Washington that the United States would intervene militarily to back up the Kuwaitis against the Iraqis. After the Iraqi invasion of Kuwait, the Iraqis discovered in Kuwaiti government papers a memorandum reportedly describing a November 1989 meeting between CIA director William Webster and Kuwaiti officials confirming agreement to take advantage of the deteriorating situation in Iraq and put additional pressure on it. The CIA admitted that the meeting took place on the date specified in the document but claimed that nothing about Kuwaiti-Iraqi relations were discussed "at this meeting."

On the last day of the Baghdad Summit, May 30, 1990, Saddam Hussein accused some Gulf countries without naming them of overproduction of oil, and claimed that driving the price of oil down in Iraq's present economic condition amounted to an act of war. He suggested that Iraq needed an increase in the price of oil and hoped that the problem would soon be resolved. "Both Abu Dhabi and Kuwait," observed an American energy consultant, "signed agreements with OPEC limiting production, and then three times broke their word; they produced substantially above their quotas, keeping oil prices several dollars below the target. They thereby reduced the income and incurred the enmity of all other OPEC countries — not just Iraq."[39]

In June 1990, President Saddam Hussein made a speech in Baghdad on the first anniversary of the death of Michel Aflaq, the ideologue and founder of the ruling Baath Party. He emphasized that the Arab Summit in Baghdad a month earlier had unanimously agreed that "there was a minimum of general Arab common interests particularly with regard to the Palestinian question, the oil wealth, Arab national development, and the requirements of common Arab security interests within the new international context, which all Arab states without exception agreed to respect." Saddam Hussein insisted that "given this unanimous undertaking, no single Arab country had the right to deviate or to violate this minimum of common Arab interests. And therefore, it was an Arab nationalist duty for the Arab states, or, in case of inability to act, for any one state capable of assuming its nationalist responsibilities, to take the initiative to repel and punish the deviant state." This, he added, was the basis of the new Arab solidarity which emerged from the consensus of various Arab orientations discussed at the Baghdad Summit in May.[40] The Iraqi President was clearly threatening that he would not tolerate the attempt to stop his modernization programme which he presented as serving the Arab nation. By equating Iraqi plans for reconstruction and military build-up with the nationalist Arab interest of building an Arab deterrence to growing Israeli might, Saddam Hussein presented opposition to Baghdad's ambitions as a threat to the entire Arab nation. As a self-proclaimed guardian of the Arab nationalist interests, he took it upon himself to punish those acting to undermine those interests.

Iraq has traditionally claimed a historical right to Kuwait, which was an administrative subdistrict of the Iraqi province of Basra in the Ottoman empire. Iraqi leaders argued that Kuwait should have been part of modern Iraq and that the creation of an independent Kuwaiti entity was an artificial creation of British colonialism bent on dividing the Arabs to weaken them and better exploit their wealth. The claim was first articulated by the Iraqi monarchy in the 1930s; it was invoked by the Iraqi regime of Abdel Karim Qassem following the end of the British protectorate on Kuwait and the proclamation of Kuwaiti independence in 1961. Only British military intervention and strong Arab League opposition deterred the Iraqi leaders from invading and annexing Kuwait to Iraq. With the downfall of Qassem in 1963, Iraq recognized Kuwait's independence and seems to have reluctantly accepted the new reality of Kuwaiti sovereignty. But it was always an undercurrent of Kuwaiti-Iraqi relations that Iraq considered that it had a *droit de regard* over Kuwaiti policy and expected it, if not to be subordinated to Iraqi orientations, to take Iraqi national security concerns into consideration.

At the Arab Foreign Ministers' Conference in Tunis on July 15, 1990, Iraqi Foreign Minister Tarik Aziz identified the immediate source of threat to the Iraqi economy and national interests and specifically accused Kuwait and the United Arab Emirates of overproduction of oil. In a 37-page memorandum Aziz enumerated a list of Iraqi grievances against Kuwait: owing Iraq $2.4 billion for Iraqi oil allegedly stolen from the Rumaila oilfield; the pumping of Iraqi oil from Rumaila was considered an act of war against Iraq; being intransigent about assistance money given to Iraq during the war with Iran which Kuwait considered a debt and wanted repaid but Iraq considered legitimate assistance for the defense of the region against Khomeini; alleged Kuwaiti collusion with foreign powers (the United States) to thwart Iraqi efforts of reconstruction and leadership of the Arab world against the growing Israeli threat; Kuwait's alleged refusal to negotiate in good faith outstanding issues of frontier delineation and the crucial issue of Iraqi vulnerable access to the Gulf, an issue dramatized during the Iran-Iraq war. In view of what Saddam Hussein had said in his June speech, the implications of the perceived Kuwaiti threats to Iraqi national security were clear and Iraq left no doubt that it was ready to act unilaterally if necessary. Shortly thereafter, Iraqi troops moved toward the Kuwait-Iraq borders.[41]

On July 25, Saddam Hussein told the American ambassador in Baghdad, April Glaspie that Washington must choose between friendly relations with Iraq or support for Kuwaiti economic warfare against Iraq. He reviewed the devastations brought upon his country by the Iran-Iraq war and suggested that the United States was supporting Kuwait in "another war against Iraq," an "economic war" which deprived Iraqis of "their humanity by depriving them of their chance to have a good standard of living." He told Glaspie that the United States should be grateful for Iraq for having stopped Iran militarily because the United States could not fight such a war. After attacking the United States for its support for Kuwait, he demanded that Washington "declare who it wants to have relations with and who its enemies are…if you use pressure, we will deploy pressure and force." He then warned that Iraq would take whatever action it deemed necessary to stop Kuwait from continuing "an economic war" against Iraq. In response to the Iraqi leader's comment that Iraq needed higher oil prices, the American ambassador said: "We understand that and our opinion is that you should have the opportunity to rebuild your country. But we have no opinion on the Arab-Arab conflicts, like your border disagreement with Kuwait...(American Secretary of State) James Baker has directed our official spokesman to emphasize this instruction."[42] The day before Glaspie's meeting with Hussein, State Department spokeswoman Margaret Tutwiler publicly disavowed any American defense commitments to Kuwait. The same disavowal was repeated by John Kelly, assistant secretary of State for Near Eastern and South Asian affairs, before a congressional subcommittee on July 31. Saddam Hussein probably concluded from these statements that "he had the green light" from Washington.[43]

In late July, an OPEC meeting convened in an atmosphere of crisis. Kuwait and Abu Dhabi were pressured by Saudi Arabia, Iran and Iraq to respect agreements on production limitations. Both countries were shaken by the combined pressure and agreed to honour their word on production limitations. OPEC ministers agreed to raise the price from $18 to $21 and keep it there until the market reaction had been determined. Shortly after the OPEC agreement, Iraq announced that Kuwait was already cheating on the agreement but presented no evidence to substantiate the charge. It seems unlikely, however, that the Iraqis could determine in a matter of days that the Kuwaitis were already violating the latest OPEC agreement. In fact, there is evidence to suggest that the Kuwaitis were planning to honour their word by cutting their production by 25 percent.[44]

Meeting in Jeddah, Saudi Arabia on July 31, Iraqis and Kuwaitis engaged in difficult negotiations that proved unfruitful. These were followed by a second meeting on August 1, which proved equally unsuccessful. The Iraqis were reportedly angered by what the Jordanians described as a defiant and intransigent Kuwaiti position while the Kuwaitis argued that the Iraqis had not come to negotiate in good faith because they had already planned to invade Kuwait. At 2 A. M. August 2, 1990, the Iraqi invasion of Kuwait got underway.

Notes

1. A. LeRoy Bennett, *International Organizations: Principles and Issues* (Englewood Cliffs, N. J., Prentice Hall, 1980), p. 192.
2. Colman McCarthy, "Israeli Justice," The *Washington Post* reproduced in the *Guardian Weekly*, July 22, 1990.
3. Thomas L. Friedman, "What the United States Has Taken On In the Gulf Besides a War," *The New York Times,* January 20, 1991, see also Thomas L. Friedman, "When War is Over: Planning for Peace and US Role in Enforcing It," *International Herald Tribune,* Paris, January 21, 1991.
4. Seymour Hersh, *The Price of Power: Kissinger in the White House* (New York, Summit Books, 1983), p. 542)
5. George Lenczowski, *American Presidents and the Middle East* (Durham and London, Duke University Press, 1990), pp. 118-119; see also Seymour Hersh, *The Price of Power: Kissinger in the White House* (New York, Summit Books, 1983), p. 542.
6. Henry Kissinger, *White House Years* (Boston, Little Brown, 1979), p.1265.
7. Christopher Hutchins, "Minority Report," *The Nation,* May 6, 1991.

8. George Lenczowski, op. cit., p. 206.
9. See Paul Balt, *Iran-Iraq: Une Guerre de 5000 Ans* (Paris, Anthropos, 1987), p. 125.
10. See Atif al-Ghamry, "Collaborators and the Careful Application of Kissingers' and Sharon's Theories in the Gulf," *Al-Ahram* (in Arabic) (Cairo), August 15, 1990.
11. *New York Times* June 9, 1981.
12. Stephen C. Pelletiere; Douglas V. Johnson II; and Leif R. Rosenberger, *Iraqi Power and U.S. Security in the Middle East* (Carlisle Barracks, Pennsylvannia,Strategic Studies Institute, U.S. Army War College, 1990), p. 54.
13. See "Crash Reveals Israel's Arms Deal with Iran," an "Insight" report in the *Sunday Times*, (London), July 26, 1981; See also the *Sunday Times*, July 29, 1981; see also the revelations made by Gary Sick in the American press and quoted in Anthony H. Cordesman, *The Iran-Iraq War and Western Security 1984-87: Strategic Implications and Policy Options* (London, Jane's Publishing, 1987), p. 31.
14. *Agence France Presse*, October 28, 1987, quoted in Behrouz Souresrafil, *The Iran-Iraq War* (Plainview, New York, Guinan Co, 198), p. 53.
15. James E. Akins, "Heading Towards War," *Journal of Palestine Studies* vol. XX, no. 3 (Spring 1990), pp. 16-30, p. 21.
16. *New York Times*, June 24, 1941, quoted in Walter LaFeber, *America, Russia, and the Cold War: 1945-1980* (New York, John Wiley & Sons, 1980), p. 6.
17. See Mohamed Sid-Ahmed, "Ambitieux et risqué, le choix de l'Egypte." *Le Monde Diplomatique*, (Paris) January, 1991.
18. Stephen C. Pelletiere et al, op. cit., p. 52; Martin Yant quotes in his *Desert Mirage* (Buffalo, New York, Prometheus Books, 1991) a *Newsday* report citing a congressional Mideast specialist who had reviewed the communications intercepts used by Shultz for his allegations and corroborrated the Army War College Study's conclusion. "George Shultz was going...way beyond the evidence," the specialist told the newspaper. p. 109.
19. *Washington Post*, September 25, 1988, quoted in Donald Neef, "The U.S., Iraq, Israel, And Iraq: Backdrop To War," *Journal of Palestine Studies* vol. XX, no. 4 (Summer 1991), pp. 23-41, p. 32
20. *New York Times* April 28, 1991, quoted in ibid., p. 32.
21. Pelletiers et al, op. cit., p. 52.
22. See Michael Klare, "Dissuasion sélective et vieilles recettes," *Le Monde Diplomatique* May, 1988.
23. The *New York Times*, January 30, 1991.
24. *Washington Post National Weekly Edition*, March 18-24, 1991.
25. Roger Cohen and Claudio Gatti, *In the Eye of the Storm: The Life of General H. Norman Schwarzkopf* (London, Bloomsbury, 1991), p. 185.
26. *Air Force Magazine*, Mars, 1991, quoted in Chapour Haghigat, "Les dessous de la guerre du Golf,"*Le Monde Diplomatique*, April 1992.
27. See *The New York Times*, February 7, 1990; see also Michael Klare, "Le Golfe, banc d'essai des guerres de demain," *Le Monde Diplomatique*, January 1991; see also *Aviation Week* and *Space Technology*, August 13, 1990.)
28. Atif Al-Ghamry. "Collaborators and the Careful Application of Kissinger's and Sharon's Theories in the Gulf," *Al-Ahram* (in Arabic) (Cairo), August 15, 1990.
29. *The Lyndon B. Johnson Security Files*, reel 7 out of 8, quoted in Fawaz A. Gerges, "Regional Security After the Gulf Crisis: The American Role," *Journal of Palestine Studies* vol. XX, no. 4 (Summer 1991), pp. 55-68, p. 65.
30. David Halvey, Scott Malone, and Sam Hemingway, Outlook Section, *Washington Post*, February 10, 1991, quoted in Donald Neef, op. cit., p. 36.
31. Dan Raviv and Yossi Melman, Iraq's Arsenal of Horrors, the *Washington Post*, reproduced in the *Guardian Weekly*, April 22, 1990.

32. Ibid.
33. Arab League, Memorandum to the United States, Tunis, May 30, 1990, translated by *Mideast Mirror,* June 8, 1990 and reproduced in *Journal of Palestine Studies,* vol. XX, no. 1 (Autumn 1990), pp. 149-152, p. 151
34. Milton Viorst, "A Reporter At Large: The House of Hashem," *The New Yorker,* January 7, 1991; see the Final Statement of the Extraordinary Arab Summit Meeting, Baghdad, May 30, 1990, translated in *FBIS,* May 31, 1990, and reproduced in *Journal of Palestine Studies,* vol. XX, no. 1, (Autumn, 1990), pp. 152-159.
35. *Time,* August 20, 1990.
36. Alain Gresh, "Ambitions irakiennes," *Le Monde Diplomatique,* May, 1990.
37. Alain Gresh, "Le monde arabe orphelin du développement et de la démocratie," *Le Monde Diplomatique,* October 1990.
38. See Doreya Awny, "La dette arabe: 208 milliards de dollars," *Le Monde Diplomatique,* September, 1990.
39. James E. Akins, "Heading Towards War," *Journal of Palestine Studies,* vol. XX, no. 3 (Spring 1991), pp. 16-30, pp. 19-20.
40. Lutfi Al-Hawali, "The Fall of the Arab Berlin Wall," *Al-Ahram,* (in Arabic) (Cairo), August 16, 1990.
41. *Al-Ahram,* (in Arabic) (Cairo), January 25, 1991.
42. *The Washington Post,* reproduced in the *Manchester Guardian Weekly,* September 23, 1990; see also the "Iraqi Transcript of Saddam Hussein's Meeting with the U.S. Ambassador to Iraq on 25 July," translated and broadcast by ABC News, September 11, 1990, and partly reproduced in *Journal of Palestine Studies* vol. XX, no. 2 (Winter 1991), pp. 163-168.
43. The *New York Times,* September 19, 1990.
44. See James E. Akins, "Heading Towards War," *Journal of Palestine Studies,* vol. XX, no. 3 (Spring 1991), pp. 16-30, p. 20.

CHAPTER SIX

Anatomy of Confrontation

On August 1, General Collin Powell, Chairman of the US Joint Chiefs of Staff, became convinced on the basis of Defense Intelligence Agency reports that Iraq was about to invade Kuwait. He told Secretary of Defense Dick Cheney to "sound the alarm at the White House." Although pressed to act, the White House decided to do nothing. Bob Woodward suggested in his book *The Commanders* that either the warning "just fell through the cracks" or the White House already had a different plan for handling the impending crisis. It may be that the White House was not anxious to save Saddam Hussein from the catastrophic trap in which he was about walk.

Once informed of the invasion, President Bush was reported to have made "an almost instantaneous" decision to intervene.[1] At the emergency National Security Council meeting of August 2, Bush forcefully stated his opposition to the invasion and made it clear that he planned to take action. When Treasury Secretary Nicholas Brady suggested ways of adapting to higher oil prices, Bush angrily interrupted: "Let's be clear about one thing. We are not here to talk about adapting. We are not going to plan how to live with this."[2] White House counsel Boyden Gray left the meeting "feeling that the military now had a real opportunity. It seemed to him that Bush was certainly going to do something."[3]

On August 2, the day of the Iraqi invasion of Kuwait, King Hussein of Jordan spoke with Saddam Hussein about the invasion. The Iraqi leader reportedly told him that he wanted to teach Kuwait a lesson and planned to withdraw his troops over the weekend. But he warned that condemnations from the Arab world would complicate his withdrawal plans because it would make it appear as if he were caving in to pressure. The same day, King Hussein flew to Alexandria, Egypt, to meet President Hosni Mubarak. The two leaders agreed with Saudi King Fahd, whom they contacted by phone, to reassure Saddam Hussein and to work to hold off an impending censure by the Islamic Conference Organization which was meeting in Cairo. They also spoke with President Bush and asked him to give them time to handle the crisis themselves. They agreed to convene a limited Arab summit in Jeddah, Saudi Arabia, with Saddam Hussein and Sheikh al-Sabah, the Emir of Kuwait, to resolve the crisis peacefully. King Hussein flew to Baghdad and obtained Saddam Hussein's approval for a negotiated settlement at the forthcoming Jeddah Conference, scheduled for Sunday August 5.[4] Prince Seilman al-Sabah of the ruling Kuwaiti family told me, however, that Saddam Hussein imposed as a condition for attending the conference that the Emir of Kuwait not be present.[5] At any rate, on August 4, King Fahd sent an emissary to Amman to confirm to the Jordanians that he saw no threat of an Iraqi invasion of Saudi Arabia.

From the very beginning of the crisis President Bush opted for militarily confronting Iraq. As early as August 3, the day following the Iraqi invasion, top officials of the Bush administration were frankly admitting that American military intervention "was rising rapidly to the top of the their list of options."[6] American officials were accordingly instructed to foil negotiated Arab solutions to the crisis. Thus, the Bush administration expressed concern at the "natural instinct of Saudi Arabia and its Gulf neighbours to bargain with Iraq."[7] At their August 4 meeting at Camp David, Bush and the top officials of his administration agreed that the American military intervention in the area, taken as a given already, must be designed to be attractive to the Arab League and presented within the context of defending Saudi Arabia because "Kuwait is not popular among the Arabs."[8] After the meeting was adjourned, Bush and the top officials of his administration — Vice-President Quayle, Secretary Baker, Secretary Cheney, National Security Advisor Scowcroft, Chairman Powel, and CIA director Webster — remained. They discussed intelligence information about Saudi Arabia and shared concerns about Saudi readiness to reach a compromise with Iraq and solve the crisis peacefully. The Arabs, the group agreed, "could not be relied on." Bush decided to phone Saudi King Fahd to "make a pitch," and apply "some pressure." When Bush placed the call, King Fahd told him that Saudi Arabia did not need American troops to defend itself. Bush decided to send a team of American officials to Saudi Arabia to expose the Iraqi threat and "increase the pressure on King Fahd" to accept massive American intervention.[9]

As he stepped off the helicopter that brought him back from Camp David on August 5, Bush shared with reporters his feelings about the direction of American response to the Iraqi invasion of Kuwait. To the surprise of General Powell who had understood that the President had committed himself only to the defense of Saudi Arabia, Bush, waving his finger and visibly angry, said: "I view very seriously our determination to reverse out this aggression.... This will not stand, this aggression against Kuwait."[10] This meant that American military intervention was not designed to play a deterrent, defensive role in Saudi Arabia, but would eventually serve for the purpose of waging war against Iraq. General Powell, who was watching the President's remarks on television, "was stunned...[and] marvelled at the distance Bush had travelled in three days. To Powell, it was almost as if the President had six-shooters in both hands and he was blazing away."[11] Bush proceeded to knock off suggestions that the crisis could be solved peacefully through negotiations, and expressed no interest in pursuing or allowing to succeed a so-called negotiated Arab settlement for the crisis. He was sharply critical of Arab leaders who had not condemned the Iraqi invasion of Kuwait, and urged all Arab regimes to "join the rest of the world in condemning this outrage."[12]

Bush recognized that Arab leaders had asked him to give them some time to handle the crisis themselves. He now indicated that he was no longer willing to wait for this Arab solution: "I was told by one (Arab) leader that I respect enormously...that they needed 48 hours to find what was called an Arab solution." He then added: "That obviously has failed."[13] The Iraqi invasion of Kuwait occurred on August 2 and on August 5 Bush was already declaring the failure of Arab efforts to end the crisis peacefully. After 3 days of Iraqi occupation of Kuwait, the American

President was in effect foreclosing negotiated options and declaring inevitable a military solution to put an end to Iraqi occupation of Kuwait.

Arab leaders had been frantically discussing a number of options to present at the Jeddah conference. One scenario suggested the referral of the Iraqi-Kuwaiti disputes to some arbitration with the understanding that Iraq was entitled to have an outlet to the Gulf water. Another scenario provided that after the Iraqi withdrawal from Kuwait and the restoration of the Kuwaiti ruling family, Kuwait would pay financial compensations to Iraq for the abusive Kuwaiti exploitation of slant drilling into Iraq's Rumaila oil fields across the border. A third option envisaged by Arab leaders provided for the establishment in Kuwait, after Iraqi withdrawal and the restoration of the ruling family, of a Kuwaiti government prepared to enter into some form of economic, political and military association with Iraq. These preparations for the negotiations in Saudi Arabia were aborted "by President Bush's decision to intervene in the crisis by immediately dispatching American troops in Saudi Arabia and the Gulf. Everybody understood, on this August 5, 1990, that the American President, excluding all possibility of negotiations, was opting for a strategy of confrontation...War was implied in his decision."[14]

President Mubarak called off the Jeddah Summit. He later explained to the Egyptian Parliament, on January 24, 1991 — as Iraq was being subjected to massive bombardments — that he had called off the Jeddah conference because King Hussein had failed to put to Saddam Hussein the condition that Iraq make a commitment to withdraw before the negotiations could begin.[15] King Hussein, however, told a different story. The Jordanian monarch said that after returning from Baghdad on August 3, he was shocked to learn that Egypt had allowed the public condemnation of Iraq. The Arab League Ministerial Council meeting in Cairo had adopted, on August 3, a harsh resolution condemning "Iraqi aggression against Kuwait," and asking for the "immediate and unconditional withdrawal of the Iraqi forces." A frustrated King Hussein phoned Mubarak in Alexandria to find out why Egypt had undermined the agreed-upon plan. President Mubarak reportedly replied that he had no choice in the matter because he had "come under intense pressure,"[16] presumably from Washington.

Shortly after the Iraqi invasion of Kuwait the Iraqis had notified the American Embassy in Baghdad that they had no intention of entering Saudi territory. President Bush, however, saw the crisis differently and, on August 3, he instructed Secretary Cheney and Chairman Powel to impress upon the Saudis the seriousness of the situation. They had called Saudi Ambassador Prince Bandar the same afternoon and shown him photography which they claimed proved Iraqi troops were heading towards Saudi Arabia. Bandar had gone to Saudi Arabia and informed King Fahd of the American belief of the seriousness of the Iraqi threat. The King was sceptical. He decided to get his own information and sent Saudi scouts into Kuwait to verify the American claim. The scouts came back and reported no Iraqi movements toward Saudi Arabia. "There was no trace," wrote Bob Woodward, "of the Iraqi troops heading toward the Kingdom."[17]

On August 5, US Secretary of Defense Dick Cheney flew to Saudi Arabia with a specific mission: "Get the King to agree to accept US forces..., get that invitation. Persuade him."[18] During the flight to Saudi Arabia, Cheney and his party rehearsed their presentation to King Fahd. Cheney told his subordinates that he had no idea whether Saddam Hussein would invade Saudi Arabia or not. However, an American intelligence officer sent to Kuwait before the Iraqi invasion had reported that the Iraqi forces had no intention of invading Saudi Arabia and had in fact began to withdraw from their forward positions on the Kuwait-Saudi borders.[19] But Cheney and his party were not above using the threat of an imminent Iraqi invasion of Saudi Arabia to "persuade" King Fahd to accept massive American military intervention.

When the American party was received by the Saudi King, Cheney went straight to the point: "Saudi Arabia faces what may be the greatest threat in its history," he sombrely warned, "If this is not countered, there will be grave consequences for Saudi Arabia, and serious consequences for the United States;" Cheney then requested Saudi cooperation for American intervention and for the strangulation of Iraq.[20] General Schwarzkopf then pulled out satellite pictures and explained that they showed Iraqi divisions positioned between Kuwait City and the Saudi border and concluded: "We think Saddam Hussein *could* attack Saudi Arabia in as little as 48 hours."[21] Cheney calmly told the Saudi King that without 200,000 American troops, Saudi Arabia, which had earlier refused to provide military facilities to the US Central Command, would become another Kuwait.[22] King Fahd and his brother expressed ambivalent feelings about the Kuwaitis. Fahd asked his brother Crown Prince Abdullah what would happen to Kuwait if they accepted American forces in Saudi Arabia. The Crown Prince said "There is still a Kuwait." "Yes," the King shot back, "but the entire population is living in our hotel rooms."[23] After some discussions, the Saudi King agreed to American intervention "as long as the Americans agreed in writing to leave when the threat passed and to get Saudi approval before initiating any offensive military action."[24]

When he was back in his quarters, Cheney phoned President Bush, told him of his success, and requested the President's approval to begin American military deployment in Saudi Arabia. Bush told him on the phone: "You got it. Go."[25] On the way back Cheney stopped in Alexandria, Egypt, where he requested and received President Mubarak's consent to the passage of the American nuclear aircraft carrier U.S.S. *Eisenhower* through the Suez Canal the very same night. And thus on August 6, 1990, the irreversible decision of military intervention began to be implemented. The military solution had not been endorsed by the American congress, nor, with the exception of British Prime Minister Thatcher, by the European Allies. America's Arab supporters had been urging restraint, but once massive American intervention began to take place, it acquired its own momentum and subordinated all other options to its more pressing logic.

During the first week of September and as officials of the Bush administration were busy sending troops to the Saudi Kingdom while trumpeting the danger of an Iraqi threat to Saudi Arabia, Peter Zimmerman, former official of the US Arms Control Agency, publicly stated that contrary to statements made by officials of the Bush administration, "we don't see anything (in the satellite pictures) to indicate an Iraqi force in Kuwait of even 20 percent the size the administration claimed." Zimmerman told the *St. Petersburg Times* that he and another satellite imaging experts could see the extensive US military deployment at the Dharan Airport in Saudi Arabia but that they "did not find anything of that sort anywhere in Kuwait. We don't see any tent cities, we don't see congregations of tanks, we don't see troops concentrations, and the main Kuwaiti air base appears to be deserted. It's five weeks after the invasion, and from what we can see, the Iraqi air force hasn't flown a single fighter to the most strategic air base in Kuwait." The Pentagon refused to explain the discrepancies, Congress did not investigate the Pentagon claims nor did it see photographic evidence to back the administration's claims, and the major national media outlets chose to ignore the *St. Petersburg Times* revelations.[26]

In the statement he made to reporters upon his return from Camp David on August 5, Bush had described the Iraqis as "outlaws and renegades," thus setting the stage for the confrontation course. Within the context of the new American strategic doctrine elaborated after the collapse of the Soviet Union and the end of the cold war, the United States was openly committed, as mentioned above, to challenging "the aggressive ambitions of renegade regimes." By describing the Iraqis as "outlaws" and "renegades" President Bush was in effect giving a signal that his administration had made a determination that the Iraqi action posed a security threat to American national interests. The Iraqis had, therefore, to be confronted — hence their elevation to the rank of *bona fide* enemies working to undermine the national interests of the United States. This was, at any rate, the assessment presented to President Bush by William Webster, Director of the Central Intelligence Agency. Webster told the president and his advisors that "Saddam poses a threat that goes beyond the immediate Kuwait crisis and extends to the critical long-term interests of the United States…The CIA evaluation is that Saddam, flush with newly seized Kuwaiti oil reserves, will become a powerful, intimidating force inside the Organization of Petroleum Exporting Countries, driving up oil prices, fuelling inflation, and possibly throwing the United States into recession and unmanageable fiscal difficulty."[27] A determination has been made from the very beginning of the crisis that "it is now in the US 'national interest' to stop Saddam."[28] Since the United States did not yet have enough military forces in the region to confront and decisively defeat the Iraqi army, the Bush Administration decided that it would pursue a strategy consisting of "a multifaceted effort to strangle Iraq's economy, foment discontent in the military, and support resistance groups inside and outside the country."[29] The president was clearly confident that his strategies would succeed. When a reporter asked him how he intended to prevent Saddam Hussein from installing a puppet government in Kuwait, he shot back: "Just wait. Watch and learn."[30]

In defending his decision to send American troops to Saudi Arabia, Bush claimed that the mission of these American troops was purely defensive and that they had no intention of initiating hostilities. This was a necessary ploy since the initial dispatch of American troops did not yet ensure that they would be able to wage the kind of massive war intended to bring about a quick and decisive victory. So it was important to lull the Iraqis into a false sense of security lest they seize the initiative and determine the time and nature of the looming confrontation. Bush therefore claimed: "I want to be clear about what we are doing, and why. America does not seek conflict, nor do we seek to chart the destiny of other nations. But America will stand by her friends. The mission of our troops is wholly defensive. They will not initiate hostilities, but they will defend themselves, the kingdom of Saudi Arabia, and other friends in the Gulf."[31] It was thus part of the American strategy to arrive in Saudi Arabia under the guise of defensive actions until such time as American forces had reached the size demanded by General Powel to wage the kind of massive war for which American strategists had been preparing.

On Monday August 6, the United Nations Security Council imposed sweeping mandatory sanctions against Iraq with a worldwide arms and oil embargo. The U.S.-inspired resolution was adopted by a 13-0 vote with Yemen and Cuba abstaining. The resolution said that the sanctions were imposed after a determination had been made that Iraq failed to comply with Security Council Resolution 660 demanding that Iraq withdraw unconditionally from Kuwait, and usurped "the authority of the legitimate government of Kuwait."

King Hussein of Jordan stood to loose a great deal from the confrontation course. A majority of his people supported Iraq and resented the wealth of the conservative monarchies of the Gulf and he was shrewd enough to be sensitive to the sentiments of his people. On the other hand, Jordan depended on the subsidies and oil deliveries it received from Saudi Arabia, which would subsequently be suspended. Hussein believed therefore that his best course of action was to remain neutral, but neutrality was precisely what Washington rejected. And it was this confrontational attitude of the Bush administration that King Hussein resented and denounced. It seemed like a replay of the ideological confrontation which dominated American relationships with the emerging Third World nations in the fifties when Iraq was the darling protogé of the West and the centre of its anti-communist Baghdad Pact. Washington was then unwilling to accept Egyptian President Nasser's position of neutrality which crusading Secretary Dulles believed was "immoral."

In a perceptive analysis of the crisis precipitated by the Iraqi invasion of Kuwait and its escalation phases, King Hussein explained that in his view: "The combination of King Fahd of Saudi Arabia's panic, President Mubarak of Egypt's obtuseness, President Assad of Syria's desire for revenge, and President Bush's narrow concentration on military measures, was a disastrous one." This "disastrous" combination led to escalation on at least three occasions: "The first was before the Iraq-Kuwait talks in Jeddah, when President Mubarak announced that he had Saddam's word that there would be no use of force against Kuwait. The announcement deprived the Iraqis of leverage, and encouraged the Kuwaitis to dig in their heels. The result was the collapse of the talks and the invasion of Kuwait the following day. The second was when Arab League condemnation of the Iraqi action scuttled a plan for a summit in Saudi Arabia over the first weekend after the invasion. At that time…Iraq was still genuinely ready to withdraw, but its reaction to the condemnation was to name the provisional government whose personnel had earlier been deliberately left unclear. The third was just before the Saudi decision to accept US troops. Again…the Iraqis were still ready for phased withdrawal, although now the 'provisional government' would have had to be represented at the talks. Then came the Saudi decision, and this was followed by the 'merger' of Iraq and Kuwait." The Jordanians said that the graduated nature of Iraqi political moves in Kuwait proves that Saddam Hussein wanted to bargain but was not given the chance.[32]

The Cairo Summit Supports Military Intervention

On the diplomatic front, Washington moved quickly to mobilize Arab support for its strategy of military confrontation with Iraq. Saudi Arabia had been won; Egyptian support was crucial and Cairo was clearly discouraged from pursuing the option of a negotiated settlement that could have offered the Iraqi leader a face-saving way out. Initially, Egyptian President Hosni Mubarak attempted to play a mediating role, first to prevent and then diffuse the Iraq-Kuwait crisis, but pressure from Washington, after the Iraqi invasion of Kuwait, left him with few options but to support the growing boomerang for confronting Iraq.

The *New York Times* was blunt in reminding Mubarak as the Arab Summit met in Cairo that his dependency on American aid robbed him of the luxury of independently charting his own course. "President Mubarak of Egypt," wrote the editors, "having tried to play a mediating role, now seems to be temporizing. Washington has a right to expect more from a country that accepts $2 billion a year in American aid. He and King Hussein of Jordan can seize the occasion of their Arab summit meeting today to get on board."[33] Egypt's support was considered crucial for the success of the confrontation drive and the effort to give it international support.[34] Egyptian officials had told American Secretary of Defense Dick Cheney that Egypt was ready to cooperate with Washington by sending troops if he could persuade other Arab countries to do the same because "we need that Arab cover."[35] The Arab summit provided the opportunity to seek and get that cover.

The Arab conference was convened by President Mubarak in Cairo on August 9. The prevailing mood of the Egyptian hosts was one of impatience with those Arab leaders who spoke of more initiatives for a political solution to the crisis; there was an obvious desire for a quick endorsement of the measures taken to isolate Iraq and to give the military option greater credibility. Thus, in an unusual move, the Summit, under Mubarak's leadership, proposed that the final resolution would be put to a simple majority vote rather than the usual consensus or unanimity rule. Furthermore, PLO leader Yasser Arafat and Libyan leader Momar Khadafy requested that the final resolution contain no condemnation of Iraq, leaving the door open for an Arab solution for the crisis. But President Mubarak "surprising everybody, forced a vote on a text condemning Iraq without allowing for a discussion, thus creating a fait accompli impossible to undo despite the very divided and nuanced opinions of half of the Arab governments. In effect, a dividing line was clearly drawn: favoring the American position were only the Gulf monarchies and Egypt, all the others had reservations or were hostile. Syria constituted a special case."[36]

Specifically, the Cairo Summit confirmed its support for UN Security Council Resolutions 660 and 661 demanding unconditional Iraqi withdrawal, imposing sanctions against Iraq and rejecting its annexation of Kuwait. The summit's final resolution also expressed total Arab solidarity with Saudi Arabia and the Arab Gulf States, and supported "all decisions that Saudi Arabia and other Gulf States could make in their legitimate self-defense in accordance with article 2 of the common defense and economic cooperation treaty between the member States of the Arab League, and article 51 of the Charter of the United Nations, and Security Council Resolution 661 of August 6, 1990."[37]

In authorizing individual Arab States to dispatch forces to defend Saudi Arabia, and in supporting all decisions and requests for assistance made by the Saudi Kingdom and the Gulf States to defend their national sovereignty against a possible Iraqi aggression, the summit was in effect accepting the American claim of an imminent Iraqi threat to Saudi Arabia, and helping to raise the stakes in the confrontation over Iraqi occupation of Kuwait. The final resolution lent legitimacy to the American preference for a military solution and to the US military build-up already underway in the region. According to the Egyptian press, this crucial resolution was supported by 12 members. Yemeni Ambassador to the United Nations Abdallaah al-Ashtall told me, however, that the resolution was supported by 11 States out of 21 States represented, with Dijibouti casting the deciding vote.[38]

Like President Bush a few days earlier, the Cairo Summit seems to have had little patience for those who spoke of the possibility of an Arab political solution to the crisis. When asked by reporters about Arafat's complaint that his peace initiative had not been presented to the Conference, President Mubarak dismissed Arafat's claim that his initiative represented a serious effort for the peaceful resolution of the crisis. He said that he had given the floor to Arafat but that when the Palestinian leader started talking about the possibility of Afghanistan and Kashmir mediation in the crisis, "I brought to his attention that we were here for the Kuwait problem. Do you have solutions now…because this Summit meeting was called to find a solution for this problem? The President of Palestine answered by saying that he had presented a solution and he sent me a piece of paper containing the names of three leaders to go to Baghdad. So I asked him 'did you discuss this with anyone? Did these people agree to go to Baghdad to mediate a solution? Then I asked him 'What will you do after the mediation?"[39] Whatever their worth, Arafat's proposals were not discussed.

As to Yemeni President Ali Abdullah Salih's peace plan, President Mubarak explained his lack of interest in it on the ground that it called on a number of Arab leaders including himself to go to Baghdad. Mubarak said that he rejected the idea of going to Baghdad because "I knew the results in advance." He also characterized the different proposals for a diplomatic solution to the crisis as "a lot of talk without preparations" and those who made them as "saying anything to delay and waste the time of the Summit." When asked if there was still a chance for a peaceful solution, President Mubarak echoed what President Bush had said a few days earlier, and said: "I would like to frankly say, and I am always an optimist, that there is no hope," and added without elaboration, "I tried the impossible to open the doors for a solution."[40]

Egypt may have taken the legally correct and morally honourable position by strongly opposing the invasion and condemning the aggression against a sovereign nation. But there was no escaping the reality of its diminished stature in the Arab world. At the end of the conference Cairo could not marshall the moral authority necessary to lead the Arabs either against foreign intervention or for a united front of common response to Saddam Hussein's invasion. "This loss of moral stature," commented leading Middle East scholar Walid Khalidi, "could be largely adduced to a perception by Arab mass opinion and the intelligentsia that Egypt, since Camp David, has evolved into the nonautonomous fulcrum of specifically American policies in the region."[41]

The editor of the semi-official Egyptian paper *Al-Ahram* called the Summit "a historical meeting" and argued that the apparent division of the Arab world was in reality a deceptive appearance. He said that all the Arab countries condemned the Iraqi invasion and demanded the withdrawal of Iraqi troops from Kuwait, even though there were reservations about the intervention of foreign forces in the area and differences on the means of solving the crisis. As a witness to what went on during the closed-door Summit meeting he gave the following summary:

The first orientation within the Summit consisted of Iraq, the PLO and the Yemen and called for an Arab delegation headed by President Hosni Mubarak to go to Baghdad to consult with President Saddam Hussein before the Summit adopted any resolutions...They claimed that President Saddam Hussein had told them that he was ready to discuss all issues.... The second orientation was represented by Libya and Algeria who maintained that although they condemned the Iraqi invasion of Kuwait because no one can justify or accept the invasion of one Arab country by another, it was wrong to give legitimacy to foreign forces to enter Arab lands to wage war against Iraq...King Fahd (of Saudi Arabia) had stated that Saudi forces would not initiate hostilities against anyone unless they were attacked. Moreover, we should not forget that Libya itself was the target of an American strike. We now reach the third orientation within the Summit...which received the support of 12 Arab States and was based on: 1) the Arab countries do not want to give any cover to foreign intervention in the region; 2) the question is not whether or not to condemn the invasion, everybody had already done that, but rather how to solve the present crisis.[42]

This third group favoured the sending of Arab troops to Saudi Arabia. The *Al-Ahram* editor justified the decision by saying that President Mubarak had no choice but to support the military option and to put it to a vote because "President Mubarak believed that if he did not respond positively to the option of Arab military intervention, the only other acceptable alternative would be foreign intervention."[43] But this rationale fails to explain why military intervention, Arab or foreign, was the only acceptable alternative to a crisis which was barely a week-old. More significantly, it does not explain how the Arab military option was going to forestall or diminish this other, apparently unpleasant alternative of foreign intervention which was already underway. The rationale in fact, derives its logic from attribution to the third group at the conference of an ill-reasoned dilemma: if we don't join the foreign forces which are being deployed right now we would appear to be encouraging them. In fact, the dilemma lay somewhere else for this third group: how to reconcile a sincere desire for a political solution which would spare Iraq certain destruction, with the pressure from the United States to support its military intervention. By giving in to the latter, the former was rendered more complicated because it was cast within a context of confrontation and escalation. In short, far from discouraging the unpleasant alternative of foreign intervention as the editor of *Al-Ahram* implied, the decision of the summit encouraged it. This was confirmed when President Bush interpreted the Arab Summit decision as justifying and strengthening the case for the military confrontation course he was already pursuing.

Alliances

From the very beginning of the crisis, Egypt unequivocally opposed the Iraqi invasion of Kuwait and rejected the possibility of material benefits accruing to Iraq from its use of violence. In so doing, it upheld a basic tenet of international law and reaffirmed its commitment to the principle of peaceful resolution of inter-state disputes, the cornerstone of the Charters of the UN and the Arab League. Meanwhile, Egyptian support for American policy preferences (although expected given the relationship that developed between Cairo and Washington as a result of the triumph of the Camp David strategy), diminished in the eyes of many Arabs whatever moral weight carried by Egyptian defense of the sanctity of international law.

Still, beyond the strategic-political cooperation between Washington and Cairo, there were compelling economic realities which the Egyptian government could not afford to ignore. A net exporter of agricultural produce, Egypt had become, in 1990, unable to feed its own people and barely able to meet the interest payments of its $50 billion-debt. Its economy was burdened with two million jobless out of a work force of 13 million, not counting massive and chronic hidden unemployment. Cairo's choice did not seem to be between siding with Iraq or with the United States, for there was hardly anybody among the Arab States who did not condemn the Iraqi invasion of Kuwait. Rather, it seemed to the Mubarak government that it was a matter of supporting the American drive for military intervention, thereby giving it credibility as Washington demanded, or trying to support a negotiated settlement as King Hussein attempted to do throughout the crisis. In the end, Cairo judged that it could not afford to alienate the United States, particularly since Washington held the promise to forgive Egypt's $7 billion military debt to the United States.

The Summit vote did, however, mark some significant shifting of alliances. Thus, King Hussein of Jordan, longtime the West's most loyal friend in the region, expressed serious reservations about the Cairo Summit's resolution. An astute analyst of Western and Arab politics, Hussein understood that his hold onto power depended more than ever on his reflecting the views of his people. The King had taken his country on the road to democracy and allowed free elections to be held in November 1989. The elections resulted in a landslide for candidates representing the Muslim brotherhood or sympathetic to their views. Now a majority of Jordanian parliamentarians resented the way the United States was handling the Gulf crisis and expressed anger at the American double standard applied to Middle East conflicts. Their resentment was shared by the man in the street as was evident from the pro-Iraqi and anti-American demonstrations which swept the Jordanian capital. Realizing that the Cairo Summit's resolution had taken the crisis a step closer to military confrontation, King Hussein warned: "I do not want to sound challenging or to provoke any action but very sincerely I am very, very afraid that what is happening now is driven to some degree by the same mentality that brought us Suez: the idea that some powers of this world can tell people you can say this or you can't say that, you can move in this way or you can't move in the other way."[44]

King Hussein's frustration was easy to understand. Jordan stood to lose the most, after Iraq, from a military confrontation which could spread to the rest of the region. Israel had threatened instant war if Iraqi troops entered Jordan. Such a war could easily give Israel the excuse it needed to expel en masse the Palestinians of the West Bank to Jordan — 60 percent of whose population was already of Palestinian origins. Economically, Jordan had lost the most, after Kuwait, as a result of the crisis and of its refusal to join the anti-Iraqi coalition. It had to absorb 250,000 Jordanians and 200,000 Palestinians who fled Kuwait leaving behind their life savings, which were estimated at $8 billion. Other Jordanian workers were forced to leave after Saudi Arabia and the Gulf States refused to renew their work permits. Furthermore, economic aid from the Gulf and Saudi Arabia was terminated and Saudi oil supplies to Jordan were discontinued, further aggravating a desperate economic situation while increasing Jordanian dependency on Iraqi oil. In addition, half of Jordan's economic activities were conducted with Iraq and Hussein's half-hearted and reluctant compliance with the economic sanctions against Iraq further damaged the Jordanian economy.[45] King Hussein decided to take his case against the war option to the American people. Writing in the *Washington Post*, he stated: "Since the Iraqi invasion of Kuwait did not occur in a vacuum, it cannot be solved in a vacuum. Any solution must address, if not simultaneously at least sequentially, the major underlying causes — namely, the dispute between Iraq and Kuwait, the imbalance of wealth in the area, the unsolved confrontation between Israel, Palestine and the Arab States, and the perilous escalation and proliferation of weapons of mass destruction...As for victors and spoils, Middle East wars have produced neither, only graveyards for illusion and the seeds for future wars...The Middle East cannot afford another war, the world should not impose another one on it."[46]

King Hassan of Morocco has been a longtime supporter of Western policies in the Arab world and has played a prominent role in facilitating the secret Egyptian-Israeli talks which paved the way for Sadat's policy of separate negotiations and separate treaty with Israel. He also played an important role in facilitating third party political and material support to Iraq during the Iran-Iraq war. Moroccan relations with the West in general and the United States in particular were very good and Hassan is described by Bob Woodward as owing his survival of the numerous plots against his reign to CIA support. On the way back from his trip to Saudi Arabia on August 6, Secretary Cheney stopped in Morocco and secured King Hassan's support for American military intervention. At the same time, Hassan was astute enough to gauge the reaction of his people to the crisis and to tamper his support for American intervention with virulent criticism of American support for Israel. In an interview with the French newspaper *Le Monde* on August 16, he said that all America's friends "were disgusted" because the American congress has always been "sickeningly" and "systematically" supportive of the extreme right-wing policy of the Shamir government. He also played down the importance of his decision to support military intervention by describing it as a "symbolic" gesture to express solidarity with the monarchies of Saudi Arabia and Kuwait.

Syrian President Hafez al-Assad, on the other hand, had consistently been vocal in his criticisms of the United States policy in the region. His decision to send Syrian troops to fight side by side with American troops against another Arab country, albeit one ruled by his traditional ideological rival, owed more to opportunism and strategic calculations than to an unshakable commitment to the restoration of the Kuwaiti ruling family. Assad, a realist who has been called the Bismark of the Middle East, made a shrewd assessment of the operational environment and the forces at play and concluded that, although popular sentiments in Syria were pro-Iraqi and anti-American, the benefits of siding with the United States outweighed the benefits of adopting a policy orientation in line with popular opinion in his country. With the collapse of the Soviet Union as a rival superpower, the Middle East was wide open to greater American influence and it was obvious that the course of confrontation chosen by Saddam Hussein would leave Iraq exposed, alone and without the military or even political support it once enjoyed from Moscow. Siding with Saddam Hussein would have simply isolated Syria with Iraq without any serious prospects of increased Syrian influence in the region. In addition, American support for a negotiated settlement with the Israelis, who continue to occupy Syrian territories, was judged necessary for the resolution of the Arab-Israeli conflict. Assad also realized that he needed American acquiescence to launch a final offensive against the forces of the rebellious General Michel Aoun who, with weapons from Iraq and Israel, challenged Syrian ascendency in Lebanon, refused to recognize the authority of the Syrian-backed government in Beirut, and launched a desperate, bloody, and ultimately losing war against the Syrian-backed Lebanese forces. Following an official visit by Secretary Baker to Damascus in October 1990, Syrian troops eliminated the last hold-outs of the Aoun-led rebellious forces, disarmed the various militias, allowed the regular Lebanese army to regain control, and established a Syrian-backed government of national reconciliation in which most of the various Lebanese factions were represented.[47]

So when Iraqis and Americans came knocking at Assad's door shortly after the Iraqi invasion of Kuwait, the choice had already been made and it was only a matter of finessing a decision which was bound to appear surprising to many. Thus, the Iraqi oil Minister Issam Abdel Rahim al-Chalabi visited Damascus on August 7, five days after the Iraqi invasion of Kuwait and only one day after the Security Council imposed mandatory sanctions against Iraq. He pleaded with the Syrians to reopen the Iraq-Syria pipeline which had been closed by Damascus shortly after the start of the Iraq-Iran war. In a desperate attempt to entice the Syrians to agree to the Iraqi request, the Iraqi Minister promised that Baghdad would share the revenues of oil exported through the Syria-Iraq pipeline. The Syrians showed little interest and argued that the reopening of the pipeline could only take place within the context of normalized relationships between the two countries. From the American side, John Kelly, US Assistant Secretary of State for Near Eastern and South Asian Affairs, visited Damascus twice in one week and seems to have struck a deal with the Syrian regime: American promises to work for the recovery of the Israeli-occupied Syrian Golan Heights, and possibly also promises of economic aid, in return for Syrian support against Iraq. Syrian government officials frankly admitted that Saddam Hussein left them no choice. "At a time when the Soviet Union has almost pulled out of the game," said one Syrian official, "Saddam Hussein has put all of us in a deadlock by imposing an impossible choice: either being completely for the United States or completely against them...The American presence is now a reality. Now all we can do is to try to make the situation less dangerous."[48] Syria supported the military option endorsed by the Cairo Summit, thus approving the presence of US troops in Saudi Arabia, and promised to send its own military contribution.

Tunisian leaders, who traditionally followed a pro-Western foreign policy, refused even to come to the Cairo Summit so as not to, as they put it, "give ephemeral legitimacy to foreign intervention which is the interest of neither the Arabs nor world peace and security."[49] Public sentiments in Tunisia were overwhelmingly pro-Iraq, even among the intellectual elites and the intelligentsia, who were strongly critical of the dictatorial nature of the regime in Baghdad. An opinion poll carried out shortly after the Iraqi invasion of Kuwait found a majority of Tunisians strongly critical of Saudi Arabia for allowing American troops in their country: 94 percent of respondents said they were opposed to the American military intervention in Saudi Arabia, and 79 percent believed that the Saudi Arabian government lost its religious legitimacy as a guardian of the Moslem holy places by allowing American military intervention.[50]

From the beginning of the crisis, the Palestinian leadership cast itself in the role of a mediator between Iraq and Kuwait. The decision was partly motivated by Arafat's reading of widespread Palestinian frustrations with American support for Israeli occupation and the growing conviction that American interests in the Arab world must be challenged before Washington would pay any heed to Arab Palestinian interests. Arafat's position of neutrality may also have been an expression of gratitude to Saddam Hussein for the material support he lavished on the Palestinian leadership after the end of the Iran-Iraq war. But the Palestinian mediatory role was also used by its leadership to cloak ambiguities and contradictions in its position on the crisis. After the Cairo Conference rejected Arafat's mediating efforts, the PLO failed to forcefully condemn the Iraqi invasion of Kuwait. In opting for this position, the Palestinian leadership missed an opportunity to repeatedly and forcefully express support for the very principle of international law from which the Palestinians under occupation drew moral and legal strength: the inadmissibility of acquisition of territory by force. Further, in getting entangled in inter-Arab disputes, Arafat violated the unwritten rule of non-interference in Arab affairs, a principle that governed the delicate and changing support the Palestinians received from Arab governments. It was a miscalculation and the PLO's detractors were quick to use it to undermine the Palestinian leadership credibility and international standing. More immediately the PLO's position cost the Palestinian people crucial and badly-needed financial support which Kuwait and the Gulf States had generously provided in the past and which had now been abruptly terminated. At the same time, Palestinian financial losses as a result of the crisis were colossal; the economic strength of the 400,000-strong Palestinian community in Kuwait, the most cohesive, politically conscious and prosperous in the diaspora and the main source of financial support for the Palestinians under occupation and in the refugee camps, was virtually wiped out. The loss in Palestinian income and assets in Kuwait alone had been estimated in the billions of dollars.[51]

Although the Cairo Summit decisions may have disappointed many Arabs including traditionally pro-Western Arabs, they, and the role played by Egypt, seem to have satisfied American demands and Egyptian needs for an Arab cover for the confrontation course chosen by Washington. As mentioned above, President Bush interpreted the summit decision as supporting and strengthening his course of military confrontation. He phoned President Mubarak on August 11 to congratulate him on the decision to send Arab forces to the Gulf and reassured him that he was not trying to overthrow the Iraqi regime.[52] The reality, however, was different. President Bush signed a CIA order directing the Agency to "do what it can to destabilize Iraq politically and get rid of Saddam Hussein by almost any means."[53]

The Soviet Position

But perhaps the most important and most dramatic reversal of alliances took place outside the Cairo Summit. The Soviet Union, longtime ideological supporter of and chief arms supplier to the Iraqi regime, was reduced to a reluctant supporter of its former chief rival.

Although prior to the crisis it was clear that the Soviet Union was a declining superpower with reduced political influence, Soviet officials continued to insist that they were bringing to their foreign policy new thinking and were as much interested in the Middle East as ever. Soviet Foreign Minister Edward Shevardnadze toured the Middle East in February 1989 and emphasized his government's commitment to playing a dynamic and constructive role in the region. The new Soviet rhetoric emphasized cooperation, negotiations and the importance of reaching a political settlement to the Middle East conflicts within the context of the international consensus to which the West officially subscribed. Moscow also moved toward improving its diplomatic relations with Israel, severed after the Israeli lightening strike of 1967. Thus, although the Soviet Union may have lost out to the capitalist system economically, its rhetoric, symbolic actions, and statements about the Middle East indicated that it did not intend to abdicate, at least diplomatically, its ambitions as a military superpower with traditionally strong interests in the Middle East.

From the first day of the Gulf crisis, Moscow's cooperation was of crucial importance to Washington's drive to isolate Iraq and put together an anti-Iraq coalition with international credibility. Shortly after the Iraqi invasion of Kuwait, the Kremlin followed the White House lead in issuing harsh condemnations of the invasion. Soviet Foreign Minister Edward Shevardnadze joined American Secretary of State Baker, who was visiting Moscow during the first week of August, in describing the Iraqi invasion as "brutal" and calling for unconditional withdrawal from Kuwait. An official Soviet statement suggested that Moscow was not totally opposed to the use of force to drive Iraqi troops out of Kuwait. The statement, published in *Pravda* on August 10, read: "We are also ready to begin immediate consultations within the framework of the Military High Command Committee of the Security Council which, in conformity with the charter of the United Nations, can fulfill very important functions."[54] In fact, Moscow's cooperation with Washington extended beyond the diplomatic and political spheres and included the sensitive area of military intelligence. On instructions from the Soviet Defense Ministry, the Soviet military attaché in Washington went to the Pentagon, on August 19, and shared with the American military chiefs crucial information on the types of armaments the Soviet Union had delivered to Iraq. In addition, the Soviet press emulated the American press in its harsh condemnations of the Iraqi action and constant denunciations of the Iraqi President who was invariably described as "a dictator," "a new Hitler," "the thief of Baghdad," and "a criminal."[55]

By the end of August, the Security Council had quickly passed a succession of resolutions imposing mandatory sanctions, declaring the annexation of Kuwait null and void, condemning Iraqi actions against foreign nationals and foreign embassies in Kuwait, and authorizing the use of force to impose a blockade to enforce the sanctions against Iraq. This dramatic and energetic succession of decisions by the Security Council would not have been possible without the cooperation of the Soviet Union which was unable to emphasize the necessity of using the United Nations conference machinery to bring about a political settlement of the crisis. On September 9, the respected Soviet commentator Stanislav Kondrachov, of the official Soviet paper Izvestia, lamented to the British television network the BBC, the decline of the Soviet Union which, he said, could no longer be considered a superpower.[56]

At their Helsinki Summit, on September 9, President Bush and President Gorbachev displayed superpower agreement on what was needed to resolve the crisis, even as they emphasized different means for achieving it. A joint declaration stated: "Our preference is to resolve the crisis peacefully, and we will be united against Iraq's aggression as long as the crisis exits. If the current steps fail to end it, we are prepared to consider additional ones consistent with the United Nations charter."[57] They seemed to disagree on two issues: while President Bush refused to rule out the use of force and continued to demand unconditional capitulation from Iraq, Mr. Gorbachev counselled more patience for a political solution; they also disagreed on whether or not there was any linkage between Iraqi occupation of Kuwait and Israeli occupation of Arab territories. While the American President continued to refuse to see any link between the two conflicts, President Gorbachev believed and said that there was a connection. Still, President Bush got the backing he needed from the Soviet President and could now claim to be assured that further United Nations measures would have the support of the Soviet Union. Washington would also be able to claim that its anti-Iraq coalition had the support of the international community and that it was not an American war against the Arabs. Gorbachev, notwithstanding his claim that the Soviet Union could not be bought for dollars, received the promise of more American economic aid. In short, it was palpably clear that Iraq could not count on its traditional ally to save it from its predicament. The unity of purpose and the convergence of interests of the two world leaders meant that Saddam Hussein was, as Gorbachev put it, "driving into a dead end."[58]

American Goals in the Gulf

President Bush articulated a number of American goals all of which were usually cast within a high moral context about the defense of principles, the necessity of upholding the rule of law and protecting the decency of inter-state relations, and the imperative of defending a new world order. "It will not be easy to defend our principles," Bush said, "it will take time and could cost us a high price."[59] A statement which prompted a respected French analyst to sarcastically observe: "Time and money will not be enough. One must first have principles. And alas, these have been only too often roughly handled by those who want to enforce their respect today."[60] More specifically, the record of American interventions and wars, against Central American countries in particular, weakened any claim to monopoly over moral principles. Aware of this reality too frequently ignored or brushed aside, respected American commentator William Pfaff observed that Presidents Reagan and Bush "are hardly qualified to teach Saddam Hussein, given their own practices in cases (Nicaragua and Panama) where the vital interests of America were less at stake than are those of Iraq in controlling Kuwaiti oil."[61]

The repressive nature of Saddam Hussein's regime was known and, indeed, supported by Washington. The violation of international law involved in the Iraqi invasion of Kuwait was neither the first such disregard for the rule of law nor the last. This of course in no way excuses it or rationalizes it, but it helps to place it within the context of the real world as opposed to the rhetorical one. The American invasion of Panama and the Soviet invasion of Afghanistan were cogent examples too recent to allow the Superpowers an unchallenged self-righteous and self-serving assertion about their concern for international law. Illegal military occupation was tolerated, and indeed effectively if not officially supported, by Washington in the case of Israeli occupation of Palestinian, Syrian and Lebanese territories, and treated with indifference in the case of Turkish occupation of Greek Cyprus, and Chinese occupation of Tibet.

Behind Washington's resolve to confront the Iraqi challenge lay the realization that the Iraqi invasion of Kuwait threatened to bring about the collapse of a whole structure of economic, political and military order which was essentially favourable to Western interests and the conservative order allied with the West, and increasingly a source of frustration to the majority of Arabs. "In reality," observed one commentator in the respected French periodical *Le Monde Diplomatique,* "it would appear that the enormity of (Saddam Hussein's) action was designed to challenge an economic and political status quo in the Middle East increasingly unfavourable to the Arabs, and exclusively profitable to an Israeli expansionism stimulated by the perspectives of the enormous transfer of population from the Jewish communities of the Soviet Union to the Palestinian territories. This is the only explanation for the vivacity of the Western reaction, and particularly the Anglo-Saxon reaction. The sudden concern for the immediate and muscular respect for the rule of law in a region where it has been held up to ridicule a hundred times in the past forty years, particularly by the Western powers, the Soviet Union, Syria, Iran, Israel, can only be understood in light of the collapse of a status quo profitable to regional and international actors."[62]

Threat to Dominant Order

With the end of the cold war and the disappearance of the communist threat, there was a realization in Washington that challenges to the status quo and the established order favourable to the United States would come, no longer from East-West rivalry, but from the North-South dichotomy with its growing inequalities and attendant discontent and frustrations.

In claiming that in confronting Iraq, the United States was defending a new world order, President Bush argued that such an order must allow all countries in the world "from North and South...to prosper and live in harmony."[63] But a North-South world order where 25 percent of the total world population inhabits the North and spends 80 percent of world income, embodies precisely the kind of "harmony" against which the South has been protesting. With 6 percent of the world's population, the United States alone is using nearly 40 percent of its wealth. The April 1992 United Nations development report indicates that the gap between the rich North and the poor South is growing and has reached a level whereby the average income per capita in the North is now 150 times that of the average income per capita in the South. This "harmony" of North-South relationship is daily inflicting various forms of violence on millions of people. Each day 40,000 children die throughout the Third World from hunger and malnutrition. Hunger, drought, epidemics and malnutrition are expected to cause the death of about 30 million people over the next ten years throughout the Third World. Many countries in the Third World are condemned to perpetual economic stagnation as a result of having to pay more than half their national income to reimburse just the interest of their crippling debt to the International Monetary Fund and the World Bank. These two financial institutions are draining $0.5 billion a year from the rich North as compared to $6 billion a year from the poor South.

This "harmony" in relationship between the rich North and the increasingly poorer South was in effect, a time bomb ticking away. Not surprisingly, American strategists reached the conclusion that the new threats to American global interests and to the preservation of American affluence would come from the Third World. When President Bush was asked before the Iraqi invasion of Kuwait about the identity of the enemy which replaced the Soviet Union in the post-Cold-War era, he unhesitatingly said "instability." This view is certain to ensure that "Washington will never be short of enemies."[64] Such a world order in which its only superpower is haunted and obsessed by enemies from around the globe is not reassuring; it is an uneasy reminder of the grim and disturbing picture Joseph Schumpter painted in his classic work *Imperialism* of the logic by which Imperial Rome was committed to fighting instability around the globe because there was no corner in the world where some interest was not alleged to be in danger; and inevitably there was no alternative except to relate to the world in increasingly negative, coercive and self-destructive ways.

The Iraqi invasion was viewed by the Bush administration within the global context of threats to "stability" and to American interests; a convenient context for the justification of the enormous American military deployment already underway. Thus, the Bush administration made a conscious decision to treat the Gulf crisis not as a Middle East crisis between two Arab countries, but as a crisis which chiefly concerned the United States whose vital interests were at stake. Accordingly, the Administration deliberately ignored Middle East specialists both in and out of government. "The president sees this not as a traditional Middle East crisis," said one administration official, "but as the first post-Cold War crisis. It involves weapons with the capability for mass destruction and has implications for world oil supplies that go far beyond the region. It requires new thinking and new concepts, and there is a feeling that it's better to talk to people who see things in global terms rather than with regional specialists whose thinking has been much slower to catch up with this kind of situation."[65]

There was a good political reason for the globalization of the crisis. Most Arabists and State Department career diplomats urged a negotiated settlement of the crisis, an advise ill-suited to an administration bent on confrontation. Middle Eastern experts from outside the government put forward realistic peace plans which involved negotiations with the Iraqis and some face-saving proposals to allow the Iraqi leadership to withdraw from Kuwait without the political risk associated with humiliation. "Invariably," said an official of the Bush administration, "these plans call for concessions that would leave Saddam in control of some of the fruits of his aggression. That goes counter to Bush's insistence that Iraq must withdraw completely from Kuwait and surrender all its ill-gotten gains before there can be any type of dialogue."[66]

The perception was that if the United States allowed any challenge to the dominant order to succeed, however symbolically, then American prestige would suffer and American credibility in the eyes of friends and foes alike would diminish. And this would set the stage for all sorts of political and economic upheavals with far-reaching consequences for American interests in the region. But the dominant order was increasingly a source of growing frustrations and anger in the Arab world; it lacked economic equity in terms of distribution of wealth between the rich Arab minority and the poor majority; it was not particularly compatible with international law in terms of American-supported Israeli occupation of Arab territories and various violations of human rights in the region; it was not particularly stable in terms of popular opposition to unpopular regimes; and it was not particularly democratic either.

George Bush and the top officials of his administration knew that they could not use the usual slogan justifying American interventions in the name of defense of democracy. In a statement reminiscent of the Congress of Vienna policy of intervention throughout Europe to crush challenges to established European monarchies, Bush said: "Kuwait is not a democracy, but it's not a question of democracy, it's a question of legitimacy."[67] But legitimacy in democratic countries traditionally derived its basis from the consent of the governed as expressed in freely-held elections. Now, if President Bush was committing America to defend legitimacy regardless of its sources and irrespective of the nature of the regime it legitimized, he was in effect articulating a policy orientation which has long characterized American interactions with the world, as critics such as William Appleman, Gabriel Kolko, Richard Barnet, Noam Chomsky, Edward Herman and others have shown. American foreign policy has often shown rhetorical interest in the ideals of democracy but real commitment to military intervention in defense of a certain political and economic order and of the regimes whose political destinies and economic interests were tied to that order, regardless of the nature of these regimes. Thus, regimes whose legitimacy rested on the wresting of power by brute force and military coups have been welcomed and supported by Washington as in Turkey (1960), South Korea (1961), Brazil (1964), Indonesia (1966), Chile (1973). In short, in saying that American intervention in the Gulf was not in support of democracy but rather in support of legitimacy as embodied in the status quo and regardless of its basis, President Bush was in effect admitting that the dominant order may be inequitable, unstable, anti-democratic, replete with violations of international law and human rights, but it serves American interests and therefore its legitimacy must be defended. Any challenges to it are considered challenges to "stability" and America had just declared that in the absence of the Soviet threat, "instability" had become America's number one enemy.

Oil

The "new thinking" and "new concepts" invoked by Bush administration officials to justify their globalization of the crisis were not evident in the list of American goals articulated by the president, Congressional leaders, and public-opinion makers. Thus, in his statement justifying the dispatching of American troops to the Gulf, President Bush explained that American national interests were at stake. Contrary to his repeated subsequent denials, Bush frankly admitted that the fight was after all going to be for oil and for the power to influence its price control mechanisms as the CIA assessment had suggested: "The stakes are high. Iraq is already a rich and powerful country that possesses the world's second largest reserves of oil, and over a million men under arms. It's the fourth largest military in the world. Our country now imports nearly half of the oil it consumes, and could face a major threat to its economic independence. Much of the world is even more dependent on imported oil, and is even more vulnerable to Iraqi threats."[68]

In addition to identifying the risk related to Iraqi influence over oil production and price setting mechanisms, Bush slipped in a statement about Iraq being the fourth largest military power in the world. A misleading and self-serving assertion. It relied on numerical comparisons of troops under arms and numbers of various weapon systems, a rather anachronistic method of assessing the power and military strength of nations on the eve of the twenty-first century. The technical expertise, the quality of training, the nature of the military-industrial complex, the professional quality of the army, and the nature of the leadership are all important factors in the evaluation of military power. If we include these criteria and add to them the historical experience showing Iraq bogged down for eight years in static trench warfare manoeuvres against Iran and unable to achieve a decisive victory, a realistic picture would emerge, revealing Iraq to be no more than a third-rate ambitious regional power. The war in the Gulf would clearly confirm the validity of this realistic assessment which I put forward during my television appearances in the midst of a flood of contrary and gratuitous self-serving assertions about Iraq's awesome power. The propaganda value of the Bush statement about Iraq being the fourth largest military power in the world would prove effective, and influential print and electronic media personalities and "experts" would uncritically repeat the statement, helping the propagandistic goal of inflating the Iraqi threat, and engineering public consent and support for a massive war against a Third World country.

Oil has traditionally figured prominently in the geostrategic calculations of the security managers of the industrialized world. Chevron penetrated Saudi Arabia as early as 1932 as a result of American support for Ibn-Saud who had expelled the British-supported Sherif Hussein and annexed his Kingdom of Hejaz in 1925. In Mexico, American secret services provided support for counter-revolutionary movements to prevent Mexican nationalization of its oil resources in 1938. Washington tried to prevent the return of democracy in Venezuela between 1938 and 1948 before finally settling for a profit-sharing scheme for oil exploitation with the Venezuelans. To break the monopoly granted by Reza Shah Pahlavi to the Anglo-Iranian Oil Company, the Iranian Parliament nationalized, in 1951, the Iranian petroleum industry and elected Mohamed Mossadegh, the extremely popular seventy-three year old leader of the National Front, as new Prime Minister. For almost two years Mossadegh vainly attempted to renegotiate with Britain new terms for the Anglo-Iranian Oil Company before finally, in despair, bringing the matter before the International Court of Justice which ruled in favour of Iran. Faced with an effective British embargo on Iranian oil and mounting threats from right-wing opposition and criminal elements, Mossadegh organized a referendum in which the Iranian people expressed their full confidence in his leadership. In August 1953, with the Shah vacationing in Rome, the CIA organized a coup which overthrew the Mossadegh Cabinet and replaced it with a an extreme-right wing government headed by General Zahedi, a former Nazi sympathizer. In the process, American oil companies eased out the English oil interests, obtained 40 percent of the Anglo-Iranian oil company, and enjoyed the unqualified support of a grateful Shah of Iran.[69] It was the beginning of a long friendship.

With 5 percent of the world population consuming 25 percent of its energy production, the United States' needs seemed insatiable, its dependency uncontainable. President Carter declared, in the late 1970s, that American dependency on imported oil was the moral equivalent of war; but the dependency only increased. Thus, in 1972 the United States imported 13.2 percent of its oil needs; by the mid 1980s it was importing 45 percent of its oil consumption, and 52 percent by 1991. And if current trends continued, proven American reserves of oil would continue to deplete at a rapid pace. In England, the North-Sea current proven and recoverable oil reserves could be depleted in 13 years.[70]

Shortly after the Arab-Israeli war of 1973 the OPEC nations instituted huge increases in the price of oil as Third World countries led by Algeria, Mexico and Iran demanded a new economic order. The Third World countries were revolting against the inequality of economic relationships between the industrialized nations and the less developed countries; they demanded a fair price for their raw materials, a mechanism for transfer of technology, more profit sharing with the multinational corporations operating on their soil, and Western help in development and industrialization. The huge increase in oil prices gave the Third World OPEC countries huge financial power and apparent political independence, thus placing them in a favourable position to mediate the transition to a new economic order. Their revenues had increased from $10 billion in 1960 to $20 billion in 1970, $133 billion in 1974, and $327 billion by 1980. But the inability of the OPEC countries to transform this huge financial power into political power, and the failure of the industrialized world to endorse and genuinely support the principles underlying the new economic order led to uncontrolled lending to Third World countries by international banks recycling the huge sums of petrodollars deposited with them. This gave rise to the most massive debt crisis in the post World War II era. Third World debt to international banks increased from $3 billion in 1970 to $128 billion in 1980. As it became apparent that many of the Third World countries were unable to meet even the payment of interests on their debt obligation, international finance moved in to restructure the world economy and institute a new economic order which bore little resemblance to the vision of an equitable partnership in development between the industrialized North and the developing South. The World Bank and the International Monetary Fund instituted rigorous "performance criteria" which imposed certain economic and fiscal conditions on debtor nations desperate to re-schedule their debt payments.

American military and political leaders multiplied the threat of military intervention to prevent a repeat of the 1973-74 oil embargo; they also successfully co-opted the cooperation of Saudi Arabia, Kuwait and other Gulf countries to influence OPEC and ultimately bring it to its knees; the success of the campaign was crowned by the repeated failures of the once mighty organization to enforce production and price quotas or to stop the collapse of oil prices by 1985-86. Saudi

Arabia emerged thereafter as a principal tool in the industrialized world strategy to influence OPEC and to maintain the stability of the established economic order.[71] The new economic order agenda had been defeated and the power accumulated by Third World oil producers defused and brought under control. With the collapse of the Soviet Union and the resulting desperate need for economic assistance in East and Central Europe, international finance extended its "performance criteria" to these areas which joined the growing number of countries convinced of the need for an open-door, capitalist-oriented, privatization-driven economic programme; this was the "invisible victory," as American strategists would proudly proclaim, of the principles valued by American corporate power and traditionally defended by American military might.

Although Kuwait produced only 3 percent of world oil production, its 9.4 percent share of world proven recoverable reserves gave it a major strategic importance, particularly when added to Iraq's 9.9 percent share of oil reserves. Thus, Iraqi control of Kuwait would have put at the disposal of Saddam Hussein roughly 20 percent of proven and recoverable world oil reserves. Given his regional ambitions and drive to build a strong army, the Iraqi leader would have exerted tremendous influence over the Gulf States and Saudi Arabia. This would naturally have had significant implications for the unfolding new economic order and would have represented a direct challenge by a Third World leader to the seemingly undisputed supremacy of the United States. And given the importance of Middle East oil to the new economic order, the Iraqi challenge had to be not only confronted but decisively defeated as well. With one bold stroke, the deployment of American troops in the Gulf brought under American influence territories that held 40 percent of the world's proven reserves and controlled 45 percent of the world's net oil exports. American power over the international oil scene had never been more dramatic at a time when American dependency on imported oil had never been greater.

Opinion-makers candidly recognized that American primary interests in the region were related to the flow of oil and to who controlled its production. The *Washington Post*, which supported the war option, editorialized in the second week of August: "For the United States and Europe, the primary interest in political stability there is the flow of oil."[72] Zbigniew Brezezinski, former national security advisor in the Carter Administration, was blunt about what he believed should be American aims in the Gulf: "In the circumstances, America must act firmly, even unilaterally, but also intelligently. Its policy must be to deter aggression but not to lead a crusade. To put it more crudely, the flow of oil is ultimately an American imperative; the liberation of Kuwait is the international community's responsibility."[73]

The American Way of Life

American military interventions abroad have traditionally been justified by a number of arguments; some were related to the perception of American leaders that the United States had been chosen by history to be the guardian at the gate; others were based on the conviction that America's "manifest destiny" was to use its power to generate and civilize mankind; and yet others sprang from the belief that economic prosperity at home was inextricably tied to American ability to have an unimpeded access to markets and raw materials abroad. Thus, history willed the annexation of Hawaii; the invasion of Cuba was an act of humanity; the invasion of the Philippines was a duty of civilization and Christianity. The Theodor Roosevelt administration expanded the Monroe Doctrine of exclusive American influence over the Western Hemisphere and gave America the prerogative of policing it by force to combat wrong doing and enforce respect for law and order. Thus, American troops invaded Panama under Roosevelt, Nicaragua under Taft, the Dominican Republic and Mexico under Wilson, and Nicaragua again under Coolidge. At one point a Mexican leader lamented the fate of his country for being too far from God and too close to the United States.

Isolationist sentiments stopped the United States from joining the League of Nations, vilified by politicians and opinion-makers as an instrument for freezing the imperialist pre-war status quo. During World War II, and even before Pearl Harbor, Franklin Roosevelt conceived plans for an expanded world police role for America, with the help of Britain. At the 1943 Teheran conference, after the Russian stand at Stalingrad stopped the Nazi invasion and assured the survival of the Soviet Union, Roosevelt proposed an international condominium composed of America, Britain, nationalist China, and the Soviet Union, to carry out the task of policing the world. Anticipating the emergence of the United States as the supreme economic power of the world, Roosevelt was attracted by the possibility of vast trade with China, access to the enormous oil resources of Saudi Arabia, and vast economic concessions for American companies. He now demanded that the British dismantle their preferential trade agreements and accept the principle of open door policy of free trade and free access to markets. It was this theme of linkage between American prosperity at home and free trade and free access to markets abroad which, more than the concept of policing the world, would ultimately be successfully invoked as necessitating American interventions abroad. Secretary of State James Byrnes articulated, in August 1945, the increasingly potent rationale of linkage: "Our international policies and our domestic policies are inseparable. Our foreign relations inevitably affect employment in the United States. Prosperity and depression in the United States just as inevitably affect our relations with the other nations of the world."[74]

Almost all arguments invoked to justify American interventions from the Spanish-American war in 1898, which Theodor Roosevelt hoped would bring empire to America, to the Panama invasion of 1989 through which George Bush made an example of a dictator and former American ally who rebelled against Washington, were cast within the all-encompassing imperative of defending American freedom and the American way of life. In explaining this basic and fundamental tenet of American interventionism, President Johnson said to American troops in Vietnam in 1966: "Everything that happens in this world affects us, because pretty soon it gets on our doorsteps." The President then expressed the basic threat to the American way of life in direct and primitive terms: "There are 3 billion people in the World and we have only 200 million of them. We are outnumbered 15 to 1. If might did make right, they would sweep over the United States and take what we have. We have what they want."[75] The American intervention in the Gulf was also cast in the familiar mould of defense of American freedom and the American way of life. Explaining his decision to send American troops to Saudi Arabia, President Bush told a Pentagon audience in August, 1990: "Our jobs, our way of life, our own freedom and the freedom of friendly countries around the world would all suffer if control of the world's great oil reserves fell into the hands of that one man, Saddam Hussein."[76]

Intervention and Military Presence

Ever since the end of World War II and the rise of the United States as the new superpower with national interests spanning the globe, American policy makers wanted to have a strong presence in the Middle East. At the same time, Washington was anxious to prevent the Soviet Union from extending its system or influence to the region. By making a public commitment to the defense of Greece and Turkey against communist aggression from outside and from inside, the 1947 Truman Doctrine was in fact making an open-ended American commitment to intervene and crush even internal challenges to the ascendency of the pro-Western regimes in the Eastern Mediterranean region. In 1954, an attempt to extend the military encirclement of the Soviet Union to the Middle East through the establishment of a pro-Western military alliance sponsored by London and based in Baghdad failed because of Arab nationalist opposition to it. By the Eisenhower Doctrine in 1957, Washington arrogated to itself the right to intervene militarily in the Middle East to support pro-Western regimes against the rising tide of Arab revolutionary nationalism. London sent troops to Jordan and Washington landed American marines in Lebanon to support pro-Western regimes shaken by the growing pro-Nasser nationalist forces. With Israel's lightening military victory in the 1967 war against its Arab neighbours, Tel-Aviv was seen as a desirable strategic ally capable of deterring Arab nationalist forces from threatening American interests in the region. When King Hussein of Jordan launched his army against the Palestinian resistance in Jordan in 1970 and Syria was getting ready to intervene in support of the Palestinians, Nixon's National Security Advisor Henry Kissinger managed to elevate Israel to the status of a strategic asset of American power by authorizing the Israelis to deploy their army and air force to deter Syrian intervention in Jordan, thus allowing Hussein to crush the Palestinians.

The substantial Arab military showing in the 1973 war, and the coordinated political use of Arab oil exports presented Washington with different challenges: how to continue to pursue its traditional goals in the Middle East in the face of a more united Arab world ready to expose the contradictions in the American approach to the region by using its strategic resources to bargain for political adjustment in American foreign policy orientations. The dilemma was resolved for Washington by Sadat's eagerness to belong to the American camp at the price of separation from the Arab camp. His policy directly led to the Camp David accords and the removal of Egypt from the Arab-Israeli conflict. The defection of Egypt, the Arab world's traditional leader, severely set back the prospect of a united military, political or economic Arab front for the pursuit of common Arab goals.

The likelihood of a replay of the 1973-74 Arab-controlled scenario had diminished considerably and Washington could look forward once more to pursuing its traditional goals in the region unhampered by manifestations of Arab political or economic unity and its attendant greater bargaining power. But the Iranian revolution in 1979 foiled the expectations of policy makers in Washington, and forced a review of American strategic calculations in the region. President Carter responded by an outright reliance on American force to protect Washington's strategic interests in the region, commonly recognized to be Arab oil, access to ports, stability of pro-American regimes, and an Israeli military hegemony over the region. He ordered the creation of the Rapid Deployment Force in 1979, an American armada ready to intervene anywhere from Pakistan to Egypt. But no country in the region was willing to take the political risk of hosting the Headquarters of the Strategic Central Command of the Rapid Deployment Force; it was finally located in Florida. Ironically, the force was fully deployed for the first time to bolster the Iraqi war effort against Iran in 1987.[77]

One of the important American goals in the military deployment in the Gulf was to demonstrate to the Gulf States the importance of American military presence which they had repeatedly refused to countenance in the past. In his appropriately titled article "The Joint Chiefs Have Been Preparing For Years," John C. Ausland observed that "the present deployment of American forces gave the Pentagon something that the Saudis had up till now refused: the right to conduct military exercise in Saudi Arabia."[78] With American military might in the region, Washington could pursue its traditional foreign policy objectives certain in the knowledge that it could militarily squash any regional challenges to its priorities, as well as deter political challenges to the contradictions inherent therein. The Camp David order which put an end to the brief period of Arab military, economic and political cooperation with its potential of a common Arab front, was now backed by awesome military power ready to enforce its domination against any regional challenges.

Sharing the Defense Burden

There were also economic considerations affecting the calculations behind the drive to confront and defeat Iraqi ambitions. American economic difficulties had repeatedly dramatized the need for budgetary restraints and fiscal responsibility. The Reagan years had taken the United States from a slight trade surplus of $1.5 billion in 1980 to a galloping trade deficit of $110 billion in 1989. As Lester C. Thurow of the Massachusetts Institute of Technology has shown, the United States passed under the happy and care-free guidance of Ronald Reagan from the first creditor nation in the world (+ $141 billion in 1981) to the first debtor nation in the world (- $620 billion in 1989). Similarly, the national debt shot up from $3,989 per every woman, man and a child in 1980 to $12,409 in 1990.[79]

Locked in his world of illusion and connected to reality through a soothing ideology, as Garry Wills showed in his thorough and amusing account in *Reagan's America* Ronald Reagan believed that victory was possible in a nuclear confrontation and that American could win a nuclear war with the Soviet Union; he took the country on perhaps the most massive and most costly rearmament programme in its history, and many, as Wells has shown, were eager to be fooled and believe in Reagan's lies. But with the end of the cold war and the collapse of the Soviet Union and its subsequent disappearance altogether, the huge military build-up begun under Reagan and the colossal American military arsenal became more difficult to justify; Congressmen began calling for reduction in the Defense budget and for the creation of "peace dividends" for diversion of defense funds to social and economic recovery projects. The Iraqi invasion of Kuwait put an end to these calls and suddenly America's huge military arsenal seemed necessary for defense against other enemies. And if these enemies could be presented, like the communist threat before, as posing common dangers to the industrialized world and its vital interests, then the growing American burden of defense could be shared by all those theoretically threatened by the new danger. "Dragging its military budget," observed an economist, "the economy of the United States was destined to loose its race with Europe and Japan. Since the Gulf crisis, the American military arsenal is suddenly revitalized. Washington can at last impose on its allies 'a share of the burden' and part of the millstone."[80]

In fact, the Bush administration may have been more successful at getting its allies to share the cost of militarily confronting Saddam Hussein than previous administrations managed to do in their drive to get America's allies to share the burden of deterring Soviet threats. In the process, the Bush administration may have waged the first American war serving perceived American economic and political interests but subsidized mostly by outside sponsors. Although it will not be admitted, but in hiring out its army to serve American-defined goals, Washington may even have made money in the deal. It also established an important precedent for its two giant economic competitors, Japan and Germany whose dependency on oil from the Middle East is now tributary of American military power. In the past, American nuclear weapons and defense guarantees underwrote the security of Germany and Japan against communist threats while they rebuilt their economies. There had always been critical voices in congress urging various American administrations to get the allies to pay more for American defense guarantees, and the issue of sharing the burden of defense remained a periodic, and occasionally acrimonious bone of contention. With American military presence in the Gulf, the United States was providing Germany and Japan with new defense guarantees, this time against threats to their economic prosperity given their dependency on Middle East oil. This ensured that the United States would remain the ultimate guarantor of the security of the industrialized world and continue to wield significant leverage in its relationship with its economic competitors.

The Israeli Factor

Israeli pressure on Washington to confront Iraq and to destroy its military capabilities played an important role in the Bush administration's decision to opt for military confrontation. "From the very origins of the present crisis," observed one commentator, "the Israeli influence in the United States was brought to bear with all its weight in favour of the strategy of confrontation with Iraq which President Bush quickly adopted. It (Israeli influence) was certainly not the least of factors which militated in favour of the decisions made by the White House."[81]

With the end of the Iran-Iraq war, Israel considered Iraq as its principal enemy and the destruction of Iraqi military power as a top priority. From the very beginning of the Gulf crisis, Israel pressured Washington to adopt a tough and uncompromising line and, throughout the crisis, the Israeli position remained unchanged, and rejectionist. Israel wanted the destruction of the Iraqi regime and its military arsenal and rejected any suggestion that it should pay in political flexibility to help cement the anti-Iraq alliance which Washington forged with Arab States. Israeli Defense Minister Moshe Arens explained at the end of August 1990 that Israel's main concern was "the imposing war machine built up by the Iraqis; I hope this military capacity will not be there in the years to come."[82]

The Israeli daily *Maarive* was even more forthright: "The only solution to the Gulf crisis is to smash Saddam Hussein's regime."[83] Israeli military officials urged Washington to strike at Iraq "massively and efficiently" because "Time is working against the United States and all of us in this situation."[84] Israeli Prime Minister Shamir came to Washington in mid-December to tell the Bush administration that it should not expect anything from Israel after the expected war with Iraq. His message was a familiar one which he and Menahem Begin had delivered to Washington many times before: no concessions to the Arabs, no negotiations with the PLO, no withdrawal from the occupied Arab territories. An observer noted that "Mr. Shamir's Defense Minister Moshe Arens has put the rejectionist line with maximum clarity: 'There is no need for new ideas'" regarding a peaceful settlement of the Arab-Israeli and the Israeli-Palestinian conflicts.[85] The Israeli ideas may be old but they enjoyed the power derived from Israel's military might and its occupation of the Arab territories. As such these were the only ideas needed and as Arens candidly put, it there was no needs for other ideas.

Israel's supporters in the United States adopted the same position and advanced the same arguments which were given wide currency by pro-Israeli influential *New York Times* commentators like William Safire, Charles Krauthammer and A. M. Rosenthall who acted as virtual spokesmen for Israel and regularly used the pages of the influential newspaper to drum up support for the war against Iraq. Pro-war newspapers such as the *Washington Post* also supported the Israeli view and urged that American war aims go beyond the UN-endorsed aim of ejecting the Iraqis from Kuwait: "A simple withdrawal," wrote the editors, "would also leave Kuwaiti territory and oil under the shadow of Iraqi power...in both situations an enduring result cannot be achieved until the Iraqi threat is not merely contained but brought to an end. The Iraqi threat, as almost all of us now understand, consists of Saddam Hussein and his huge army and his gas-missile-nuclear complex."[86]

Henry Kissinger, not surprisingly, urged the expansion of the anticipated war aims to include those advocated by the Israelis. In an article in the *Los Angeles Times*, he praised the Bush administration's decision of massive troop deployment and argued that "even attainment of the UN objectives might provide only a breathing space if Saddam Hussein remains in office and Iraq continues to build up its nuclear and chemical weapons potential." He gravely warned against any backing off because "any withdrawal, however dressed up, without achieving US objectives, would be ignominious [and] would end America's stabilizing role in the Middle East." To continue to play that "stabilizing role," so dear to Kissinger, the former national security advisor urged the Bush administration "to consider a surgical and progressive destruction of Iraq's military assets-especially since an outcome that leaves Saddam Hussein in place and his military machine unimpaired might turn out to be only an interlude between two aggressions."[87]

This convergence of views between influential American figures and opinion-makers, on the one hand, and, on the other hand, the Israeli position urging war and the destruction of Saddam Hussein's regime and military capabilities, did not lead to a debate about American national interests in the Middle East and the best course of actions to defend them. Very few people commented on whether or not American interests would be served by a maximalist position consistent with what

the Israelis had been demanding. Very few people worried about the contradictions in a contemplated UN-endorsed military operation whose major war objectives were being greatly influenced by the views of a country that consistently
defied and vilified the United Nations. One of the few people who raised questions
about those pushing the Israeli view was former national security advisor in the
Carter administration Zbegniew Brezezniski. He argued that for many among the
supporters of the Israeli view, the occupation of Kuwait was "a convenient excuse,"
and warned that "such a reckless undertaking" does not advance American national interests.[88]

A more vocal, if lone, critic of the supporters of the Israeli views was conservative columnist and television commentator Patrick Buchanan. He described
Capitol Hill as "Israeli-occupied territories" and violently denounced the pro-war
camp because "only two groups are drumming up support for war — the Israeli
Defence Minister and his yes-men friends in the United States...The Israelis want
the war for us to destroy the Iraqi war machine. Our relations with the Arabs are
of no interest to them." As usually happens in the United States when a well-
known figure capable of influencing public opinion criticizes Israel, Buchanan was
promptly accused of anti-Semitism by Rosenthall of the *New York Times*.[89] This was
the extent of the debate on such crucial an issue as American war aims in a military
operation advertised as ushering in a new world order. In the end, the Bush administration accepted uncritically, and without adequate explanation and much
less a debate, the Israeli view of the necessity of destroying Iraq's military-industrial complex.

Notes

1. *Time* magazine, January 7, 1991.
2. *International Herald Tribune,* March 4, 1991.
3. Bob Woodward, *The Commanders,* (New York, Simon and Schuster, 1991), p. 229.
4. *Ahkbar al-Yum* (in Arabic) (Cairo), February 9, 1991.
5. Conversation in Cairo with Kuwaiti Prince Seilman al-Sabah, 1991.
6. *New York Times,* August 4, 1990.
7. Thomas Friedman, "US Seeking to Forestall Any Arab Deal for Kuwait," The *New York Times,* August 5, 1990.
8. Bob Woodward, *The Commanders,* op. cit., pp. 252-53.
9. Ibid., pp. 253-54.
10. Ibid., p. 260.
11. Ibid., p. 261.
12. The *Washington Post,* reproduced in the *Guardian Weekly,* August 12, 1990.
13. David Hoffman and Dan Balz, "Bush Seeks How Best to Topple Hussein," The *Washington Post,* reproduced in the *Guardian Weekly,* August 12, 1990.
14. Paul-Marie De La Gorce, "Golf: une guerre l'arraché?" *Le Monde Diplomatique,* December, 1990.
15. Al-Ahram, (in Arabic) (Cairo) January 25, 1991.

16. For the text of the Arab League Ministerial Council Resolution on the Gulf Crisis on August 3, see *Journal of Palestine Studies* vol. XX, no. 2, (Winter 1991), p. 178. For King Hussein's version of what happened see *The New Yorker,* January 7, 1991.
17. Bob Woodward, op. cit., p. 259.
18. Ibid., p. 259.
19. *US News & World Report,* January 20, 1992.
20. Bob Woodward, op. cit., p. 267.
21. Bob Woodward, op. cit., p. 268.
22. *New York Times Magazine,* January 27, 1991.
23. *New York Times* "After the War: Reconstructing the Crucial Decisions," March 3, 1991.
24. Ibid.
25. Woodward, op. cit., p. 273.
26. See Martin Yant, *Desert Mirage* (Buffalo, New York, Prometheus Books, 1991), pp. 91-92. Yant also quotes Eugene Carroll, retired U.S. Navy rear admiral with the private Center for Defense Information in Washington saying to the *Toronto Globe and Mail* that "in terms of passing through Kuwait and heading into Saudi Arabia, I see no evidence whatsover that he (Saddam Hussein) had that in preparation." p. 90.
27. David Hoffman and Dan Balz, "Bush Seeks How Best to Topple Hussein," *The Washington Post* reproduced in the *Guardian Weekly,* August 12, 1990.
28. Ibid.
29. Ibid.
30. Woodward, op. cit., p. 260.
31. The *Washington Post,* reproduced in the *Guardian Weekly,* August 19, 1990.
32. Martin Woollacott, The paradox of king and country, The *Manchester Guardian,* August 26, 1990.
33. *New York Times,* August 9, 1990.
34. *New York Times,* August 8, 1990.
35. *Newsweek,* August 20, 1990.
36. Paul-Marie De La Gorce, La quête désespérée d'un dénouement diplomatique, *Le Monde Diplomatique,* December, 1990.
37. *October* magazine (in Arabic) (Cairo), No. 721. August 19, 1990. p. 39.
38. Interviews with Yemen's Ambassador to the United Nations, Ambassador Abdallaah al-Ashtall. New York, 1991.
39. *Al-Ahram* (in Arabic) Cairo, August 12, 1990.
40 Ibid.
41. Walid Khalidi, "The Gulf Crisis: Origins and Consequences," *Journal of Palestine Studies,* vol. XX, no. 2 (Winter 1991), pp. 5-28, p. 7.
42. *Al-Ahram,* (in Arabic), (Cairo), August 12, 1990.
43. Ibid.
44. *Al-Ahram,* (in Arabic), (Cairo), August 13, 1990. See also The *Manchester Guardian Weekly,* August 19, 1990.
45. See Marc Lavergne, "Les Jordaniens exposés en première ligne," *Le Monde Diplomatique,* January 1991.
46. *Washington Post,* reproduced in the *Guardian Weekly,* September 30, 1990.
47. See Ghassan Elezzi, "Quand l'armée israélienne 'sauvait' le Liban," *Le Monde Diplomatique,* June 1992; see also Ghassan Elezzi, *L'invasion israélienne du Liban, origine, finalités et effets pervers* (Paris, L'Harmattan, 1990).
48. Françoise Chipaux, "Syria prepares to return to the Western Camp," *Le Monde* August 18, 1990, reproduced in the *Guardian Weekly,* September 2, 1990. See also Noura Boustany, "Syrians Unhappy at Link With U.S.," *The Washington Post,* reproduced in the *Guardian Weekly,* November, 11, 1990.

49. The Manchester Guardian, August 19, 1990.
50. See Nadia Khoury-Dagher and Aziza Dargouth Medimegh, "Pourquoi, en Tunisie, la rue a soutenu Baghdad," Le Monde Diplomatique, March, 1991.
51. See George T. Abed, "The Palestinians and the Gulf Crisis," Journal of Palestine Studies, vol. XX, no. 2 (Winter 1991), pp. 29-42.
52. Al-Ahram, August 12, 1990.
53. Newsweek, August, 20, 1990.
54. Amnon Kapeliouk, "L'Union soviètique est-elle encore une grande puissance?," Le Monde Diplomatique, October, 1990.
55. Ibid.
56. Ibid.
57. The Manchester Guardian, September 16, 1990.
58. Michael Dobbs, "The Two Presidents Who Needed Each Other," The Washington Post, reproduced in the Guardian Weekly, September 16, 1990.
59. International Herald Tribune, August 10, 1990, cited in Le Monde Diplomatique, September, 1990.
60. Claude Julien, "Guerres saintes," Le Monde Diplomatique, September, 1990.
61. William Pfaff, The Village Voice, August 14, 1990, quoted by Serge Halimi in "L'opinion américaine, si loin du Proche-Orient," Le Monde Diplomatique, November, 1990.
62. Georges Corm, "La longue litanie des ruptures au Proche-Orient," Le Monde Diplomatique, October 1990.
63. Cited by Claude Julien, "Un gendarme ambigue," Le Monde Dipomatique, October, 1990.
64. Richard Barnet, "Les objectifs fondamentaux de l'Amérique," Le Monde Diplomatique, October, 1990.
65. John Goshko, "U.S. Arabists Ignored," The Washington Post, reproduced in the Guardian Weekly, December 2, 1990.
66. Ibid.
67. James E. Akins, "Heading Towards War," Journal of Palestine Studies vol. XX, no. 3 (Spring 1991), pp. 16-30, p. 24.
68. The Washington Post, reproduced in the Guardian Weekly, August 19, 1990.
69. See Claude Julien, l'Empire américain (Paris, Grasset, 1968); see also Gabriel Kolko, Confronting The Third World: United States Foreign Policy 1945-1980 (New York, Pantheon Books, 1988); see also Homa Katouzian, Musaddiq and the Struggle for Power in Iran (London, I. B. Tauris, 1990); see also Farhad Diba, Mossadegh, A Political Biography (London, Croom Helm), 1989.
70. Denis Clerc, "Le pétrole et l'injuste partage," Le Monde Diplomatique, October, 1990; see also "The Gulf Crisis: The Oil Factor, An Interview with Pierre Terzian," Journal of Palestine Studies, vol. XX, no. 2, (Winter 1991), pp. 100-105.
71. See Georges Corm, "Les habits neufs de la domination néocoloniale," Le Monde Diplomatique, April 1992.
72. Washington Post, reproduced in the Guardian Weekly, August 19, 1990.
73. Washington Post, reproduced in the Guardian Weekly, August 26, 1990.
74. Raymond Dennet and Robert K. Turner, (eds.) Documents on American Foreign Relations, VIII (1945-1946), (Princeton, 1948), pp. 601-602) quoted in Walter LaFeber, America, Russia, and the Cold War: 1945-1980 (New York, John Wiley and Sons, 1980), p. 27.
75. New York Times November 2, 1966, quoted in Richard Barnet, Internvention and Revolution: America's Confrontation with Insuragent Movements Around the World (New York, New American Library, 1972), p. 38.
76. Wall Street Journal, August 30, 1991.

77. See Alain Gresh, "Modeler dans la guerre un ordre de paix au Proche-Orient?" *Le Monde Diplomatique*, February, 1991.
78. John C. Austland, "The Joint Chiefs Have Been Preparing For Years," *The International Herald Tribune*, August 22, 1990.
79. See Claude Julien, "Le risque et la raison," *Le Monde Diplomatique*, November, 1990.
80. Ibrahim Warde, "Les dividendes de l'oépration," "Bouclier du désert," *Le Monde Diplomatique*, November, 1990.
81. Paul-Marie de La Gorce, "La défense israélienne en état d'alerte," *Le Monde Diplomatique*, September, 1990. See also Joel Brinkely, "Half of Kuwaitis replaced by Iraqis, Israelis say," *The New York Times*, October 6, 1990.
82. Alain Frachon, "Israelis fearful of closer American ties with the Arabs," *Le Monde*, September 2, reproduced in the Guardian Weekly, September 9, 1990.
83. Ibid.
84. Jackson Diehl, "Israelis Think U.S. Should Strike Quickly," *The Washington Post*, reproduced in the *Guardian Weekly*, August 26, 1990.
85. *Manchester Guardian Weekly*, December 23, 1990.
86. *Washington Post*, reproduced in the *Guardian Weekly*, August 26, 1990.
87. *Los Angeles Times*, reproduced in the *Guardian Weekly*, August 26, 1990.
88. Zbegniew Brezezinski, "Patience in the Persian Gulf not War," *New York Times*, October 7, 1990.
89. See Henri Pierre, "Media Heavyweights fight a Gulf duel," *Le Monde*, September 30/October 1, reproduced in the *Guardian Weekly*, October 7, 1990.

CHAPTER SEVEN

Negotiations or War?

Realizing that of his five neighbours only Iran and Jordan have not aligned themselves with the anti-Iraq coalition but that they were coming under increasing pressure for a stricter adherence to the economic sanctions imposed on Iraq, Saddam Hussein was desperate for allies. The sanctions and the blockade were slowing strangulating Iraq which imported 70 percent of its food before the crisis. He turned to his arch-enemy, Iran. And in the ultimate act of pragmatism and cynicism, he decided to give up all the questionable gains of his unedifying eight-year war with Iran. Hussein announced that he now accepted the 1975 Algiers accords by which Iran and Iraq had agreed to share sovereignty over the Gulf straits of Shatt al-Arab, an agreement which he had torn up when he launched the war against Iran in 1980. Baghdad also announced that it was withdrawing its forces from occupied Iranian territories and freeing the remaining Iranian prisoners of war. Radio Baghdad said that this decision was made so that Iraq would be "free to confront the others."[1] But "confronting the others" was a most unwelcome obligation which Saddam Hussein did not fully expect and from which he was desperate to retreat if only, given his enormous pride, he could do it without loosing face.

Saddam Hussein began therefore to send signals of his readiness to negotiate his way out of Kuwait. The first Iraqi offer of a negotiated settlement was made through two Iraqi-born American citizens who were in Baghdad at the time of the Iraqi invasion of Kuwait. The two Arab-American businessmen, Michael Saba and Samir Vincent, carried a proposal from Baghdad which offered a realistic chance for the peaceful settlement of the crisis by providing for Iraqi withdrawal in exchange for guarantees that Iraq would be given access to the Persian Gulf, retain control of the Rumalia oilfield, and negotiate an acceptable oil price with the United States. The plan was first presented by Michael Saba to the White House on August 10. At the same time Samir Vincent contacted former CIA director Richard Helms who transmitted the plan again to national security advisor Brent Scowcroft on August 21. To make the plan more attractive, the Iraqis decided on August 23, to release all foreign "guests" held in Iraq. But "there was nothing about this [peace initiative] that interested the US government," said Richard Helms. Washington was simply not interested in any negotiations with Iraq and Helms frankly admitted: "The US government did not want to make a deal."[2]

As the American military build-up in the region continued to grow, and as Egyptian forces began to arrive in Saudi Arabia to be followed by Moroccan and Syrian forces, the Iraqi regime made a significant retreat from its grandiose and defiant rhetoric. On August 16, Iraqi Foreign Minister Tarik Aziz announced to an American Television Network that Iraq was ready for "unconditional negotiations with the United States."[3] In other words, Iraq was no longer demanding an American commitment to freeze the military buildup in the region. The unconditional offer of negotiations was ostensibly designed to take the edge away from the seemingly relentless drive to a war Iraq was certain to loose, and give Iraq what it really wanted to accomplish by the invasion: to negotiate with Washington from a position of relative strength. This offer too was quickly rejected by Washington which insisted on unconditional withdrawal or war. On August 17, tens of thousands of foreign nationals in Kuwait and Iraq were ordered by the Iraqi regime to report to designated hotels for possible dispatch to "civilian and military installations." The intent seemed to be to use these "foreign guests," as the Iraqi radio called them, or "hostages" as the Western media called them, to deter the United States and its allies from launching military attacks against Iraq or Kuwait. The move was widely criticized as a blatant violation of the rules of international law and served only to strengthen Western public support for the tough stand taken by Washington.

A few days later, on August 28, President Saddam Hussein offered to release all American and European nationals detained in Iraq in return for an American undertaking not to attack Iraq. This offer too, like the previous one, was quickly dismissed by President Bush who repeated his demand for unconditional Iraqi withdrawal from Kuwait. In September, the Iraqi regime allowed the departure of all foreign women and children from Iraq, a move that won Saddam Hussein no substantive change in the hard line adopted by the Bush administration.

In addition to Iraqi offers of unconditional negotiations and to the peace plan communicated to Washington by Baghdad through Sabba and Vincent, there were other peace plans that could have provided a basis for negotiations between the American-led camp and the Iraqis. Thus, on August 28, a PLO-Jordanian initiative proposed the transformation of Kuwait into "a Monaco of the Gulf," "a constitutional monarchy that would sign an agreement with Iraq giving it control of certain administrative aspects, on the understanding that the principality, mirroring the relationship between Monte Carlo and France, would have self-rule." The Palestinian-Jordanian initiative called for the simultaneous withdrawal of Iraqi forces from Kuwait and the American-led forces from Saudi Arabia, to be followed by the deployment of Arab peace-keeping forces. It also called for a plebiscite in Kuwait on turning it into "a free zone" and the form of sovereignty it wanted to have. Iraq accepted the plan but there was no indication that the United States was prepared to give the plan a chance, not even as a basis for negotiations, insisting on unconditional Iraqi withdrawal from Kuwait. The London-based Saudi newspaper *Al-Sharq al-Awsut*, scornfully dismissed the plan and quoted an unnamed diplomat as saying that a "strike that will close the page on Saddam Hussein's regime in its entirety" was needed.[4]

On August 31, at an extraordinary meeting of 13 Arab foreign Ministers in Cairo, the Arab league proposed its own five-point peace plan. It mirrored the American conditions for a settlement on the basis of unconditional Iraqi withdrawal from Kuwait, restoration of the Kuwaiti ruling family, and Iraqi compensations to be paid to Kuwait. The Arab League meeting was boycotted by Iraq, Jordan, the PLO, Yemen, Algeria, Tunisia, and Mauritania. On September 1, Libya presented the most detailed peace plan any country had put forward since the beginning of the crisis. It called for: a) withdrawal of Iraqi troops from Kuwait to be replaced by UN forces; b) the withdrawal of the American-led forces from Saudi Arabia to be replaced by Arab forces; c) the lifting of the UN embargo against Iraq; d) the Rumaila oilfield and Bubyian Island claimed by Saddam Hussein to be given to Iraq; e) Kuwaitis to exercise the right to self-determination; f) Arabs to agree on a unified Arab oil policy with a mechanism to deter violations of oil production quotas; g) issues of debt and compensation between Iraq and Kuwait to be solved through negotiations between the two countries. The plan was drawn up after consultation with Iraq, Jordan, and Sudan. Washington showed no interest.

The Iraqis have also reportedly communicated to the White House through Iraqi intermediaries another peace plan, the essential elements of which were put forward in an interview given by Abu Iyyad, Yasser Arafat's deputy in the Fatah organization of the PLO, to the French newspaper *Libération* (September 4). The Iraqi plan called for : a) a US guarantee that it would not attack Iraq, or stage an air strike against its chemical plants and nuclear laboratories; b) foreign nationals detained in Iraq to be freed; c) Iraq to withdraw from all of Kuwait except the island of Bubiyan, thus giving Iraq the access to sea it needed; d) Iraq to keep the disputed Rumaila oilfield; e) the ruling family not to return to Kuwait but the people of Kuwait to freely decide on the form of government they would like to have. Although this Iraqi plan was generally considered by Western observers as a realistic basis for a negotiated settlement of the crisis, the United States rejected it and the Bush administration repeated its position of unconditional Iraqi withdrawal from Kuwait or war.

Linkage as a Way out of the Crisis

Washington's leadership role in confronting Iraq and pushing the military option highlighted fundamental American foreign policy contradictions and a dual approach to foreign policy issues depending, not on a set of clear principles and guidelines, but on who and what is involved. A brief review and analysis of how the United Nations was used is instructive. The speed with which the United States led the drive to get the Security Council to condemn the Iraqi invasion of Kuwait, impose mandatory sanctions, and authorize a military blockade against Iraq, contrasted sharply with the American record on Israeli violations of international law and Israeli occupation of Arab territories. Between 1972 and 1990 the United States used its vetoes no less than 33 times to prevent United Nations Security Council resolutions condemning Israeli actions in the occupied Arab territories and in Lebanon.

Let's briefly consider the record. On August 3, 1990 the United Nations Security Council condemned Iraq's invasion of Kuwait and, on September 16, 1990, it condemned Iraq's "aggressive acts" against diplomatic missions in Kuwait. Between 1975 and 1990, the same UN Security Council, when it was not blocked by American vetoes, adopted eleven resolutions condemning Israeli aggression against Lebanon and other Arab countries. On August 9, 1990, the Security Council declared Iraq's annexation of Kuwait "null and void" under international law. In August 1980, the same Security Council declared Israel's annexation of Jerusalem "null and void" under international law. In December of the same year, the General Assembly adopted a similar resolution supported by 143 countries and opposed only by Israel. In December 1981, the Security Council declared Israel's annexation of the occupied Syrian Golan Heights "null and void" under international law. In December 1988, the General Assembly adopted a resolution condemning Jewish settlements in the occupied Arab territories; it was supported by 149 countries and opposed only by Israel. On August 3, 1990, the Security Council condemned Iraq's occupation of Kuwait and demanded the immediate and unconditional withdrawal of Iraqi forces. The same UN body condemned Israel on three separate occasions and demanded the immediate and unconditional withdrawal of its forces from Lebanon. In January 1976 and in April 1980 Security Council resolutions calling on Israel to withdraw to its pre-1967 lines as part of a two-State settlement of the conflict were vetoed by the United States. On August 18, 1990, the Security Council condemned Iraq's detention of foreigners and on October 29, it condemned its hostage-taking and mistreatment of foreigners. The same Security Council adopted no less than seven resolutions deploring Israeli deportation of Palestinians living in the occupied territories, and two resolutions deploring Israeli practices of "opening of fire…resulting in the killing and wounding of defenceless Palestinian civilians."

The General Assembly repeatedly condemned Israeli violations of Palestinian human rights. It adopted resolutions condemning Israel's refusal to recognize the applicability of the Geneva Convention to the occupied territories (December 1988); its forcible removal and resettlement of Palestinian refugees living in the occupied territories (December 1988); Israel's "arbitrary detention and imprisonment of thousands of Palestinians" (December 1988); and Israel's "continued massacre" of Palestinian civilians in the occupied territories. This last resolution was adopted in October 1989 and was supported by 149 countries and opposed only by Israel and the United States. On the question of sanctions, the Security Council voted for arms and economic embargo against Iraq on August 6 and voted, on September 25, to also impose an air embargo against Baghdad. In January 1982, a Security Council Resolution calling for arms and economic embargo against Israel for its annexation of the occupied Syrian Golan Heights was blocked by an American veto. The United States also blocked another Security Council Resolution in June 1982 threatening sanctions against Israel for failure to withdraw from Lebanon. Another Security Council resolution in August 1982 urging an arms embargo as a first step against Israel for failure to withdraw from Lebanon was vetoed by the United States which also blocked another Security Council resolution in August 1983 threatening sanctions against Israel for its Jewish settlement policy. No amount of self-righteous rhetoric or manipulation of logic will be able to deny the similarities and the link between Israeli and Iraqi violations of international law.[5] There is, however, a difference: the Israeli record of violations is impressively unique in the post World War II era.

Consider further the attitude of the Security Council in 1980 when the Iran-Iraq war broke out. The Security Council waited six days after the war broke out on September 22, 1980 before it held its first meeting; and after ten days of slow proceedings it calmly decided to simply remain seized of "the evolution of the situation between Iran and Iraq."[6] It took the Security Council two years to vote on a ceasefire resolution on July 13, 1982. The war continued with all permanent members of the Security Council providing armaments to the belligerents, with Washington providing intelligence and military support to both sides in the conflict.

The Gulf crisis was different. The speed with which Washington moved to get the United Nations to impose sweeping sanctions and a military blockade, the resolve shown by the Bush administration for confronting Iraq and cutting it down to size, the helpless attitude of the Soviet Union, and Egypt's ability to get the Arab League to sanction the military option, dramatized to the Iraqi regime the extent of its isolation and the degree of its miscalculation. Saddam Hussein began sending signals that his invasion of Kuwait was meant as a bargaining chip for economic and security concessions for Iraq and that he was ready for negotiations. A mention has already been made of the Iraqi "back-doors" peace offer through two Iraqi-American businessmen. On August 12, Saddam Hussein publicly announced an Iraqi initiative for a peaceful solution of the Gulf crisis: "I propose that all questions of occupation or questions presented as occupation in the region be solved on the basis of principles and rules decreed by the Security Council on the following lines: First, preparing withdrawal principles on the same basis for the immediate and unconditional Israeli withdrawal from the occupied Palestinian, Syrian and Lebanese Arab territories, the withdrawal of Syria from Lebanon; the withdrawal of Iranian-Iraqi forces. Second, the immediate withdrawal from Saudi Arabia of American forces and other forces which responded to the American conspiracy and their replacement with Arab forces. Third, the freezing of all decisions of sanctions and blockade against Iraq..."[7]

Many in the Arab world and in the international community welcomed the initiative, seeing in it a first step toward a possible peaceful solution of the crisis. Many more could not disagree with the fundamental premise contained in the Iraqi plan with regard to the necessity of applying the same standards of international legality to Israeli occupation of Palestinian, Syrian and Lebanese territories. The plan sparked a debate on what came to be known as the issue of linkage: linking the withdrawal of Iraqi troops from Kuwait with the withdrawal of Israeli forces from the occupied Arab territories.

Saddam Hussein may not have invaded Kuwait to solve the Palestinian problem, but the linkage which he insisted on establishing between Iraqi occupation of Kuwait and Israeli occupation of Arab territories served to at least highlight another fundamental contradiction in the American approach to the conflict. The international community including the Soviet Union and France recognized the existence of such a linkage; the United States was virtually alone, with Israel, in insisting that there was no political linkage between these two conflicts. Egypt was also opposed to linkage. Its Deputy Prime Minister Dr. Boutros Ghali told me that Egypt rejected linkage as a way of solving the crisis for legal and political reasons: "The different resolutions of the United Nations were asking for unconditional withdrawal. If we added this linkage it would have been in contradiction with the UN Security Council resolutions, mainly Resolution 660. Secondly, we opposed linkage because it would have complicated the whole problem. For us what was important was to find a quick solution to the crisis so that we can move forward with the search for a solution to the more important problems and in particular the Palestinian problem. Therefore we had a legal objection and a political objection to the notion of linkage."[8]

In effect, the issue of linkage became, throughout the crisis, the rocks on which floundered all efforts at a negotiated settlement largely because of American opposition to it. On August 13, President Bush rejected outright the Iraqi leader's proposals. On August 15, the CBS reported, quoting Jordanians sources, that Saddam Hussein sent a message to King Hussein of Jordan containing another Iraqi initiative. Iraqi leaders were ready to attend a conference to discuss Iraqi withdrawal from Kuwait in return for a commitment by President Bush to freeze the number of American soldiers in the region, thus reducing the chance of an American-led attack against Iraq.[9] Washington expressed no interest. Two weeks later Saddam Hussein softened his position on linkage by no longer insisting on immediate Israeli withdrawal from the occupied Arab territories and suggested that Iraqi withdrawal from Kuwait and Israeli withdrawal could be handled seriatim, not simultaneously.[10] Washington remained uninterested.

But Washington's Western allies did not share its adamantine opposition to linkage. In the most realistic peace plan to come from the American-led camp, French President François Mitterand, speaking at the United Nations on September 24, pleaded for replacing the "logic of war" with the "logic of peace." He called for an Iraqi declaration of intent to withdraw from Kuwait to be followed by a UN-supervised withdrawal, the freeing of foreign nationals detained in Iraq, the restoration of Kuwaiti sovereignty, and the confirmation of the democratic will of the Kuwaiti people. His plan provided for dialogue between the countries of the Middle East to address the problem of Lebanon, the Palestinian conflict, and the question of security for Israel. Mitterand also established, not a simultaneous but rather a sequential linkage between the Gulf crisis and the Palestinian and the Arab-Israeli conflicts. He presented his plan in stages: "First of all...let Iraq declare its intention to withdraw its forces, to free the hostages and everything becomes possible. In a second stage, the international community...would...guarantee the implementation of the military withdrawal, the restoration of the sovereignty of Kuwait, as well as the democratic expression of the Kuwaiti people. The third stage could then proceed, the one that the whole world is expecting...I have in mind the Lebanon [sic], which has still failed to regain its full sovereignty throughout its territory...I have in mind the Palestinians, who are in the throes of despair...At the end of the road one finds oneself with the idea of an international conference which would guarantee the implementation of the agreement and act as the catalyst of any successful negotiation."[11] The Mitterand plan offered a compromise solution which seemed to go half-way toward meeting some of the Iraqi demands. It did not insist on the unconditional return of the ruling Kuwaiti family; it did not mention the destruction of Iraqi chemical arsenals or the overthrow of Saddam Hussein, as demanded by Bush and British Prime Minister Margaret Thatcher, and it offered the Kuwaitis the opportunity to exercise self-determination as Iraq seemed to accept in its "back-doors" plan communicated to the White House. Most importantly, the French plan went a considerable way toward establishing the link Saddam Hussein insisted on making between Iraqi occupation of Kuwait and Israeli occupation of Arab territories by suggesting the convening of a peace conference to address the Arab-Israeli conflict after the Iraqi troops had withdrawn from Kuwait.

President Saddam Hussein expressed interest in the French plan and said that "Iraq would contact France to seek and offer clarifications of the two nations' positions."[12] Iraqi officials indicated that they saw an opening in the French plan for a resumption of the thwarted Arab efforts at a negotiated settlement. They believed that a joint Soviet-French initiative supported by the Arab countries, outside of Egypt and the Gulf countries, as well as by Germany and Japan, who showed little enthusiasm for the war enterprise, could lead to a negotiated settlement of the crisis. But the attempt at an Arab-mediated political solution on the basis of ideas acceptable to France and the Soviet Union was unsuccessful because of the opposi-tion of Washington and its allies. "Once more," wrote one analyst, "an inter-Arab solution was proposed, this time by the King of Morocco. And, once more, Egypt foiled it," by opposing the proposal for an Arab summit; Washington rejected Iraqi interest in the French peace plan as nothing more than propaganda and "an effort to divide the U.S.-led opposition to his annexation of Kuwait."[13] Washington rejected the French plan for a number of reasons: a) it failed to provide for the un-conditional return of the Kuwait family, which was after all largely financing the military operations in the Gulf; a) it seemed to promise a peace conference to ad-dress the Arab-Israeli conflict, thus linking the resolution of the Gulf crisis to move-ment on the Palestinian question, a linkage adamantly opposed by Israel; c) perhaps more importantly, even if Washington could overcome Israeli opposition, no small obstacle, the French plan would still be unattractive because it promised to give Saddam Hussein a negotiated way out of his impasse and thus allow him to emerge out of the crisis claiming some moral victory, and live to mount another challenge to the established order. And this ran counter to the American deter-mination to seize the opportunity of his helpless predicament to finish with him, his military power, his potential influence over the region, and his challenge to the established order once and for all.

Another serious opportunity for a negotiated settlement was foiled by Washington in October. Saudi Arabia's Defense Minister Sultan Ibn Abdulaziz declared shortly before Egyptian President Hosni Mubarak arrived in Saudi Arabia that Arab countries were ready to grant Iraq "all its rights," adding that "Saudi Arabia sees no harm in any Arab country giving its Arab sister land, a site, or a position on the sea," provided that Saddam Hussein accepted Iraqi forces' unconditional withdrawal from Kuwait.[14] It was the clearest indication yet of a Saudi conciliatory position aimed at offering the Iraqi regime a way out of the crisis. The Bush administration was not amused. Prince Sultan had al-ready caused consternation in Washington in September when he said that he did not want to see Saudi Arabia used as a launchpad for an attack against Iraq. Officials of the Bush administration moved quickly to ensure that the Saudis were not backing away from support for the American confrontational strategy. And "at Washington's express request (Prince Sultan) had to deny his own statements."[15]

Brief Linkage

Ironically, as politicians and analysts were discussing the question of linkage on which a peaceful settlement seemed to hinge, and as Israel and its friends in Washington were increasing their opposition to any linkage, the violent realities of the Israeli repression of Palestinian nationalism managed to briefly bring the Pales-tinian question back to centre stage and establish, at least psychologically, the linkage Washington so adamantly opposed.

On October 8, "The Movement of the Faithful to the Temple Mount and the Land of Israel" used the occasion of a Jewish holiday to advertise its goal of demolishing the two Mosques of Arab Jerusalem's Temple Mount to make way for the reconstruction of an ancient Jewish temple. Palestinians demonstrated their angry opposition and clashed with the Israeli police who shot and killed 21 Palestinians and injured 140. Later, the same day, 3 more were killed by the Israeli army in separate clashes. These were the most single-day causalities suffered by the Palestinians since the Palestinian uprising began in December 1987. The UN Secretary-General Pérez de Cuéllar said he was "shocked and greatly dismayed by the bloodshed and by what appeared to have been an excessive use of force by the Israeli authorities."[16]

After five days of protracted negotiations at the United Nations, the Security Council adopted Resolution 672 which condemned "in particular the acts of violence committed by the Israeli security forces." The resolution empowered the "UN Secretary-General to send a mission to Israel to make recommendations so as to ensure the security and protection of the Palestinian civilians."[17] Israel promptly announced that it would not allow any UN mission to investigate the killings. Prime Minister Yitzhak Shamir angrily rejected the UN decision. "Jerusalem is the capital of Israel," he affirmed, "Our sovereignty on the mosque of the Temple Mount and the other sacred places is complete. The United Nations have no right to interfere in what does not concern them."[18] Israel's claim to sovereignty over Jerusalem is of course rejected by both the United Nations and the international community including the United States. But it is instructive to note the nature of the position of the Israeli government, rejecting any role for the UN to protect Palestinians against Israeli repression, but strongly urging UN interference to go beyond ejecting Iraqi troops out of Kuwait and militarily put an end to the Iraqi regime.

The prompt rejection of the role and right of the United Nations Security Council, the same body which authorized economic and military measures against Iraq, has for long been a feature of Israel's relations with the United Nations. The statement of the Israeli prime minister and the apparent acquiescence by the United States, the leader of the anti-Iraq coalition for the defense of the rule of law, dramatized the charges of double standard that critics of American foreign policy have been making. Jerusalem is indeed a case in point. Shortly after the Israeli annexation of Arab Jerusalem in April 1968, the Security Council adopted, on May 21, 1968, Resolution 252 ordering Israel to renounce all measures designed to change the character of the city. On August 20, 1980 the Security Council repeated its order in Resolution 478, rejecting the Israeli parliament law declaring all of Jerusalem the capital of Israel. As Alain Gresh, a leading commentator in France, put it in Le Monde Diplomatique: "We are still waiting for the sanctions which will convince the Jewish State to apply these [UN] resolutions."[19]

The reluctant American support for Resolution 672, after Washington considerably watered down its condemnation of Israel, marked the first time the United States supported a Security Council Resolution condemning Israeli behaviour since the Israeli invasion of Lebanon in 1982. Washington deviated from its traditional practice of vetoing resolutions condemning Israel as a price for maintaining the cohesion of the anti-Iraq coalition whose Arab members would have been placed in a politically embarrassing position had Washington blocked the resolution. The United States was also anxious that the Palestine question get off the agenda in order to get the attention of the Security Council and public opinion directed back to the Iraqi occupation of Kuwait, because the longer the Palestine issue remained the focus of world attention the more readily public opinion would start to perceive the linkage between the Gulf crisis and the Israeli-Palestinian conflict. In fact, France was already recognizing that there was no escaping the reality of that linkage, notwithstanding Washington's objections. "The Americans have succeeded in reducing the shock caused by the butchery in Jerusalem," wrote the respected French newspaper *Le Monde*, "but the event has nonetheless shown, as France's Foreign Minister Roland Dumas pointed out last Friday, that 'by the very force of things' there is a connection, in any case, a conjunction of facts, between the Palestinian problem and the Gulf crisis."[20]

But Washington continued to oppose even the appearance of linkage. Thus, it threatened to veto a Security Council Resolution calling for the convening of an international peace conference including Palestinians and Israelis. In early December, the non-aligned States inserted in the proposed resolution a formula judged acceptable to the United States, stating that the Security Council considered "that the convening at an appropriate time of an international conference, properly structured with the participation of the parties concerned," would facilitate a peace settlement. Although US diplomats initially agreed to the formula, it seems that the White House came under attack from Israel and its friends in Washington because the same American diplomats at the United Nations threatened to veto the resolution. And this despite the fact that the language of the text concerning the convening of an international conference reflected official US policy. A compromise was finally struck whereby the President of the Security Council issued a non-binding statement on behalf of the members supporting an international conference. In return for removing the offending language from the text, Washington promised to support "moves to protect Palestinians in the occupied territories."[21] The promise remained just that.

Washington's rejection of Iraqi, Arab and European initiatives for the peaceful resolution of the crisis of Iraqi occupation of Kuwait, and its adamant opposition to any linkage, bespoke the extent of Bush's determination to confront and defeat Saddam Hussein. It was obvious that a peaceful resolution of the crisis could have been achieved had Washington not consistently preferred the confrontational course. This much had in fact been recognized by a Congressional report prepared in January 1991 and based on American intelligence information. The report recognized that Saddam Hussein may have invaded Kuwait as a way of bargaining from a position of strength for a settlement of Iraq's disputes with Kuwait. "The Iraqis apparently believed that having invaded Kuwait," the report said, "they would get everyone's attention, negotiate improvements to their economic situation, and pull out." The report recognized that if the White House had agreed, "a diplomatic solution satisfactory to the interests of the United States may well have been possible since the earliest days of the invasion." Instead, the Congressional report continued, "The NSC (National Security Council) apparently concluded on the basis of a psychological profile of Saddam Hussein, and to avoid seeming to in any way reward the invasion, to refuse any negotiations with him, concluding that they would be fruitless until the US had backed Saddam Hussein into a corner from which he could not escape."[22] Having cornered Saddam Hussein, the American strategy was to move in for the kill, not retreat and point out an escape route of negotiations.

The Drive for War

Washington's position never changed: unconditional Iraqi withdrawal from Kuwait, and therefore humiliation the Iraqi regime was unwilling to accept, or war. All Arab efforts at an Arab solution were consistently thwarted. Prince Hassan of Jordan complained that: "Every time the King and other leaders say they have a package, the Americans knock it down."[23] President Ali Abdullah Salih of Yemen also strongly criticized the American opposition to a negotiated settlement which he said was entirely possible if Washington removed its opposition. "It is still possible to find a solution for the complete withdrawal of all Iraqi forces from Kuwait and all foreign forces from the region," said the Yemeni President, "I know Iraq is ready for dialogue…"[24]

But Washington was not. By early November, the number of American troops in the Gulf had reached 230,000. On November 8, President Bush announced that he was ordering an additional 200,000 American troops to the region. He also announced that he was changing the official mission of American troops in the region. He now ordered them to be ready for "offensive capabilities." It will be recalled that American forces were originally dispatched to the region for the ostensible reason of defending Saudi Arabia against the perceived threat of an Iraqi invasion, a threat which the Saudis themselves were not able to verify. Now that the American military build-up was completed, their real mission of waging war against Iraq was openly declared. The announcement was greeted with unease among Washington's allies, with the exception of Israel which of course welcomed it. During his eight-day tour of the Persian Gulf and Europe, American Secretary of State James Baker was told by many members of the Washington-assembled anti-Iraq coalition that more time was needed for sanctions to work. Baker responded by saying that Washington had all the legal authority necessary under the United Nations Charter to act alone if necessary. But most members of the coalition urged that if the confrontation came to war it would be best to enter the hostilities under the United Nations umbrella.

In early December, Washington once more had little difficulty in getting the Security Council to adopt a resolution essentially endorsing already operative American policy. Resolution 678, adopted by 12 votes to two, set a January 15 deadline for Iraqi withdrawal from Kuwait, and authorized the use of "all necessary means to uphold and implement Security Council Resolution 660 (1990) and all subsequent relevant resolutions and to restore international peace and security in the area." University of Iowa law professor Burns Weston told a meeting of the American Bar Association that Resolution 678 in effect "gave the appearance of the U.N. having been used as a tool of US foreign policy…and raised questions about the extent to which the U.N. has been allowed to keep faith with its own charter.[25] The United Nations was increasingly perceived as being used as an instrument of American foreign policy. The text of Resolution 678 set no restrictions to the kind of 'necessary means' to be used against Iraq, made no demands that whatever actions were taken be subject to the collective authority of the Council, and made no restrictions on the use of force against civilians. In short, the United States managed to obtain from the international organization a *carte blanche* to give its foreign policy orientation the cover of legality. There is nothing in the charter which authorizes the Security Council to delegate the responsibility of defining the war aims and the means of attaining them to one of several members of the United Nations. And this, as Richard Falk noted, "is in total contradiction with the mission of the UN which consists in saving the humanity from the scourge of war."[26]

As the drumbeats of war got louder, the war fever swept aside the one success story of this whole crisis: the effective worldwide imposition of sanctions and blockade against a country which invaded its neighbour. William Webster, Director of the American Central Intelligence Agency and no critic of American foreign policy, believed that the sanctions were working and urged that they be given a chance. Webster told the House Armed Service Committee on December 5, that sanctions have cut off more than 90 percent of Iraq's imports and 97 percent of its exports, and that they had seriously reduced its ability to feed its people. Iraq was expected to be able to produce less than half the grains it needed; Iraqi shops were expected, by the spring, to have hardly any poultry, sugar, or cooking oil. The sanctions were clearly effective and were hurting Iraq. Webster also testified that "Iraq's military could maintain its current combat readiness for no more than nine months if economic sanctions continued to hold, and that the ability of the Iraqi Air Force to fly regular missions could decline within three months."[27] But the war machine was already in march and no other success story or competing vision of a new world order was likely to stop it.

After the adoption of Resolution 678 gave the American war enterprise the cover of international legality, the Bush administration set out to give the appearance that it was "going the extra mile for peace" by sending Secretary of State James Baker to meet Iraqi foreign Minister Tarik Aziz in Geneva. The meeting took place on January 9, that is, less than a week before the expiry of the ultimatum given to Iraq to withdraw from Kuwait or face war. It lasted for six hours as hundreds of reporters from around the world waited in an atmosphere of tension and anticipation. But Bush had specifically instructed Baker that the American position was "no negotiations, no compromise, no attempts at saving face and no reward for aggression."[28] This left nothing to negotiate about between the American and Iraqi delegations. Baker seems to have essentially delivered a message conveying the seriousness of the ultimatum and the extent of destruction that Iraq faced if it refused to capitulate and withdraw unconditionally. In effect, Baker had come to deliver a public *dictate* to the Iraqis: withdraw unconditionally or face destruction. But it was good public relations to continue to engage in diplomatic manoeuvres, appearing to be exhausting all channels of peaceful solutions while in fact rejecting all proposals for a negotiated settlement. National Security Advisor Brent Scowcroft frankly admitted that such was the essence of the American strategy when he told Saudi Ambassador Prince Bandar, in December, that "[b]asically the President has made up his mind," and referring to the diplomatic efforts, Scowcroft said: "these are all exercises."[29]

Although officials of the Bush administration may have accepted the argument that the sanctions against Iraq have been effective, they nonetheless were not interested in giving them a real chance because even if they resulted in an Iraqi withdrawal from Kuwait they would still not accomplish American and Israeli goals. Indeed, the sanctions, as Ignacio Ramonet observed, "can weaken Iraq and lead it to withdraw from Kuwait, but they cannot by themselves destroy Baghdad's military industry. And increasingly this seems to be one of Washington's major objectives..."[30]

A last-minute effort by Algerian President Chadli Benjedid to avert the war ended in humiliation when Washington reportedly refused even to receive the Algerian President. Although Saudi Arabia had already refused to receive him in December, President Benjedid had planned a shuttle between Baghdad and Washington in a last-minute attempt to avert the war which, following the collapse of the Aziz-Baker talks in Geneva, was all but certain. On January 13, two days before the fateful deadline, reporters were summoned to Algiers airport to travel with the Algerian President. But the trip to Washington never materialized. As President Benjedid's motorcade arrived at the airport "a message came through that Washington would not see him."[31] Bush had already authorized the air attack. He and his advisors believed that they had adequately prepared the American and international public opinion for war and had shown that they had gone "the extra mile" for peace. Washington thus judged that there was no longer any point in engaging in additional "exercises" of diplomacy.

The War Against Iraq

In leading a coalition of countries to war against Iraq, the Bush administration's objectives included but were not limited to the removal of Iraqi troops from Kuwait. The destruction of Iraq's military capabilities and the removal of Saddam Hussein, goals Israel and its friends articulated and advocated from the very beginning of the crisis, were prominent among American war aims. As early as the second week of August 1990 "highly placed sources" within the Bush administration were admitting that the American war objective will be to use air power "to flatten Iraq." "The aim," said the same official, "is to destroy Iraq's war-making potential and to inflict such damage...the Iraqi military will overthrow Saddam."[32] This position received the support of congressional leaders. Senator Richard Lugar of Indiana, one of the Republican Party's most influential legislators on foreign policy, candidly stated that Saddam Hussein "does have to leave the leadership of the country, and beyond that, many of the forces that he has aggregated have to be removed as a threat."[33]

From the very beginning of the war against Iraq on January 17, it became obvious that the United States was pursuing objectives that went far beyond the declared goal of evicting the Iraqi troops out of Kuwait. The latest in weapon technology, cruise missiles, smart bombs, Stealth fighters, and camera-equipped planes sending photos of missiles finding their way to their targets through open doors, were unleashed against Iraqi military, industrial and social infrastructures. American officials frankly admitted that the Iraqi military-industrial complex and alleged nuclear and chemical plants were targeted in the first raids "to insure that they would be destroyed *even if President Saddam Hussein complied quickly with the United Nations resolution commanding him to withdraw from Kuwait*."[34] (emphasis added). It was also conceded that such a war aim was the price Washington had to pay to placate and obtain that Israel, a nonbelligerent country on whose urban centres some Iraqi missiles were launched and caused some minor damage, refrain from any military retaliation which could have unforeseen consequences, particularly for the Arab regimes participating in the American-led war against Iraq. Israel had responded to Iraqi Scud missile attacks by presenting Washington with a $13 billion bill of which $10 billion in the form of loan guarantees to resettle Soviet Jewish immigrants and $3 billion for estimated losses during the Gulf crisis. More ominously, Israeli leaders ordered their mobile missile launchers armed with nuclear weapons and deployed in the direction of Iraq ready to launch.[35] The Bush administration offered Israel money and several batteries of the successful anti-missile Patriot missiles. In addition, it undertook to make the destruction of all Iraqi Scud missiles a top targeting priority. On January 23, President Bush declared that there were no limits to American war aims and that American forces were going "all the way:" "There can be no pause now that Saddam Hussein has forced the world into war," said Bush, "[w]e will stay the course and we will succeed — all the way."[36]

For the first two weeks of the war, the American-led forces conducted an air war, possibly the most massive in history, at the rate of one mission every minute, every hour, twenty four-hours a day.[37] The bombardments were directed against military but also against Iraq's industrial and social infrastructures and seemed to be deliberately aimed at destroying whatever industrial capacity Iraq had developed in the last quarter of a century. The Soviet Union, China and Arab allies in the anti-Iraq coalition expressed concerns about the relentless destruction of Iraq and its infrastructures. To maintain and present to the world continued super-power agreement, American and Soviet officials met in Washington and agreed on what appeared to be conditions for cessation of hostilities. In a joint communiqué issued on January 29 at the end of three days of talks, Secretary Baker and his Soviet counterpart Minister Bessmertnykh said that they "continue to believe that a cessation of hostilities would be possible if Iraq would make an unequivocal commitment to withdraw from Kuwait. They also believe that such a commitment must be backed by immediate, concrete steps leading to full compliance with the security council resolutions." Both ministers "agreed that in the aftermath of the crisis in the Persian Gulf, mutual U.S.-Soviet efforts to promote Arab-Israeli peace and regional stability...will be greatly facilitated and enhanced."[38]

Although administration officials quickly dampened any hope of a pause in the bombardments to allow Iraq to rethink its position or to enter negotiations with the United States, some American allies seem to have interpreted the communiqué as offering conditions for a cease-fire which depended on obtaining a firm "commitment" from Iraq to withdraw from Kuwait. Moreover, it was possible to read in the reference to the promise that following the Gulf war American-Soviet efforts to promote Arab-Israeli peace would be greatly facilitated, an indication that the two countries would cooperate to bring about that international conference Israel had adamantly refused to accept. Israel and its friends and lobbyists were furious. Pressure was brought to bear on the administration to publicly state that it had no such intentions in mind. The White House had to deny that there was any change in its position of unconditional Iraqi withdrawal from Kuwait and total rejection of any linkage between the Iraqi-Kuwaiti crisis and the Arab-Israeli conflict.

The air war against Iraq continued with sustained fury. American B-52 bombers engaged in carpet bombings of Iraqi troops and installations. Baghdad and major Iraqi cities were subjected to merciless bombings day and night. Outraged, the Iraqis sent a strongly-worded protest letter to the United Nations Secretary-

General. In it, Foreign Minister Aziz condemned the "deliberate and brutal attacks launched on behalf of the United Nations by forces of the criminal Zionist-imperialist alliance on civilian, economic, humanitarian, medical, cultural and religious targets and on citizens and their families in all parts of Iraq." He said that the Iraqi government held the UN Secretary-General Prez de Cullar personally responsible "to history and mankind," for what the letter described as "the heinous crimes being committed against the noble people of Iraq." Aziz placed much of the responsibility for the UN-endorsed war against Iraq on the dramatic changes taking place in the Soviet Union which removed Moscow's balancing role in international affairs and opened the way for "arrogant former colonialists and new imperialists once again to impose hegemony and intimidation."[39]

Even European members of the American-led war coalition began to express serious concerns about the relentless destruction of Iraq and its industrial infrastructures. On January 29, French Defense Minister Jean-Pierre Chevènement resigned to protest against "the logic of war" which "threatens to drive us further and further from the objectives established by the United Nations." Chevènement was "particularly alarmed that a military offensive originally authorized by the United Nations to liberate Kuwait now appeared aimed at overthrowing the government of Saddam Hussein and destroying much of Iraq."[40] Chevènement had repeatedly appealed to the United States on the eve of the war to make "the very small gesture" of offering Baghdad the pledge of an international peace conference on all Middle East problems in exchange for withdrawal from Kuwait.[41] But his appeals, like President François Mitterand's peace plan earlier, had fallen on deaf ears in Washington.

There was no respite in the systematic and massive destruction and punishment being visited upon Iraq. The apparent impunity with which the American-led forces were carrying out their mission led President Bush to take pride in what he believed was an important demonstration of both American power and American credibility to would-be challengers of American interests. In a speech on February 1, 1991, he stated: "When we win, and we will, we will have taught a dangerous dictator, and a tyrant tempted to follow in his footsteps, that the US has a new credibility, and that *what we say goes.*"[42] (emphasis added). Bush was suggesting to the Third World, presumed hot-bed of that dreaded "instability," the nature of the new world order and the role he assigned to the United States in it. The question of credibility has traditionally preoccupied American foreign policy planners, all the more so because in the nuclear age the various defense doctrines relied heavily on the credibility the potential enemies assigned to them. At the same time, superpower relations during the cold war were characterized by, among other things, a drive to influence and dominate Third World regions. And in that drive the credibility of the superpower as a guarantor of a certain socio-economic and political order and as a supplier of weapons and defender of certain conceptions of security, played a major role. "Since 1950," observed historian Gabriel Kolko, "'credibility has been by far the most dangerous and unpredictable variable in the way Washington conducts its foreign policy and military policies. The doctrine of credibility eliminates all rational calculations of global interests, objectives and priorities. The war against Iraq is the first pure manifestation, unsullied by remotely rational ideological considerations, of how deeply imbedded the credibility fixation has become in Washington's calculations."[43]

In addition, Washington also sent a message that it was clearly in charge even if the war was nominally fought in the name of the United Nations. Thus, from the very beginning of the war, the United Nations was relegated to the background and was allowed no involvement in how the war was conducted. In fact, the Security Council did not even meet to discuss the war until February 14, almost a full month after the war started. The meeting was called by Cuba and Yemen who circulated a peace plan calling for a halt to the bombing of Iraq and for the appointment of a Security Council commission to examine ways of ending the fighting. Washington first opposed the meeting but finally agreed to it on the condition that it be held behind closed doors. The Cuba-Yemen proposal, however, was not put to a vote because of American opposition to it.

Arab Opposition

At the same time Bush was affirming America's new credibility and warning the Third World: "what we say goes," the Arabs, including those in the coalition against Iraq were impressed by Saddam Hussein's steadfast and defiant attitude against overwhelmingly superior odds in a war which it would be more appropriate to call a punishment from the air against basically helpless targets. The *New York Times* correspondent in Saudi Arabia found that "many Saudis feel a begrudging admiration for the Iraqi leader, and enormous relief that he was not totally crushed in the initial days of the allied invasion." A Saudi professor told the *New York Times* reporter: "In all our wars, the Arabs were stopped or ultimately spared by superpower intervention. But Mr. Hussein is steadfast against the world's only superpower and the 28 countries fighting alongside it."[44]

By February, the United States-led relentless air war had dropped on Iraq bombs which, according to the *New York Times*, were "generally believed to exceed what was used in all of World War II." When asked for a reference point from previous wars, Maj. Gen. William (Gus) Pagonis said: "It is almost at a point where there is no comparison."[45]

The massive scale of the destruction inflicted upon Iraqi infrastructures elicited anger among the Arabs where massive anti-American demonstrations broke out in Jordan, Tunisia, Algeria and Morocco. There were also widespread demonstrations of protest in many Egyptian universities. Rifaat el Saeed, a spokesman for the eight opposition parties in Egypt and senior official of the Progressive Alignment Party circulated a petition signed by all opposition parties, except the Social Democratic Wafd Party, calling for an end to the war which they described as "a savage American attack against the Iraqi people."[46] The Soviet Foreign Minister also expressed concerns that the war was extending beyond the UN-sanctioned objective and presenting "a growing danger to Iraqi civilians."[47] In Morocco, where 300,000 people took to the streets shouting anti-American and pro-Iraqi slogans, King Hassan II, who had sent 1,500 troops to Saudi Arabia to show his solidarity with the rich Gulf monarchies and the West, prudently tampered his support for the war with sympathy and support for the Iraqi people. "Although our position on Iraq's invasion of Kuwait is opposed to theirs," said the Moroccan King, "our hearts are with the Iraqis. Our hearts are with them because they are our brothers, Arabs and Muslims."[48]

An opinion poll carried out in February as Iraq was being subjected to massive bombardment day and night, found that 93 percent of Tunisians supported Iraq in one form or another. What was remarkable about this support was that it was not based entirely on the understandable sentiment of inter-Arab solidarity for a sister Arab country being systematically destroyed. Rather, the support derived its strength from beliefs in the legitimacy and political and economic justice the respondents assigned to the Iraqi invasion of Kuwait. Thus, an overwhelming majority of Tunisians supported Iraq on the basis of the legitimacy of its annexation of Kuwait; 57 percent of respondents considered the annexation as recovery of Iraqi territory; 14 percent thought of it as constituting a just redistribution of Arab wealth and another 14 percent considered it as a justified response to the Kuwaiti stubbornness in the Iraqi-Kuwaiti negotiations; 53 percent of respondents believed that the Iraqi stand against the American-led war was a stand against Western imperialism. "It is a war of colonizers against colonized," observed one Tunisian intellectual, "the role assigned to the colonized as an aid recipient and dependent is only possible if the colonized remains at his historic place, dependent and unequal. Now, for the first time the colonized is colonizer, but the world order cannot accept this reversal of roles." Similarly, in his January 26 speech, Tunisian President Ben Ali seems to have reflected many of the unarticulated sentiments of the Tunisian people. The real objectives of the aggression against Iraq, he said, consisted in preventing the Arab nation "from acceding to progress and mastering science and technology so that it will forever remain condemned to dependency."[49]

In Jordan, King Hussein lashed out against the war which he described as being "against all Arabs and all Muslims and not against Iraq alone." In a televised speech to the Jordanian people on February 6, the king praised the Iraqi people and the Iraqi army "as they defend us all and raise the banner that says: God is great." King Hussein compared the American-led war enterprise to the secret Anglo-French Sykes-Picot agreement which divided the Middle East into areas of French and English domination and symbolizes for the Arabs the height of Western betrayal and duplicity. He also strongly condemned the bombings of trucks carrying Iraqi oil to Jordan through the Iraqi-Jordan highway. "There were new attempts to deprive us of our needs of oil," he said, "and that was one way of imposing sanctions against us for no reason except our basic position" of neutrality. Jordan is not willing, he said, "to dance to the tune others play without being able to freely express our opinion, which we will not give up."[50] Hussein criticized Egypt, Saudi Arabia and Turkey, strong supporters of the US role in the war, as countries that brought shame upon Islam by supporting the United States in the destruction of an Arab country. Significantly, he also repeated his charge that a diplomatic Arab solution to the crisis was foiled because the United States and Israel were bent on the destruction of Iraq: "We now realize fully the real reasons why we, the Arabs, were deprived of our right to solve our problems, and why the United Nations was prevented from fulfilling its role, and why the doors were shut against any sincere political attempt to resolve the Gulf crisis. It is claimed that every effort possible was made to solve the crisis during the first five months before the war. This is not true...All the good offices of Jordan and others who were concerned for the future of our nation were aborted. Why? Because the real purpose behind this destructive war, as proven by its scope, and as attested to by the declaration of the parties, is to destroy Iraq, and rearrange the area in a manner far more dangerous to our nation's present and future than the Sykes-Picot Agreement."[51]

The day following King Hussein's speech, the Bush administration announced that it was reviewing all economic aid to Jordan. An Arab recipient of American aid does not have the luxury of independently charting his country's own political course and of rejecting America's war plans. The *New York Times* bluntly reminded both President Mubarak of Egypt and King Hussein of Jordan of this reality on the eve of the Cairo Summit, and the Bush administration has just taught Jordan a lesson in the realities of their relationship for daring to oppose the war. Israeli leaders, however, may contemptuously and angrily reject American peace plans for the Arab-Israeli-Palestinian conflict, refusing to concede any link between massive American aid and American-sponsored peace plans in the region; they may then turn around and demand, and receive, an increase in American economic and military aid.

Moscow humiliated-Withdrawing Iraqis Bombed

On February 12 President Gorbachev's special envoy Yevgeny M. Primakov arrived in Baghdad with a special message from the Soviet leader appealing to President Saddam Hussein to withdraw Iraqi forces from Kuwait and save his country from further destructions. Radio Baghdad quoted Saddam Hussein as giving this encouraging response: "Iraq is prepared to extend cooperation to the Soviet Union and other nations and agencies in the interest of finding a peaceful, political, equitable and honourable solution to the region's central issues, including the situation in the Gulf."[52] The United States responded by increasing the pressure. On February 13, American Stealth fighter-bombers destroyed a concrete building in a residential neighbourhood of Baghdad, killing hundreds of civilians. American officials claimed that the building was a legitimate military target because it had been used as a communication centre for the command of military forces. But Peter Arnett, reporting from Baghdad for the *Cable News Network*, said that the building "had housed civilians at night since the first days of the allied bombing. He indicated that the site had become a nightly gathering centre for civilians fleeing the allied strikes, which have destroyed three major bridges in the centre of the city in recent days."[53]

An Associated Press reporter who spoke to witnesses at the scene described the attack thus: "the first bomb struck the entrance of the building about 4 A. M.; jamming the only escape route. Ten seconds later, a second bomb smashed through 10 feet of reinforced concrete and exploded in the windowless bunker below." The bombing raid lasted twelve hours and was one of the most intensive raids of the war. Arnett reported that Iraqi officials said that 200 bodies had been recovered and that there were about 300 more inside.[54] Even the *New York Times* seemed baffled and, addressing the Bush administration, asked: "why not stop bombing the cities?"[55]

Iraqi leaders continued to explore the opening given to them by the Soviet Union in an attempt to end the relentless destruction. On February 18, Iraqi Foreign Minister Tariq Aziz went to Moscow to be briefed on the Soviet peace plan. He returned to Baghdad, discussed the plan with the Iraqi leaders, then returned

to Moscow to deliver Iraq's response to the plan. On February 22, Moscow announced that Iraq had accepted the Soviet peace plan on the basis of "full and unconditional withdrawal" from Kuwait and an end to UN sanctions against Iraq.
Baghdad dropped its demands for a Middle East peace conference, Iraqi reparations from Kuwait, and for the withdrawal of Western forces from the region. The
Soviet peace plan was greeted with relief by the international community, anxious
to forestall the land war the United States seemed about to launch. Bush's first
response was to express concerns about the Soviet plan. The American President
clearly wanted to avoid having to prematurely end the war in a way which would
rob Washington of the glory of a total victory which seemed close at hand. He also
wanted to keep the sanctions against Iraq even after withdrawing from Kuwait so
as to use them as leverage to pressure the Iraqi people into overthrowing Saddam
Hussein, a now publicly stated American war aim.

On February 22, Bush issued an ultimatum which, as *Newsweek* put it, "was
meant to be unacceptable." He demanded that Iraqi troops start pulling out of
Kuwait the same day and complete their withdrawal within one week, and gave
the Iraqi leader a 24-hour deadline to expire the following day at noon, eastern
time. If the Iraqis complied, they would be humiliated by the hasty withdrawal imposed on them by Washington and by the necessity of having to abandon much of
whatever was left of their heavy equipment to comply with the restrictive deadline. The spectacle of Iraqi soldiers putting down their arms and running home
would preempt any Iraqi claims of a valiant stand for the defense of the mother-
land and for the honour of the Arabs. It would also rob Baghdad of the claim that
withstanding the merciless pounding and bombardment by the forces of a superpower leading twenty-eight nations in a grossly unequal confrontation represented a moral victory in itself, a view which many of Saddam Hussein's
opponents were willing to grudgingly concede.

Iraq had been for all practical purposes crushed by perhaps the most massive
air campaign in history and the Iraqis had announced their acceptance of unconditional withdrawal from Kuwait, the ultimate admission of defeat. But Bush's conditions were designed to do more than simply achieve the unconditional Iraqi
withdrawal. If accepted, the ultimatum and its attendant sever humiliation of Iraq
would enhance the profile of the American "victory" and its credibility to potential
and future challengers to the American-supported order. If refused, this would provide the convenient excuse for launching the land war and completing the destruction of whatever was left of the Iraqi forces. In either case, Bush wanted to leave no
doubt in the minds of the Iraqi people as to the extent of the defeat the Iraqis had suffered at the hands of the American-led forces. The Soviet Union responded by
modifying its peace plan to incorporate many of the conditions advanced by the
Bush administration and forwarded the new plan to Baghdad, giving Iraqi troops
three weeks to complete their withdrawal; the Iraqi leadership accepted the added
condition of an accelerated withdrawal timetable. But the Bush administration was
clearly annoyed by the Soviet effort to stop the war and, as Bush perceived it, rob
him of an imminent "total victory" in the war. Administration officials were irritated
by the Soviet Union's belated-attempt at peace brokering which they described as
designed "to prevent the United States from achieving its political aims in the
Gulf."[56] An official of the Bush administration confided that in two phone conversations with the Soviet leader, President Bush "told Gorbachev, nicely, to bug off."[57]

The helplessness and humiliation Soviet leaders suffered in their aborted attempt at ending the war added to the sense of frustration and impotence in the face of the systematic destruction of one of their major allies in the Middle East. Soviet criticisms of the war and of American goals came into sharper focus. Washington was clearly placing its own strategic designs in the region above its newly-found cooperation with Moscow. "This war was launched by the United States," observed the Soviet newspaper *Pravda* on February 25, "to establish its leadership in the world. Notwithstanding the beautiful intentions proclaimed by Washington, this is a dirty war, like the war in Vietnam."[58] As the bombardments of Iraq intensified and the destruction grew apace, Soviet commentators' criticisms of Washington's objectives became belatedly more strident. "This is not a storm," wrote the distinguished Soviet commentator Stanislav Kondrachov in the *Izvestia*, "it is a massacre in the desert, a massacre in Basra, a massacre in Baghdad, and we are on the side of the assassins."[59]

George Bush's determination to ensure that the victory of the United States forces was unambiguously decisive was partly motivated by considerations related to America's new strategic doctrine of confronting Third World regional powers. The national security policy review ordered by Bush when he came to power had concluded that the United States must confront and *decisively defeat* Third World challenges to its interests: "In cases where the US confronts much weaker enemies, our challenge will be not simply to defeat them, but to defeat them decisively and rapidly," the national security review concluded, "for small countries hostile to us, bleeding our forces in protracted or indecisive conflict or embarrassing us by inflicting damage on some conspicuous element of our forces may be victory enough, and could undercut political support for US efforts against them."[60]

Washington was determined, therefore, not to let Moscow spoil a "good war." Shortly after the 24-hour ultimatum expired, the United States-led forces launched the previously planned ground assault on Iraqi forces in Kuwait and inside Iraq itself. Although Bush spoke on the phone with Gorbachev on Saturday shortly before the deadline expired, he chose not to inform him of the exact time for the ground offensive. A State Department official candidly admitted that the reason for launching the ground attack even though Iraq had accepted to withdraw from Kuwait unconditionally was related to the American political objectives of destroying Iraqi military potentials and removing Saddam Hussein: "We are trying to create an environment that either ensures that the people of Iraq understand it is not in their interest to keep him (Saddam Hussein) around or that ensures that he cannot be a threat to any other country."[61] When asked if the United States intended to carry out the equivalent of the de-Nazification of Germany after World War II Secretary of State Baker said that was "a political aim" of Washington. [62]

On February 25, Radio Baghdad announced that Iraq had ordered its troops to withdraw immediately in conformity with the Soviet peace plan. However, the Bush administration rejected the Iraqi offer of unconditional withdrawal and insisted on continuing the war.[63] Shortly thereafter, the Iraqi News Agency announced that Iraqi Foreign Minister Aziz asked the Soviet Ambassador "to convey a message from President Saddam Hussein and the Revolutionary Command Council to achieve a cease-fire and put an end to the criminal behaviour of the United States and its allies and collaborators."[64] But the Bush administration was in no mood to end the war. "We continue to prosecute the war" said Marlin Fitzwater, the White House spokesman, minutes before an urgent meeting of the Security Council called by the Soviet Union was scheduled to discuss the latest Soviet proposals, incorporating many of the American conditions and accepted by Iraq. A *New York Times* headline was instructive: "Allies See Pullout Signs, but Keep Pounding Departing Iraqis."[65]

Accordingly, the bombing and the killing continued even as the Iraqis were desperately fleeing Kuwait. To justify their insistence on continuing the war, American officials claimed that the Iraqis were still fighting when in fact they were simply running for their lives. The *Washington Post* revealed the existence of "a public-relations campaign managed by the US Central Command" to term the disorganized withdrawal of the Iraqi forces a "fighting retreat" to justify the merciless bombing on February 26 of a six-lane traffic jam of Iraqi tanks, passenger cars, and ambulances trying to get out of Kuwait.[66] There were so many Navy, Air Force and Marine planes competing to destroy the withdrawing convoy that the "killing box" had to be divided in half by air traffic controllers to avoid mid-air collisions.

Other stories emerged after the war and revealed a level of inhumanity and a penchant for barbaric cruelty difficult to reconcile the noble ideals of a new world order, even one ushered in by a war of massive and systematic mechanized destruction. Thus, reporters later discovered that another fleeing convoy had been mercilessly destroyed by B-52 bombing runs along a second road connecting Kuwait to Iraq. It was also later established that the American army division that broke through the Iraqi front lines in Kuwait used earthmovers and ploughs mounted on tanks to bury approximately 6,000 Iraqi soldiers, some wounded but many still alive, in more than 70 miles of trenches.[67]

Unconditional Surrender

On February 27, Iraq offered to relinquish all claims to Kuwait, release war prisoners, and accept responsibility for war reparations in return for an immediate cease-fire and the lifting of international sanctions. But the war raged on as the Iraqis were mercilessly hunted down, surrounded and killed, and as massive and increasingly destructive bombardments continued unabated. The American-led forces were bent in totally destroying the Iraqi military-industrial and social infrastructures and crippling any capacity of industrial or military recovery. The *New York Times* described the growing level of destruction even at this stage of unconditional Iraqi capitulation and withdrawal as "practising arms control by brute force."[68] Washington responded to the Iraqi offer of surrender with one of the most devastating bombardments of the war against Baghdad. The blasts and the explosions were so great that the Rashid hotel, where Western reporters were staying, "heaved and shuddered."[69] A few hours later, at 9 P. M. Eastern time, President Bush appeared on national television to proclaim victory and order a suspension to the offensive military operations against Iraq.

The following day the Pentagon announced that 4,000 of Baghdad's main battle tanks had been destroyed, and that all of the 42 Iraqi divisions assembled to defend Kuwait had been destroyed, captured or rendered unfit for battle. The number of Iraqis killed and wounded was estimated to be between 100,000 and 150,000. The real numbers are probably much higher. Thousands of civilians have been killed in Iraq and Kuwait.[70] The claims about Iraq's army being the fourth most powerful army in the world, and the claims about huge stockpiles of chemical and biological weapons turned out to be gross exaggerations, deliberate propaganda ploys to inflate the threat of the enemy, engineer consent for the massive war, and magnify the victory of the American forces. During the 100-hour ground war, when at last the combatants confronted one another after six weeks of merciless punishment from the sky, the Iraqi army had fielded only 185,000 men against the 700,000 troops of the American-led coalition forces.[71] Moreover, hundreds of thousands of American-led troops combed Kuwaiti and Iraqi territories for the much-advertised Iraqi chemical and biological weapons but found nothing. "It is a great mystery," said Gen. Steven Arnold, senior operations officer in Operation Desert Storm.[72] Reporters who visited the scene were shocked by the horrors of killings and destruction. The *New York Times* run a story appropriately headlined: "7 Miles of Carnage Mark Road Iraqis Used to Flee."[73] The American military congratulated themselves on the realization of their military objectives and looked forward to some "long-term American military presence in the Gulf."[74]

On March 10, eight Arab Foreign Ministers met in Saudi Arabia and sanctioned American military presence in the region. They endorsed the four-point plan outlined by President Bush in his address to a joint session of the Congress a few days earlier. President Bush had called for an expanded American naval presence in the Persian Gulf as well as "continuing American participation in joint exercise" with Arab Gulf countries "involving both air and ground forces." The Bush plan also called for arms control agreements, economic development programmes to bridge differences between the Arab haves and have-nots, and negotiations between Israel and Arab States and Palestinians on the basis of trading Israeli-occupied Arab lands for peace with Israel. The statement of the Arab Foreign Ministers endorsing the American plan was rightly viewed as "something of a breakthrough in Arab-American relations," even though Secretary Baker who attended the meeting said: "This is not the appropriate time" for an international peace conference on the Arab-Israeli-Palestinian conflict. Baker also announced an agreement to replace the 500,000 American troops still in Iraq and Kuwait by an Arab peacekeeping force made up of the six Arab Gulf States, Egyptian and Syrian troops, and an enhanced American naval presence in the Persian Gulf. A few days later an agreement was reached with the Gulf States to move the headquarters of the United States Central Command from Tampa, Florida, to an unspecified site in the Middle East.[75]

Iraq Relegated to the Pre-Industrial Age

Officials of the Bush administration described to the *New York Times* the extent of civilian damage they estimate to have inflicted on Iraq: "Iraq's electrical power industry may have been damaged well beyond the intentions of allied war planners...In addition, allied war planes wrecked Iraq's civilian telecommunication system, described as a total loss by one estimate; and the bombing campaign seriously damaged the national network of roads and bridges, crippling commerce in a nation that straddles two major river valleys."[76]

But the damage observed by independent envoys from the United Nations seems to have been a great deal more than what the administration was willing to concede. On March 20, a United Nations team returned from Iraq where it surveyed civilian damage caused by the war. The UN report submitted by UN Under-Secretary-General Martti Ahtisaari read in its general conclusion: "I and the members of my mission were fully conversant with media reports regarding the situation in Iraq and, of course, with the recent WHO/UNICEF report on water, sanitary and health conditions in the Greater Baghdad area. It should, however, be said at once that nothing that we had seen or read had quite prepared us for the particular form of devastation which has now befallen the country. The recent conflict has wrought near-apocalyptic results upon the economic infrastructure of what had been, until January 1991, a rather highly urbanized and mechanized society. Now, most means of modern life support have been destroyed or rendered tenuous. Iraq has, for some time to come, been relegated to a pre-industrial age; but with all the disabilities of post-industrial dependency on an intensive use of energy and technology."[77]

Following the press conference at which he discussed his report, I asked Mr. Martti Ahtisaari to describe in details the kind of "near-apocalyptic" destruction he and his team witnessed in Iraq. Mr. Ahtisaari talked about hospitals without electricity and water; power stations completely destroyed, bridges blown up, modern communication systems annihilated, and desperate needs in terms of basic health and medical support, food and shelter for thousands of homeless people. When I asked him to comment if the kind of destruction he witnessed was necessary for the achievement of the United-Nations-sanctioned aims in Kuwait, he chose to limit his answer to the humanitarian needs of the Iraqi people. When I pressed him on that question, Mr. Ahtisaari claimed that he was not concerned with political or military decisions but that the destructions he saw in Iraq were "real and horrendous."[78] When I showed Ahtisaar's UN report to Amr Moussa, then Egypt's ambassador to the United Nations, and asked him for his views on it, he said that he was "very saddened by it;" but he refused to blame the United States for the way it conducted the war and insisted on placing the blame only and entirely on Saddam Hussein.[79]

Iraq Out of Kuwait But Sanctions Continue

The post-Gulf war American strategy was to try to accomplish through various means of pressures, such as the military occupation of about 20 percent of Iraqi territories and continued enforced sanctions against Iraq, what the war had failed to accomplish, namely, the removal of Saddam Hussein.

In his dogged pursuit of the goal of personal defeat of Saddam Hussein and his ouster from power, President Bush thoughtlessly called on the Iraqi people to rise against Saddam Hussein and implied American support for such a popular revolt. But Bush was reminded by advisors and allies alike that the collapse of the central government in Baghdad could conceivably lead to the dismemberment of modern Iraq into a number of ethnically-based States, an arrangement which American policy has traditionally not favoured. Moreover, Egypt, Syria, and Saudi Arabia made it clear to Washington that they opposed such an outcome. They certainly did not want to see the Shiits in the south, supported by and linked to Iran, topple the central government and emerge as the dominant force able to establish an Iran-like Islamic republic in Iraq. Turkey, an American ally with the largest Kurdish minority in the region, may have contemplated with excited anticipation the prospect of laying claim to the oil-rich Mosul region in northern Iraq in case of Iraqi dismemberment, but it certainly feared and opposed the dangerous precedent of giving Iraq's Kurds an independent status which could only encourage Turkey's large Kurdish minority, oppressed by President Turgut Ozal's repressive regime and emergency rule. The Bush administration decided then that its best interests indeed lay in maintaining Iraq's territorial integrity, in weakening Saddam Hussein's regime sufficiently so as to foreclose for a longtime to come, Iraqi regional ambitions but not enough to allow the uprisings in the south or in the north to succeed and bring about the dismemberment of Iraq. In other words, Washington agreed to continue the same "cynical enterprise" the Congressional Report (the Pike Report) had condemned during the secretly-supported destabilization campaign in Iraq ordered by the Nixon-Kissinger team during the seventies.

Accordingly, no attempts were made to militarily help the Shiits or the Kurds to overthrow the central government in Baghdad. The best outcome from Washington's point of view seemed to be for the removal of Saddam Hussein, but not his regime, and his replacement by another military leader willing to cooperate with Washington and the emerging new Arab order. With this in mind, an American campaign of sanctions and military intimidation was designed, as American officials willingly recognized, "to send a strong message to Mr. Hussein military commanders and the Iraqi Baath Party elite that they should drive him from power."[80]

Once again the United States had no difficulty in getting the Security Council to adopt, on April 3, 1991, a cease-fire resolution essentially reflecting the American strategy of continued sanctions, increased pressure and stiff military conditions designed to complete the disarmament of Iraq started by, as the New York Times put it, "brute force." Iraq was to be completely eliminated as an Arab military power to contend with in the region and for this purpose the United States demanded the destruction of whatever real and potential Iraqi offensive power may have escaped destruction during the war. Accordingly, the cease-fire resolution imposed on Iraq the mortgaging of its future oil sales to pay for war reparations, maintained the sanctions — except for food and medicine — in place, and demanded that Iraq agree to the destruction of ballistic missiles, chemical and biological weapons, nuclear-weapon-grade material and all related research and manufacturing facilities. The resolution called this condition a step toward "establishing in the Middle East a zone free from weapons of mass destruction."[81]

But one does not have to be a cynic to deride this statement. It is illusory to speak of ridding the region of weapons of mass destruction at a time when American Arab allies and Israel were speeding up their armament programmes and adding to their already huge lethal arsenals. In addition, Israel, it will be recalled, has steadfastly refused to ratify the Nuclear Weapon Non-Proliferation Treaty and was certain to continue to oppose any real attempt at regional control of weapons of mass destruction that would control its nuclear and biological armaments programmes. In fact, after paying lip service to the need to regulate the flow of conventional weapons to the Middle East, Washington quickly backtracked, arguing that its allies in the region were opposed to the idea and were demanding more sophisticated weapons, and in larger quantities, for their self-defense.

Washington agreed to supply Saudi Arabia and the Gulf States with American weapons worth more than $20 billion. The end of the cold war will not, after all, put an end to the mindless militarization of the Third World.

The cease-fire resolution was in reality designed to punish Iraq and strengthen the deterrent power of the dominant economic, political and military order in the Middle East.[82] Abdallah al-Ashtall, Yemen's ambassador to the United Nations and the only Arab member of the Security Council, told me that the resolution was "very vindictive.... [it was] like kicking someone who is already on the ground...The United States is trying to do through diplomacy what they haven't accomplished by war."[83]

With Iraq's acceptance of the conditions contained in the resolution the war formally came to an end. Saddam Hussein turned his attention to quelling the Shiite rebellion in the south and the Kurdish insurgency in the north. Washington's acquiescence in the repression of the popular uprisings it had encouraged elicited strong criticisms at home for calling on the Iraqi people to revolt and overthrow Saddam Hussein and then failing to come to their help when they needed it. The Bush administration decided to intervene militarily in the north but only to set up what was called "safe havens" for the Kurdish refugees who fled en masse to the mountains and to the Iranian and Turkish borders. The refugee camps set up by American and British troops in northern Iraq became the temporary safe havens for the Kurds while their leaders negotiated and reached agreement with Saddam Hussein on some form of autonomy for the Kurdish region in northern Iraq.

In the meantime, the United Nations renewed the sanctions against Iraq as more Iraqi civilians were dying from malnutrition and epidemics. A medical team from Harvard University visited Iraq from April 26 to May 6. Its report warned that 170,000 Iraqi children under five were likely to die from infectious diseases as cholera and typhoid epidemics spread. Another United Nations team also went to Iraq in July. The mission was headed by Prince Safruddin Aga Khan who warned in his report that unless averted immediately the food crisis in Iraq would cause massive starvation throughout the country.[84]

Thus, the Gulf war formally came to an end. The ruling Kuwaiti family was restored to power, the conservative monarchies of the Gulf were preserved, the United States obtained the military bases it had sought for over a decade for its Rapid Deployment Force Strategic Central Command, the Israeli objective of eliminating the last potentially serious Arab military challenge to its military domination of the region achieved, and the ascendency of the pro-American Arab regimes confirmed. An important and bloody lesson had been given to a Third World leader who dared to challenge American interests. And although Saddam Hussein himself managed to cling to power, Washington promised to continue its campaign of pressures, psychological warfare, destabilization and secret plots to eliminate the defiant Iraqi leader. The lesson would not be lost on the rest of the Third World which Washington assumed to be the source of new challenges to American interests around the globe. Ambitious Third World leaders will now think twice before daring to challenge the established order.[85]

Notes

1. *Al-Ahram,* August 16, 1990.
2. Robert Parry, "The Peace Feeler that Was," *The Nation,* April 15, 1991.
3. *Al-Ahram,* August 17, 1990.
4. See *Manchester Guardian,* "Ways out without war," September 16, 1990.
5. See Norman Finkelstein, "Israel and Iraq: A Double Starndard," *Journal of Palestine Studies,* vol. XX, no. 2 (Winter 1991), pp. 43-56); see also Ligue internationale pour le droit et la libération des peuples, *Dossier Palestine. La question palestinienne et le droit international* (Paris, La Dcouverte, 1991).
6. Ahmad Salamatian, "Affaibli, le régime iranien choisit la prudence," *Le Monde Diplomatique,* September 1990.
7. *October Magazine,* (Cairo, in Arabic) No. 721. August 19, 1990. p. 42.
8. Personal interview with Boutros Ghali in Cairo, 1991.
9. *Al-Ahram* August 16, 1990.
10. James E. Akins, "Heading Towards War," op. cit., p. 23.
11. French President François Mitterand, Address to the UN General Assembly, New York, September 24, 1990 reproduced in *Journal of Palestine Studies,* vol. XX. no, 2. (Winter 1991), p. 168-170; see also The *Washington Post,* reproduced in the *Guardian Weekly,* October 7, 1990.
12. Ibid.
13. Ibid.
14. *Manchester Guardian,* October, 28, 1990.
15. Paul-Marie De La Gorce, "Golf: une guerre à l'arraché?" *Le Monde Diplomatique,* December, 1990.
16. *Manchester Guardian,* October 14, 1990; see also David Hirst, "Divided Arabs use deaths to support their positions on Iraq," the *Manchester Guardian,* October 14, 1990.
17. *Le Monde,* October 14-15, 1990.
18. Alain Gresh, "Le butin du conquérant," *Le Monde Diplomatique,* November, 1990.
19. Ibid.
20. *Le Monde,* October 14-15, 1990, reproduced in the *Guardian Weekly,* October 21, 1990.
21. See Jane Rosen, "Israeli lobby leans on the US," *Manchester Guardian,* December 16, 1990.
22. *The Nation,* April 15, 1991.
23. *The New Yorker,* January 7, 1991.
24. *Washington Post,* reproduced in the *Guardian Weekly,* December 2, 1990.
25. Martin Yant, *Desert Mirage* op. cit., p. 130; see also *Manchester Guardian,* December 9, 1990.
26. See Richard Falk, "La force au mépris du droit, Les Nations unies sous la coupe de Washington," *Le Monde Diplomatique,* February, 1991.
27. *New York Times,* December 6, 1990.
28. Richard Falk, *Le Monde Diplomatique,* February, 1990.
29. Woodword, *The Commanders,* opt, cit, p. 345.
30. Ignacio Ramonet, "Menaçante anomie," *Le Monde Diplomatique,* January 1991. See also Kimberly Elliot, Gary Hufbauer and Jeffrey Schott, "Judging from History the anti-Saddam Sanction Can Work," *International Herald Tribune,* December 11, 1990.
31. Peter Hiett, "Chadli fails too," *Middle East International,* January 25, 1991.
32. *Newsweek,* August 20, 1990.
33. *Wall Street Journal,* August 30, 1990.
34. *The New York Times,* January 30, 1991.
35. Seymour M. Hersh, *The Samson Option: Israel's Nuclear Arsenal and American Foreign Policy* (New York, Random House, 1991), p. 318.

36. *New York Times*, January 25, 1991.
37. *New York Times*, February 5, 1991.
38. *New York Times*, January 31, 1991.
39. *New York Times*, January 29, 1991.
40. *New York Times*, January 30, 1991.
41. Robert Parry, "The Peace Feeler That Was," *The Nation*, April 15, 1991.
42. Gabriel Kolko, "Obsessed with Military 'Credibility'," *The Progressive*, (Madison), (March 1991), pp. 24-26..
43. *New York Times*, February 1, 1991.
44. *New York Times*, February 4, 1991.
45. *New York Times*, January 25, 1991.
46. *New York Times*, January 25, 1991.
47. *New York Times*, February 6, 1991.
48. Nadia Khoury-Dagher and Aziza Dargouth Medimegh, "Pourquoi, en Tunisie, la rue a soutenu Baghdad," *Le Monde Diplomatique*, March, 1991.
49. *New York Times*, February 7, 1991.
50. *New York Times*, February 13, 1991.
51. King Hussein, "Address to the Nation," Amman, February 6, 1991, reproduced in *Journal of Palestine Studies* vol. XX, no. 3 (Spring 1991), pp. 148-49.
52. *New York Times*, February 14, 1991.
53. *New York Times*, February 14, 1991.
54. *New York Times*, February 14, 1991.
55. *New York Times*, February 25, 1991.
56. *New York Times*, February 25, 1991.
57. *New York Times*, February 23, 1991.
58. Amnon Kapliouk, "Le grand débat à Moscou sur la guerre du Golf," *Le Monde Diplomatique*, March, 1991.
59. Ibid.
60. *New York Times*, February, 23, 1991. George Black, an editor at the *Nation* was one of the few critical writers at the height of post-war public euphoria. In a *Los Angeles Times* artilce he quoted the review of national security policy that Bush ordered at the start of his presidency and sarcastically pointed out that it was unencumbered by "any sentimental nonsense about democracy." He concluded: "From Truman to Reagan, every postwar US president has cloaked his crusades in the language of democracy. Bush appears to prefer a more direct approach. One of the minor cultural artifacts of this war was a button that read, quoting the president, 'America kicks butt.' The question is, does it any longer know how to do anything else?," quoted in Martin Yant, *Desert Mirage*, op. cit., p. 184.
61. *New York Times*, February, 25, 1991.
62. Ibid.
63. *New York Times*, February 26, 1991.
64. Ibid.
65. *New York Times*, February 26, 1991.
66. *Washington Post*, March 11, 1991.
67. *Manchester Guardian*, September 13, 1991, quoted in Galal Amin, "On the Gulf War, Machiavelli and Israeli Efficiency," *Al-Ahram Weekly*, January 2, 1991.
68. *New York Times*, February 27, 1991.
69. *New York Times*, February 28, 1991.
70. *New York Times*, March 1, 1991.
71. Jacques Isnard, "Golf: la guerre réévaluée," *Le Monde*, May 2, 1992 and Marie-France Toinet, "Comment les États-Unis ont perdu les moyen de leur hégémonie," *Le Monde Diplomatique*, June, 1992.

72. Martin Yant, *Desert Mirage* op. cit., p. 110; see also *New York Times*, March 4, 1991.
73. *New York Times*, March 3, 1991.
74. *New York Times*, March 1, 1991.
75. *New York Times*, March 11, 1991.
76. *New York Times*, June 3, 1991.
77. *Report to the Secretary-General on Humanitarian Needs in Kuwait and Iraq in the Immediate Post-Crisis Environment* by a Mission to the Area led by Mr. Martti Ahisaari, Under-Secretary-General for Administration and Management, March 20, 1991. United Nations, New York.
78. Interview with UN Under-Secretary General Mr. Martti Ahtisaari, United Nations, New York, 1991.
79. Interview with Amr Moussa, Egypt's Ambassador to the United Nations. New York, 1991.
80. *New York Times*, March 23, 1991.
81. Personal communication.
82. See Adel Safty, "Stranglehold on UN no way to a new world order," *Globe and Mail* (Toronto), April 5, 1991.
83. Interview with Ambassador Abdallah al-Ashtall, Yemen's Permanent Mission to the United Nations, New York, 1991.
84. *Guardian Weekly*, August 4, 1991.
85. Norman Friedman, *Desert Victory. The War for Kuwait* (United States Naval Institute, Annapolis, Maryland, 1991).

CHAPTER EIGHT

The New World Order

Aftermath of the War Against Iraq

The war against Iraq and the new world order it helped shape completed the American ascendency in the Middle East and made it unchallenged and unequal since the Franco-British imperial domination of the Middle East following the end of World War I. Ironically, it was American President Woodrow Wilson who opposed, but was unable to stop, Franco-British colonial designs on the region, arguing that the game of balance of power had been discredited and peoples could only be governed by their consent. After the war against Iraq, Washington found itself free to chart the future of the region and control the direction of the Arab-Israeli-Palestinian conflict as it saw fit. It could insist on the principles of justice and of international law as a basis for the resolution of the pestering Palestinian conflict — and there is no shortage of UN Security Council Resolutions — or it could succumb to the temptation of using a uniquely favourable balance of power as the basis for a settlement. Washington chose to praise the former in official statements but to rely on the latter for effective policy decisions.

Washington assured its continued access to ready and cheap oil resources and confirmed the supremacy of the established balance of power, dominated by Israeli and American military and economic interests. It was partly against that balance of power that Saddam Hussein had revolted in an attempt to militarily challenge it to place himself in a more favourable bargaining position in the post Cold-War era. There was nothing pioneering in his balance of power calculations. They were the same calculations that informed the Zionist approach to Palestine and more specifically the philosophy of the founders of the State of Israel. David Ben Gurion believed, preached and effectively acted upon one constant and unshakable strategy: "military faits accomplis [are] the basis of political achievements." But Israel was able to rely on Western and particularly American support to play and profit from a balance of power strategy that assured its hegemonic domination of the Middle East. Saddam Hussein relied on Moscow, the ultimate loser in the larger balance of power game, at a time when the regional realities of the post Camp-David Arab world and the international realities of a collapsing Soviet Union militated against his calculations. Saddam Hussein may have been taken aback by the speed with which the Soviet Union collapsed into insignificance, and its subsequent disappearance altogether; indeed, never in the history of empires had an imperial power undefeated militarily and master of the latest weapon technology self-destroyed so rapidly. At the same time, even the timid political support expressed by the French for a political solution to the crisis could not be translated into effective action capable of stopping or even slowing down the steam-roller of war. Indeed, the nascent European Union was unable to assert any measurable political independence during the Gulf crisis; like the moribund Soviet Union it was relegated to irrelevancy, neutralized, and finally brought aboard the international coalition, lending legitimacy to the war option.

In his book *The Arab Predicament*, Fouad Ajami presents an insightful if somewhat indiscriminate cataloguing of Arab failings. He argues that the Arab dilemma resides in the pull between the Arabs' fascination with and attraction to the West's power and material success, on the one hand, and, on the other hand, the impulse to resist integration, and therefore subordination, retreat into their own universe, and develop their own values. History, geography, fate or divine intervention placed the Arabs close to the fire, Ajami argues, and the Arabs do not have the luxury of stepping out and passively observing their own destiny. They must make choices and commitments and take sides. In taking sides against the Iraqi invasion of Kuwait, the Arab State system, like other State systems, acted out of calculations of self-interest. It supported the principle of sovereign equality of all States and rejected the use of force as a means of inter-State conflict resolution. It was a rational response motivated by the instinct of self-preservation and fitted well within the context of an ideal and orderly international system of relations governed by the rule of law which many nations hopefully expected to result from the end of the cold war.

But there was no escaping the reality that the very nature of the Gulf crisis, the absence of the moral stature required to resolve it peacefully, and the falling in line behind a military solution the logic of which was far from compelling, exposed some of the long-ignored fundamental shortcomings of the Arab system and its social woes: the inability to develop some sort of a cohesive mechanism for democratic rule and genuine popular participation in the political process; the continued concentration of autocratic power in the hands of rulers whose power base remained the armed forces and not popular consent; the inability to address the popular resentment for the betrayal of pan-Arab ideals, supported by popular masses but appropriated for rhetorical and selfish use by autocrats and potentates primarily interested in the consolidation of their own power; the gross economic inequalities between the excessively rich few of the Gulf and the poverty of the overwhelming majority in the rest of the Arab nation and all the attendant feelings of frustration and anger; the failure to develop a common and realistic response to the Western economic, political and ideological challenges; the chronic inability to translate rhetorical denunciation of effective American support for Israeli occupation of Arab territories into any programme of coordinated political and economic actions, thus making possible the continuation of contradictory American foreign policy goals in the region: thus Arab strategic resources were made available to the American military-industrial complex and massive Arab investments continued to make significant contributions to the American economy while American money and weapons continued to make possible the Israeli occupation of Arab territories.

The failure of the Arab State system was also dramatized by the inadequacy of its response to the challenge of Muslim groups who remain virtually the only cohesive and organized groups claiming, and convincing growing numbers of adherents, that they offer better alternatives to the discredited social-nationalist-military ideologies, on the one hand, and the ill-understood and indiscriminately-applied free-trade and privatization-driven capitalism *à outrance* programmes demanded by international finance, on the other. When Le Front islamic du salut (Islamic Salvation Front) won a majority in the parliamentary elections in Algeria in 1991 and was poised to form the next Algerian government, a military coup barred its way to power, cancelled the dreaded elections, abolished the democratic reforms, arrested Muslim leaders, and imposed military rule. Perhaps more than anything else, the triumph of the Islamic Salvation Front bespoke the extent of popular sentiments of powerlessness, betrayal, disaffection and frustrations with the usual representatives of the Arab State system.[1]

One of the most recurring themes in the Arabic newspapers during and after the war against Iraq has been the certainty that the Arabs will emerge once more as the losers, their ranks more divided than ever, their power potential more dissipated than ever, and their future more dependent on outside power than they thought possible or acceptable. After the war, Egyptian officials I spoke with confirmed Egyptian commitment to an all-Arab security system for the region consistent with the March 1991 Damascus Agreement between the Gulf countries, Egypt and Syria. But as the Gulf countries' preference for reliance on American military presence and secret agreements with Washington became clear, many in the Arab world began to talk about a secret American agenda in the region. Invariably, feelings of frustrations and humiliation at the hands of the United States were expressed even in those countries that supported the American-led war against Iraq. The continuation of the sanctions against Iraq, the repeated statements that the Iraqi regime should be brought down, the public suggestion that Saddam Hussein should be tried for war crimes, and the cynical way in which the West seemed to be targeting Libya, are giving the Arabs the uncomfortable feeling that more than ever, bashing the Arabs continues to be fair game.

The targeting of Libya has aroused particularly angry sentiments throughout the Arab world. American investigators of the bombing of a Pan American World Airways jet over Scotland, in 1988, accused two Libyans of involvement; Washington and London insisted that Libya hand over the two suspects for trial in the United States and England. The case against Libya rested on rather thin and ambiguous evidence and, indeed, some American officials criticized the targeting of Libya as motivated by political considerations. Even Vincent Cannistraro, former head of the CIA's investigation of the bombing, said that the targeting of Libya was "outrageous."[2] Under pressure and threats from Washington and London, Libya put forward some legal proposals to resolve the conflict over who should try the two Libyan suspects, but Washington was unmoved and continued to insist on its demands while making threats and mobilizing the UN Security Council to impose sanctions against Libya.

Arab masses could not help but feel anger and powerlessness. Even in Egypt, the leader of the anti-Iraq Arab coalition, feelings of humiliation were widely expressed and not only by the Muslim coalition or the opposition groups, but increasingly in government papers as well. Describing the helplessness and humiliation which pervades the Arab world and the anger at Western double standards with the Arabs and Israel, a writer commented in *Al-Ahram*: "It seems that one of the conditions that the Arabs must meet to be eligible for membership in the 'new world order' is to join hands with the West in isolating and overturning specific Arab regimes that, like Iraq, are not toeing the Western line."[3] Another *Al-Ahram* columnist commented bitterly that in rejecting Libya's proposals for a legal settlement, the West was turning the "new world order" into a system of "codified international piracy." Another Egyptian commentator angrily remarked that the Western campaign against Iraq and Libya was not simple electioneering by Bush but rather part of "a grand design aimed ultimately at terminating the Arab national bond, doing away with even the minimum level of Arab solidarity, and melting the Arab entity into a looser, larger entity called the Middle East, so that the Arab region will in the future become nothing more than a mass of clashing mini-States among which Israel can exist and over which it can hold sway."[4] The *Al-Ahram* writer may or may not have been aware of the Zionist Plan for the Middle East discussed in chapter one, but what he described as an American objective bore a peculiar resemblance to the Zionist Plan's goal of dismembering the Middle East States along ethnic and confessional lines into small satellites, weak, divided, dependent, and controlled by the dominant power in the region, Israel.

With the elimination of Iraq as a potential deterrence to Israeli military domination of the region, Israel's military might stood wholly and completely unchallenged. Never since the establishment of the State has Israeli power so dominated the region; never since the beginning of the Arab-Israeli conflict in 1948 has the combined Arab potential of deterrence been reduced to such insignificant levels. Israeli leaders could contemplate with confidence a continued consolidation of the occupation of Arab territories even as they continue the peace negotiations with the Palestinians and the Arabs. They know that "things have changed since Camp David," and seem prepared to calmly act accordingly. Instructive in this regard was the controversy caused in Israel by Israeli Health Minister Ehud Olmert's statement on March 17, 1991 at the annual meeting of the powerful America-Israel Political Action Committee (AIPAC) in Washington, that Israel would be ready "to negotiate all the issues, all the claims, all of the demands, including the territorial demands of the Syrian..." The following day, Israeli Prime Minister Shamir clarified his government position on negotiations and on the real meaning it assigned to them. Referring to the Syrians he said: "They could say to us 'We want the Golan Heights' and we'll say 'We won't give it to you.' So here are your negotiations."[5] After his defeat in the June 1992 election, Shamir admitted that he had planned to drag the peace negotiations for ten years while consolidating Israel's hold on the occupied Arab territories and implanting there half a million Jews.[6]

American officials and public opinion makers welcomed the electoral victory of the Israeli Labour Party led by Yitzhak Rabin. The June 24 issue of the *New York Times* reported that officials of the Bush administration had said that the real winners of the Israeli elections were the Middle East peace negotiations. The paper also reported that American officials were pleased because they viewed Labour leader Rabin as flexible, willing to freeze settlements, trade land for peace, and negotiate seriously the issue of Palestinian autonomy. Yet, in its analysis of Rabin's flexibly and his fundamental policy differences which set him aside from Shamir, the same issue of the influential paper reported: "Rabin has promised to stop the construction of 'political settlement' not vital for Israel's security," and recognized that Rabin "has not specifically defined 'political settlements'," but that Labour has ported settlements in areas like the Jordan Valley and the environs of Jerusalem."[7] These "fundamental" differences between Labour and Likud may be important enough to get the Bush administration to agree to provide Israel with the $10 billion in loan guarantees Washington had tied to a freeze in settlement activities, but they are not substantive differences when it comes to the basic question of the Palestinian right to freedom and independence. Palestinians under occupation may legitimately ask: what does it matter if Jewish settlements built on confiscated and seized Palestinian lands are considered "political settlements" or "strategic settlements" if the ultimate result of both varieties is the dispossession of the Palestinians and the reduction of the territorial basis on which they may be able to reconstruct their shattered society. What does it matter if the Palestinians continue to be dispossessed and dominated in one form or another, in the name of biblical promises or strategic considerations?

It is estimated that there are today approximately 230,000 Jewish settlers in the West Bank, Gaza, and East Jerusalem and that more than 60 percent of the occupied Arab territories have been seized by Israel for exclusive Jewish use.[8] This *fait accompli* is not likely to be affected by the differences separating the Likud leaders from the Labour leaders. At the Ottawa session of the peace-talks in early 1992, Israeli negotiators clearly based their position on this new reality, correctly and forcefully arguing that "things have changed since Camp David." And indeed they have. Not only are there ten times as many settlers today as there were in 1978, but also the Arabs have never been more militarily subordinated to the dictates of Israeli military power; they have never been more dependent on the United States whose money and weapons make the Israeli occupation possible. Consequently, Israeli negotiators refused even to discuss, let alone negotiate, the question of the Palestinian right of return which was not even mentioned in the final communiqué of the Ottawa peace conference except indirectly in a restatement of relevant United Nations resolutions. The expected "flexibility" of Labour leaders is only relative to the total intransigence of the Likud leaders, but Labour thinking does not differ substantially from Likud's on the fundamental question of Palestinian national rights and right of return. These questions require some truly visionary and courageous Israeli leaders capable of the kind of concessions that come from strength and the honest recognition that the victim has suffered enough injustice. There are growing numbers of Israelis urging on their government this kind of generous and enlightened realism.

The New World Order

At the end of World War II, the United States stood supremely confident, wielding unparalleled power matched by no other country or group of countries in the world. It was the only superpower with military bases around the globe possessing the most powerful navy, the best equipped ground forces and the largest air force in the world. It was the only country to possess the ultimate weapon of destruction which it had just used in Japan over Hiroshima and Nagazaki, more as an intimidating demonstration of power to the Soviet Union than out of an absolute necessity to subdue an already defeated Japan. With its block of friendly Latin American votes the United States controlled the United Nations. The Charter of the international organization was carefully drafted to ensure, through the in-

corporation at American insistence of Article 51, that American freedom of intervention in Latin America — traditionally guaranteed by the unilaterally-declared
and self-serving Monroe Doctrine — and in other areas as well, would not be
hampered by legalism or Soviet obstructionism at the Security Council. The United
States also controlled the World Bank and the International Monetary Fund (IMF)
and thus controlled and imposed its economic and trade terms on foes and friends
alike, dismantling the British-dominated Sterling trade bloc and insisting on an
open world market, presumed to be vital for the successful international function-
ing of the capitalist system.

Europe had been ravaged by the war and was preoccupied with the urgent
task of reconstruction for which it desperately needed American help — finally
given under the terms of the Marshall Plan. The Third World had not yet
awakened and much of it remained controlled by the weakened but still ambitious
European colonial powers. China was still pro-American and had not yet been
"lost" to the communists. Although the Red Army stood astride Eastern and much
of Central Europe, the Soviet Union had lost 20 million people in the war; its
economy was virtually ruined; much of its infrastructures devastated; many of its
towns and villages destroyed, and it faced an enormous and costly task of
reconstruction. The United States stood on top of the world. It intended to
dominate it, shape it on its image and open it to its trade and corporate prophets.

When the Soviet Union refused to cooperate and open Eastern and Central
Europe to American trade and influence, and subsequently emerged as a military
superpower, the cold war ensued. It was mainly a struggle between two competing
ideological systems of economic and political organization and was largely fought
in the new emerging Third World, for its resources, its markets, its strategic
facilities and its political loyalties. The two competing superpowers also fought by
proxy many "hot" wars to the death...of their overarmed Third World allies, but
wars between them became unthinkable. Their nuclear arsenals could assure their
mutual destruction. And this certainty of Mutual Assured Destruction (MAD) became the basis of a global balance of power and terror that was publicly endorsed
by a more or less cordial entente between the two superpowers, but constantly undermined by their machinations and incessant manipulative attempts at enhancing their respective advantages.

At the end of the war against Iraq, the United States stood supreme in its
military domination of the post-Cold War era. It had led a massive war — thanks
to the financial support of allies, the political paralysis of a former superpower, and
the helpless acquiescence of the United Nations — and had achieved success as a
self-appointed coalition leader. It may be true, however, that the United States is experiencing economic, social and moral decline, as many Europeans claim.[9] Consider for instance the fact that in 1960 the United States accounted for 40 percent of
the world gross national product; in 1990 it was down to less than 25 percent; in
1985 the United States became the first and largest debtor nation in the world for
the first time since 1913, owing the outside world one trillion dollars. Japan and
Europe, ravaged and devastated by World War II, are today economic giants seeking to play a more assertive political role in a world no longer dominated by
American corporate power. Still, the United States had waged a cold war and an
arms race which bankrupted its chief rival. It had fought and destroyed the first
challenge from an ambitious regional power to its newly-established supremacy in

the post-Cold-War era. The Soviet Union has gone and the Third World and the Non-Alignment Movement are in disarray. The massive war against Iraq and the impressive display of unmatched weapon technology provided American leaders with the backdrop necessary for laying exclusive claim to charting the course of the new world order.

A former State Department official, writing as a private citizen and therefore expressing no official views, claims that the new world order consecrated the United States as the supreme power of the world, and thus marks the end of history and the last stage of human socio-political evolution. And this is because "in all its crucial fundamentals, the US constitutional order of liberal democracy and economic system of entrepreneurial capitalism define the end point of human political history, the very end of technological time. This is it: the goal of several millennia of human groping and searching and dying in the dark — through wars, utopian experiments, eugenic pogroms, authoritarian bureaucracies, philosopher kingdoms, nationalist frenzies, revolutionary purges, totalitarian horrors — looking for the one true way, the way according best with the real intrinsic nature of the human being." Apparently dismissing the new world order if it accepted the sovereign equality of non-democratic nations, scorning the United Nations as a reactionary alliance, rejecting notions of cultural and moral relativism in favour of the superiority of Judeo-Christian ideals, the author writes: "The universalist moral codes of the Judeo-Christian tradition, with their revolutionary claim of basic equality and moral autonomy for all individuals, are the foundation of liberal democracy and the new global system."[10]

But other people, and there are other peoples whose different visions emanate from their own cultural, historical, and socio-political experiences which cannot simply be dismissed as irrelevant or *passé* because of the collapse of one superpower or the rise to uncontested hegemony of the other, may not see the new world order in this light. In his book *Une certaine ideé de la République m'amène à...* former French Defense Minister Jean-Pierre Chevènement quoted President Charles de Gaulle, who jealously defended French independence against American conceptions of a world order, saying to French writer and Minister of Cultural Affairs Andér Malraux in 1969: "The day when the Americans will become consciously the masters of the world you will see how far their imperialism will go..."[11] The extension of the American military, economic and cultural power to vast areas of the world may not always be welcomed with unrestrained enthusiasm by cultures and societies that have experienced only coercive relationships with the United States. Announcing the ultimate, final and irreversible triumph of the current capitalist economic model and the constitutional order of liberal democracy, and anticipating their adoption by the rest of the world is too indiscriminate, definitive, and complacently ethnocentric a view of the current stage of human development. The capitalist economic model and the liberal political order have not sprung from some higher infallible moral authority overnight; they have evolved over hundreds of years not without pains, sufferings, economic depressions, aggressive competitions, colonizing ventures and outright wars.

In his criticism of Cartesian epistemology, eighteenth-century historian Giambattista Vico suggested that all history is essentially the history of thought, ideas and human relations; there is no prior plan of unrealized intention which is gradually taking shape and inexorably moving towards a finite end or an ideal eternal of perfection similar to that created by Plato's God. Unlike the realm of physical nature which will always elude total comprehension because it remains external to man, the field of history is defined by the man-made ideas, their evolution, their growth and the visions they encompass and articulate. Certainly it is more comprehensible to man than physical nature but it is also as dynamic a process as human thoughts and ideas and the interactions of human communities; it remains an eternal ideal whose course is driven by the history of all nations and their interactions. To argue, as Francis Fukuyama does in his end of history thesis, that the present stage of evolutionary progress defines the end point of human history is to presumptuously set limitations to the creative, regenerative, and liberating power of the human spirit and the human will.

The triumph of the basic proposition that what is good for the individual is good for the society does not negate nor banish from competitive real and potential existence the validity of the various cultural and spiritual definitions of what is "good" in the first place. The revolutionary claim of the basic equality of all individuals has indeed been at the foundations of liberal democracy, but it is a self-evident truth that the existence of a claim does not guarantee its application. Consider the history of slavery, of anti-Semitism, of colonial domination and of the Black civil rights struggle; in these intercultural, economic and political encounters liberal democracy was guided more by selfishly-defined and coercively-implemented ethnocentrist interests than by that revolutionary claim of basic equality of all human beings.

In his monumental 52-year project *A Study of History* Arnold Toynbee, arguably the most distinguished historian of the twentieth century, summed up the multiple and competing historical tendencies of socially-organized communities in two principal currents. In the new age the dominant note in the corporate consciousness of communities is that of being parts of some larger universe; in the past age the chief characteristic of their consciousness was that of aspiring to be universes in themselves. The validity of this observation and the dynamic conflict between these two tendencies are not negated by the collapse of one superpower or the triumph of the system of economic and socio-political organization of the other. There is no telling what the last stage of human socio-political evolution will be like nor when it will be reached, but the constant striving for improvement to the human condition will assuredly have gained a great deal when the enlightened liberal ideals are backed by an active, unambiguous, and unwavering commitment to the overriding interest of the world as a human community rather than as a collection of competing entities wielding individual monopolies over the instruments of violence, and selectively promoting and defending narrowly defined national interests. History as a registry of conflicts, crimes and human follies perpetuated in the name of *raison d'état* will cease to exist when liberal democracy's claim of basic human equality is backed by the resources and the political will necessary to liberate humanity from the oppression of injustice, poverty, malnutrition, and wars.

In their *Toward A Just World Order*, Richard Falk, Samuel Kim and Saul Mendlovitz discuss the various studies for the World Order Project compiled and published throughout the 1970s under the title *Preferred World Orders for the 1990s.* Their conceptual framework produces a global entity in which the world is materially, ecologically and spiritually integrated to make the *unity* of the human species the starting point of prescription. Their world order values are implicit in the postulate of human solidarity against conditions of oppression, mass poverty, and ecological and geopolitical dangers. To achieve a just world order they called for fundamental structural changes to the existing framework of international relations in which power is distributed unequally while authority is shared among legally equal sovereign states. A central feature of the required structural change is the relinquishing of State monopoly over warmaking prerogatives and the creation of a world police force answerable to some form of world government which preserved the autonomy of nation-States in other matters. The selective diminution of State power will be accompanied by the valorization of the underlying diversity of planetary life, creating a blend of centralization and decentralization, dismantling the system of global militarization and replacing it with one based on human solidarity for the creation of a just world order. But beneficiaries of the State system showed neither receptivity nor political will to diminish the State system monopoly over the instruments of violence.

The end of the cold war and its vicious circle of ideological rivalry and self-perpetuating arms race created unique opportunities for renewed efforts to move towards a new world order. The need for urgent action was dramatized by the fate of former Yugoslavia where Bosnia was being victimized by Serbian attacks and daily scenes of blood baths, a drama which moved the United Nations to slow action while Washington took its time to "consider" its options. Unfortunate Bosnia does not have oil. Consequently thousands of Muslim Slavs and Croats were being killed and, as the *New York Times* aptly put it, the world watched murder. The drama moved UN Secretary General Boutros Ghali to present to the Security Council a set of proposals aimed at strengthening the United Nations' original mandate of peaceful resolution of disputes and maintenance of peace and security. Ghali called for more binding arbitration by the World Court to prevent disputes from erupting into wars; he also proposed the strengthening of the UN peace-keeping force by activating the dormant UN Military Staff Committee, expanding multinational force at the disposal of the Security Council and requiring delinquent members to pay up their UN dues. The *New York Times* called Ghali's proposals "an example of the new leadership needed in this new era."[12]

American leadership will set the tone, shape the form, and provide the direction of the new world order. The United States has a particular responsibility and a unique ability to facilitate the implementation of these and other proposals and move the United Nations towards some form of genuine international multilateralism. Or, alternatively it can succumb to the temptation of using the United Nations as an instrument of its foreign policy. It can opt for a strong UN organization in which responsibilities are shared, power is wisely and democratically exercised and where the human, economic and ecological problems of the world are tackled with the unity of the human race as the starting point of action. Or it may rely on its preponderance of power, in a system of balance of power where American might rules supreme, as the ultimate guarantor of a *Pax Americana* while the basic problems of militarization, poverty, unequal distribution of wealth remain fundamentally unresolved. It may display the wisdom of mature strength or succumb to, as the late William Fullbright put it, the arrogance of power; promote collective internationalism or opt for hegemonic American unilateralism.

Two crucial documents recently prepared by officials from the Pentagon, the State Department and the White House and clearly representing official American thinking, provide what may be considered an American blueprint for the new world order. The first is a classified 46-page document prepared by the Pentagon in conjunction with the National Security Council and in consultation with the President and his advisors. Its drafting was supervised by Paul D. Wolfowitz, the Pentagon's Undersecretary for policy. The second document was prepared by a committee of experts headed by Admiral David Jeremia, Assistant to the Chairman of the Joint Chiefs of Staff General Collin Powell. Both documents spell out in detail various scenarios of conflicts and possible challenges to the United States' undisputed supremacy, and articulate a set of American political and military objectives and policy guidelines. As such, they provide an authoritative and clear exposition of official American thinking about the new world order and the American role in it which may be summarized in the following points:

1. The unique position of the United States as the only superpower left after the collapse of the Soviet Union must be preserved against all challenges from anywhere in the world. To this end, the first political and military objective of the United States in the new world order must be "to prevent the emergence of a new rival, either in the territory of the former Soviet Union or elsewhere…" Specifically, the "less visible" victory over communism which facilitated a greater integration of Germany and Japan into a U.S.- led system of security, has created a situation where the United States must prevent these two powers from possessing nuclear weapons, and thus from being able to challenge, or even compete with the United States world leadership.

2. American domination of the new world order must be clear, unequivocal and American leadership strong and assertive, if America is to maintain its supremacy unchallenged. To achieve this, regional powers in Europe and elsewhere must be discouraged from trying to change their present status or challenge American domination. The United States must therefore strive to "convince potential competitors that they need not aspire to a greater role" in the new world order. With regard to advanced industrial nations, the United States must convince them that the established order sufficiently serves their interests so as to "discourage them from challenging our leadership or seeking to overturn the established political and economic order."

3. The United States has in effect become the only power capable of enforcing respect for the established order and while it may not wish to act as a policeman redressing every wrong, it will nonetheless decide which wrongs may be overlooked and ignored and which transgressions must be redressed by force if necessary: "We will retain the pre-eminent responsibility for addressing *selectively* those wrongs which threaten not only our interests, but those of our allies and friends, or which could seriously unsettle international relations." (emphasis added). First among the vital interests identified as requiring forceful action was the "access to vital raw materials, primarily Persian Gulf oil…"

4. The United States must support the spread of capitalism and the move towards the generalization of market-based economies in Eastern Europe as the best way of guaranteeing that "no hostile power is able to consolidate control over the resources within the former Soviet Union…" American strategy in Europe must "refocus on precluding the emergence of any potential future global com-

petitor." To this end, the United States will rely on its massive nuclear strategic arsenal and will have its strategic nuclear weapons "continue to target vital aspects of the former Soviet military establishment," because Russia will remain "the only power in the world with the capability of destroying the United States." The United States must therefore continue its armament programmes and must strive for the "early introduction" of the global anti-missile defense system (popularly known as Star Wars).

5. Although it is now commonly recognized that Western Europe is no longer threatened by any power from the East, the United States does not want to dismantle NATO which served to institutionalize its dominant role in Europe. As a result, the United States will oppose any European move toward greater independence vis-à-vis Washington and will insist that NATO continue to provide the basis of any security system in Europe and remain "the channel for US influence..." Accordingly, the United States must "seek to prevent the emergence of European-only security arrangements which would undermine NATO..." In short, as American opposition to European-based Security initiatives at the NATO Conference in Rome in November 1991 clearly demonstrated, there will be no defense of Europe unless it is based on American doctrines and priorities. Still, the French and the Germans moved in the direction of greater independence anyway and, in May 1992, agreed on the formation of a Franco-German army as the nucleus of a European army to be formed by 1995. Secretary Cheney expressed American displeasure and repeated the commitment to maintaining the NATO structures.

6. The United States should in fact extend its pre-eminent role in Western Europe to the former territories of the Soviet Union and to East European countries which used to belong to the defunct Warsaw Pact. To this effect, the United States should provide a security guarantee to Eastern and Central European countries "analogous to those we have extended to Persian Gulf states," and seek to facilitate their integration into NATO.

7. Asia is now the region with the heaviest concentration of political and economic beliefs at variance with the American system. The United States intends to maintain an imposing military posture there to ensure that no regional threats are posed to its interests and friends in the region. The United States must therefore maintain its "status as a military power of the first magnitude in the area," to prevent the emergence of any power seeking to dominate the region or to challenge the established order.

8. The United States will use force if necessary to prevent the proliferation of nuclear weapons and other weapons of mass destruction particularly to countries such as North Korea, Iraq, and the republics of the former Soviet Union.

9. In the Middle East, the overall American objective is to ensure that the United States "remain the predominant outside power in the region and preserve the US and Western access to the region's oil." The war against Iraq demonstrated that it was "fundamentally important" to prevent any hostile regional power or alignment of powers from dominating the region. It is therefore the intention of the United States to continue to rely on military presence and military alliances in the region to deter any challenge to the established order.[13]

There is little mention in the American blueprint for the new world order of international law, collective internationalism, or democratic management of international affairs. The emphasis is clearly and unambiguously on the reliance on American military power as the principal instrument of preserving American domination of the new world order. There is no mention of the United Nations even though the organization was effectively used to give a cover of legality to a massive war which supposedly ushered in the new world order. There is a brief mention in the Wolfowitz document about the fact that coalitions "hold considerable promise for promoting collective action" as in the war against Iraq, but far more significant is the emphasis the document places on American ability to intervene militarily with or without international backing. And this because of "the sense that the world order is ultimately backed by the United States," and therefore "the United States should be postured to act independently when collective actions cannot be orchestrated." The new world order has room for only one dominant military power and therefore American leaders "must maintain the mechanism for deterring potential competitors from even aspiring to a larger regional or global role..."[14]

In effect, American military preponderance is so great there is not even the usual need for grounding American actions in a semblance of legality and international legitimacy; power seems to provide its own justification. The primary mission of the United States in the new world order is not to ensure that collective internationalism is accepted through a reinvigorated United Nations, but rather to ensure American monopoly of preponderant power, prevent the emergence of a global competitor, forestall and foil any attempt at reconstructing the Soviet Union, prevent the European allies from developing an independent system of security which could enhance their independence and induce them to aspire to some global leadership role, and stop the emergence of any regional power or coalition of powers capable of challenging American domination. To accomplish this, the militarization of American foreign policy must continue and traditional American penchant for military interventions to *selectively* redress wrongs must be backed by a growing military arsenal. Given the United States' relative economic decline and growing dependency on foreign investments and strategic resources including oil, the determination to perpetuate American military supremacy and to prevent any challenges to it may grow as the need to preserve a precarious balance of economic power becomes increasingly founded on military might as its ultimate guarantor.

Conclusion

The Iranian revolution in 1979 and the removal of Egypt from the Arab-Israeli conflict after the Camp David treaty, brokered by Washington and excluding the Soviet Union and the United Nations, radically altered the geostrategic considerations that prevailed in the Middle East up till the end of the 1970s. Iran was no longer part of the American strategic axis. Egypt had been for some time no longer allied with the Soviet Camp.

In fact, Egypt became, thanks to Camp David, the leader of the so-called "moderate" Arab regimes and as such became an essential pillar of the new American strategic axis encompassing Israel, Egypt and Turkey. At the same time, American preoccupation with the preservation of their traditional interests in the region shifted from the primary need to ensure Israel's military domination of the region, to the imperious necessity of defending America's oil interests. The shift of emphasis came as a result of the consequences of the 1973 Arab-Israeli war and the unwelcome display by the Arabs of a capacity for coordinated political and economic actions which presented an opportunity and a challenge to American policy makers. The opportunity was to separate Egypt from the Arab camp, a process which Kissinger commenced with the Sinai I and Sinai II disengagement agreements he engineered with Sadat's enthusiastic support. The process put an end to Egyptian belligerent status with Israel and neutralized its role in the Arab-Israeli conflict. At the same time the agreements were followed by the most massive American military and strategic commitments to Israel, transforming its huge superiority into military supremacy over the region. With Israeli supremacy assured, American policy planners focused their attention on access to, and influence over Middle East oil.

The 1973 Arab-Israeli war also presented a serious challenge: it showed the potential for coordinated Arab and Third World economic actions, particularly with regard to crucial resources as Middle East oil. Huge increases in the price of oil following the war had serious economic repercussions in the industrialized nations but, more significantly, it represented an affirmation of economic independence from a Third World increasingly insistent on a new economic order. As pro-Zionist commentator Robert Tucker, urging greater militarization of American foreign policy, put it in *Commentary* (January 1975), the crisis went beyond American need for and Arab control of Middle East oil; it fundamentally had to do with the growing pressure of the rapidly multiplying people of the Third World for a greater share of the cake. The challenge had to be confronted lest it set an example for similar challenges with the potential of upsetting the established economic relationship between the industrialized nations and the Third World countries. Secretary of State Henry Kissinger and Secretary of Defense James Schlesinger multiplied the threat of American military intervention to take control of Middle East oil fields. But with Sadat co-opted and speeding along the path of a separate agreement and separation from the Arab world (the sixth world power) and pro-American conservative petromonarchies willing to cooperate, the Ford administration thought it had diffused the potential for another political use of Arab economic power. The threat came from wholly unexpected direction: Iran. By the end of the 1970s, American traditional foreign policy goals in the Middle East of ensuring Israel's superiority and having ready and cheap access to the region's oil had become uneven on the scale of priority: Camp David had ensured the first, the Iranian revolution had threatened the second.

The Iran-Iraq war seemed like a good opportunity for weakening both the Iranian threat to the pro-American oil-producing conservative monarchies of the Gulf, and the so-called radical Arab threat to the Camp David order. Iran threatened to export its Muslim revolution and its anti-American ideology to the traditionally pro-American regimes of Saudi Arabia and the Gulf Emirates. Iraq had led the campaign to ostracize Egypt from the Arab camp after Cairo signed a separate peace treaty with Israel, and threatened to lead disaffected Arabs against accommodation with Israel. Iran and Iraq were left, and indeed helped, to prolong their war and weaken each other as much as possible. But the war brought Iraq closer to Egypt and the conservative Arab regimes: Iraq fought the war largely with money from Saudi Arabia and Kuwait, and partly with the military help of Egypt whose regime accepted to provide a security commitment to deter any Iranian military threat to the Gulf region.

But it was an alliance of convenience. It ended when the Iran-Iraq war came to an end. The political philosophy which brought Egypt into the American camp and ensured a close relationship between Saudi Arabia, Kuwait and the United States, was in sharp contrast to the one advocated by the ruling Baath regime in Iraq. Whereas Cairo, Riyadh and Kuwait saw in the collapse of communism and the disintegration of the Soviet Union a vindication of their political vision which relied on the alliance with, and was necessarily subordinated to, the interests of the United States, Baghdad, and particularly Saddam Hussein, who had relied heavily on support from Moscow, reasoned correctly that the end of the cold war consecrated the domination of the only superpower left, the United States. Regional powers such as Iraq could therefore only rely on themselves and had either to accept the primacy of American interests, vision, and political priorities or place themselves in a position of relative strength from which to bargain with the United States. Saddam Hussein opted for the latter, gambling that his bid for regional power status will not be challenged given the price he paid in blood, as he often claimed, to defend the Arab regimes of the Gulf. But Iraqi ambitions of regional superpower status carried with them the inevitability of affecting Iraq's bilateral relations with weaker neighbours such as Kuwait with whom historical disputes had never been satisfactorily resolved. An Iraqi-Kuwaiti clash occurred with Kuwait accusing Iraq of bullying, blackmail and extortion, and Iraq accusing Kuwait of collaboration with Washington in an economic warfare designed to stifle Iraqi efforts at economic reconstruction and military modernization.

A similar collision occurred between the Bush administration and the Saddam Hussein regime. Whereas the end of the Iran-Iraq war ended Baghdad's usefulness to Washington, Iraq was interested in building on the military and strategic cooperation it received from the United States during the war. Saddam Hussein argued that in defending the petromonarchies of the Gulf against the Iranian threat he has assured the survival of pro-American regimes and defended American interests in the region. Washington, however, and given the nature of the special Israeli-American relationship, was necessarily more sensitive to the Israeli argument that the real threat in the Middle East did not come from Israeli repression of Palestinian nationalism nor from continued Israeli occupation of Arab territories but rather from the emergence of Iraq as an ambitious regional power ready to challenge the status quo. Since American policy planners had defined the new threat to American interests in the post Cold-War era as coming from "instability," any challenges from regional powers like Iraq to the "stability" of the dominant order in the Middle East became of necessity a threat to American vital interests. As Israel's friends in the Congress initiated an anti-Iraq campaign and an obliging and collaborative media began a process of demonization of Iraq as a dangerous State that must be confronted, the United States and Iraq were set on a confrontation course.

When the Iraqi-Kuwaiti collision occurred and Iraqi troops invaded Kuwait, Washington moved in to quickly foreclose the possibility of a negotiated settlement and oppose Arab attempts at a political settlement that could get Iraqi troops out of Kuwait but leave Iraqi ambitions unchanged and unchallenged.

Confrontation with Iraq was decided upon by the Bush administration "almost instantaneously," and the question became how to sell the confrontation course to the American and international public opinion. As John MacArthur showed in his book *Second Front,* John Fialka in his *Hotel Warriors,* and Martin Yant in his *Desert Mirage,* the management of the confrontation was masterful; the control of information and disinformation calculated, purposeful, and deliberate; the Orwellian rhetoric brilliantly constructed, self-serving and rigorously sustained, the "army of metaphors" rich, evocative, and provocatively effective in communicating their own "truth" about the conflict and the war. Arab and European peace initiatives, often accepted by Iraq as a basis for negotiations were almost systematically rejected by Washington which adopted a single, unchanging, unvaried, and unalterably adamantine position: unconditional capitulation or war. But to soften the harshness of such an irrational stand, the Bush administration went through the motion of diplomatic "exercises" to show a willingness to go the "extra mile" for peace. In reality, as the American position at the Baker-Aziz talks in Geneva revealed, Bush remained immovably intractable in his ultimatum of capitulation or war.

Washington's ability to marshall support and its confidence that it could see through and win a major war with Iraq were of-course largely facilitated by the international environment. The collapse of communism fundamentally modified the balance of power in the United Nations which moved with unprecedented resolve and speed to condemn Iraq and impose sweeping sanctions and a blockade against it. A new world order was being shaped at the United Nations, but it was not an order based on the fundamental principle of peaceful resolution of disputes on which the Charter of the organization was based. Rather, it was an order based on the foreign policy orientation of the only remaining superpower. The United Nations organization, vilified, maligned, and violently denounced for its dictatorship of majority when Third-World nations used it to voice their grievances, became a rejuvenated, respected and hailed international organization when it marched to the drums of its undisputed dominant power. It obligingly enacted binding Security Council Resolutions that often reflected already effective American foreign policy orientations and decisions. Thus, Bush was so confident of automatic UN support that he decided, in early November, to send an additional 200,000 American soldiers to Saudi Arabia, and change the American forces' mission in the Gulf from defensive to offensive, before he went to the United Nations to seek authorization for the use of force   which he did not do until December.

From the very beginning of the war against Iraq in January 1991, it was clear from the massive scale of the attacks and from the targets being hit, that the American war aims went well beyond the eviction of Iraq from the Kuwait. They clearly encompassed the destruction of Iraq's military power and its industrial-military base in such a way as to completely eliminate Baghdad's regional power ambitions. Specifically, a crucial war aim was the destruction of Baghdad's real and potential power to challenge the Israeli-dominated military order and the conservative Arab regime-dominated economic order in the region. Both the Soviet Union and the United Nations were kept at bay and reduced to bit players in this unfolding first military test of the new world order. Moscow's feeble attempts to save Baghdad from the added humiliation of a ground war after Iraq accepted to unconditionally withdraw from Kuwait, were politely rebuffed by Bush who told Gorbachev to "Bug off." Before the war, Washington had agreed to go through the motions of some diplomatic initiatives which were candidly described by National Security Advisor Brent Scocrowft as just "exercises" for the sake of winning public support for the confrontation course. Now that the war was going well and Washington was close to what was considered a total victory, the diplomatic initiatives, particularly those of a former superpower, could safely be treated with disdain.

There was no room for even marginal political manoeuvres in the new balance of power, advertised as a new world order, to lend respectability to the pretence of great power cooperation when there was only one real great military power. Cooperation with a former superpower was far less important than the administration of a bloody and humiliating lesson to a regional Third World leader who dared to challenge the new world order. And this served the credibility George Bush was anxious to preserve when he said that after the war "what we say goes." The war has thus demonstrated the risk inherent in disregarding the realities of the new balance of power and the danger of challenging them.

By challenging the political, economic and military order in the Middle East, Saddam Hussein believed that he could negotiate with the United States improvements to the economic and security position of his country. Further, by challenging Israeli military hegemony in the region when he threatened to respond to any Israeli attack with all weapons including missiles, and by insisting on linking his occupation of Kuwait with Israeli occupation of Arab territories, Saddam Hussein was putting into devilishly daring practice an old reality of inter-State relations articulated as a major concept in the classic writings of the nineteenth century Prussian military theorist Karl von Clausewitz, namely that war is the continuation of politics by other means. But Saddam Hussein's fatal miscalculation lay in his assumption that *Iraq* could emulate great power behaviours. In the American and Israeli eyes, Saddam Hussein committed the unpardonable error of violating the cardinal cosmic rule of the inequality of nations, enforced for their own benefit by the great and the mighty: *quod licet Jovi non licet bovi,* which roughly means that what is permitted to the Gods is not permitted to Swine.

And Washington intends to make sure that the lessons of the war against Iraq are not lost on the Third World, the former republics of the Soviet Union or for that matter even the friendly advanced industrialized nations. The new world order is and will be dominated, alone, by the United States. To enforce this new world order, the United States intends to ensure that its military might is ostentatiously present around the globe sending the important message of deterrence that the United States is a military power "of the first magnitude." Even the European allies will be discouraged from trying to disengage their security system from the American-dominated NATO and from even aspiring to leadership roles.

After the war against Iraq, the Bush administration succumbed to the temptation — and Israeli demand, that the uniquely favourable balance of power be used as the basis for any negotiated settlement of the Arab-Israeli conflict. Accordingly, Washington rejected calls for an active role for the United Nations in the Middle East Peace Conference, convened in Madrid in October 1991. The international organization, built on the primacy of the principle of peaceful resolution of disputes, seems to have been an effective instrument through which to wage total war against Iraq, but somehow was judged a liability for negotiating peace in the Arab-Israeli-Palestinian conflict. By excluding an active role for the United Nations, Washington essentially downgraded the importance of the principles of justice and international law embodied in the various UN resolutions with regard to the

Palestine and Arab-Israeli conflicts. Instead, the Bush administration gave in to Israeli demand that the parties negotiate alone without outside interference, neither from the United Nations nor from the United States itself whose official policy is, after all, opposed to Israeli occupation of Arab territories.

The direct bilateral negotiations between Israel and Syria, Israel and Lebanon, and Israel and a joint Jordanian-Palestinian delegation, was in fact cast within the context of the existing power relationship between these parties individually and collectively, on the one hand, and Israel, on the other hand. Now, the balance of power in the region has never been more heavily tilted in favour of Israel: Israel's military domination of the region has never been greater. With the elimination of Iraq as a military power, the last of the so-called confrontation States, Arab military challenges to Israeli hegemony has never been weaker. They are virtually nonexistent. Egypt has a treaty with Israel; Syria could not recapture its Golan Heights from Israel in 1973 when it fought along side Egypt; without Egypt, it is today even less likely to even contemplate the military option. Jordan and Lebanon are both militarily insignificant. The leadership of the Palestinian people has been excluded from the negotiating table. Politically, the only superpower sponsoring the peace talks has been Israel's traditional and virtually unconditional supporter. The Soviet Union, the Arabs' traditional supporter, no longer exists. The United Nations, whose resolutions recognize the legitimacy of Palestinian demands, is excluded. The European Community which supports the international consensus, UN resolutions and Palestinians' right to self-determination, has been neutralized. At the same time, as the negotiation process continues, Israel continues its policy of building or expanding Jewish settlements, whether these are called "political" or "strategic" settlements, continuing the process of occupation and dispossession. Moreover, Israel made it clear that the fact that the United Nations voted, in late 1991, to repeal its 1975 resolution qualifying Zionism as "a form of racism," would not affect Israel's disregard for the international organization: "If, because of this vote," said the Israeli delegate in New York, "we are now asked to give the United Nations a place in the peace process, our answer is a very clear 'no', nothing has changed."[15]

Secretary Baker admitted, in a television interview on PBS that the Middle East peace conferences which the United States convened were "basically constructed on Israel's terms."[16] If the basis of negotiations at these peace-talks were to continue to exclude the UN and its resolutions on Palestine and the occupied Arab territories, and rely on what the parties themselves, alone with no outside interference, left to their own devices and power, can agree on, the distribution of relative power between the negotiating parties will fundamentally be the ultimate arbiter, just as it was at the Camp David negotiations. But since the parties bring to the negotiation table vastly unequal military and political power, the asymmetry is even greater here than it was at Camp David. And that is because at Camp David Saddat offered Israeli leaders at least the strategic advantages inherent in his removal of Egypt from the Arab camp and the consequent opportunity of consolidating Israeli occupation of Arab territories. The Palestinian and Arab parties have no such tangible goestrategic cards to play; they could only invoke the justice of their cause and the support of the international community for their international law-grounded demands. In a rational world this should be enough to ensure reasonable success. But we live in this world. Given their context, the negotiations will therefore necessarily be reduced to what the Israelis are prepared to give and what the Arabs and the Palestinians have increasingly fewer options but to grudgingly take it or leave it. Such an outcome would reflect the realities of power, not of shared values.

Such an outcome would be regrettable and would do little to advance the interests of peace-defined positively as a community of interests and shared values. Power has unfortunately only too often determined the nature of peace between former adversaries and although the present context of Middle East peace negotiations seems grounded on the relative power between the negotiating parties, there is an alternative and competing vision based not on the relationship of power but rather on a shared value: the equality of peoples and their rights to live in freedom and dignity. Such a vision can materialize if a courageous American administration working with a generous Israeli leadership, animated no longer by ideological parochialism but increasingly by enlightened realism, can agree that an Arab-Israeli-Palestinian peace negotiated on the basis of justice and international legitimacy would produce a peace of satisfaction. And this would be a more reliable basis for peaceful co-existence.

Notes

1. See Lahouari Addi, "Algérie: le dérapage," *Le Monde Diplomatique*, February, 1992; see also Jacques Berque, "Que veulent les islamistes au Maghreb?," *Le Monde Diplomatique*, February, 1992; see also Ignacio Ramonet, "Algérie: dernière chance avant le chaos," *Le Monde Diplomatique*, December, 1991; Lahouari Addi, "L'armée au secours de la démocratie en Algérie?, *Le Monde Diplomatique*, August, 1991.
2. "The Untold Story of Pan Am 103," *Time* magazine, April 27, 1992.
3. Mohamed Sid-Ahmed, "Greater Challenges for Arabs in 1992?" *Al-Ahram Weekly* January 2, 1992.
4. See David Hirst, "No Time to put the boot in," *Guardian Weekly*, March 29, 1992.
5. Prime Minister Yitzhak Shamir, "Remarks on the Golan Heights, Jerusalem," March 18, 1991, *Mideast Mirror*, March 19, 1991, reproduced in *Journal of Palestine Studies* vol. XX, no. 4 (Summer 1991), p. 176.
6. *CNN*, June 27, 1992.
7. *New York Times*, June 24, 1992.
8. See Paul Kessler and Joseph Parisi, "L'avenir compromis des Palestiniens," *Le Monde Diplomatique*, February, 1992.
9. See Marie-France Toinet, "Comment les États-Unis ont perdu les moyens de leur hégémonie," *Le Monde Diplomatique*, June, 1992.
10. Francis Fukuyama, *The End of History And The Last Man* (New York, Free Press, 1992), reviewed by George Gilder in The *Washington Post* reproduced in The *Guardian Weekly* February 9, 1992.
11. Paul-Marie De La Gorce, "De la liberté des nations," *Le Monde Diplomatique*, February, 1992.
12. *New York Times*, June 28, 1992.
13. See the *New York Times*, "U.S. Strategy Plan Calls For Insuring No Rivals Develop," March 8, 1992; see also the Pentagon's Plan: "Prevent the Re-Emergence of a New

Rival," reproduced in the *New York Times,* March 8, 1992; see also *International Herald Tribune,* March 9, 1992, and February 18, 1992.

14. *New York Times,* March 8, 1992.
15. *Le Monde,* December 18, 1991.
16. PBS, April 1, 1992.

INDEX

ABC Nightline, 143, 149, 159, 165
ABC Television, 50, 159, 164
Abdel-Fadil, Mahmoud, 65
Abdullah, Crown Prince of Saudi Arabia, 200
Abdullhadi, Rami S., 39n
Abed, George T., 225n
Abu Dhabi, 192, 194
Abu Ghazala, Field Marshal, 129
Abu Iyyad, 229
Abu-Jihad, 165, 169
Abu-Lughod, Ibrahim, 14
Achille Lauro, 125
Adams, Michael, 7
Addi, Lahouari, 271n
Afghanistan, 97, 105, 182, 204, 212
Aflaq, Michel, 192
Aga Khan, Prince Safruddin, 250
Aghouri, 110
Ahmad, Eqbal, 54
Ahtisaari, Martti, 7, 248
Aid, Adel, 108, 109
Akins, James E., 195n
Al-Ahali, 91n, 118
Al-Ahram, 48, 110, 126, 129, 204, 257
Al-Akhbar, 48, 110, 118
Al-Ashtall, Abdallaah, 7, 204, 250
Al-Baghdadi, Abdel-Latif, 99
Al-Bahrawi, Said, 135n
Al-Baze, Oussama, 94n
Al-Chalabi, Issam Abdel Rahim, 208
Al-Dawa, 108
Al-Ghamry, Atif, 195n
Al-Hakim, Tawfiq, 48, 124
Al-Hassan, Hani, 35
Al-Hawali, Lutfi, 196n
Al-Jumhouria, 118, 122
Al-Mashat, Abdul-Monem, 135n
Al-Sabah, Prince Seilman , 7, 197
Al-Sabah, Sheikh Jabir al-Ahmed, Emir of
  Kuwait, 197
Al-Sadawi, Nawal, 120
Al-Shafii, Hussein, 99
Al-Sharq al-Awsat, 228
Al-Tahriah Palace, 55
Al-Telmissany, Omar, 120
Al-Tuhamy, Hassan, 61, 68
Alexandria, 60, 65, 76, 106, 113, 128, 197, 199, 200
Algeria, 105, 205, 216, 228, 256
Algiers, 164, 169, 238; accords, 183, 227
Ali, Abdel Monem Said, 137n
Ali, Shafiq Ahmad, 135n
Allon, Yigal, 30; Plan, 31
America-Israel Political Action Committee, 257
American Council for Judaism, 29
American goals in the Gulf, 211

American Israel Public Affairs Committee
  (AIPAC), 169
Amiel, Barbara, 173n
Amin, Mohamed Fahim, 118
Amin, Samir, 93n
Amman, 31, 129, 164, 198; summit, 129
Anglo-Arab compact, 12
Anglo-French Declaration, 12
Anglo-Iranian Oil Company, 215
Anti-Semitism, 146, 149, 223, 261
Antonius, George, 37n
Aoun, Michel, 208
Apartheid, 155
Appleman, William, 214
Aqaba, Gulf of, 161, 162, 163
Arab and Palestinian positions on the conflict,
  21
Arab Defence Pact, 129
Arab League, 74, 87, 101, 104, 182, 189, 193-202,
  228, 231
Arafat, Yasser, 25, 35, 125, 128, 159, 164, 165,
  169, 204, 209, 229 Arens, Moshe, 221
Arnett, Peter, 243
Arnold, Steven, General, 247
Aron, Raymond, 34
Aruri, Nasser, 91n
Assad, Hafez al, 207, 208
Aswan, 55, 71, 116; Declaration, 71
Ausland, John, C., 220
Austland, John C., 226n
Awad, Muhsin, 109, 126
Aziz, Tarik, 193, 228, 237, 237, 238, 240, 243, 245,
  268

Baath Party and government, 180, 192, 249, 267
Bab el-Mandeb, 55
Badeau, John, 188
Badi, Joseph, 40n
Baghdad; 1, 2, 6, 180-267; Pact, 180, 209;
  Summit, 130, 192
Baha Eddin, Ahmad, 48, 68
Baker, James, 7, 18, 32, 169, 194, 198, 208, 210,
  236, 237, 238, 239, 245, 247, 268, 270
Balfour, Arthur, Lord, 14; Declaration, 1, 12, 14,
  58, 132, 139, 140
Balt, Paul, 195n
Baltimore program, 14
Balz, Dan, 224n
Bandar bin Sultan, Prince, 199, 237
Bantustans, 69
Bar-Lev, Haim, 163
Bar-On, Mordechai, 156
Bar-Zohar, Michael, 16
Barak, Aharon, 75
Barnet, Richard, 214
Basel Conference, 58
Basheer, Thaseen, 95n

YEAR 501

The Conquest Continues

Noam Chomsky

In Noam Chomsky's characteristic style, *Year 501* offers a succinctly written, logical analysis, firmly grounded in the documentary record. Noting that the current period has much in common with the Colombian age of imperialism, during which western Europe conquered most of the world, Chomsky focuses on various historical moments in this march of imperial power, up to an including the current axis where the United States, Germany, and Japan share world economic control with the United States, revelling in a virtual monopoly of military might.

250 pages
ISBN: 1-895431-62-X   **$19.95**
ISBN: 1-895431-63-8   **$38.95**

IMAGINING THE MIDDLE EAST

Thierry Hentsch

Translated by Fred A. Reed

Thierry Hentsch examines how the Western perception of the Middle East was formed and how we have used these perceptions as a rationalization for setting policies and determining actions. He sees our ideas of the other and our ethnocentrism not simply as innocent myopia but as our whole way of viewing the world. The book concludes with the consequence of this imagination on the Gulf war and its aftermath.

Dr. Thierry Hentsch teaches international relations at the Université du Québec and is a well-known specialist on the Middle East.

256 pages, index
Paperback ISBN: 1-895431-12-3   **$19.95**
Hardcover ISBN: 1-895431-13-1   **$38.95**

SHOCK WAVES

Eastern Europe after the Revolutions

John Feffer

Covering Poland, Hungary, Czechoslovakia, Romania, Bulgaria, Yugoslavia, and the former East Germany, Feffer provides an incisive historical background to the current crisis and offers critical and guardedly hopeful speculation about the future of the region.

John Feffer is an associate editor for *World Policy Journal* at the New School for Social Reseach in New York. He has studied in the Soviet Union, worked for the Polish Academy of Science, and travelled throughout Eastern Europe on behalf of the American Friends Service Committee. He is the author of *Beyond Détente*.

300 pages, index
Paperback ISBN: 1-895431-46-8   **$19.95**
Hardcover ISBN: 1-895431-47-6   **$38.95**

MASK OF DEMOCRACY

Labour Rights in Mexico Today

Dan LaBotz

An ILRERF Book

Following scores of interviews with Mexican rank and file workers, labour union officials, women's organizations, lawyers, and human rights activists, Dan LaBotz presents this study of the oppression of workers' rights in Mexico. By focusing on wages, unemployment, health and safety issues, women workers, child labour, and democratic unionizing, LaBotz illustrates the precarious position of workers in the Mexican economy of the 1990s.

Dan LaBotz is a writer and activist living in Cincinnati, Ohio. As a truck driver during the 1970s, he was a founder of Teamsters for a Democratic Union. He has also written a study of the Teamsters reform movement entitled *Rank and File Rebellion: Teamsters for a Democratic Union*.

270 pages, index
Paperback ISBN: 1-895431-58-1 $19.95
Hardcover ISBN: 1-895431-59-X $38.95

BEYOND HYPOCRISY

Decoding the News in an Age of Propaganda
Including A Doublespeak Dictionary for the 1990s

Edward S. Herman

Illustrations by Matt Wuerker

In a highly original volume that includes an extended essay on the Orwellian use of language that characterizes U.S. political culture, cartoons, and a cross-referenced lexicon of *doublespeak* terms Herman and Wuerker highlight the deception and hypocrisy contained in the U.S. government's favourite buzzwords.

240 pages, illustrations, index
Paperback ISBN: 1-895431-48-4 $19.95
Hardcover ISBN: 1-895431-49-2 $38.95

THE NEW WORLD ORDER AND THE THIRD WORLD

edited by Dave Broad and Lori Foster

The New World Order analyses the problems and possibilities for Third World revolutions within the historical context of US imperialism. This work is an up to date, indispensable resource drawn from the experiences of internationally recognized authors.

In addition to the editors, contributors include Ed Herman, Thomas Bodenheimer, Robert Gould, Samir Amin, Susanne Jonas, Dave Close, and Doug Booker.

160 pages
Paperback ISBN: 1-895431-16-6 $19.95
Hardcover ISBN: 1-895431-17-4 $38.95

BLACK ROSE BOOKS

has also published the following books of related interests:

The Political Economy of Human Rights, Vol. 1. The Washington Connection and Third World Fascism, *by Noam Chomksy and Edward S. Herman*

The Political Economy of Human Rights, Vol. 2, After the Cataclysm: Postwar Indochina and the Reconstruction of Imperial Ideology, *by Noam Chomksy and Edward S. Herman*

The Fateful Triangle: Israel, the United States and the Palestinians, *by Noam Chomksy*

Turning the Tide: The US and Latin America, *by Noam Chomsky*

The Culture of Terrorism, *by Noam Chomsky*

Language and Politics, *by Noam Chomsky, edited by Carlos P. Otero*

Pirates and Emperors: International Terrorism in the Real World, *by Noam Chomsky*

Radical Priorities, *by Noam Chomsky, edited by Carlos P. Otero*

Common Cents: Media Portrayal of the Gulf War and Other Events, *by James Winter*

Germany East: Dissent and Opposition, *by Bruce Allen*

The New World Order and the Third World, *edited by David Broad and Lori Foster*

Voices From Tiananmen Square: Beijing Spring and the Democracy Movement, *edited by Mok Chiu Yu and J. Frank Harrison*

Toward a Humanist Political Economy, *by Harold Chorney and Phillip Hansen*

Culture and Social Change: Social Movements in Québec and Ontario, *edited by Colin Leys and Marguerite Mendell*

Dissidence: Essays Against the Mainstream, *by Dimitrios Roussopoulos*

The Radical Papers, *edited by Dimitrios Roussopoulos*

The Radical Papers 2, *edited by Dimtrios Roussopoulos*

The Anarchist Papers, *edited by Dimitrios Roussopoulos*

The Anarchist Papers 2, *edited by Dimitrios Roussopoulos*

The Anarchist Papers 3, *edited by Dimitrios Roussopoulos*

Send for our free catalogue of books
BLACK ROSE BOOKS
C.P. 1258, Succ. Place du Parc
Montréal, Québec
H2W 2R3
Canada

Printed by
the workers of
Ateliers Graphiques Marc Veilleux Inc.
Cap-Saint-Ignace, Qué.
for
Black Rose Books Ltd.